Understanding
the
New Testament

REVISED

Francis Bayard Rhein,

B.S., M.DIV., S.T.M.

RECTOR, TRINITY CHURCH, UPPERVILLE, VIRGINIA

BARRON'S EDUCATIONAL SERIES, INC.

WOODBURY, NEW YORK

MAPS
Palestine: In New Testament Times and
The Missionary Journeys of Paul,
courtesy of Thomas Nelson & Sons.

Contents

PART III

PREFACE

This book was written to present the New Testament in terms that do not require prior training to be understood. It does not attempt to settle the great debates of Biblical scholarship, nor does it make claim to originality in its interpretations. Directed to undergraduate study where students cannot reasonably be expected to show concern for the intricacies of advanced Biblical research, simplification is achieved by accepting established scholarship without including lengthy substantiating data. Where dates, authorship, and interpretation are open to question the position which seemed to represent the most modern consensus has been taken, but the minority report is also included.

The book is indebted to the men whose lives have been devoted to research in the field, the great scholars whose dedication and learning have produced the material from which such simplifications can be made. Much of the material on the life of Christ was taken from Maurice Goguel's *Life of Jesus*. The interpretation of the parables follows largely the position taken by B. T. D. Smith in his work, *The Parables of the Synoptic Gospels*. The chapter on the Synoptic Gospels follows closely the subject division and analysis of Frederick C. Grant's, *The Gospels, Their Origin and Their Growth*. Doctor Grant has graciously consented to the use of his outlines in their entirety. The section on John's Gospel is indebted to R. H. Lightfoot's Commentary. The Acts of the Apostles is explained through the position taken by Burton Scott Easton in his work, *The Purpose of Acts*. The sections on the Epistles come from many different scholars, three of whom should be mentioned; Herbert Newell Bate, *A Guide to the Epistles of St. Paul*; Albert E. Barnett, *The New Testament, Its Making and Meaning*; Morton Scott Enslin, *Christian Beginnings*.

The paraphrases of the Epistles are neither an attempt at literal translation, nor vernacular. They seek to act as commentary retaining sufficient identity with the R. V. for a student to read the two in parallel without difficulty.

Lastly, the book owes its greatest debt to Doctor Martha Fodaski of the English Department of Brooklyn College whose skillful editing of the manuscript made lucid much which the author left obscure.

F. B. R.

Part I

I

Introduction

GENERAL BACKGROUND

THE STAGE

Geography

Before the curtain rises the stage is set. Lights are arranged and a musical background produces a mood for what is to come. These things are not only a matter of custom, but also a matter of necessity if the play is to be fully enjoyed and understood. New Testament study is the study of a great drama. It cannot be properly undertaken without a clear understanding of the set. The ear must be tuned to the sound of the times and the eye must see the land of ancient Palestine. The clang of Roman armour in the market place tells of an occupied territory. The wailing song of temple worship rouses folk memories of a subjugated people who call for deliverance. The cadent murmuring of a class sitting at the feet of a scribe, learning by endless repetition makes the sacred law of Judaism live. A beggar's cry speaks the ageless story of poverty. A fat merchant rich with trade calls forth a bargain and a lamb led by bleats its way to sacrifice.

So the prelude is played and the curtain rises on a set that could be Death Valley of American pioneer fame, Salt Lake,

Utah, where another group of deeply religious people have gathered, the sunny steppes of Southern California where grape and grain grow well, or the rough defile of America's great canyon where a misstep means death. Palestine is all of these. It is a land of violence. It is a land where the day can be stifling hot and the night winds pull wraps around those who watch, whether Semite shepherd or Roman legionnary. Here the temperature ranges from 130° to the freezing point, sometimes within twenty-four hours.

The words of the script are in many tongues—a worldly Greek in the cities, Latin for the government records, Aramaic amongst the lower classes, Hebrew in the temple, and dialects of all, the gamut of ancient polyglot. All these come to us, now shouting, now laughing, now crying through the years of history. The drama is a tragedy, but unlike the Greek Oedipus, the English Hamlet, or the American Willie Loman, the hero goes down at last, not because of his weakness, but because of his strength. The play is a first run. It has not changed since the stage was first set and the principals first walked into history. History itself went around the corner and was changed. The play goes on. New Testament study is existential. It is a living study of a constant, living relationship.

Walk then into the Palestine of century one. The climate is the same today; the people have not changed; even the politics are familiar—only the names are a little different. In the fifth century, B.C. the land was already called Palestine. This is the name Heroditus used and that of the Jewish historian, Josephus, nearly one-half a millennium later. Nearer our tongue is the Roman Palestina, a land with many separate names for different localities within: Judea, Samaria, Galilee, and Peraea. The soft word *Palestina* does not fit the land's harsh character. Palestine is a rugged country principally characterized by a great trench formed by the Jordan Valley and the Dead Sea. The trench is trisected by three rivers, the Harmuk, the Jabbok, and the Arnon. At one end the Sea of Galilee is forever famous because of the men who fished there. Peter, the Big Fisherman, drew his nets in its waters. At the opposite end the Dead Sea cannot support life. Like Salt Lake in Utah, its brine is so saturate that a man need not swim to float. The whole distance from the Sea of Galilee to the Dead Sea, approximately seventy-five miles, lies roughly from 700 to 1300 feet below sea level. The land itself is neither fertile nor soft except in spots. The climate is not easy and the people are not by temperament gentle. This is Bedouin country, fought over since before recorded history. It was the corridor between the great civilizations of the Tigris-Euphrates Valley and the Nile. It was also the path followed by Indo-European peoples when they poured into Persia and Egypt. The Sumerians, the Chaldeans, the Hyksos, the Hittites, the Assyrians, the Babylonians, the Medes, the Persians, and the Children of Israel have all known her soil. Sennacherib, Nebuchadrezzar, Cyrus—each took his turn there. Alexander marched his armies through the gateway on his way to Egypt and made the land captive. The Romans followed to write *finis* to Hebrew history.

Today Rome is no more. The proud Pharaohs are gone, but Egypt and the Arab League would drive the new Hebrew nation into the sea. Suez is a canal of tremendous strategic value. Oil and transportation are a new kind of wealth. The fight for control continues. Many loyalties, languages, and many religions still tear the land to pieces. Troops still march in the corridor.

Political Background

In the year 586 B.C. Nebuchadrezzar conquered the land of Judah and laid waste the temple. Thus, the heart of Judaism was still. To make certain it would not stir again, the Babylonian king finished the work which his battering rams had begun. Not only was the city brought to the ground, but also the men and women who lived there were exiled to far-off places. The wealth, the religion, the leaders, the brains of the Hebrew people were moved to Babylonian colonies. Had Babylonia stayed in power, Hebrew religious history would have ended, but the spotlight swings now to a small kingdom, a province of the Medes, Anshan by name. Here, east of Zagros mountains ruled Cyrus, soon to be known as "the Great." With the bold stroke of sudden revolt, he became master of the Medes. Croesus, king of Lydia, was the next to fall. In 539 B.C. Cyrus conquered the mighty Babylon and became master of Mesopotamia, Syria, and Palestine. Under his benevolent rule, the Jews were allowed to return to Palestine. Not all elected to do so. The luxury and wealth of mighty kingdoms seemed to many preferable to the poverty and insecurity of their native land. Palestine was a poor man's country not comparable in culture to Persia, Babylon, Phoenecia, or Egypt. Clearly more milk and honey could be found in the centers of Babylonian wealth than in the promised land. The journey home was a matter of religious fanaticism coupled with racial pride and, where appetite was dulled by foreign fleshpots, the Hebrew people were not sufficiently motivated to move.

Some, however, elected to do so. In 536 B.C. the foundations of the temple were laid in Jerusalem. The national religion began, at first faintly, but soon with great strength to pulse again through the blood of the people. The last epoch of Hebrew history began. In the next two hundred years the nation produced some of its strongest and most glorious religious literature, while at the same time great heroes, both prophetic and military, were born. Not strong enough to be of concern to Persian power, its people were allowed to prosper unmolested by foreign rule.

Two hundred years passed before world power was to shift again. The birth of a son to King Philip of Macedon brought about the change. Philip was assassinated at the wedding feast of his daughter Cleopatra and the king of Epirus. His son, barely twenty and Alexander by name, wrote violent history for thirteen years. His armies marched first in the name of liberation to free the Aegean coast from the hand of the Persian Darius. Next Phoenecia, Egypt, Syria, Mesopotamia and Assyria fell before a young man's destiny. Thence Alexander, now " the Great," moved to conquer and marched east, we are told, to the Indus where at last his exhausted and mutinous armies forced a halt. In a decade the world belonged to Alexander, but at the age of thirty-three Alexander, a victim of fever, was dead.

A struggle for power followed, but no man was able to acquire all. The various city states were a rich legacy that was to be divided by the sword amongst the warring generals of Macedon, three of whom—Antigonus, Seleucus, and Ptolemy—founded dynasties. At first Seleucus ruled in the north; Antigonus, Asia Minor, Syria, and Mesopotamia; and Ptolemy, the region of Africa. Thirty years later the lines were drawn. Assassination, intrigue, and revolution had taken their toll. Seleucus died by an assassin's hand to be succeeded by Antiochus I. The line of Antigonus survived in Macedonia until its conquest by Rome 197-168 B.C.; and the Ptolemy's rule did not end until an asp's fatal strike on Cleopatra's breast. The stinging poison gave Egypt to Rome and Mark Anthony to Caesar Augustus.

Palestine was a battle ground in the struggle for power that raged until Rome's legions brought quiet to the world. In the year 300 B.C. the *Pax Romana* had not come. The Ptolemies and the descendents of Antiochus pushed the pendulum of power back and forth across the land. Not for a century was the conflict to be settled. When Antiochus III came to the throne, again the title of "Great" was bestowed by history. Alexander had brought Greek culture to the lands that he had conquered. Those who followed continued to do so. Judaism, by its nature, cannot tolerate the imposition of a foreign culture. Religion and politics were inseparable to the Jew. From the earliest days God demanded his first and final allegiance. Bitter conflict between Hellenization and Judaism was inevitable.

Antiochus, " the Great, " was succeeded by Antiochus Epiphanes,[1] a man fanatically Greek. Dog and cat were put in the same arena. Fur was soon to fly. Epiphanes was a headstrong man of great administrative ability, if not diplomatic

[1] Antiochus IV, 175 B.C.

understanding. Under his rule, the temple was destroyed and an altar to Zeus replaced the great altar of sacrifice that had belonged to Jehovah.[2] In the campaign to accomplish this terrible destruction, the country was ravaged, women and children were captured and sold into slavery. The pressure was too great. Rather than the destruction of Hebrew culture, the campaign created a major revolt. A priest, Mattathias, and his sons withdrew to the country and began what are now known as the wars of the Maccabees.[3] The fighting spirit and the luck of the ancient Joshua were with these people. Though outnumbered ten to one, they were able to defeat the Syrian king four times.

Antiochus Epiphanes died in 163 B.C. while hastening from Persia to settle the great revolt, and so for a time the Hebrews were free from outside pressure. Judas, son of Mattathias, succeeded in uniting the ancient kingdom of Israel once again. Not since the days of David had such a thing been done. He defeated the Idumeans in the south and the Ammonites east of the Jordon. He was, however, defeated in 161 B.C. by the Syrians. Jonathan, another son, now became an actor in the play. By diplomacy, he attempted to succeed where military endeavor had failed. He was murdered by a Syrian general, and a third son, Simon, took the lead. In 141 B.C. Simon assumed the title of both governor and high priest, and the Hasmonean[4] dynasty was at last successful in its struggle to come to birth.

Sadducees and Pharisees

The Maccabean revolt and subsequent Hasmonean rule were the last flash in the pan. For a few years Israel flourished, but a lasting shift in power did not occur. The Hebrews were not to become a major world power. In this period two parties,

[2] Known as the "Abomination of Desolation"; Book of Daniel 9:27, 11:31, 12:11 and Mark's Gospel, 13:14, Mt. 24:15, I Mac. 1:54.
[3] Maccabaeus meaning "hammerer" was a name given to his son Judas. Bailey & Kent, pp. 313 ff., *A History of the Hebrew Commonwealth.*
[4] The name is derived from Hasman, surname of Mattathias.

well known to New Testament literature, came to birth—the Sadducees and the Pharisees. The Pharisees' origin is somewhat obscure. Sometime in Jonathan's day a group of religious people known as the Hasidim objected to policies of state that were not in accord with the best interests of the national religion. They put religious motivation ahead of secular politics. Later, these people became separatists opposed to Jonathan, and were known as Pharisees. The Sadducees were not as large a party. They represented the priestly aristocracy and the political party in power.

The Hasmonean flame burned brilliantly for less than fifty years. Then Simon was assassinated by his brother-in-law who nearly succeeded in destroying the entire family. Simon and two of his sons died in the coup, but a third son, John Hyrcanus thwarted the play for power. John succeeded in winning the people of Jerusalem to his support and reigned from 134 to 104 B.C. The flame flickered and was soon to die. Hyrcanus was followed by the short reign of his son Aristobulus, whose degenerate rule lasted less than a year. Another son, Alexander Jannacus [103-76B.C.], carried on in the grand style of his father for a few years more, but the last of his reign was marked by severe internal strife. Strong opposition to his policies came from a plot to bring about his overthrow. The next to come to power was a queen, his wife, Salome Alexandra [76-67 B.C.]. Civil war between her two sons Hyrcanus II and Aristobulus II was to extinguish Jewish political autonomy forever. In reply to a request from both parties, each of which hoped to benefit, the Roman Pompey took over Palestine in the year 63 B.C. His massacre of 12,000 Jews was a sad harbinger of things to come.

Palestine was not again to be an independent state. Henceforth, it was a land of military government and puppet kings. Even the high priest was Rome's quisling. Pompey's dictatorship was not absolute. Hyrcanus II and Aristobulus II continued unsuccessful quests for power. Eventually, Pompey was defeated by Caesar, who was assassinated in 44 B.C. by Brutus and Cassius, and Caesar Augustus became emperor.

With the backing of Roman legions, Herod, the Idumean, became king of the Jews in 37 B.C. He was a puppet king hated by those over whom he was chosen to rule. He established power by ruthless removal of all who opposed him. His first appointment to high priest, Aristobulus, he removed from office by drowning. He arranged the murder of his wife Marianne. Half the Sanhedrin[5] were put to death. He ruled until 4 B.C., when he was succeeded by his three sons: Herod Antipas, ruler of Galilee and Peraea; Philip, ruler of the land north and east of the Sea of Galilee; and Archelaus, ruler of Samaria and Judea. Archelaus was not permitted the title of king by Rome, but instead was made ethnarch, which simply means ruler. He was removed for inefficiency and replaced by Pontius Pilate in 26 A.D. Pilate himself aroused the ire of Rome because of his Samaritan massacre and was recalled in the year 36 A.D.

Religious Background

In the American army of World War II, a man had the choice of three religious classifications, Protestant, Catholic or Jew. A Roman soldier at the time of Jesus Christ owed his military allegiance to the emperor who was also god,[6] but his belief was not limited. If he were stationed in Palestine, a wide choice was his and both his conscious and subconscious minds were subjected to many religious influences. Pythagoreanism, the teaching of the Orphic cults, mystery religions, Zoroastrianism, Mithraism, and the superstitions of the times could all be part of his religious understanding. Demons lurked in the dark and deserted places. Further, the state itself demanded loyalty somewhat similar to that demanded by communism today. In Palestine, amongst the Hebrews, Judaism was dominant. A strong and intensely legalistic religion, it was the protagonist as well as the antagonist of the Christian movement.

[5] Sanhedrin: a religious and civil court composed of priests, Sadducees and Pharisees.
[6] See p. 178.

GREEK PHILOSOPHIES AND RELIGIONS

Epicureanism

Epicurus was born on the Island of Samos in 341 B.C. Today the philosophy brings to mind good things to eat. A more sophisticated understanding allies Epicureanism with all sensuous pleasure. "Eat, drink, and be merry for tomorrow you die," is thought to summarize the position. Epicurus' system, however, was more profound than such clichés imply. True, the aim of his philosophy was to guide mankind in the pursuit of happiness, but he felt that "not all pleasure is worthy of being chosen, not every pain ought to be avoided." [7] Mental pleasures were more important and greater than those of the flesh. Such qualification is quite contrary to the popular understanding of his position. Epicurus felt that all things are produced by natural rather than supernatural means. Death is the end of everything.

Stoicism

Of far greater significance to the early Christian movement was Stoicism. In many ways it is the opposite of Epicureanism. Zeno, who founded the school, was born in Citium on the Isle of Cyprus in 336 B.C. Against the hedonism[8] and naturalism[9] of the Epicureans he sought harmony with the universe as the greatest good. His philosophy was highly rationalistic and moral. Love of one's neighbor was a good in itself. Stoicism understood religion and philosophy in the same terms.

[7] Frank Thilley and Ledger Wood, *A History of Philosophy.*

[8] Hedonism: the doctrine that pleasure is the highest good.

[9] Naturalism: a world understanding that denies the supernatural and feels nothing has more than natural significance. Natural desire and instinct are determinative.

It found a strong following in Rome during the first century. Seneca, Epictetus and the Emperor Marcus Aurelius can be counted among its followers.

In contrast to Epicureanism, Stoicism was strongly ascetic. Thus, it was a philosophy for hard times. Further, it strongly emphasized an all-ruling divine wisdom and the essential brotherhood of man. The similarity to Christian theology is striking.

Pythagoreanism

Nearly all Americans are exposed to plane geometry and algebra as part of their required schooling. For that reason the name of Pythagoras is familiar to them. It was he who first demonstrated the geometric proof that the square of the hypotenuse of a right triangle is equal to the sum of the squares of the other two sides ($H^2 = A^2 + B^2$). Actually his fame comes not from his mathematical formulae, but through the fact that he founded a religious cult and a school of philosophy that sought to explain reality in terms of numbers. At the time of Christianity he was perhaps better known for the cult than for the other things. Pythagoras was born in Samos around 575 B.C. and emigrated to the Greek colonies in Southern Italy where his school was founded.

The Pythagoreans had much in common with Orphic belief; and it is astonishing that Pythagoras, a man of such genius in some fields, should be so primitive in others. For example, note some of the rules of his order: do not stir fire with iron; do not look in a mirror beside a light. These things were evidently part of an ascetic system in a particularly licentious age.

Orphism

Orphism was an outgrowth of the worship of Dionysus. Similar to the mysteries and even identifiable with them, the earliest forms were concerned with fertility. Rather than the original orgiastic customs, the Orphic cults attempted to transfer the emphasis to spiritual channels. Primary to the faith was transmigration of the soul.[10] The body was seen as the prison of the soul while the sins of a previous life were supposed in some fashion to be responsible for the punishments received in the present. The body is death because it confines the soul. The cult evolved a system of purification to achieve liberation. They believed a world of true reality to which the soul aspired existed above the senses.

Gnosticism

The word gnosticism is derived from the Greek *gnosis* meaning knowledge. The religion which bore the name was established before Christianity and became a serious rival to it in the second century. One might assume from the word *wisdom* that the gnostic was characterized by a highly rational approach to God and the supernatural. Such is not the case. The connotation is quite the opposite. The type of knowledge to which reference is made was a mystical affair which was thought to bring about spiritual enlightenment and insight. Knowledge was achieved through initiation ceremonies and the mechanics of ritual. Gnosticism was strongly syncretistic,[11] combining in its early days Persian dualism,[12] mystery religions, and aspects of the Orphic cults. It accepted much of the Christian faith, but perverted Christology[13] to create one of the most dangerous heresies faced by the church. The position was taken that Christ revealed God to man, but was not really involved in the material world which was regarded as evil. His appear-

[10] Metempsychosis: the belief that the soul passes from one body to another at death and birth.

[11] Syncretism: "The reconciliation or union of conflicting religious beliefs, or an effort intending such." Webster, *Third International Dictionary*.

[12] Spirit and mind are good—matter is evil—belief in a god of light and a god of darkness, one good, the other evil. See Zoroastrianism.

[13] Christology: pertaining to the nature of Christ.

ance was ghostly in line with the Docetistic belief.[14] Thus, Christ's essential manhood was denied.

Mystery Religions

The mystery religions developed from fertility cults whose original concern was the assurance of productivity. A primitive culture cannot survive unless the crops are bountiful and the warriors numerous. Early rituals were highly sexual in character and in some phases sexual union was part of the cultus. In the Christian era the mysteries had become more spiritual. Esoteric and complicated ceremonies were continued, but emphasis on the mother corn goddess was no longer extreme. The exact form of ritual varied with the location. The cults were widespread throughout the ancient world. Perhaps the earliest were the Eleusian Mysteries whose mother god was Cybele. Her son[15] Attis also played a large part in the cult. In the early eras voluntary castration was part of the priesthood.

Astralism

One step above the superstitions of the time was astralism. Although no educated person takes it seriously today, the ancients saw a close connection between the stars and the destiny of man. The configuration of the stars at the time of birth was thought to be significant. Prediction of the future was based on the appearance of stars and constellations. The science of astronomy was in its infancy, but far enough advanced to lend credence to superstition. The phases of the moon were known and predicted. Eclipses were accurately forecast as early as Thales 640 B.C.[16] Thus, it was an easy mental jump to the as-

[14] Docetism: an early Christian heresy that Christ's body was spiritual rather than physical (natural) and that as a result He only appeared to suffer crucifixion and death.

[15] See Fraser, *The Golden Bough*. Fraser feels that Attis was considered son; others place Attis as the consort of Cybele.

[16] Thales: Father of philosophy and founder of the Milesian School; 640 B.C. Miletus, a seaport on the coast of Asia Minor.

sumption that accurate forecast in one area could assure the
same in another. It is perhaps for this reason that astrology has
had such a strong hold on man's imagination throughout the
ages.

Zoroastrianism

The exact date of Zoroaster's birth is uncertain, but the
great beauty and tremendous influence of the religion which
he preached is without doubt. Sometime in the sixth century
B.C. his ministry began in Media. He taught the existence of
one supreme god, Ahura Mazda. Mazda was a god of light who
fought against the forces of evil and darkness led by Ahriman.
Ahriman was a counterpart to the devil and was probably the
origin of the traditional conception of Satan. The religion was
thus strongly dualistic and in this respect contrary to Christian
theology. It found a great following in Persia and was the established religion of Iran at the time of Alexander. In the Christian
era, Mithraism was immensely popular amongst Roman troops.
Its similarities to the Christian belief made it a strong rival.
Mithras was understood as an agent of Ahura Mazda in somewhat the same way Christ might be seen as an agent of the First
Person of the Trinity.[17] In the war between light and darkness
Mithras generaled the powers of light. The cult became both
militant and secret in character. Worship took place in underground sanctuaries and involved animal sacrifice. Roman soldiers returning from eastern duty established it in the heart of
Rome.

[17] God, the Father.

II

Judaism

The Covenant

As surely as the New Testament story can be seen as a great drama unfolding in history, so can the Old Testament be seen as a passionate love story between God and man. "And I will walk among you and will be your God and ye shall be my people." [1] At the time of the prophets, the relationship is so well established that prophetic language, in its desperate attempts to call the people back to God, becomes in many instances the language of lovers. Hosea cries that the people have been untrue, that they have gone awhoring after other gods. "Go take unto thee a wife of whoredoms and children of whoredoms; for the land doth commit great whoredom, departing from the Lord." [2] Jeremiah tells the children of Israel that their offerings are no longer pleasing in God's sight. "Can a maid forget her ornaments? Can a bride her attire? Yet my people have forgotten me." [3] "Turn O backsliding children, saith the Lord; for I am married unto you; and I will take you one of a city, and two of a family, and I will bring you to

[1] Leviticus 26:12.
[2] Hosea 1:2.
[3] Jeremiah 2:32.

Zion." At the center of this faith is the belief that God had revealed his will not only to the Hebrew people through their history, but finally to all mankind. At the last the Hebrews felt that they were God's instrument for the purpose of making his will known.

The story of Judaism begins with the Exodus from Egypt sometime in the middle of the 13th Century B.C., circa 1260.[4] This is when the actual history of the Hebrew nation begins. True, Genesis gives folk memories that stretch to a much earlier period and undoubtedly much of the law codified by Moses may have already been familiar, not only to the band of refugees that fled from Pharaoh, but also to their cousins in the wilderness. True, also, the Hebrew Bible, The Torah, or the first five books of the Old Testament include Genesis narratives, but the people were not yet unified nor was the covenant established.

The establishment of the covenant was to become at the time of Christ the basis for the interpretation of the law and the intense legalism which resulted. Careful adherence to the law was necessary to keep a right relationship with God. What then is a covenant? The word might nearly as well be translated "contract." In modern times a contract is always a two-way street, or it is not legally binding. Something is given and something must also be received in return. The covenant relationship with the God, Jahweh, at the time of Moses also had a double requirement. "You worship me on the one hand and I will look after you on the other."

Covenants were bound between people and between tribes. Often these were sealed with the letting and mingling of blood. In such a fashion blood brothership was established. The phrase "cut a covenant" was a matter of common usage. Covenants were established to unite tribes in war against a common enemy. The conception among primitive peoples was easily transferred to the Deity.

First, Jahweh was a warrior god who assured the Israelites

[4] This date is generally now accepted, although a few scholars may favor a date in the 15th century B.C.

victory in battle as they wandered through the wilderness and then over the people who already inhabited the land of Canaan. Victory over the local desert tribes was a logistical possibility, but success over the advanced, urban, Canaanite people presented different odds. Walled cities and large standing armies led by kings wise in the ways of war were a combination that did not always fall before the Hebrew onslaught. When unsuccessful, the Israelites searched first for their sin. What else could cause God to break his contract? In some fashion the people must have been untrue.

Throughout the years they succeeded in conquering Canaan and establishing themselves in the land. Certainly they married Canaanites. Certainly they also adopted Canaanite customs and religious practices, but also they were constantly reminded by their religious leaders of the need to remain true to Jahweh. From the monolatry[5] of the Mosaic period, they moved at last with the major prophets to monotheism. But it was only as a result of their removal from the promised land by the Babylonian, Nebuchadrezzar, and their life in exile that they came to understand God not only as one God, but also as a God of all peoples who judged all peoples, including the Hebrews, with equal justice. Only at this point in history is their faith properly described as ethical monotheism. Always, however, the Hebrews considered themselves God's chosen people with the obligations involved and the protections afforded.

The Messiah

The Hebrews came to understand themselves first as the servants of God and after the Exile, as his suffering servants.[6] As a result of the covenant relationship, they naturally expected that the situation in which they found themselves would

[5] The worship of one god without denying the existence of other gods also is known as henotheism. The first of the ten commandments is henotheistic. "Thou shalt have none other gods, but me" implies that other gods exist to be had; otherwise the command is pointless and redundant.

[6] 2nd Isaiah. See Ftn. 16, p. 20.

eventually change. Jahweh had not let them down except where they had first failed him. If now they were properly loyal, then a reversal of the existing order must follow. Cyrus permitted their return to Palestine, and the temple was rebuilt. When would the nation be established as a leader on earth with the ability to proclaim Jahwism to all mankind? Perhaps another leader would be born, strong in arms and steadfast in faith, to lead the people once again in victory. Had not Moses won over Pharaoh? Had not Joshua succeeded in routing the forces of Canaan? Had not the Judges thrown off the various yokes of oppression suffered by tribal units in the years following? All these things were accomplished in Jahweh's name. Why not again?

Alexander dashed all hopes for world dominance, but a dream prevailed. The order of things must somehow change. For years the nation suffered under the Hellenization of its Seleucid rulers. Then one day the High Priest Mattathias could stand religious insult no longer and succeeded in revolt. To those who had no understanding of world power, it may have seemed possible that the time of deliverance was at hand. With the Maccabean revolt and the establishment of the Hasmonean dynasty, the new order might have begun, but when Pompey came to power with Rome in the ascendancy, it was clear that no ordinary man could ever lead the Hebrews to world victory. How then was Jahweh to be vindicated? How was his rule to be established? If not by ordinary means, then by supernatural. In this fashion the conception of a Messiah came into being.

Throughout Hebrew history the process of anointing was a means of bestowing authority. The High Priest in Leviticus was called the *anointed priest*. Saul and David were anointed to kingship. But the Hebrew word "anointed" could also be transcribed "Messiah." This religious one, this anointed one, was to have supernatural power conferred by the Deity. As in most cultures, the Hebrew kings had also in the past been seen in part as divine. The step to Messianic understanding was not long. He had to be general, king, priest, and God's special agent with powers bestowed by the Deity. The Messiahship of Jesus was a different thing and military characteristics were absent, but at present we are dealing with the expectation which proved quite different from the eventual actuality.

God

As history had shown, God was all powerful. Furthermore, he was understood to be just and merciful as indicated by the teachings of Scripture.[7] He created the world, ruled the world of his creation, and revealed himself not only through the machinations of history, but also directly through the voice of his prophets. Under the covenant God was always available to hear the prayers and to receive the sacrifices of the penitent. God could neither be manipulated by sacrifice, nor bribed in any fashion.[8]

Perhaps also some Persian influence colored the Hebrew conception of God. The forces of evil were a problem to the ancient mind as they arc today. If, however, a god of evil existed, the Jew was sure he did so only on Jahweh's license. Jahweh was supreme.

The Old Testament conception of God was highly anthropomorphic. He was visualized in the same glory as the most magnificent oriental potentate. This was as far as imagination could go, but God stood clearly above and beyond mankind.[9] So great was the exhaltation of God that it was sometimes difficult for the Hebrew to see how he could have anything to do with this world. The result was the creation of a hierarchy of lesser supernatural beings. At the time of Christ, angels and demons were accepted as part of the order of things.

Further, God was felt to be near at hand.[10] In the ancient days he was thought to inhabit both the heavens and the temple. At the time of Moses and Joshua the presence of the Deity

[7] Deuteronomy 4:31.
[8] Deuteronomy 10:17.
[9] Daniel 7:9, Baruch 4:10, 14:22.
[10] Deuteronomy 4:15.

in the ark[11] was accepted as fact. The transfer of this concept to the Holy of Holies in the temple was a matter of course.

Demons

The lower spiritual beings took the form of both good and evil agents. The Hebrew tradition that each person was assigned a guardian angel is an appealing conception. The angel which led Peter and John from prison is in this tradition.[12] A recording angel kept track of man's activities to be reported to God, and thereby helped in the administration of divine justice. Demons, on the other hand, were thought to cause mental disease by taking possession of the body just as a hermit crab inhabits a crustacean shell. Springing from early animism,[13] belief in such beings was widespread. They were thought to inhabit dark and deserted places and were an ever present threat to man's health and happiness. These spirits were in revolt against God, under the leadership of a master demon, Satan.

Heaven, Hell, and Immortality

The Hebrew conception of after life appears late in the development of Judaism. The first five books of the Old Testament [14] say nothing about immortality. The law exhorts man to lead a good life that "your days may be numbered long on this earth." Where overtones of immortal life are heard, the song is spiritual, but the tune a dirge. The Hebrew conceived of body and spirit as a dualism which split at the moment of death. The spirit left the body and went to reside in Sheol.

---

[11] The Ark: A sacred wooden chest in which the early Hebrews believed God to reside—carried always in battle, the presence was supposed to assure victory. The box contained the tablets of law.

[12] Acts 5:19, 12:7.

[13] Animism: The conception that inanimate objects possess personalities, consciousness, or souls of their own.

[14] Genesis, Exodus, Leviticus, Numbers, and Deuteronomy.

This was not a place of either punishment or reward, but a sort of nether region somewhere within the earth where nothing takes place. Existence in Sheol was shadowy and colorless. The witch at Endor brought Samuel back from such a realm to advise Saul on his future.[15] The conception is in line with the Greek Hades where existence after life on earth was also thought to be an underground cave, the best of which was far worse than the worst on earth. In each case, life without a body was conceived as utterly gloomy and boring.

Not until after the Exile did a doctrine of reward and punishment begin to emerge in terms of after life. The development was evolutionary, growing out of the circumstances of history. In Deutero or Second Isaiah[16] and the period following, God became universal and highly transcendent; and, yet, he was not beyond concern for the individual. Some sort of heavenly abode was the natural corollary of transcendence. And a transcendent God, yet one still anthropomorphic,[17] could hardly be conceived as inhabiting the dark interior of the earth.

Sometime in the era of the Maccabees, doctrines of heaven and hell probably began to emerge. In the apocalypse of Enoch, which comes from this period, a clear doctrine of heaven and hell first occurs.[18] With the failure of the Hasmonean dynasty to establish Jahweh's kingdom on earth and with the failure of a Messiah to appear, it became clear that rewards and punishments were not entirely affairs of this earth. The wicked often prospered in life and the good weren't always rewarded, but that justice was not finally served by Jahweh was inconceivable. The heroic Hebrew must have some reward, if not here, then certainly elsewhere. By similar reasoning those who did not serve the righteous cause must surely be punished. At the

---

[15] I Samuel 28.

[16] Although the Old Testament contains only one book of the Prophet Isaiah, the writings can be divided into four or more from the point of authorship coming from different eras. Chapters 1-40 are pre-Exilic; Chapter 13 an insert; Chapters 40-55, 56-66, post-Exilic.

[17] Anthropomorphic: Ascribing human form to God—also assuming that the deity follows human conduct and motivation.

[18] Henry Thatcher Fowler, *Origin and Growth of Hebrew Religion.*

coming of God's kingdom, then, it was assumed that spirit and body would be reunited. The righteous would be raised up to live again on this earth. The evil would go elsewhere. The Hebrews were not in agreement on this point. Traditionally the Pharisees believed in immortality, whereas the conservative Sadducees, remaining in the spiritual climate of the law, did not. Among the Greek Jews of Alexandria primitive Platonism influenced the developing doctrine of immortality.

Nature of Man

Belief in an anthropomorphic deity is strong in the Old Testament,but not absolute. Unfortunately Biblical fundamentalism has greatly exaggerated the conception that God exists in a form which corresponds to man; and although the Jew himself may have visualized his God as a patriarch, the earliest literature did not intend to create such an image. The emergent doctrine of man will be misunderstood if the concept is maintained. The language which describes man as made in the image of God is no doubt poetic and is not, as many assume, an attempt to describe the details of creation. The Hebrew doctrine of man developed concurrently with the doctrine of God and the conception of the covenant already discussed in earlier chapters.

The kinship between God and man in Old Testament literature is spiritual, not biological. The words sought to make clear a special relationship which was different from that which existed between God and the rest of creation. The act of creation was felt to come from God's need to overcome loneliness, and man's function was to be a companion to the Deity. Overtones of this can be seen in the conjugal relationship the Hebrews felt existed between God and the nation. Man was God's minion whose life found meaning only in terms of God's will.

At the instant will was posited in reference to God, a compulsion came upon man. If God's will is meaningful, then obedience to it must be of paramount importance. Herein is a clue to the nature of man. Obedience to God's will would create the favored and desired relationship. If man was to have spiritual fellowship with God, obviously he must obey God. As he was created for fellowship, only through obedience could he be fulfilled or become fully man.

To the Hebrew mind this right-relationship was the equivalent of blessedness. (A blessed man is a fulfilled man. The carpenter becomes blessed as he creates a piece of furniture worthy of his skill as a craftsman. Until he has done this he is not yet a carpenter. Similarly, the surgeon who saves a life, having left his bed in the small hours of the night, fulfills himself and achieves blessedness. The saint in prayer, the mother nursing her newborn babe, the painter with brush and canvas, the author at work on his manuscript—all are examples of blessedness. In these activities each man makes a part of his being complete.) Similarly, man was thought to fulfill his entire being by obedience to God's will.

Fellowship with God was another aspect of the same conception. Again it is a mistake to interpret Old Testament references as meaning physical fellowship even though this is what they may seem to describe. God was too exalted for that. Certainly physical fellowship was never conceived as possible with a God whose face it was impossible to gaze upon. In both cases where Moses experiences a theophany,[19] even though God appeared indirectly, the experience is described as unbearable. In one instance God appeared in a burning bush, in the other as a great light that left Moses a transfigured man.[20] Later, when God was thought to inhabit the ark, so great was his power that a person touching the sacred box suffered death upon the spot.[21]

Between God and man lay an insurmountable barrier whose magnitude was commensurate with the difference between the finite and the eternal. God was transcendent—above all that he had created. "What is man that thou art mindful of him?"[22]

---

[19] The appearance of God to man.
[20] Exodus 3:2-3, 34:35.
[21] 2 Samuel 6:6-7.
[22] Psalm 8:4.

The answer was a forerunner of the Christian doctrines of prevenient grace to be systematized by Augustine (354-430 A.D.) and Calvin (1509-64 A.D.). Fellowship was possible through God's grace alone. It was God who reached across the barrier to man.

Body and Spirit

Man was thought to be a combination of both body and spirit. Primitive religion understood spirit to be associated with breath for the obvious reasons that when breath leaves the body, i.e., when respiration ceases, the body is dead. The Hebrew word for spirit, *ruah*, also means breath or wind. Early Greek philosophy also developed a theory for the nature of matter based on the assumption that air was basic to life. In the development of Judaism spirit came to mean more than breath. Spirit was closely associated with character. "Create in me a clean heart O God; and renew a right spirit within me." [23] Spirit dominated the body and was separate from it. For example, because the prophets assumed that the spirit of God came upon them, they felt justified in couching their message in terms whose introduction was "Thus spake the Lord." The conception that demons could occupy the body has already been discussed. The possibility that the spirit of God could be superimposed upon man's spirit or perhaps better substituted for it can be properly understood as a positive counterpart.

Sin

Obedience and disobedience have no moral significance unless man has the ability to make choices. The Old Testament understood man's will to be free. As a result man could resist God's will. Sin comprised any act that was not in harmony with the Deity. Thus sin broke the relation of fellowship and was related to defiance and rebellion.

[23] Psalm 51:10.

A secondary or derived aspect of sin developed with the evolution of ritual and religious legalism. Breaking the rules concerning sabbath observance, unclean food, and unclean associations came to be called sin. Further, the law was concerned with moral offences for which ritual acts alone were not sufficient for absolution. A contrite heart was also necessary and where such did not exist, or where sin was committed on purpose, a ritual act alone was not considered efficacious. The basic and terrible character of sin, however, resulted from its identification with disobedience and rebellion. By breaking the relationship of fellowship with God, sin destroyed blessedness and compromised manhood.

Sin was always understood in reference to the Deity except where it of necessity involved others by implication and association. Where a man's sin lowered all society, the act automatically became a sin against man as well as God, and as all men are part of society, any sinful act must have been seen to some extent as sin against man.

Punishment for sin might come through God's wrath and the resulting catastrophe which he could inflict upon man and nation, but first and always was the certain and horrible punishment—the inevitable loss of blessedness. Where God's punishment was thought to take place, the purpose was disciplinary rather than penal. Punishment was redemptive. By correcting the character of the sinner it could make the right relationhip to God possible, but punishment was never considered an atonement in itself.

Sacrifice

Sacrifice to God took many forms—thank offerings, sin offerings, peace offerings, guilt offerings, and what might be described as daily, routine offerings made simply to maintain a right relationship. Thank offerings were not an expiation, but were made simply in return for boons received. In the parlance of the 20th Century market place, sacrifice was a means of keeping the relationship between God and man sweet.

Sacrifice demonstrated the attitude of the worshipper toward God, but it possessed the characteristics of a sacrament. In a mechanical sense it did something for the donor. It became in part the outward and visible sign of some invisible action on God's part, but the action was felt to be impossible without penitence. Although God alone could save man, the act of sacrifice was felt to be necessary in order to make the saving grace possible. Worship was a two-way street in every sense.

$$\text{SACRIFICE (with penitence)} \left(\begin{matrix} \text{to} \longrightarrow \text{God} \\ \longleftarrow \text{God's grace to man} \end{matrix} \right) = \text{SALVATION}$$

Lastly, it was felt that occasions might exist where sacrifice as a mediating factor between God and man was not necessary, or rather that there were occasions where God might deal with man directly. Sometimes God seemed to have accepted penitence and acted accordingly. Sometimes punishment came directly as a result of sinful action. David, who sinned in his relationship with Bathsheba and in his indirect murder of her husband, Uriah,[24] felt God's wrath when Bathsheba's child died.[25]

Worship

The first century Jew did not go to church with the suburban attitude of today's culture, nor did the activity associated with the temple have much in common with modern protestant or orthodox practice. Until the sack of Jerusalem and the exile under Nebuchadrezzar, worship was confined to the temple. It was the center for all sacrifice. The frequency and occasion of sacrificial worship were not geared to the Sabbath in the sense that Sunday is considered a Christian day of obligation, nor did the form take that of preaching and liturgical response —rather, sacrifice was a mechanical process performed by the

[24] 2 Samuel 11:1-17.
[25] For a more complete summary of the nature of man see H. H. Rowley, *The Faith of Israel.*

priests for the purpose of creating and maintaining a right-relationship with God. A special offering for ministerial support was also absent. Unlike today's ministers, the Jewish priesthood was a hereditary class supported by tithes and a share of things offered for sacrifice.

After the temple was rebuilt under Cyrus, it continued in its function until 70 A.D. and was, therefore, active at the time of Christ. The Exile, however, created a second place and mode of worship. Since the Jews in exile could not worship in the temple and as they lived in colonies which followed their ethnic customs, it was natural that they should gather for instruction and worship to fill their religious needs. Sometime during this period the synagogue was born and grew up to become an official institution of Judaism. In it worship developed a liturgical pattern familiar to modern times including prayers, reading lessons, and sermons. Priests were relegated to a minor position, their principal function being to pronounce the benediction and to sound trumpets on special occasions. Rather than by priestly oversight, the synagogues were ruled by a "head" and sometimes by a committee. Salaried officials presided over the services. The importance of the synagogue to Judaism cannot be exaggerated. Perhaps it even saved the life of Jewish religion during the Exile and has served as its inspiration and guide in years since.

The Literature of Judaism

The literature of Judaism is threefold. The basic writings of ancient days were thought to contain the revelation of God's will to man. These comprise the Torah or Pentateuch,[26] —and formed the law. Law, however, by itself is functionless. It can have meaning only when applied to the life of man, and application necessitates interpretation. Different circumstances can change meaning; what may be a practical application in one instance, may prove absurd in another. The letter and spirit of the law may be different. Of what value is the Con-

[26] Genesis, Exodus, Leviticus, Numbers, and Deuteronomy.

stitution of the United States and the Bill of Rights without
the system of American jurisprudence based on English common law to administer and interpret it?
So also was the Torah interpreted by oral tradition which
became a sort of religious common law. Although at first it
was forbidden to write the oral tradition, written records began to appear as the centuries passed. Somewhere near the end
of the second century, Hebrew copies of the oral Torah became acceptable. This codification is known as the Mishnah.
The Mishnah in turn was the object of commentary known as
Gemara. The last two were formulated together by the Phari-
saic rabbis to form the Talmud in the period 200-600 A.D.
Written collections do not appear in the first century as universally accepted authoritative material, and only the Sadducees
held that the Torah needed no interpretation. It follows that
although at the time of Christ the beginnings of the Talmud
were known, interpretations differed among different sects and
groups. Rather than a theology, the Jewish codes were legalistic interpretations to assure proper conduct before God.

Essenes

The Essenes were a sect within Judaism, and can best be
described as a type of Jewish monasticism. Opinion is divided
as to whether they were actually a celibate order. Philo indicates that they were. Josephus mentions variations among the
sect where marriage took place, and excavations of the Qumran
community have disclosed a burying ground for women. That
the order followed the strict type of discipline commonly associated with the history of Christian monasticism is without
doubt. In at least one instance the sect lived within a walled
community. Its members did not hold personal property and
the community, headed by a superior or superintendent, required a period of probation as well as vows of profession. In
recent years the discovery of the Dead Sea Scrolls has added a
great deal to knowledge of the sect. In 1947 a Bedouin goat-
herd, Muhammad Adh-Dhib, by accident found a cave in the

Qumran area that contained a storehouse of ancient scrolls. Fortunately at the time he was unaware of the magnitude of his discovery. A decade of research has now produced rich material for the New Testament scholar as well as for the Old. The greatest treasure is a complete scroll of the prophet Isaiah. Also discovered were a rule for the community, a commentary on Habakkuk, hymns,and various other fragments.

The Qumran community does not exactly correspond to the accounts of the Essenes given by Josephus and Philo, but little doubt exists that they describe a similar sect. So much language in the New Testament corresponds so closely to Essene or Qumran writing that a hypothesis has been advanced which links Christ, himself, with the community. The evidence at hand cannot, however, substantiate this possibility.

Immediately after the discovery of the Qumran community at the time when similarity of expression was first observed, the point was used to cast a shadow not only upon the integrity of the gospel, but also upon the foundations of the Christian faith. That Christ should have quoted Essene sayings was thought to indicate a lack of originality in Christian teaching. What difference this makes to the basic Christian message is not clear. Jesus Christ was a Jew among Jews. His continual reference to and quotations from the Old Testament have not in the past been considered grounds for doubting the potency of his teaching. Instead they give credence and authority to the gospel story. After all, what other form of expression could have been used? The Essenes must have been well known to his time and even if he were not closely associated with the group, its strongly religious nature,coupled with the fact that it was spawned within Judaism, would have made points of similarity certain. Absence of such similarity would be far more suspicious than their existence.

Zealots

The Zealots are credited with triggering the revolt against Rome known as the "Great Rebellion" in 66 A.D. The rebellion ended in utter disaster when Vespasian undertook the destruction of Jerusalem. An experienced commander with ample forces at his disposal, he forced a successful campaign. Returning to Rome before the city's fall, he let his son Titus deliver the final blow. The subsequent sack was one of the bloodiest in history. In a final surge of fanaticism the Jews refused offers of clemency on the condition of surrender. Thousands of men, women and children, diseased and starving from the siege, were put to the sword.

How far back in history the Zealots can be traced remains a matter of question. Probably an outgrowth of the separatist movement, their spirit certainly extends to the days of Seleucid persecution. Their inspiration comes from the heroism of the Maccabean period, and their nationalism was a sustaining force to Judaism. Unfortunately Zealot revolutionary policies were for the most part destructive and fanatical. The name indicates what type of people belonged to the party.

III

Evolution of
the New Testament

The word *Bible* comes from the Greek *biblion* meaning little book. The plural form is *biblia*, twenty-seven of which form the New Testament. The word *gospel* is a translation from the Greek meaning "good news." [1] A study of the New Testament must have as one of its chief concerns an effort to determine what the good news is through an investigation of content in the light of historical setting, a study of the slant given by authorship, and a careful evaluation of the actual writings themselves. How many times were they copied? How many times translated from one tongue to another? What writings and sources were available for the original? How many were chosen to constitute the Bible and who chose them? To read the Bible without a thorough understanding of these things is almost certainly to read it with misunderstanding. Some of the message will not come through the ages clearly. Some may not come through at all. Compare, for example, a

[1] Streeter, *The Four Gospels,* p. 497. Streeter suggests that the usage whereby the word " gospel" became the call name for the biography of Christ came about as a result of the early world-wide circulation of Mark's writings. Jewish practice referred to books or sections of books by some striking word that might occur in the opening sentence. Mark's introductory words are, "The beginning of the gospel."

Russian interpretation of the Berlin crisis with that presented by the United States. Discuss the American Civil War and evaluate the Georgia campaign using first Northern and then Southern sources. Try to reconstruct with accuracy the events that took place in Atlanta or Gettysburg simply on the basis of hearsay without recourse to written record. The New Testament presents a similar difficulty. The earliest writing can be dated around the years 50-60 A.D. Some of it is late as 150 A.D. Jesus Christ was crucified close to 30 A.D. To further complicate the problem, the writings themselves have been copied countless times by hand. The fidelity of the printing press was fifteen hundred years away. Each hand could add or delete what seemed fitting. No copyright office stood by to assure accuracy and to credit authorship. When a different tongue was added, the resulting version might vary greatly from the original while the original itself could be quite different from the fact it sought to portray.

In broad outline, New Testament writings consist of four Gospels, three of which are so similar as to be known as the Synoptic Gospels—Matthew, Mark, and Luke—whereas the fourth, John, can be seen even on superficial reading as a work quite different in character from the others. The Gospels are primarily concerned with the message of Jesus, but they include as a matter of narrative necessity many other things of tremendous interest. They tell of the relationship between Christ and his followers; they tell something of the life and custom of the times; they describe methods of teaching; they include some history; they describe eyewitness accounts of momentous events and attempt to interpret them; and they tell a little of the evangelists themselves. They can be read literally and in the light of history and context. They also must be read between the lines.

Beside the Gospels is the Acts of the Apostles, a book whose title describes well its content. Acts tells of the early Christian era and is the first Christian book. Christ's ministry was within Judaism. Christianity did not exist until after the resurrection experiences and these did not take place until after Christ's ministry. The remaining portion of the New Testament includes some of its earliest writings—a group of writings in letter form devoted to particular problems of the times; a few short letters known as the Pastoral Epistles ; and a book entirely different in character from any of the rest, Revelation.

Formation of the Canon

During the life of Christ, those who became his followers received his teachings directly. As a result of the immediacy of his teachings and through the fact that a large portion of Jewish religious teachings by tradition always remained oral, they felt no need to record his words. Word of mouth and memorization by rote were accepted means of communication and record. In the first days following his crucifixion, the feeling of immediacy persisted. His predictions (perhaps misunderstood) of a changed world order were thought to apply to the contemporary time.

Even the most obtuse reading indicates that the early Christians were filled with tremendous enthusiasm. Their motivation is clearly spiritual. The resurrection experiences were so real to many and so close to many more that an unshakable conviction was fired and forged among the followers. The Holy Spirit was upon them and they were not of this world.

Almost at once legal fences were built around the community of Christians. Requirements for membership came into being. The new way of life was a communal affair, both in spirit and in worldly fact. Ananias and Sapphira held out some of their goods with disastrous results.[2] Already the penalty for non-conformity was death. The Christians felt that God had fulfilled his prophecy coming from Old Testament days. The Messiah had come. The new order had been ushered in. True, the events were not quite what was expected. The Messiah had

[2] Acts, Chapter 5.

been nailed to a cross by the very authorities Judaism had hoped he would overthrow, but then he had risen from the dead. This was vindication. Furthermore, he had promised to come again. At any instant the event might take place and God's judgment would rest upon all men alike. This news was indeed urgent and Christians staked their lives upon the fact.

For the converted Jew, God had fulfilled his prophecy, but the converted Jew was not for long to be the foundation of the Christian movement. Almost at once dissension arose over the Gentile question. Was Christianity to be a movement within Judaism or was it to spread to the Gentile and pagan world? Could a man become a Christian without first becoming a Jew? [3] The early church[4] answered in the affirmative. For many Gentiles the message and life of Christ were not so much the fulfillment of a prophecy as a fresh and original religious revelation. Of what concern was the prophecy of Isaiah and the religion of dispersed Jewry to the worldly Greek or Roman? Could St. Paul substantiate his message in Corinth before an audience steeped in the traditions of Greek philosophy by reference to a prophet whose people had been vanquished six hundred years before? Was Stoic Rome to buy his religious product because it was sold in the name of Judaism? The teachings of Christ for such as these must have stood on the conviction and skill of those who spread his gospel. Again the teaching was immediate, existential, taught and understood in terms of the current historical situation.

Time passed. The first century days were gone. The words and deeds of Jesus Christ were memory, and the new order did not seem to have come. The need to record and evaluate the history and teaching of Jesus was apparent now. St. Paul had written his epistles. Mark's Gospel had been written. Other gospels and epistles followed from many hands. Special treatises and apologetic writings were the spawn of reli-

---

[3] Acts 11:1-18.
[4] Term applied to Christian communities, not to be confused with church buildings, none of which existed at this time.

gious controversy. These were to hatch many and various traditions. Many were close to the gospel stories and well-written. The Didache, also known as the Teaching of the Twelve Apostles, was composed some time near 100 A.D. It is an authoritative work including not only history and teachings, but also descriptions of early Christian services. Others still used by modern scholars were an Epistle from Clement, Writings from Hermas (The Shepherd of Hermas), and the Epistle from Polycarp. These were not, however, to survive as canonical literature.

In the second century the influence of other religions was strong. Early convictions were replaced with questions. Statements concerning the nature of Christ and the events of his ministry became contradictory. Lines had to be drawn. Some writings were thought to be authentic with sound historicity; others did not ring clearly. Some portrayed accurately the teachings and interpretations, others did not. Thus, not without bitter controversy, slowly, over a long period of time, some were cast aside, others kept. Oddly enough, one of the first lists was compiled by a heretic, Marcion. Active in Rome during the second century, he gathered a large following. The list was a guide for his followers. It included Luke and the Pauline letters, but not the Epistle to the Hebrews or the Pastorals. A letter to the Laodiceans, which he did include, has not survived in the canon. Another list is known as the Canon of Muratori, named after its discoverer, an Italian priest of the 17th century. Individual lists, popular heresies, Montanism, Gnosticism—such things as these forced the ecclesiastical hand, but the canon could not be fixed until some recognized authority existed to fix it. Thus, formation of the canon did not take place finally until after the church councils. The first great general council was held in Nicea 325 A.D. and not until Easter of 367 A.D. did a canonical list similar to that recognized today appear. This was issued on Easter of that year by Bishop Athanasius of Alexandria. It is to be noted that the church created the Bible and that the Bible did not create the church.

The Text

Since the last part of the 19th century, textual criticism has become an exact science. It is now possible to appraise early writings with an accuracy unknown before our time. The new versions of the Bible are better than those of centuries past. At first this seems the opposite of what might be expected. The closer one is to an event in history, the more accurate the reporting should be. The ancients, however, did not have at their immediate disposal all the information we now have at ours. Communications, which we take as a matter of course, did not then exist. They could see only one facet while we can view the whole. Any one author had only a limited number of sources from which to choose. We have them all.

Most of the original writings were on papyrus. This vegetable material made from reeds crumbles with time. Few of these writings have survived and these only in fragmentary form. In the 4th century, vellum came into use. This made possible a book form similar to that of the present day. Furthermore, the skin is vastly more durable than reed. Because of the leaf form, writings on vellum are known as a *codex* (leaf) or codices. The papyri manuscripts were rolled.

The original language of the books is Koiné Greek, the common language of the Graeco-Roman world and one quite different from the classical Greek of earlier times. As the gospel spread to far off places, a demand for different translations was created: for Syria, the Syriac translation; for Egypt, the Coptic versions, and for the area of Africa that had once been Carthage, Latin. Some say the early texts even found their way to England, there to be repeated in the Celtic tongue.

At the request of Pope Damasus, St. Jerome (Eusebius Hieronymous Sophronius) journeyed to Africa. Using the available sources, he completed a Latin version in 386 A.D. Although fought by many, Jerome's Bible, the Vulgate, finally won acceptance and became the official version of the Roman Church to remain so until today. The Biblical train now goes into a tunnel and does not emerge for over half a millennium.

Not until the 8th century is new Biblical literature written, and the early English versions are still later. Some of the first are closely mixed with legend surrounded by tales of the supernatural. Caedman, the poet, is supposed to have been given divine gifts of meter and rhyme in order to put the Holy Scripture into poetic form. Eadhelm, Bishop of Sherborne, translated the Psalms into Anglo-Saxon; and Ebgert, Bishop of Holy Island, made a translation of the Gospels. Legend had it that the Venerable Bede, an aged monk and famous scholar, dictated a translation of John's Gospel on his death bed. After working night and day, he concluded the last sentences with his dying breath.[5] King Alfred is said to have translated parts of the Bible under the title, Alfred's Dooms, which forms the beginning of his Laws for England. The translations of this period were efforts to make the Scripture intelligible to the people and were written in simple and colloquial language. This sort of version is not to reappear until our present time with current efforts in modern vernacular.

Darkness falls again, shrouding the Holy Scripture from the light of scholarship. William the Conqueror crossed the channel, the Battle of Hastings was fought (1066), and England became a Norman land. Norman clergy replaced the native ministry. No need was felt to translate the Bible. The amalgam of Anglo-Saxon and Norman-French was to produce not only a new culture, but also a new language before the Bible emerged in rough form recognizable as the immediate ancestor of our present text.

In the last part of the fourteenth century, John Wycliffe lit a powder train that was to result in one ecclesiastical explosion after another. The thunder crashed for nearly two centuries before the Holy Bible was given officially to the people of England and Europe in their own language. Men were murdered by stealth and burned openly at the stake in the name of orthodoxy. In spite of persecution and trial, John Wycliffe produced the first complete English Bible.[6] This was a translation of the

---

[5] J. Paterson Smyth, *How We Got Our Bible*.
[6] Ibid.

Latin Vulgate which appeared in 1382. Although his Biblical work was good, his sectarian following in later years became radical. Wycliffe's work fell into ill repute. After his death, he was called, among other gross epithets, the organ of the devil and the idol of heretics. By order of the Council of Constance, his body was exhumed, the remains burned, and the ashes flung into the Swift River.

Two things were necessary to make Scripture properly available to the people—first a version that was something more than a translation of Jerome's first work, and secondly, a means of reproducing the new version once made. History was soon to fill both needs at once. Constantinople fell to the Turks in 1454, forcing Greek scholarship into Europe; in the same year the movable type printing press was invented. Once again after a thousand years of silence, scholarship was to speak. Greek sources were investigated, pens were active, and new versions of the Bible were born. Gutenburg produced the first printed edition (1450-61). The Gutenburg Bible or the 42 line Bible is also sometimes known as the Mazarin Bible because a famous copy belonged to the library of Cardinal Mazarin in Paris. Erasmus wrote his Greek New Testament in 1516. The next editions of importance are those of the famous printer and scholar Robert Stephens (Etienne, Stephanus), who published three editions in Paris (1546, 1549, 1550). This work, known as the Textus Receptus, was largely based on the fourth and fifth editions of Erasmus.

Although Wycliffe blazed the trail, William Tyndale was the real hero of the English Bible. His bones were not exhumed and burned; instead the man himself was strangled at the stake and burned for his pains. His story reads with the excitement of a modern detective thriller. Pathos and humor stand side by side. Inspired by Erasmus, he set about a translation from the Greek and Hebrew of the early manuscripts. This was a time when the foundations of Rome were rocked by the Reformation. The powder keg exploded when Luther nailed his theses to the door of his parish church. Never again was the Roman Ecclesiastical structure secure. Tyndale could not obtain permission for his translation from the English church authorities. The future of orthodoxy was too uncertain at the time. Rather than give up his project, Tyndale left England in 1524 to pursue his work in Hamburg, Germany. Here he completed a version which he took to Cologne to be published. The process had actually begun when word leaked to the church from the printers and Tyndale was forced to flee. At Worms, the sanctuary of Protestant reform, he succeeded in printing his first edition.

Hundreds of Tyndale's Bibles were smuggled to England, although every effort was made to prevent their reaching the public. At one time, in a desperate effort to stop the flow, the Bishop of London offered to purchase the Bibles from the printer and so destroy them at their source. The order was accepted, but the money was used to print Bibles in greater volume. The gate was down. In both Europe and the British Isles, the Holy Scriptures were no longer esoteric documents to be read by a few in high places. The word of God now came directly to the people at the price of Tyndale's death. He refused offers of safe conduct in England and continued to live in Germany, where he was betrayed by a friend. Imprisoned in the Castle of Vilvorden, he languished, old and miserable, until the day of his execution on October 6, 1536.

From Tyndale's time to ours, the Bible has developed both in the integrity of translation and the numbers produced until today it is the world's best seller. In 1535, Myles Coverdale, a man within the church, who became Bishop of Exeter, produced an English version in part from Latin. Much of the work, particularly in the New Testament, came directly from Tyndale. In 1537 a Bible was printed by one John Rogers. These works were immediately followed by "The Great Bible," a version produced by Coverdale and officially authorized by the Church of England in 1539. This was, through the process of copy and reference, almost entirely Tyndale's work. Strangling and the stake had failed.

Many works were to follow from both Isle and Continent. From Geneva came the "Breeches Bible," known better as the Geneva Bible, a product of the Reformation. J. Paterson Smyth tells that the Barker edition renders Genesis 3:7, where Adam and Eve "sewed fig leaves together and made breeches," this being the source of the title. On the continent Luther made a German version. In 1604, the King James Version was begun. By far the most beautiful in language, this Bible combines the best scholarship and research with exquisite English and remains a classic in our time. The needs of semantics have produced more recent versions, the Revised Version, the American Revised Version, but the King James still remains the most popular. Lastly, scholarship has produced many admirable translations in modern English, which are easily read and true to text. Among the better known are the New Testament translations of Goodspeed, Moffatt, and Phillips.

Sources, and the Problems of Research

An examination of the Gospel writings reveals that three are very similar, in fact nearly identical in many places, while the fourth is very different in language and content. The question arises, why the close similarities; why the differences? Scholars of the New Testament call this the synoptic problem. Some differences are to be expected. Experiments in psychology reveal the impossibility of obtaining exact duplication of description from different witnesses of the same occurrence even when the evidence is given immediately. The Gospels were written years after the actual events from different sources of information. Herein is a clue to the problem.

If the three Synoptic Gospels—Matthew, Mark, Luke— are placed side by side in parallel columns, a striking fact is at once discernible. All three contain the material which constitutes Mark. Further, parallel material exists in Luke and Matthew which does not exist in Mark; and lastly, both Luke and Matthew contain material which distinguishes them from Mark and from each other.

An analysis of these facts is not difficult. Matthew and Luke were no doubt written from a source which was also used by Mark, or were taken in part directly from Mark. Scholarship agrees on the latter. Secondly, it is clear that Matthew and Luke used a source not known to Mark. This source has been given the title Q.[7] Lastly, Matthew and Luke contain sources and sayings of their own. Thus, the Synoptic Gospels develop from at least four sources, Mark, Q, and the sources of Matthew and Luke which are designated M and L respectively.[8]

GOSPEL COMPOSITION CHART

Matthew	Mark	Luke	SOURCE
xxxx	xxxx	xxxx	Ur Marcus—Mark 65 A.D.
Q		Q	Q—50 A.D.
xxxx	xxxx	xxxx	Ur Marcus—Mark
		LLLL	Luke 80-85—L 60
MMMM			Matthew 80-85—M 60

xxxx = common material

The exact date at which any of the Synoptic Gospels took form cannot be given. Agreement, however, exists within narrow limits. Mark is undoubtedly the earliest of the three and is dated 65-70 A.D. The Gospel was written in Rome for the particular needs of Christian groups there. Matthew was probably written in Antioch around 80-85 A.D., although some have placed it as late as the turn of the century. Luke falls in the same period. Q, also of Antiochene origin, is the earliest, coming from near 50 A.D. M and L were written around 60 A.D.

The writings come to us by the devious route of redaction, translation, version, recension, conflation, interpolation, assimi-

---

[7] Q is derived from the German word *quelle* meaning source.

[8] Although this may represent an over-simplification, certainly the theory is basic to the facts. Even the best scholars are not in agreement on further divisions. Some feel that an early form of Mark may have existed from which Matthew and Luke were derived in part rather than from the familiar Marcan Gospel. This has been given the title Ur-Marcus. Streeter makes a strong case for an early gospel composed of L and Q from which Luke was derived termed Proto-Luke.

lation, extrapolation, gloss, and simply copying.[9] The uninitiated student must learn a new vocabulary, but once he has learned it, he can evaluate the text in a manner otherwise impossible. These are the terms of *Formgeschichte*, or form criticism.[10]

The word criticism does not denote a lack of truth, but in this case means examination. The story of form criticism is a history in itself, but it is a story that opens windows of understanding closed tight to scholars of earlier ages by the dictates of traditional orthodoxy.

Biblical criticism poured from the hot crucible of eighteenth century learning. A new age was cast, and as the children of the enlightenment grew to maturity, a new science of Biblical understanding grew up with them. The English Deists, Voltaire in France, the Encyclopedists, Holbach, Rationalism, the Enlightenment in Germany—these things ignited the minds of men creating a great heat of learning that first scorched the yoke of ancient dogma and then burned it away altogether. The first essay in Biblical criticism comes from the pen of Herman Samuel Remarus (1694-1768) with the date line Hamburg, Germany. The methods of criticism are accepted today, but a problem solved always seems simple in retrospect. The quickest way of putting a puzzle together is to turn the pieces right side up and then arrange them by color and type. Soon similarity of color and shape can be observed and the pieces begin to fit together. As the process continues a picture takes form which itself gives clue to the location of the remain-

[9] Redaction. The changing of the spoken word into written form.
Translation. The changing from one language to another.
Version. The new form resulting from translation.
Recension. A particular version of a text resulting from a revision.
Conflation. The bringing together from diverse sources.
Interpolation. The corruption by addition of new material.
Assimilation. The forcing of conformity to another text.
Extrapolation. The projection by inference.
Gloss. Translation, explanation, or interlinear commentary that has become part of the text in reproduction.

[10] Fuller prefers the translation, "form history," or the "history of tradition." Reginald H. Fuller, *The New Testament in Current Study*, p. 1.

ing parts. This is the method of form criticism where the pieces are the multitudinous manuscripts from different ages and areas of the ancient world, and the picture which emerges is the gospel itself.

The early manuscripts were handwritten documents (designated MS singular and MSS plural). These are sub-divided into groupings contingent upon the type of writing used, uncials and minuscules or cursives. The uncials are composed of large, block letters which are unconnected while the cursives, as the word suggests, use connected handwriting. Uncials constitute the earliest of the writings which range from the 4th to the 10th centuries. Some 170 of these are available to scholarship. Another group are the Greek lectionary texts, written between the sixth and eleventh centuries, of which 1500 or more have been found. The minuscules which immediately precede the age of printing, number to over 2300.

Most important to history are the six primary uncial Codices which have, for ease of identification, been given symbols of capital Roman letters. A is the Codex Alexandrius which rests in the British museum. B, the Codex Vaticanus is the property of the Vatican, Rome. C, the Codex Emphraemi Receptus in Paris. D, Codex Bezae in Cambridge, England. W, the Washington Codex. Lastly, the Codex Sinaiticus which takes its name from the area of its discovery.[11] This document designated Aleph takes its name from the first letter of the Hebrew alphabet. Originally held in Petrograd, it was sold to the British Museum in 1933-34 for the sum of one hundred thousand pounds (approximately half a million dollars), the largest sum ever paid for a book.

The puzzle itself has been put together in various manners. One of the accepted solutions is that of Wescott and Hort (1881). Another is that of the great Biblical scholar, Tischendorf. The relationship between the original writings and our present texts is somewhat as follows. Four families of manu-

[11] Discovered by Tischendorf in a monastery near Mount Sinai.

scripts have been classified: one, the Byzantine Text, also known as the Syriac, which is found only in late documents and which needs correction by critical comparison with others; two, the Western Text which is found in early old Latin and old Syriac; three, the Neutral Text which is seen in the old documents, Aleph, A, B, and C, and lastly, the Alexandrian Text found in part in Aleph.

A simplified diagram of Westcott and Hort's theory follows:

ORIGINAL

ALEXANDRIAN   NEUTRAL   WESTERN

SYRIAN REVISION (Early 4th C)

BYZANTINE TEXT

ROBERT STEPHENS

(Middle 16th C)

TEXTUS RECEPTUS

No portion of the New Testament can be properly evaluated unless the history of its component parts is understood. What was changed by translation? What was deleted by scribes who felt the material was not in accord with the Christian message? What was added by later ages as marginal notes, but eventually copied into the body of the text? What was added simply as an embellishment by a monk's pen more concerned with devotion to Christ than historical accuracy? What actually fraudulent material was added to promote a particular theology? What was lost in the archives of antiquity? What added to fulfill Old Testament prophecies? Answer these questions and a text of absolute integrity can be reconstructed, but these questions cannot always be answered. Take a comparatively simple problem as an example. Matthew and Luke include narratives concerning the nativity of Jesus, while Mark, the earliest Gospel, does not. Both Matthew and Luke suppose Jesus was a Galilean from Nazareth, yet the nativity stories fulfilling an Old Testament prophecy tell of his birth at Bethlehem. Why these contradictions? Clearly the date of the writing, the bias or slant of the author, the readership, all these things enter into the picture.

IV

The Quest for
the Historical Jesus

The uninformed New Testament student may object to the heading of the section. Why should a text for New Testament study find difficulty in presenting the life and personality of Jesus Christ as taken from the Gospels written about Him? Is the word *quest* not a misnomer? The answer is an emphatic no. The word quest is used advisedly and the modern consensus is clear on the point that the life of Christ cannot be reconstructed from the Gospel material, nor yet from that added by Acts and the Epistles. The quest is endless. The necessary material simply is not available. The Gospels do not contain it. If all the days described by them are added together, the period thus created is approximately one month. Further, the passages dealing with the nativity are subject to question. They are contradictory and inconclusive. Complete chronology of the life following is non-existent. The original writings did not have as their purpose the introduction of an unknown person to subsequent generations, but were written for first century Christians. They are not, therefore, a source of Christianity, but a product of it. On top of this, a great deal of the material dealing with the life of Christ as we find it in the accepted modern texts is from early manuscripts in which certain dogmas and conceptions were promulgated for a purpose which the Scripture was enlarged or glossed to serve. In short, new ideas were written into the old framework. For example, that Christ was baptized seems to be without doubt and a description of the occasion might certainly be expected. It does, in fact, appear but Matthew does not stop with the occasion. Either he or his source turns the affair into an announcement of Messiahship. Clearly this could not have been the case, for Messiahship could not have been a consideration at a date prior to the beginning of Christ's active ministry.

Nevertheless, Jesus Christ is certainly central to any study of the New Testament, and, although it may be impossible to write a biography from the available material, a great deal can be said with reasonable certainty. It is to these things that the study now turns.

Approximate Date and Place of Christ's Birth and of His Crucifixion

The man in the street today would have difficulty placing the birth of George Washington, or Abraham Lincoln on the basis of hearsay alone, and yet the chances are that he might be more accurate than most statements concerning the birth of Jesus. The time span between the event and the recording in the Gospels is roughly the same, and the Gospels themselves have undergone considerable change over nearly two millennia. To fix the date of Christ's birth with a margin of error less than five years is not possible. One thing is certain. Christ was not born in the year 1 A.D.

Two thousand years ago the Roman calendar was composed of months correlated with the phases of the moon. These alternated in length between 25 and 30 days. The year followed the seasons which corresponded with the earth's orbit of the sun. Julius Caesar designed a new calendar in 47 B.C. This calender did not have weeks, which were an innovation belonging to the time of Constantine (325 A.D.). Although other changes took place in the calendar's development, the most important one was made by a Roman monk, Dionysius Exiguus, in the sixth century. Dionysius felt that the years should be numbered from the birth of Christ. Looking through the records to find what year should be numbered "one" he found a statement by Clement of Alexandria placing the birth of Christ in the 28th year of Caesar Augustus. Caesar Augustus became emperor in the year 726 of the Roman calendar. By simply adding 28 years to this date, Dionysius came up with 754 as the year of Christ's birth, but he did not reckon the years Augustus ruled using the name Octavian. Hence Dionysius started the Christian calendar off with a four-year error which moves the date of Christ's birth back to 4 B.C. Such a reckoning assumes that Clement of Alexandria accurately dated the nativity which, however, is open to question.

Maurice Goguel, the French Biblical scholar feels that the stories of Christ's nativity as they appear in Luke and Matthew are too legendary to be of value for the purpose of date approximation.[1] No chronological data appear in either Mark or the Fourth Gospel. If Goguel is followed, the inquisitive student is left with only a small clue from Luke 3:1: "Now in the fifteenth year of the reign of Tiberius Caesar." The notation does not refer to Jesus, but to John the Baptist. Nevertheless it permits an approximation of the date for Christ's birth and ministry. Tiberius assumed the throne sometime between 28 and 29 A.D. At the time Jesus was an adult.

For those who feel justified in pursuing the matter from the early data in Matthew and Luke, a closer approximation is possible, but whether this procedure is legitimate is questionable. In Matthew we read that the birth took place in the days of Herod, the king. The date of Herod's death can be accurately fixed. Josephus makes a statement that Herod died after an eclipse of the moon. Astronomy places this event in the year 4 B.C. Thus, Christ must have been born prior to that date. Records have been discovered which indicate that the taxation Luke mentions might have taken place in the year

[1] Maurice Goguel, *The Life of Jesus*.

8 B.C. Matthew tells that Herod ordered all children two years and under to be slain.[2] Add the two year period to the date of his own death and the year 6 B.C. is indicated. Luke also places the date as 6 B.C., the time of the census by Quirinius.[3]

The Star of Bethlehem, also mentioned in Matthew, has been identified by Kepler (1571-1630 A.D.) as the conjunction of Jupiter and Saturn which took place in the year 7 B.C. More recent astronomical studies indicate that the conjunction was a triple effect: the two stars conjoined three times before finally passing. The date corresponds with Kepler's, but it has now also been discovered that in 6 B.C. an even more unusual grouping took place, that of Mars, Jupiter, and Saturn. If all this data is evaluated, the birth date probably lies between 4 and 8 B.C. with the consensus placing it near to 6 B.C.

If the evidence of "Shepherds keeping watch over their flock at night," [4] is accepted, we can assume that the birth occurred in the spring during lambing, otherwise the shepherds would have been asleep. Any speculation as to the month and day is too farfetched to be worthy of serious consideration. The earliest tradition for Dec. 25 comes from Hippolytus, around 200 A.D.

The day of the crucifixion can be more accurately fixed, but here again divergence of opinion exists. According to the Synoptic Gospels, Jesus was crucified on Friday. [Mk. 15:42, "And now when the even was come, because it was the preparation, that is the day before the Sabbath." Mt. 27:62, "Now the next day, that followed the day of preparation," Lk. 23:54, "And that day was the preparation, and the Sabbath drew on."] The day of preparation was Friday and the Jewish Sabbath was Saturday. The month and the date ac-

---

[2] Mt., 2:16 "Then Herod, when he saw that he was mocked of the wise men, was exceeding wroth and sent forth, and slew all the children that were in Bethlehem, and in all the coasts thereof, from two years old and under."

[3] Lk. 2:1-2.

[4] Lk. 2:8.

cording to the Johanine tradition was the 14th of Nisan—according to the Synoptics the 15th of Nisan. Thus, the date must have been the day of, or the day after, the spring full moon in one of the years of Pontius Pilate's administration while Caiaphas was high priest, sometime between 26 and 36 A.D. What day fits these requirements? Astronomy solves the puzzle to give two dates, one based on the Johanine tradition and the other on the synoptic—3rd April A.D. 33 and 7th April A.D. 30. Eusebius has made the date 33 popular; it has generally been accepted because of John's description of the Passover. The synoptic identification of the " last supper" as a Passover celebration seems unlikely for, as in this event, the crucifixion would have profaned the feast. All dates, however, which are based on the Jewish calendar may be questioned. Based on a lunar year, the calender was subject to periodic and arbitrary correction by the Sanhedrin, on those occasions when the lunar year became too far removed from the solar year and the seasons.

Goguel suggests an interesting and accurate means of fixing the year of the crucifixion. On the occasion when Jesus cleansed the temple, the Jews challenged his authority. In reply Jesus said, "Destroy this temple, and in three days I will raise it up." [Jn. 2:19]. The key line follows [Jn. 2:20], "Then said the Jews, Forty and six years was this temple in building, and wilt thou rear it up in three days?" As the Temple of Herod was not completed until sometime in the years 62-64 A.D., this line becomes senseless unless the translation is mistaken. It seems highly probable that the original line actually said, "For 46 years this temple has been a-building." If this is the case, simple addition can give the date. Herod began construction of the temple in the year 20-19 B.C. The Passover was near when the conversation recorded in John took place which gives the date 27-28 A.D. This date fits the reference in Luke to the fifteenth year of the reign of Tiberius Caesar. It seems quite certain, therefore, that the crucifixion took place somewhere between 28 and 33 A.D.

The place of Christ's birth is no less controversial. Christmas card art and hymnody have conditioned the public mind to an acceptance of Bethlehem as the town of the Holy Nativity. A tradition is no more reliable than the source from which it comes; in this case the source is open to so much question that it cannot be accepted by the scholar. Matthew and Luke fulfill the demands of Jewish Messianic expectation by placing the birth in Bethlehem, but they alone of all New Testament writings make this claim. It seems hardly possible that Mark, John, and Paul would have failed to mention the fact were it generally known.

What seems probable is that the early Christians believed Jesus to be the Messiah so strongly that they wrote the birth place into the gospel. The source then for the Bethlehem story is no doubt Christian conviction and not geographical reference. Micah 5:2 gave the prophecy which they felt must have been fulfilled. "But thou Bethlehem Ephratah, though thou be little among thousands of Judah, yet out of thee shall he come forth unto me that is to be ruler in Israel; whose goings forth have been from of old, from everlasting." The date of the Marcan and Pauline writing being much earlier than either Matthew or Luke indicates that they were not under pressure coming from early dogma and tends to substantiate the validity of their omissions, as opposed to the embellishments found in the others. A far stronger tradition and one far more acceptable places the birth of Jesus in Galilee—specifically in Nazareth.[5] The gospel accounts of "the virgin birth" probably come into being on a basis similar to that of the Bethlehem tradition. Note that in the Septuagint [6] Isaiah 7:14 makes a prediction, "A virgin shall conceive and bear a son." The Church has since made use of the tradition to substantiate its doctrinal position that Christ's birth was not only unique in history, but was sinless. The dogma has meaning only if it is assumed that sin is an inherited characteristic of man. These

[5] Mt. 2:13-23, 21:11; Mk. 1:9, 1:24; Jn. 1:45, 46; Acts 3:6, 4:10, 10:38.

[6] The Pentateuch translated into Greek by seventy Jewish scholars under the direction of Ptolemy II, Philadelphus on the isle of Pharos— An Alexandrian version of the Old Testament.

things are not the province of a study which attempts an historical approach to the life of Christ.

As in the case of the dates for birth and death, Christ's birthplace remains uncertain, whereas the place of the crucifixion is generally accepted. Undoubtedly, Jesus was tried at Jerusalem and crucified some place outside the city, according to the custom of the times. Tradition is very strong for the site of Calvary—the north side of the city. Furthermore this is the only side on high ground which fits the Biblical description.

Jesus the Man

Although the life of Christ is clear on the points of birth and death, the period between remains obscure. The years of actual ministry are perhaps an exception, but even these lack continuity. Rather they are represented by a few occasions which the authors found significant from the point of teaching. The Gospels were not written to convey biographical information. Where it occurs, biography is always incidental to their purpose. They were written to preserve the teachings and sayings of Jesus and to demonstrate certain facts concerning his nature. To add further obscurity, the structure of the accounts was designed to group together traditions which were originally independent, with the intention of making them coherent. In this attempt the authors were not always successful.

As a result, what is known about Christ's early youth is practically nothing. Even the origin of his name presents a problem. Although the Christian feels his name to be sacred, the unconverted do not. The name, Jesus, was common in Palestine at the time of Christ's birth and is still frequently used. The word Christ is undoubtedly a title. The "Christ" has a clear etymology following the historical development of Messianic conceptions.

The origin of Christ's family is totally obscure. Again the need to fulfill ancient prophecy seems to have slanted the record. Frequent references to the Son of David cannot be taken as indications of ancestry.[7] It seems certain that the references to David's descent come from Jewish traditions that the Messiah would spring from David's lineage. The majority of such references belong to Matthew and are not followed in parallel accounts in Mark and Luke [Mt. 12:23 versus Lk. 11:14; Mk. 7:26 versus Mt. 15:22; Mk. 11:9-10, Lk. 19:38 versus Mt. 21:9]. Arguments have been raised to show Jesus was an Aryan. Certainly no data other than the obvious are available to substantiate his racial background. He was accepted as a Jew among Jews. His family observed Jewish feasts and seems to have attended synagogue worship. The temple was familiar to him. It is unbelievable that the Gospels would not have mentioned anything so unusual as strong Aryan characteristics, had these existed. The New Testament makes no mention whatsoever of Christ in a descriptive manner that could be used to indicate race. That the people of Galilee were a racial mixture is without doubt, but equally certain is the fact that the preponderance of their blood line was Semitic.

What can be seen through the gospel narrative is a humble family typical of the lower class in Palestine. The accounts describe Jesus as an artisan—a carpenter.[8] He belonged to a large family. The existence of both sisters and brothers is indicated. In the descriptions of Christ's birth, Luke refers to him as the firstborn, not as the only child.[9] Mark mentions brothers and sisters in large number.[10] "Is not this the carpenter, the son of Mary, the brother of James, and Joses and of Juda, and Simon? And are not his sisters here with us?" The only reference that can be found to his youth does not fit the picture so established. A carpenter's son who became himself a carpenter is not the type of child one might expect to find

[7] Mt. 9:27-31, 12:23, 15:22, 20:30-31; Mk. 10:47-48; Jn. 7:41-42; Rom. 1:3, etc.
[8] Mt. 13:55; Mk. 6:3.
[9] Lk. 2:7.
[10] Mk. 6:3.

questioning scribes at the age of twelve.[11] Caste and protocol would forbid such activity. On the other hand, Jesus does emerge in his manhood not only as a teacher, but also as one learned in the law and the ways of the synagogue.[12] Somewhere along the line he must have spent much time in study and contemplation, and quite possibly he began at an early age. In any case Luke's description is all that can be found about the boy Jesus. Apparently he was an independent lad with interests of his own making, not known or understood by his parents.

When next he is to be seen, we meet a man whose personality dominates every scene of which he was a part. Here is no pale, emaciated weakling. Ecclesiastical art has done history a disservice. Carpenters are not weak people. Jesus did not live in the days of power tools and rubber-tired transportation. His hands must have been iron strong and hard with calluses. He walked countless miles in a land where the sun is a close fire made a blow torch by the wind. He slept under the stars on hard ground, unsheltered from air turned chill by night. He associated with rough strong men as their equal. Fishermen and those who go down to sea in ships are not frail. Military men recognized his authority in an age when men under arms fought hand to hand, while cold steel and muscle tipped the balance between life and death. Beaten and bleeding he hung on a cross through the midday heat before his breath failed and he died. What manner of man is this? The answer is not what Christmas cards or Renaissance imagination have conjured up for the 20th century Christian.

Duration and Location of Jesus' Ministry

All clues as to the length of Christ's ministry indicate a period of almost incredibly brevity—at the least six months [Luke], at the most a little over two years [John]. The exact

[11] Lk. 2:42.
[12] Mk. 6:2; Jn. 7:15.

time is not of great importance. The result of his work is what matters, and this cannot be evaluated in terms of man hours. The course of history was changed by what he said and did. The lives of millions upon millions of people have been lived in an entirely different environment from that which would have existed without his life on earth. Although the hours of his ministry were short, his personality made them eternally long.

The route of his travels cannot be exactly determined. A quick summary of John's account reveals at once the problems raised by any attempt to reconstruct Christ's journeys from the Gospels. According to John, after Jesus met John the Baptist in Peraea, he performed the miracle at Cana of Galilee [2:1-11]. Next he appeared at Capernaum. In ch. 2:13 the proximity of the Feast of the Passover is indicated, which fixes a point for chronology. Jesus went to Jerusalem. From there he returned to the area of the Jordan Valley with John and then went once again to Galilee through Samaria. In ch. 5 he went back to Jerusalem for an unspecified feast, and was active on the eastern shore of the lake of Gennesaret. Ch. 6:4 mentions a second occurrence of the Passover indicating the lapse of twelve months. Jesus stayed in Galilee until the Feast of Tabernacles which occurs in the fall. Ch. 7:14 tells that he was in Jerusalem for the Festival of Tabernacles. Ch. 10:22 finds him still there at the Feast of Dedication. Ch. 10:40-42 tells that he journeyed to Peraea and ch. 11:54-57 takes him to Ephraim. The raising of Lazarus is supposed to have taken place in Bethany, ch. 11:1-53. He then returned to Jerusalem on the eve of a third Passover, ch. 11:55. The synoptic material, even less explicit and more brief, depicts a Galilean ministry of uncertain length followed by a short time in Jerusalem.[13]

A compromise between John and the Synoptics suggests that the journeys so described probably lasted about eighteen months. Clearly the material is totally inadequate for a day-by-day reconstruction of Christ's ministry. There are no reports

[13] Mt. 15:21; Mk. 1:9, 1:14, 1:21, 1:28, 2:1, 3:7, 5:1, 8:27, 11:1, etc.

on activity between the occasions mentioned. The material is, in fact, inadequate for anything other than the broadest type of conjecture concerning the activities in the months under consideration. The points which are certain show that he was active in the area around Jerusalem less than two years, and that his ministry concluded with the crucifixion.

Jesus Christ, the Teacher

Christ's spoken words were more than teaching. In one sense they were propaganda; in another they were an apologia; in another they were instruction; and, for the most part, they partook of all three. They were propaganda in that they were designed to spread a particular belief. They were an apologia in that they defended this belief against the attacks of Jewish orthodoxy and they were teaching in that they were presented frequently to inner groups so that the initiated might then carry out the first two functions on their own.

Mark describes his words as spoken with something more than the characteristic of repetition so familiar to teaching methods of the times. "And they were astonished at his doctrine: for he taught them as one that had authority and not as the scribes." [14] The statement is substantiated by his audience. No matter how skilled the speaker and no matter how inspired he may seem to be, no man can command large audiences of mixed social and intellectual groups day after day unless he has a message that is authoritative. The teacher must have something to teach.

Coupled with great skill was a strong sense of prophetic vocation. Lengthy tomes have been written in an effort to pinpoint the exact time when Jesus became aware of his Messiahship. Although it is difficult, if not impossible, to determine that Christ believed himself to be the Messiah, he certainly seems to have considered himself a prophet; and if Luke's description of the early episode in the temple is taken as authentic, Jesus

[14] Mt. 7:29; Mk. 1:22.

felt his vocation as early as the age of twelve.[15] [See Messianic Consciousness of Jesus, p. 80.]

Jesus was an artist in communication. He spoke within the context of every conceivable emotion, from pathos to anger, from deep sorrow to intense joy. His speech was rich and warm and above all existential. He moved from near feminine gentleness to withering sarcasm. He soothed the sorrowful with tearful sympathy and blasted the hypocrite with violent indignation. Throughout, his style remains simple—never wordy. Each sentence, each word is chosen for a purpose and speaks directly to the point. "His words are the supple and transparent garment of his thought." [16] His examples are well chosen for his audience. Simple, homely images abound for his flock of nomads. The political issues of the day are turned into moral teachings.

Today his methods have been given a title—experience centered. Modern education has discovered the need for relating instruction to life. Otherwise it often remains meaningless. Although his format is basically from the Old Testament, he is not bound by tradition. He adapts words, phrases, and stories of Judaism (Hebrew religious history) to his particular purpose. Although an artist in language, he never speaks simply for the sake of his artistry. The Gospels reveal an accomplished strategist who makes the best use of his weapons. Like the master at chess he moves the necessary strength to the fore. His opponents hear the word *checkmate* before they realize that the trap has been sprung. Small wonder the established ecclesiastical authorities hated him so heartily. Until he appeared on the scene, theirs had been the position of intellectual superiority, but when challenged, the simple and youthful carpenter could make fools of them all.

Perhaps the largest portion of Christ's teaching is done through the use of parables. The form was not new. The parable as a means of teaching had been long accepted. It also served as a memory device in an age that was largely illiterate

---

[15] Lk. 2:42-49.
[16] Goguel, *The Life of Jesus.*

and without written record. Typical of the oriental mind, many of Christ's parables were in fact already familiar to the people of Palestine. Christ's applications, however, are his own.

A parable is a story with certain characteristics important to the New Testament student. Basically it is an expanded metaphor. In most parables the word *like* connects two factors. "The kingdom of heaven is *like* a mustard seed." [17] The story is given a frame in the first sentence and the frame usually makes historical sense, but the frame need not be significant to the teaching. Although the story is not necessarily a transcript of a life situation, it must be credible. The point to be made is self-evident if the parable is well presented. This brings up an obvious question for anyone who has read the Gospels.

Mark seems to feel that Jesus made use of parables as a means of conveying information to a chosen few while excluding the rank and file who were also listeners. The parables thus become a means of obscuring the gospel message, which is contrary to their intention. "And he said unto them unto you it is given to know the mysteries of the Kingdom of God, but unto them that are without all these things are done in parables." [18] The statement becomes absurd when the parables themselves are read. Beside its technical form a parable may be further defined as a means of making a point clear by leading the listener from the familiar to the unknown or by explaining a general truth in terms of a specific example. The parables must have been understood by Christ's audience.

Several theories have been advanced to account for the Marcan statement. Apparently Mark felt a need to explain why Jesus was not immediately followed by all who were exposed to him. Mark's dilemma is easily understood. If the people understood Jesus, why were they not converted? As they nailed him to a cross, they must not have understood. Mark does not want the reader to question the divinity of Jesus that might thus be placed in doubt. He may also have felt that the passion and crucifixion were necessary for the redemption of the

[17] Mt. 13:31; Mk. 4:30-32; Lk. 13:18-19.
[18] Mt. 13:11-13; Mk. 4:11; Lk. 8:10.

world (the atonement). He, therefore, used an artificial device to force his point, not realizing that Christ's apparent failure in the first instance came about through the sin of an entire culture rather than as a result of his inability to teach. Accordingly, most scholars feel that Christ's references to the parables as secret teachings are Mark's innovation. Others feel that the sayings which include similar references in Luke and Matthew represent the position of an early Gentile community which had in fact lost the meaning of the parables and found them obscure. A few feel that they were intentionally secret, directed at Christ's immediate group of followers who comprised a cult somewhat similar to the Essenes. Of the three suggestions the first seems to be the most likely solution to the problem. Mark added the commentary in Christ's words for his own purposes.

A closely related teaching device is allegory. At first reading the form may appear similar to the parable, but there are important points of difference. An allegory may have what appears to be an historical frame, but the story itself does not need to be credible and usually is not. An allegory can be understood only when a key is supplied. Each character and element in the story represents something else. This means that once a story has been established as an allegory, each detail needs to have meaning. In a parable, on the other hand, details may be freely added to embellish the story, making it more real and accordingly more emphatic.

Although most of Christ's parables are clearly identifiable as such, some border on allegory or have allegorical sections, while at least two are certainly allegories. Some schools have attempted to allegorize all the parables, with completely confusing results. One clear example of allegory is the story of a man whose vineyard is managed by wicked husbandmen. The problem of absentee landlords, true of all ages, is used to demonstrate a relationship. The man's tenants are not good and withhold the profits. Periodically the landlord sends servants to check on the operation and to collect the fruits of the vineyard. Each time the messengers are stoned and badly beaten.

The Lord of the vineyard then sends his son whom the husbandmen decide to kill in order to attain the inheritance.[19] First the parable does not begin with a similitude. Secondly, it is totally incredible as an historical occurrence. Why would a man send his only son unprotected into such an obviously desperate situation? Even more astonishing, why would the husbandmen expect to receive the inheritance from a man whose son they had murdered? Although Dodd argues to the contrary and assumes this to be a legitimate parable, the story makes far better sense as an allegory. The servants become the Pharisaical class, priests, scribes, etc. The messengers become prophets and the son is the Christ. As an allegory, however, the parable makes sense only in a Christian era.

Another example is the story of the Wise and Foolish Virgins (bridesmaids).[20] In this story some of the virgins (the foolish ones) run out of oil and their lamps go out. The wedding party continues on to the bridegroom's house while they go in search of oil. The virgins who arrive late find the door closed and are not admitted to the feast. The penalty doesn't seem to fit the crime. The face value of the story as a parable is clear enough. A door once closed may not easily be opened again. Opportunity knocks but once. This is secular wisdom rather than religious. If allegory, which seems more likely, the virgins are the Church of which many branches exist. These are linked to the bride, the main branch, and the bridegroom is the Christ.

The parable of the Sower is also probably allegorical.[21] Here a man sows seed not all of which grows to maturity. Some falls on the wayside, some is eaten by birds, some is undernourished and withers away, some falls among thorns, and only a small remaining portion yields fruit. As an allegory, the story seems to convey the message that not all mankind is saved.

The story in Luke centering around table manners has

[19] Mt. 21:33-41; Mk. 12:1-9; Lk. 20:9-16.
[20] Mt. 25:1-13.
[21] Mt. 13:3-9; Mk. 4:3-9; Lk. 8:5-8.

little, if any, religious significance.[22] One is advised to sit in a low position at banquets until invited to move nearer the head, lest the reverse take place. The directive makes such good secular sense that it could come from a modern manual on how to win friends and influence people. Both Bultmann and Smith see this as an ancient piece of wisdom mistakenly included in the text.[23]

In the story of the Unwilling Guest,[24] because the invited guests did not show up, the host bade his servants bring people in from the streets. One is expelled from the party as a result of improper attire. This seems rather unjust for there is no reason why the man should have been clad for a feast. The story is senseless without a key. Perhaps the meaning is that final blessedness can be achieved only in the robe of righteousness. Whenever parables are interpreted allegorically disagreement arises as to their meaning. In earlier days of Judaism the prophets frequently acted out their teachings. Isaiah walked "naked and barefoot" in the market place in a desperate effort to help keep Judah from entering into war with the Assyrians. He attempted to indicate the sort of condition the people would find themselves in if they continued to trust in power politics rather than the Lord, their God. Similarly, Christ's triumphal entry into Jerusalem[25] is probably an acted parable rather than the opening phase of military revolution. Although this type was known to the times, this incident seems to have been misunderstood by a great many people.

In dealing with the scribes and Pharisees, Christ consistently beat them at their own game. They were professionals in the field of Scripture, yet Jesus always produced a revolutionary Roland for each orthodox Oliver. Where they substantiated a position by quotation, he superseded it by the same authority. After quoting from Psalm 110, "The Lord said unto my Lord, sit thou at my right hand, until I make thine enemies

[22] Lk. 14:7-11.
[23] *The Parables of the Synoptic Gospels*, B. T. D. Smith, p. 208, Cambridge University Press, 1937.
[24] Mt. 22:2-14; Lk. 14:16-24.
[25] Mt. 21:1-9; Mk. 11:1-10; Lk. 19:29-38; Jn. 12:12-15.

thy footstool," He left the Pharisees dismayed.[26] They had said that the Christ must be the Son of David. If this be so, then why does David in the Psalm call him Lord? Unable to beat him intellectually, they inevitably used force.

The frequency with which Jesus turned chance encounter into the most potent lesson is striking. Over and over again he seized the opportunity of turning major incidents of criticism to his own advantage. He was seen eating with people of low degree, or he failed to observe the dictates of legal cleanliness.[27] These actions were outrageous to the Jew who was sensitive in matters of ritual cleanliness and social stratification. Jesus ate with publicans (Roman tax collectors) and sinners, he ate with a Pharisee without washing, and he permitted his disciples to pluck corn on the Sabbath.[28] When the criticism came for such action he was ready. He showed the law to be improperly used and interpreted, "For laying aside the commandment of God, ye hold the tradition of men," [29] or he accused the Pharisee of hypocrisy. "Ye Pharisees make clean the outside of the cup and the platter; but your inward part is full of ravening and wickedness." [30] When accused of eating with sinners he answered, "They that are whole need not a physician, but they that are sick." [31] Or he changed the emphasis from sin to salvation. "For the Son of man is come to seek and to save that which is lost." [32] Jesus succeeded not only in emerging the victor in debate, but also in making his own point clear.[33]

Occasionally he used shock treatment by making radical and bizarre statements that were for the moment unanswerable. His boast that he could build the temple in three days falls into this category. Here he struck at the very core

[26] Mt. 22:41-46.
[27] Mt. 9:10-13; Mk. 2:15-17, 7:1-2; Lk. 11:37, 38, 19:7.
[28] Mk. 2:23-28; Lk. 6:1-5.
[29] Mk. 7:8.
[30] Mt. 23:25; Lk. 11:39.
[31] Mt. 9:12; Mk. 2:17.
[32] Lk. 19:10.
[33] Son of man was an accepted title for the Messiah at the time of Christ. With one exception [Jn. 12:34] the title is used only by Christ himself in the Gospels.

of Judaism. Of all traditions that of the temple was the oldest and most sacred. The temple had been destroyed and rebuilt at the cost of an exile and the expenditure of countless wealth and hundreds of lives. It was a monument to faith which stood ageless in the Jewish mind. Now Jesus could build it in three days. What could be said to this?

Lastly, he frequently used the gambit and dilemma. He put the opposition into such a position that they had to give one of two answers either one of which resulted in defeat. A simplified version of the technique is seen in the old lawyer joke, "Answer yes or no. Have you stopped beating your wife?" On one occasion the elders and chief priests tried to trap him by questioning his authority to speak.[34] Jesus replied with a question that created a gambit. "If you answer my question, I will answer yours. The baptism of John the Baptist came from heaven or man?" If they answered from heaven they were placed in the position of repudiating God because they had repudiated the Baptist. If they answered from man they would arouse the disfavor of the people who believed in John. Their refusal to answer directly gave Jesus the opportunity to do likewise.

The modern reader may have difficulty with Biblical prose. Certainly this will be the case if he tries to understand it in terms of the measured and concise paragraphs of news print, or the direct report of contemporary history. Christ's teachings are for the most part presented in poetic form. The form not only lends itself to memorization, but serves to make the point expressed more emphatic. Hebrew poetry is filled with repetition, balance, and antithesis as well as meter and rhythm. These things are a natural part of Christ's speech.

As the entire Gospel follows this form a few examples should suffice. Matthew 5:13-15 gives a series of parable-like sayings using doublets. Jesus says the same thing twice in a different way. "Ye are the salt of the earth; but if the salt have lost its savour wherewith shall it be salted?" He follows the

<hr />

[34] Mt. 21:23-27.

statement almost immediately with another of identical meaning. "Ye are the light of the world, a city set on a hill cannot be hid." Sometimes the language develops into a triplet as in Matthew 5:22. "Whosoever shall be angry with his brother without cause shall be in danger of judgment: and whosoever shall say to his brother Racca,[35] shall be in danger of the council; but whosoever shall say, Thou fool, shall be in danger of hell fire." The Beatitudes are a perfect example of rhythm, balance and antithesis. "Blessed are the poor in spirit; for theirs is the kingdom of heaven. Blessed are they that mourn; for they shall be comforted, etc." [36] The parable of the house built on sand and the house built on rock uses antithesis.[37]

Jesus Christ, the Healer

The question of miracles or, as some term them, the mighty works of Jesus, has been controversial in this century. Early orthodoxy accepted them all as they appeared in the first text and the Church continued to do so until the age of natural science either explained some or completely repudiated others, while form criticism removed still others from the text altogether. A miracle is an event in the physical world which cannot be explained by any of the known laws of nature. The event must, therefore, be the result of a supernatural agency. By this definition one might assume that events which appear miraculous from limitations of understanding might not appear so, were all the facts known. Thus, the forward movement of an automobile without the help of a horse might appear miraculous to the ancients or even to a present day aborigine. Television today remains miraculous to those whose minds cannot grasp the intricacies of electronics. This is not what is meant by miracle. In true miracles the natural order is altered by the supernatural; it is this definition that brings about questions in respect to Christ's mighty works.

[35] A vain fellow—a Hebrew word of great scorn.
[36] Mt. 5:3-11.
[37] Mt. 7:24-27.

Many of his miracles have been explained or rationalized away by modern understanding of the universe. Certainly no one any longer believes that mental disease is caused by demons. In recent years rapid advances in psychosomatic medicine indicate that many diseases of the body are the result of maladjustments in the mind.

Real physiological disturbances such as sinus trouble, migraine headaches, ulcers, colitus, even loss of speech, blindness, and paralysis may have mental origin. Once the mind is healed, the physiological symptoms often disappear with *"miraculous"* speed. The temptation to apply current analysis to cases described in the Gospels is great. For those who have done this, Christ becomes the great psychologist. Any such approach to the healing miracles is completely unjustified. The evidence is not sufficiently clear, sufficiently reliable, or sufficiently complete to make any valid diagnosis possible. Furthermore, Christ was not a psychologist and his miracles do not follow the form of accepted psychiatric procedure. A secondary question asks whether Jesus himself believed in demons. No evidence exists to substantiate the fact that he did not. Jesus was a man of his times; his cosmology was that of the first century. Were the case otherwise he would have been omniscient which is contrary to accepted Christian doctrine.

Rationalization is sometimes used in an effort either to change the reporting completely or to substantiate what is recorded. A rational explanation of Jesus walking on water,[38] is that he was walking in the shallows or perhaps walked on the shore and was obscured by mist. Concerning the parable of the loaves,[39] theories have been advanced that each of the multitude had brought food and the resulting supply produced an overabundance for the communal meal.[40] No evidence exists for such assumptions. They are pure speculation.

The evidence which does exist may be questioned. Per-

[38] Mt. 14:25; Mk. 6:48.
[39] Mt. 14:17-20; Mk. 6:38-43, 8:7-10; Lk. 9:13-17; Jn. 6:9-13.
[40] It is commonly accepted that all the feeding stories are different accounts of the same event put to different uses by the authors.

haps many of the so-called miracles never occurred at all. Perhaps they were tricks. Speculation of this sort is fruitless. What we know is a better foundation for evaluating the miracles than what can be assumed or questioned. First we know that healings and mighty works are described by all four Gospels and that they do not seem to be questioned by the original authorship. Further, more healings took place in the early New Testament times after the crucifixion.[41] A close scrutiny of the record indicates that those mighty works which are recorded form categories which were of particular significance, but which were not necessarily taken from single occasions of each event. Undoubtedly a great many more instances of this sort of thing took place than the Gospels record.

Obviously something unique took place. These occurrences were signs of the times, no matter what they were in point of fact. In the Synoptics Jesus does not use miraculous ability in order to magnify himself or substantiate his claim to Messiahship. Rather, he asks that the healed go their way and say nothing.[42] Some of the healings took place without his presence,[43] and in one instance he is not aware of the affair until it has been accomplished.[44] If the Christian position throughout the ages is valid, that is, that in the person of Jesus God was incarnate, then the miraculous activities associated with his person become quite natural.

The mistake must not be made, however, of putting the Biblical cart before the critical horse. Some have said that the miracles must be true as recorded because they are described in the Bible which they feel is the revealed word of God. But the Bible is supposed to be the revealed word of God, among other reasons, because of the miracles it describes. The argument goes around in a circle and proves nothing.

In conclusion, the miracles can neither be substantiated nor disproved on the basis of available evidence. Their inclusion in

[41] Acts 3:1-10, 9:32-35, 36-42, 14:8-10, 28:8.
[42] Lk. 5:14, 8:56.
[43] Mt. 8:1-13; Lk. 7:2-10.
[44] Mk. 5:28; Lk. 8:44.

the gospel narrative has as its purpose not the depiction of Christ as a faith healer, but rather simply as evidence to substantiate his divinity. They were signs of the times and were duly recorded as such.

Jesus and John the Baptist

The real relationship of Jesus to John the Baptist was a source of embarrassment to the early church and presented difficult problems to the authors of the gospel. First the church could not accept any tradition which placed Jesus in a position of subordination and secondly, the obvious doctrinal question arose—if Christ were sinless, why should he be in need of repentance and baptism? The Synoptics are in agreement that Jesus was baptized by John,[45] but Matthew makes the protocol clear by John's question, "I have need to be baptized by thee, and comest thou to me?"[46] The fourth Gospel minimizes the Baptist's activity to such a degree that Christ's baptism as an individual is not described.[47]

Almost certainly Jesus was at first part of John's following. The gospel narratives are clear. Christ walks onto the stage of history surrounded by Baptist followers, is heralded by the Baptist, and is himself baptized. In an effort to make the superiority of Jesus clear the authors have written contradictory reports. The Synoptics are all in agreement that John was given a sign. Not only did he forecast the arrival of Jesus,[48] but also the impression is given that something unique took place on the occasion of the baptism itself.[49] If the Holy Spirit descended upon Christ "like a dove," John must have been emotionally obtuse or weak in memory, because later he sent messengers to Christ asking if he were the Messiah.[50] As usual Jesus gave an answer that forced the conclusion upon the ques-

[45] Mt. 3:13; Mk. 1:9; Lk. 3:21.
[46] Mt. 3:14-15.
[47] Jn. 3:23.
[48] Mt. 3:11.
[49] Mt. 3:16-17; Mk. 1:10-11; Lk. 3:22.
[50] Mt. 11:2-3; Lk. 7:20.

tioner without committing himself. "Go and show John again those things which ye do hear and see; the blind receive their sight, and the lame walk, the lepers are cleansed, and the deaf hear, the dead are raised up, and the poor have the gospel preached unto them. And blessed is he, whosoever shall not be offended in me." [51]

John the Baptist was a recognized authority before Jesus became famous. He was a popular preacher whose impact on the culture aroused the interest and finally the antagonism of kings. He achieved success in his mission and prepared the way for a revolution within Judaism.[52] His message of repentance was already in conflict with the established order when Jesus began his ministry.[53] So great was his following that many thought him to be the Messiah.[54]

The origin of John, like that of Jesus, remains a matter of speculation. His description in the Gospels suggests an eccentric or a member of a religious sect.[55] Locust and wild honey are not a conventional diet, nor were his garments altogether in keeping with the times. He may have been a Nazarite,[56] or possibly an Essene. Similar to the Essenes, his baptism had a double emphasis—purification and initiation. Those who repented were baptized as a sign of admission to the cult. On the other hand, the Essenes wore white robes and John's garb of camel's hair and animal skin does not fit the picture. Luke tells that he was of priestly origin,[57] but the story of his later days does not bear this out. The priests were a hereditary clan connected with the temple, and although some of them may have appeared there only occasionally, all did, in fact, appear. No reference to John and the temple occurs in the gospel narrative.

[51] Mt. 11:4-6; Lk. 7:22-23.
[52] Lk. 11:1.
[53] Mt. 3:7-10; Lk. 3:7-15.
[54] Lk. 3:15.
[55] Mt. 11:18; Mk. 1:6, 2:18.
[56] A man in ancient Judaism set apart by particular vows which forbade alcohol, fruits of the vine, hair cutting and proximity to a corpse. Some say that Samson was a Nazarite.
[57] Lk. 1:5-13.

In conclusion, the evidence is clear that Jesus began as a member of John's following and continued with him for some time before branching out on his own. John probably regarded Jesus as one of his followers until near the end when he sent messengers from jail. Lastly, Jesus recognized John as a great prophet and more,[58] but in the end he linked him with the old rather than the new order.[59]

Days in Galilee

Although chronology and geography must forever be uncertain, a broad reconstruction of Christ's ministry places its beginning sometime after he had been associated with John the Baptist in the vicinity of the Jordan River. Probably early in the spring Jesus left John, returned to the area of Galilee and began to preach on his own. At this point his message was not much different from John's. His unique message developed later.

Every indication in the Synoptics suggests that Capernaum[60] was the headquarters for his work. He traveled by foot and his message spread by word of mouth. These circumstances limited his ministry to the region in the immediate vicinity—a circle with a diameter of approximately twenty miles. On occasion he may have spent a night or two on the way, but even if he journeyed for a week, he couldn't have gone very far.

The impact of his teaching was apparently great even in this early stage. With a magnetism similar to John's he attracted a hard core of followers almost at once. These formed a shock corps who were willing to follow him no matter how bold the journey, no matter how great the risk. At first to be a follower involved little more than spiritual awakening and the understanding of a new and tremendously happier way of life. No doubt even the early gatherings, however, were made

---

[58] Lk. 7:24-27.
[59] Mt. 11:11; Lk. 7:28.
[60] Capernaum—probably the present day Tell-Hum.

exciting by religious awe, wonder, and fear. The presence of something tremendously mysterious may have been felt. As the word was passed, the meetings grew larger and other followers developed, the kind who came to hear and see in crowds, but who were only partially sold on the message. They may have been pleased with what they were able to understand, but they were not sufficiently impressed to change their way of life and certainly they had no intention of undergoing any risk for the cause. A front must be very popular to command enough allegiance for its followers to be willing to have their heads cut off.

Decapitation or crucifixion were popular means of execution in this age of the absolute ruler. Herod Antipas, the tetrarch,[61] was one such tyrant. He had already had trouble with John the Baptist, and then word came that a similar type of movement was beginning under Jesus' leadership. Like most ancient rulers he didn't consider benevolence a virtue because the life of the common man was one of servitude and misery. Large gatherings of any kind could easily become the first stages of serious revolt, particularly when popular leadership was coupled with the tremendous power of religious fanaticism. The Hasmonean uprising was not forgotten. The day that Herod saw another revolutionary in the making marked the end of the first stage of Christ's period in Galilee.

No longer could he journey peacefully to and from Capernaum. He was a marked man. The Herodians were after him, no doubt with orders either to break up his assemblies or, if this were to fail, to arrest him that he might be brought before Herod and summarily disposed of. Christ was only one step ahead of the authorities. A central headquarters was now impossible. He was driven to the outlying regions. Leaving Galilee, he moved to the eastern shore of the Sea of Galilee (Lake Gennesaret), thence into Decapolis, to Caesarea Philippi, to the borders of Tyre and finally to Judaea.[62]

[61] A Roman governor of limited authority; ruler of one fourth of a province.
[62] Mt. 14: 34, 19:1; Mk. 6:53, 7:24, 31, 8:27, 9:30, 33, 10:1; Lk. 13:31.

A Fugitive in Jerusalem

Because Jesus seems to have been a fugitive during his last days in Galilee, the reason for his moving on to Judaea and Jerusalem is not clear. Certainly pressure in the city would have been greater. Jerusalem was the seat of government, the location of the Roman garrison, and most important of all the home of both the Sanhedrin and the temple, a combination that formed the heart of the great religion that his preaching, if accepted, must still. Even though his message may at that time have meant only to reform Judaism, so completely did he change the emphasis of religious feeling that the established authorities would have perished. Such a thing would have been intolerable to them. Why then did he go to Jerusalem?

No one reason can be given. It may have been that the Herodians were making things too hot for him in Galilee, but it is hardly likely that this in itself would have been enough even were their opposition fortified by that of established Jewry. Trouble from these sources would not have been less in Judaea and certainly from the Jews it would have been greater. The Gospels indicate that he went up for a religious feast—Tabernacles or the Passover. Here is reason enough for a quick visit from a devout Jew, but John's Gospel indicates more than a quick visit; he records a period of several months.

Possibly Christ's following in Galilee became large enough to make him restive. Greater work could be accomplished where the population was greater. He may have felt that the time had come when he could make a direct assault on the established religious authorities. He may have hoped for a reform within orthodoxy. All were good reasons for moving.

Some Christian traditions say that he went to declare himself the Messiah. The Gospels themselves can be read to substantiate this position. If this were his purpose, he badly miscalculated the situation. His Messiahship was not accepted, he was unsuccessful in making it widely known, and he was put to death. The Synoptic Gospels depict the introduction to the triumphal entry stories in miraculous terms. Christ's prediction that a mount would be freely given for the asking proved true.[63] The implication is clear that the events form part of a divine plan for his Messiahship, trial, and crucifixion which accomplished an atonement for the sins of mankind that could take place in no other way. Is this not a Christian answer? Jesus could not have been aware of such doctrinal ramifications in respect to his life. He made no statements signifying such a point of view. More likely the prediction is a doctrinal gloss coming from many decades after the event.

It may be that he felt compelled to move into Jerusalem in order to prove himself. He may have seen the inevitable end to the conflict with both Jewish orthodoxy and Roman secular authority. On the one hand a declaration of Messiahship was blasphemy, on the other sedition. The Jews recognized no Messiah and the Roman Emperor was god. To challenge either authority was to court death, but no alternative existed. If Jesus backed down and did not stand true to his teaching, the message would have been lost and forgotten. Only if he were willing to die for his convictions could the faith be proven. He may have felt that the time had come to declare and prove himself. His predictions concerning the outcome of his visit and his unwillingness to avoid the issues as they arose substantiate this position.

The Synoptics and John's Gospel are not in agreement concerning the length of time that he spent in Jerusalem before the crucifixion. If the Synoptics are accepted, the period is short, a week or less. By their account Jesus appeared in Jerusalem with a large and enthusiastic following.[64] He immediately created a crisis by his activity in the temple.[65] Pilgrims came to the temple from many lands. Money changing and "dove marketing" (the sale of doves for sacrifice) were permitted in the outer courts of the temple. Driving the money changers out of their seats must have created a violent disturbance looked upon with disfavor by Roman and Jew alike.

[63] Mt. 21:3; Mk. 11:1-6; Lk. 19:30-32.
[64] Mt. 21:9; Mk. 11:9-10; Lk. 19:37-38.
[65] Mt. 21:12-13; Mk. 11:11; Lk. 19:45-46.

Shortly thereafter he left the city for the night.[66] The lines were quickly drawn and plans were made to bring about his arrest. In the meantime Jesus apparently remained in seclusion with his disciples to whom he preached his last sermons. Although the discourse known as the Little Apocalypse [Mk. 13:5-37] is probably not authentic, he did undoubtedly brief his close lieutenants on what the future might bring that they might be prepared to carry on after his death. A few days later he permitted himself to be found and was arrested.

Even with the increased time span given by John's Gospel the period is hardly long enough for all the events packed into it. The descriptions are typical of the Gospels which, it must be remembered, were not attempting either history or biography as these things are understood today; they were compiled for the sake of preserving a point of view, and to demonstrate certain facts. History and biography, where they occur, were contrived for the sake of continuity and, therefore, are for the most part artificial.

John makes Christ's late ministry longer than the Synoptic accounts. Jesus probably went up to Jerusalem for the Feast of Tabernacles in late September or early October. He remained in the area until the Feast of Dedication in December and then left for Peraea. During these weeks he undoubtedly raised a large following. The last sad days and the birth of the Christian movement shortly after his crucifixion give evidence to the fact. Luke records that the populace saw his death as a disaster. A great company of people, both men and women, followed him with much lament to the cross.[67] Large numbers of close followers are recorded in Acts.[68] Even on the occasion of his arrest he was not found in the presence of his close associates alone. Others were there, some of them strangers to him.[69] Although he was much beloved, he had also aroused vociferous and violent opposition. The crowds were not all

---

[66] Mk. 11:15-19.
[67] Lk. 23:27-28, 48.
[68] Acts 1:15.
[69] Mk. 14:51.

friendly. An atmosphere of strong antagonism surrounds his presence as well as devotion and love. Orthodox Jewry was after him hard and fast. Theirs was a drum head justice and the order to execute would have been carried out by mob violence on many occasions had it not been for the presence of his sympathizers ("The Jews took up stones again to stone him").[70] During the last days he was a fugitive from both the mob and from formal arrest.[71]

The situation could not continue for long. Either Jesus had to leave Jerusalem, give up preaching, and seek seclusion in a sympathetic area until the heat of controversy cooled, or he had to face the forces that were against him directly and prove his position once and for all. The story tells that he did both. His visit to Peraea represents a time of withdrawal and decision. It must have been clear to him that a return to Jerusalem could have only one conclusion, but he elected to follow that course. In making this decision he became the Messiah.

About a week before the Passover he returned to Jerusalem. John's account describes no miraculous activity. Although he mentions great acclaim, John's chronology makes the occasion more a welcome home than an initial entry. The opposition was waiting and ready. The trap was soon to spring. The quick arrest, the speed of the trial and the immediate execution, all before the Feast of the Passover, indicate a well planned frame. Jesus didn't waver in his decision and remained steadfast to the end.

The Last Supper

The exact character of "the last supper" is widely controversial. The matter is complicated by statements of dogma and doctrine which developed after the event. Furthermore the evidence of the Gospels is conflicting; and although volumes have been written to justify one point of view or another, none is finally conclusive. Two determinative facts are in ques-

[70] Jn. 10:31.
[71] Jn. 10:39.

tion: one, the nature of the repast—was it a paschal feast or fellowship meal? and two, the day on which the meal took place—was it on the evening of the fourteenth of Nisan or before?

If the feast were a Passover meal, the date would have been the 14th of Nisan which was the first day of unleavened bread, and the crucifixion would have followed on the 15th. Although the Synoptics make clear that the supper was a Passover celebration,[72] much doubt can be cast on the reporting. First, neither Matthew nor Mark mention features of the meal that must have appeared were the Feast properly observed. The bread is not unleavened and no mention of a lamb is made. The strongest objection comes from the chronology which their assumption demands. If the meal took place on the Sabbath eve, the crucifixion must have taken place on the Sabbath, the day of the Passover, and all the activities of the trial in which the Jews took part must have been on the same day. Such a situation is completely incredible. Because the activities would have profaned the Sabbath in countless ways, the Jews would have had no part in them.

John gives different evidence. He states clearly that the meal took place "before the Feast of the Passover." [73] Also when he describes Pilate presenting Jesus to the Jews during the trial, he refers to the eve of the Passover.[74] The time is specified as the sixth hour—mid-day. The Jews are shown as unable to enter the Praetorium[75] because of defilement which would have prevented their taking part in the feast.[76] Furthermore, the Synoptics are all agreed that the day of resurrection —the day the empty tomb was discovered—fell on the third after the crucifixion, which they place on the first day of the week, Sunday. In accordance with their statement, the crucifixion must have occurred on Friday and "the last supper" the

[72] Mt. 26:17-21; Mk. 14:12-16; Lk. 22:7-13.
[73] Jn. 13:1.
[74] Jn. 19:14.
[75] The Praetorium was the official residence in Jerusalem of the Roman procurator—a Gentile house and therefore unclean.
[76] Jn. 18:28.

day before. The references to Christ's burial also fit this chronology.[77]

Once again the critical scholar is forced to conclude that early Christian apology wrote the reporting concerning the preparation for the feast. Like the description of "the triumphal entry," the accounts are slanted for a doctrinal purpose. That Jesus should have celebrated the Passover with his disciples and was himself crucified on the Passover fits the conception of his death as a paschal sacrifice to atone for the sins of the world. If, as the evidence in John seems to indicate, the meal took place sometime before the day of preparation, its significance is no less important, but the emphasis is quite different. The secret meeting of Christ and his disciples is an expression of fellowship.

If the Gospels are viewed from a distance rather than with close focus on isolated events, "the triumphal entry", "the cleansing of the temple" and "the last supper" can all be seen as acted parables. When they are understood as such, a great many of the critical problems are solved. If Jesus contrived a triumphal entry of the magnitude indicated by the Synoptics, why did not the Roman authorities take immediate action? Certainly the garrison would not have permitted an incipient revolution in its midst. In the case of the temple, a complete cleansing of money changers would have created a riot that the priests could not have overlooked. An immediate and overt response should have been forthcoming. Only "the last supper" was a private affair, a small and intimate gathering.

However, the first two events were probably also confined to the presence of Christ's immediate following, because neither of the established authorities showed concern for them at the time. What all three events have in common is an assertion of Messiahship.[78] Christ actually declares himself in the case of the entry and at the supper. The implication also is clear in the case of the temple, for the conception of the Messianic age was coupled with its re-establishment as sacrosanct

---

[77] Mk. 15:42-43; Lk. 23:50-56; Jn. 19:31, 42.
[78] See Messianic consciousness of Jesus, p. 80.

to Jew and Gentile alike. The message was not fully understood. Because Christ's Messiahship was not what the Jews
expected, his actions were overlooked until perspective and
interpretation were changed by the Christian era.

The Trial and Crucifixion

From the *upper room* Jesus moved with his disciples to
the Garden of Gethsemane, a park-like area near the Mount of
Olives. The garden apparently was a popular place to meet in
the cool of the evening on the occasion of feasts and political
gatherings. There his arrest was accomplished under conditions
reminiscent of secret police activity today. That the arrest took
place at night is significant. Evidently Christ's following was
so large that a public arrest during the daylight hours would
have caused trouble. The speed of the events which followed
indicates the probability that a plan had been carefully laid,
and the accounts of the hearing and trial give the impression
that, at least as far as the Jews were concerned, the verdict had
also been previously determined.

After a minor scuffle in the garden, Jesus' friends, for all
purposes, deserted him.[79] With the story of Peter's denial the
Gospels make the circumstances clear.[80] That none of his following stood by him shows that few, if any, understood the
full implication of his message or saw him for what he was.
Rather than "the Christ," the picture is a discredited and defeated revolutionary. Jesus' first interrogation seems to be
illegal.[81] More in the nature of a private questioning than a
legitimate trial, it was perhaps an effort to obtain a confession
in order to speed the procedure of the trial before the complete
Sanhedrin later. Both the crowd and the officers were hostile.
Jesus was ridiculed and badly beaten as he was moved from one
place to another.[82] On the next day he was brought before the

[79] Mt. 26:50-52; Mk. 14:42-56; Lk. 22:50; Jn. 18:8-10.
[80] Mt. 26:72 ff; Mk. 14:70 ff; Lk. 22:57 ff; Jn. 18:25 ff.
[81] Lk. 22:54; Jn. 18:12-13.
[82] Lk. 22:63.

Sanhedrin.[83] (Mark's account omits some stages of proceedings and takes him to the Roman court early in the morning.[84]) The Jews placed two charges against him, both of which amounted to the same thing. He was first accused of threatening the destruction of the temple which could be construed as a Messianic act, and he was secondly accused point blank of declaring himself the Messiah. "Art thou the Christ?" [85] "Art thou then the Son of God?" [86] Jesus finally answered in the affirmative which to the Jew was blasphemy.

He was then taken to the Roman Court. Pontius Pilate was not concerned with Jewish religious intrigues unless they involved a movement that was seditious in respect to the authority of Rome. His questions follow that line: "Art thou king of the Jews?" Jesus parried the question with "Thou sayest." [87] Although the Romans used puppet kings, Jesus was not so identified. To have declared himself any type of secular king without Roman authorization would have been a crime against the state.

The Gospels are agreed that Pilate found no fault in Jesus.[88] He made every attempt to release him, offering the multitude another prisoner, Barabbas, for crucifixion instead. Although the Synoptics show a sympathetic crowd on the way to the cross and at the crucifixion, the people at the Roman court cry madly for blood: "Crucify him, crucify him." [89] (The trial before Herod is recorded only in Luke's Gospel.[90] The speed of the events plus the single recording casts doubt on this account. It may be that the story belongs to the early period of antagonism between the king and Jesus at the time of his Galilean ministry.)

The Gospels show that, rather than making a formal sen-

[83] Lk. 22:66.
[84] Mk. 15:1.
[85] Lk. 22:67.
[86] Mk. 14:55-57, 61; Lk. 22:70; See p. 81, Son of Man.
[87] Mt. 27:11; Mk. 15:2; Lk. 23:3; Jn. 18:37.
[88] Mt. 27:17-18; Mk. 15:9-10, 14; Lk. 23:4; Jn. 18:38, 19:15.
[89] Mt. 27:20-23; Mk. 15:13-15; Lk. 23:18-21; Jn. 18:40.
[90] Lk. 23:7-11.

tence, Pilate wrestled with a decision which was finally made for him by the machinations of the Jews. The decision to crucify Jesus developed in the absence of negative action, almost by default. The trial was suddenly over and Pilate let the course of events lead to the conclusion which was then inevitable. The accounts are graphic and the picture of a man tormented and tortured, staggering to a terrible death, is quite clear. Crucifixion had long been the official Roman form of capital punishment for slaves and malefactors. It was an extreme torture with many variations. Sometimes the prisoner was tied to the cross, sometimes nailed; sometimes he was hung head down; sometimes a simple pole was used, sometimes a wall, but always an agonizing death came slowly from shock and exhaustion or more often from circulatory failure, the formation of fluid in the lungs and subsequent strangulation. Beside the terrible physical agony, crucifixion had also the psychology of a pillory. The body was hung naked, exposed to all the indignities that mass sadism can produce. So Jesus died.

Although the accounts of the trial and crucifixion are more detailed than most gospel writing and although general agreement exists in the descriptions, one obvious critical question remains unsolved. Jesus Christ was crucified under Roman authority. This means his executioners were Roman. (Were Christ to have lived today, the Christian symbol would be the electric chair or the gas chamber.) If the only charge which finally stood up in court was blasphemy, why was he not dealt with by the Jewish authorities? He would have been stoned. It may be that Pilate, a weak governor whose position was not secure, found it expedient to carry out the will of the Sanhedrin. Neither the Gospels nor history answer the question.

Jesus was quickly buried before the Sabbath.[91] Many New Testament historians feel that the narrative of his life should end at his point. Furthermore, this juncture marks the differentiation between a movement which before Christ's death was a reform within Judaism and the movement which, as a result of his execution, became the Christian religion. Only after the

[91] Mt. 27:57-60; Mk. 15:45-46; Lk. 23:53-54; Jn. 19:31.

resurrection and the formation of the early communities described in Acts does the word *Christian* properly become an adjective. The accounts of the resurrection can be taken as the beginning of a new era rather than as the end of the old.

The tendency of the early church to see in Christ's death the fulfillment of prophecy has perhaps influenced treatment of the crucifixion narrative. The similarity between passages in Mark (Matthew) and Psalm 22 is striking. The last words of Jesus in each are identical. Compare Psalm 22:1 with Mark 15:34. [Matthew 27:46] "My God, my God, why hast thou forsaken me?" On the other hand these may well have been his last words in light of the fact that he was a deeply religious person steeped in Old Testament traditions and scriptural learning. The cry of a devout Jew in his hour of need might come from Psalms. Lamsa translates the words from Aramaic to say "My God, my God, for this was I spared?" [92] Less easily explained are the other similarities. Psalm 22:18, "They parted my garments among them, and cast lots upon my vesture," is close to Mark 15:24 and to Luke 23:34, and Matthew 27:35: "And when they crucified him, they parted his garments, casting lots among them, what every man should take." Notice also that Psalms 22:7-8 says, "He trusted in the Lord that he would deliver him, let him deliver him, seeing he delighted in him." Mark 15:28-30 as well as Matthew 27:42-43, and Luke 23:35 say, "And they that passed by railed on him wagging their heads, and saying, Ah, thou that destroyest the temple, and buildest it in three days, save thyself, come down from the cross." Again the student may be reminded that the Gospels are not biographical accounts. Clearly all of the conversation between Christ and his followers is not recorded.

[92] *The Modern New Testament from Aramaic*—George M. Lamsa—Holman.

V

The Teachings of Jesus

The Messianic Consciousness of Jesus

The exact time in Christ's ministry when he became aware of a sense of Messianic mission has been the object of scholarly research and controversy. Many still feel that a proper understanding of his teaching is dependent upon the date. If he spoke as the Messiah, his teachings have one significance, if as a Jew within Judaism another. Are his sayings prophetic in the sense that he foretold the future? As scholarship has improved and research has added data, startling conclusions have been drawn. Although the fundamentalist may find them difficult to digest, the end result of scholarship is a stronger and more credible gospel rather than one weakened by conclusions that cannot be substantiated by the available evidence.

A review of the Gospels reveals one certain fact concerning the question of Messianic consciousness. The evangelists who wrote them never made any attempt to enter the mind of Jesus. Nowhere do they presume to interpret either his teaching[1] or his emotions. As they were closer to him than we can ever be, the obvious corollary indicates that this century should not presume to attempt what the first either found im-

[1] Certain enlargements of the parables might be considered interpretation, but certainly the earliest traditions let Christ's teaching stand alone.

possible or felt to be completely undesirable. That the emphasis was elsewhere might well be taken as a guide to contemporary students of the New Testament.

Unfortunately so much weight has been placed on the issue that the question cannot be left so easily. The student uninitiated in Biblical scholarship may at once point out many countless references which seem to indicate Jesus' Messianic consciousness. Not only is the idea implicit in Jesus' acts, but also in many instances the Gospels make direct references. Times and places can be accurately identified. The Gospels indicate again and again the claim and the secret of Christ's mission. "Verily *I* say unto you," "But *I* say unto you." These words are the preface to teaching which goes beyond the law. By what authority? The implication is obvious.

Christ calls the disciples from their diverse occupations and stations in life with the facility and authority of a commanding officer ordering his troops into action. "The triumphal entry" and "the cleansing of the temple" have already been seen as acted parables which are meaningless unless the chief actor is more than a simple prophet. The appeals to the sick are clearly relevant. No doubt exists in the supplicants' minds as to whom they address their needs. Demons recognize him and flee from his authority,[2] the crowds at his trial, the opposition of the Jewish authorities, Pilate's sign, "King of the Jews"[3]—all these things cry out a claim that cannot be ignored.

Jesus himself frequently uses the title, Son of man.[4] Here a secondary controversy in scholarship arises. What does the phrase imply? Some assume it to be synonymous with the word mankind. Thus, Jesus simply identifies himself with the human race. The term is, however, more likely derived from Jewish apocalyptic literature.[5] The Son of man[6] comes from

---

[2] Mt. 8:29; Mk. 5:7.

[3] Placing the indictment over the gibbet of the executed was customary with Roman authority.

[4] Mt. 11:19; Mk. 2:10, 28.

[5] The adjective *apocalyptic* is derived from the word *apocalypse*, meaning revelation or disclosure. Literature so designated belongs to a particular period of Judaism beginning in the 2nd century B.C. and run-

beyond this world to judge it and with his judgment a new age is begun. The term as Jesus uses it (if authentic) is indubitably a Messianic confession. In face of this evidence, what conclusions can be drawn?

First, a careful scrutiny of Christ's message, although it comes rewritten by history, reveals certain consistencies. Nowhere is his message finally dependent on his rank. When analyzed his position is never a prerequisite to the acceptance of his word. Secondly, if all the evidence given in the Gospels had been available to Pilate and the Jews, it seems hardly likely that they would have had any difficulty in presenting it at court, and yet the accounts of the trial which are the most detailed sections of the Gospels indicate that so little evidence was presented that Pilate found no fault in Jesus. If Christ's opponents had so much trouble proving that he made Messianic claims, his friends might have been equally confused.

Bornkamm[7] draws a clear conclusion. Reasonable doubt is cast on the authenticity of all instances which indicate Messiahship prior to the resurrection experiences. The absolute reply, "I am," given by Jesus when questioned by the Sanhedrin as to whether he were indeed the Christ;[8] Peter's confession, which he accepted;[9] the Son of man statements;[10] and the

---

ning through to the fourteenth. The early period is of concern to an analysis of the gospel narrative. The language is characterized by highly imaginative and poetic forms usually in reference to the glory, judgment, and omnipotence of God. The format followed the visions associated with the early prophets. These were often the result of trances induced by whirling, hypnotism, and intoxication (from fermented substance or noxious gas) as well as by religious ecstasy. After the 3rd century B.C. the Jewish canon was fixed and much of the intertestamental writing claimed authorship from past authority in order to obtain a hearing. Thus, the designation pseudepigraphical has been applied to certain sections. (See also Apocalyptic Literature, p. 358.)

[6] Daniel 7:13, "I saw in the night visions, and, behold, one like the Son of man came with clouds of heaven, and came to the ancient of days, and they brought him near before him."

[7] *Jesus of Nazareth* by Günther Bornkamm, Prof. of New Testament, University of Heidelberg—Ch. 8—"The Messianic Question."

[8] Mk. 14:61-62.

[9] Mt. 16:16-17.

[10] Mk. 2:10, 28.

Marcan Messianic secret conception[11] are all open to such serious question concerning authenticity that responsible scholarship can no longer accept them as evidence. In every instance criticism considers them to be of post resurrection origin. Certainly the facts must not be construed to mean that Jesus was not in fact the Messiah. To the Christian he was, and is, and with his life a new age began on earth, but he was not what the Jews hoped for or expected. "The Messianic character of his being is contained in his words and deeds and in the immediateness of his historic appearance.[12] The problem which faced the early church in its efforts to record Christ's teachings is still with us. We live in the atmosphere of the resurrection. Although it is difficult today not to see Christ's life from that perspective, the fact is none the less clear that Jesus' followers had no foreknowledge of the events of the last days; nor can it be assumed that Christ was omniscient in this respect.[13]

The Kingdom of God

The watchword of Christ's message was repentance, and the citadel to which it assured entry was the kingdom of God. The zero hour was fast approaching. "The time is fulfilled and the kingdom of God is at hand: repent ye and believe the gos-

[11] See p. 94, Purpose.
[12] Bornkamm, Günther, *Jesus of Nazareth*, p. 178.
[13] The conclusion that Jesus never considered himself to be the Messiah seems to contradict the text and presents a problem for the critical student. In this study "the triumphal entry", "the cleansing of the temple", and "the last supper" have been categorized as acted parables. If Jesus acted in these, was he not then assuming the role of Messiah? The paradox is resolved in the statement of the question itself. Jesus acted the role to be sure, but this does not mean that he considered himself to be the character which he portrayed. What Jesus seems to be doing throughout his entire ministry is to act as a sign of God's time. Again and again he announced the kingdom of God. His acted parables are an announcement for his generation of a situation which did not become fact until after his resurrection and which was as a result only properly described by the Council of Chalcedon centuries later.

pel." [14] The primary significance of the announcement was that God's absolute rule over all of life was about to take place. Christ's words were spoken as a Jew to the Jews of Palestine in a Scriptural frame applied to contemporary life. He called the disciples who were fishermen to be fishers of men. He spoke to farmers in terms of grain sown and harvested, to vintagers in terms of vineyards and grapes, to landlords in terms of servants and slaves, to Pharisees of food eaten with people of low degree. He told of shepherds seeking the lost lamb. He assaulted the greatness of the temple, but he recognized the authority of Rome. In all he took Judaism for granted and did not bother to explain his terms except where they changed accepted tradition. The kingdom of God was not a new conception. God's omnipotence had been clear to the Jew for generations. His glory was the inspiration for religious poetry. "Verily, there is a reward for the righteous; verily he is a God that judgeth the earth." [Psa. 58:11]. "The Lord reigneth, he is clothed with majesty." [Psa. 93:1].[15] Israel had for centuries been religiously prepared for God's rule to break upon the earth. Concurrent with this expectation, the nation visualized not only the arrival of absolute justice to assure destruction of its enemies, the unrighteous who did not worship Jehovah, but also of reward for those who believed.

God's reign on earth meant that at last his will would be accomplished.[16] To the Jews as well as to Jesus, the arrival of God's sovereignty meant more than a shift in world power and a change in religious emphasis. The kingdom of God represented a new era—an entirely new world, the result of a new creation. The kingdom of God on earth meant the death of an old age and the birth of something new. In Jesus' teaching a

[14] Mt. 4:17; Mk. 1:15. Note the slight difference in language between the two evangelists. Matthew substitutes "heaven" for "God." Although the meaning is identical, the change is made for different readership. Mark's Gospel was addressed to a Christian mission, Matthew's to a Jewish-Christian group.

[15] See also Psalms 94, 96, 103:19; Isa. 52:7.

[16] "Thy kingdom come, thy will be done" (Mt. 6:10; Lk. 11:2).

radical point of departure from the traditional conception was his lack of Jewish nationalism. The hope that the nation would be put on top of the world to rule for and by God's will is not fulfilled in his teaching. Perhaps it was for this reason that he was so often misunderstood and finally rejected by the Jews.

Although nationalism does not appear, the idea of God's judgment is strong. The ancient psalmists welcomed judgment because they understood themselves and the nation to be plaintiffs in God's court, rather than defendants (as do Protestant Americans). Jesus called for repentance that all might find themselves in a proper position before God. The creation of a right relationship was desperately important for the kingdom was close at hand.[17] The jargon of our time is close to the sense of Christ's teaching. "It is later than you think." The message was urgent. Certainly Jesus felt as did his followers in the early Christian Church that action on God's part would be witnessed and understood within the generation, but the exact time was not set.[18] The arrival of the kingdom would be a surprise. Hence it might momentarily break into history. In retrospect Jesus can be seen as part of the kingdom, al-

[17] Parables concerned with the new time:

Mt. 24:32, 33; Mk. 13:28, 29; Lk. 21:29-31. The fig tree shows new life in the spring.

Mt. 12:29; Mk. 3:27; Lk. 11:21, 22. A powerful man will not voluntarily permit others to alienate his property.

Mt. 24:43, 44; Lk. 12:39, 40. No sane man would ever be robbed if he knew when a thief was coming.

Mt. 25:1-13. Opportunities do not repeat themselves. Ten virgins (bridesmaids) unprepared for the wedding feast whose lamps run dry find the door closed by the time they have obtained oil.

[18] Mk. 13:34-37. Be prepared at all times. A servant in charge of a household can never know when his master may unexpectedly return.

Mt. 5:25-26; Lk. 12:58, 59. Prepare for eventualities. Settle out of court rather than face the possibility of unfavorable judgment.

Lk. 13:6-9. The last opportunity not taken results in negative judgment. Israel has reached its last chance for repentance.

Lk. 16:1-9. Prepare for eventualities. The crooked overseer builds up favor for himself at his master's expense. The parable does not advocate dishonesty, but is emphatic on preparedness.

Mt. 11:5, 6, Jesus made his understanding plain that the times were transitory in his message to John the Baptist.

though the question of his awareness of the fact has been violently debated.[19] The fact that he occasionally linked himself with the kingdom creates a problem.[20] (Did he consider himself a symbol or the fulfillment of prophecy?)

The kingdom will not be the result of man's efforts, but comes as a result of God's action,[21] and its inheritance is a matter of God's selection.[22] A likeness to growth is made in the parable of the Sower and in the parable of the Mustard Seed.[23] The farmer knows that he cannot make seed germinate and crops to harvest. Also the magnitude of the end product in comparison to the beginning is made plain. Furthermore, although the difference between the beginning and the end is great, the two are connected by the continuity of growth and are clearly related to each other.[24]

---

[19] See Messianic Consciousness, p. 80.

[20] Mt. 11:4-5. The Prophet Isaiah's promise (Isa. 35:5).
Mt. 11:6.
Mk. 3:27.
Lk. 10:23, 11:20, 17:21.

[21] Mk. 4:26-29. The arrival of the kingdom similar to the growth factor in plants is not a matter of human agency. The parable of the farmer is a prelude to the mustard seed story and tells of a farmer who carefully cultivates his crops but who cannot actually observe the growth of the seed and does not know how it takes place.

[22] Mt. 13:24-30. Judgment is God's: Those who shall inherit the kingdom do so on God's sanction and it is not possible to tell before hand who they will be. The story of the tares tells of a man whose enemies sowed weeds in his garden. Rather than pull up the good plants, he harvests all and then separates the good from the bad.

[23] Mt. 13:31, 32; Mk. 4:30-32; Lk. 13:18-19. The eventual kingdom cannot be fully understood from present beginnings. A mustard seed is very small, but grows into a large bush. By the seed, the size of the plant cannot be foretold.

[24] Other parables of the kingdom:
Mt. 13:33; Lk. 13:20, 21. This parable is very similar to the story of the seed; a little leaven accomplishes a great deal. The end is more than what one might expect from the beginning. (It is noteworthy that the action of yeast creates fermentation which the Jews considered a corruption process. Actually the basic substances of starch and sugar are broken down by the enzyme.) In the rabbinic tradition the simile is for evil. Jesus twists the meaning to his own purpose.
Mt. 18:23-35. God expects man to act toward his fellows with the same grace that they expect to receive from him. A master forgives his servant's indebtedness, but the servant in turn refuses such clemency to

The Beatitudes and the Sermon on the Mount

The Beatitudes[25] follow a familiar Old Testament line. The prophetic literature and the psalms portray the humble and degraded position of Israel as finally vindicated by God. An inverted ethic developed in the Hebrew mind which interpreted poverty and humble position as virtue and beheld wealth and power as sinful things.[26] Poverty became synonymous with piety.[27] Although wealth and power may certainly contribute to sinfulness, it does not necessarily follow that they always do. Bornkamm feels that the construction of the Beatitudes is not based purely on this development.[28] The poverty-stricken and the humble are those who have no fruits of this world. Their lives are barren and hopeless in their present environment. They, therefore, have everything to expect in the next. These people have been driven to the edge of the world. In a sense they are already beginning to live in the next. Thus their lives are based on something other than worldly values, a circumstance which certainly does not hold for the rich and mighty. The poor and meek are accordingly blessed [29] in a way impossible of the others.

The implication is strong that a change in status comes about as a result of God's action. The doctrine of grace is implicit in Christ's statements, and the kingdom is no longer

---

his own debtors. When the master discovers his servant's behavior he punishes him most dreadfully.

See also footnotes pp. 88, 89.

    Drag Net
    Laborers
    Pearl Merchant
    Hidden Treasure
    Unbidden Guests

[25] Mt. 5:3-11; Lk. 6:20-22.
[26] Isa. 49:13, 57:15 ff.; Lk. 16:19-31; Ps. 113:5 ff.
[27] The rich find it difficult to be righteous. Mt. 19:24; Mk. 10:25; Lk. 18:25.
[28] *Jesus of Nazareth*, Günther Bornkamm, Harper & Row.
[29] See p. 22 on blessedness.

solely for the Jews, that is, for the particular religious righteousness which the orthodox claimed to represent. The idea of a holy remnant to receive God's special favor is lost for the most part in Jesus. His message and the kingdom come to all who are ready to receive them — tax collectors, harlots, Gentiles, rich, poor and even members of the hated military occupation forces.[30]

Repentance

Not only was repentance a matter of urgency,[31] but also the motivation for it was quite different from that understood by the Jews. With Jesus salvation came from God and was a present state—God sought the sinner. While the Jews felt that repentance was a means of obtaining salvation, in Jesus' teaching the action is reversed; it is initiated by God's saving grace. The sinner is sought and found by God; he is like a shipwrecked mariner helpless on a raft until he's rescued. Joy is experienced on both sides as a result of salvation. The mechanistic understanding of law which had grown into the Hebrew religion is cleanly excised.[32] At the same time the great worth and joy of the kingdom is emphasized. Its value, above all things and worth the total of life,[33] demands immediate attention.[34]

[30] Mt. 8:11-13, 13:47-50; Mk. 2:17; Lk. 14:16-24, 18:9-14. The story of the net and fishes caught, some of which are cast out, is often misconstrued as a direction concerning judgment. Smith feels that the judgment section is probably not original and that the parable is simply a direction to gather all with the Gospel. Fish for all men as the net catches all. Note that in the early phase of his thinking, Jesus gives some indication of being exclusively Jewish. [Mt. 15:24; 10:5, 6; Mk. 7:27.] B. T. D. Smith, *The Parables of the Synoptic Gospels*, Cambridge University Press, 1937.

Mt. 20:1-16. The story of laborers who received the same compensation for different hours of labor. God is free to give the same benefits to all in his kingdom as he may see fit. Similar to John the Baptist's message.

[31] Mt. 3:1-3; 3:8; 4:17; 12:41.

[32] Mt. 6:28, 23:13-33; Lk. 11:44.

[33] The parable of the Pearl Merchant and of the Secret Treasure speak to the point. In the case of the Pearl Merchant a pearl of tremendous worth is discovered and he sells all that he had in order to acquire one of greater value (Mt. 13:44-46).

The hidden treasure is difficult for some to understand as overtones

Repentance and the process necessary to be part of the kingdom are matters of other worldliness. He who has successfully made the transition is no longer of this world and, therefore, is no longer beholden to it; nor is his life any longer determined by this world's values. The kingdom is the only important thing. Life is changed.[35] Repentance means humbling oneself before God by putting his will first.

The coming kingdom is a joyful event. The sinner found and rehabilitated is a joyful creature. The practice of religion and the means of obtaining salvation are no longer matters of gloom, self-pity and misery.[36] Jesus' teaching again breaks with the past tradition: no longer is fasting a public ordeal, nor is a long face a sign of virtue. Mechanical acts without spiritual motivation are not to be mistaken for piety. The news that the kingdom is coming, the news of imminent salvation is good and happy news. The call to repentance is also then a call to rejoice.

In light of these circumstances the urgency of preparedness is obvious. An intelligent person confronted with the imminence of the kingdom would feel the need of making himself ready quickly. Certain parables stress this fact so pointedly that they have presented difficulties to the pious Protestant of post Reformation times. Luke 16:1-9 tells the story of an overseer who is guilty of shady business practice. Why does Jesus use a man who perpetrates a fraud as a good

---

of fraud occur in the transaction described. A man discovering a hidden treasure in a field sells all that he has in order to obtain the treasure obviously without divulging its presence to the owner. The story similar to the wicked overseer story describes sharp practice (Lk. 16:1-9), but this is not primary to the lesson. The point stresses the extent of preparedness and sacrifice to be given for the kingdom.

[34] The version of the parable telling the story of guests who failed to show up for a party and who were replaced by people drawn from the streets is different in Matthew and Luke, but is clearly the same parable. It was probably addressed to the religiously righteous who nonetheless did not respond to the call for repentance and who accordingly lost their place in the kingdom to the unprepared (sinners). In the end preparedness is stressed again (Mt. 22:2-14; Luke 14:16-24).

[35] Mt. 4:17; Mk. 6:12; Lk. 13:1-9, 18-20; Acts 2:38, 39, 3:19, 8:22, 17:30, 26:20.

[36] Mt. 6:16.

example? Seeing himself soon to be dismissed, the overseer writes the debts of many others off his master's books in order to obtain bargaining power and a favored position for future need. The emphasis is not on the fraud, but on the need for preparedness. To be prepared is wise.[37]

Perhaps the most difficult conception which develops from the teaching of Jesus is that concerned with the time when the kingdom will appear. Religious sects have been founded on the assumption that a key to the date had been found. Early Christians were convinced that the occasion was to be within their generation. The time of the kingdom is paradoxically both present and future. One conception sees the new age cutting unexpectedly and suddenly into history, the movie of time stopped in mid-action.[38] Two women grind corn together; one is taken the other is left.[39] Two men sleep side by side; one is taken the other is left.[40] On the other hand Jesus frequently spoke as if the kingdom had already broken into the present time.[41]

The paradox has been resolved in different ways. Psychological explanations describe the various teachings as manifestations of different emotional trends in Christ's thinking—with perhaps his expectation jumping to belief in fulfillment. Such speculation has already been shown to be invalid.[42] Another explanation suggests that the differences come from

---

[37] Another similar parable where the motif at first might appear to recommend dishonest action can be seen in the Hidden Treasure, Mt. 13:44.

In each case, however, the point is preparedness and urgency. Other parables of the new times are:

Fig tree—Mt. 24:32, 33; Mk. 13:28, 29; Lk. 21:29-31.

The Strong Man Beaten—Mt. 12:29; Mk. 3:27; Lk. 11:21, 22.

The Children of the Bridechamber—Mt. 9:14, 15; Mk. 2:18-20; Lk. 5:33-35.

The Sneak Thief—Mt. 24:43, 44; Lk. 12:39, 40.

[38] Lk. 17:24 ff.

[39] Lk. 17:35.

[40] Lk. 17:34. Also the Lord's Prayer posits the kingdom as coming. Mt. 6:10 ff; Lk. 11:2 ff.

[41] Mt. 11:5 ff.; Mk. 2:18; Lk. 8:18; 10:23 ff.; 11:20.

[42] See p. 80 of this work on entering the mind of Christ.

different periods in his teaching. Still another explanation comes from the claim of textual criticism which attempts to show that the writings which create the paradox are either an interpolation or a gloss coming from the Christian era. None of these answers explains the textual contradictions satisfactorily. The answer is to be found in the paradox itself which makes certain specifications about the kingdom—that is, the kingdom does not come with specific and recognizable signs[43], and that it is relevant to both present and future. Present and future can only be understood in terms of each other. The present reveals the future, while the future gives motivation and hope to the present. Decisions made at any given instant bind the future, while the future will stand in judgment on the present. The immediacy of Christ's message is clear. "Take ye heed, watch and pray: for ye know not when the time is." His words are an earnest and a promise of a new status for the repentant. Man must wait in readiness. He must change his life, and in so doing he brings on the kingdom.

[43] Lk. 17:20.

VI

The Gospels

MARK'S GOSPEL

Background

The Biblical order, Matthew, Mark, Luke, and John, suggests that Matthew's Gospel might be first in chronology. As has already been shown in earlier chapters, such is not the case. Mark is the earliest Gospel. Agreement is general that it was written in Rome about the year 70 A.D. or possibly a little before. Papias, Bishop of Hieropolis, writing sometime in the first half of the second century, even attributes some of Mark to a direct contact with Peter. In his exposition of the Divine Oracles [III, 39. 15] he quotes an early source:

> "This also the presbyter used to say: 'Mark, indeed who had been the interpreter of Peter, wrote accurately, as far as he remembered them, the things said or done by the Lord, but not however in order,' for he had neither heard the Lord nor been his personal follower, but at a later stage as I (Papias) said, he had followed Peter, who used to adapt the teachings to his needs, but not as though he were drawing up a connected account of the oracles of the Lord so that Mark committed no error in writing down some of them just as he remembered them. For he had only one object in view, viz., to

omit none of the things which he had heard and to falsify none of them."

The statement certainly places Mark and his sources very early in the Christian era, probably in the first generation after the immediate followers of Christ. Although the Gospel is the first of the Synoptics it is by no means the earliest of the gospel type writings. Certainly many came earlier. The work probably lies in a mid-position between the earliest records of Jesus' teaching and the other Gospels. The language is Greek, but Greek that does not reach the standards that might be expected from a man of evident education. One explanation is derived from the fact that the writing follows Aramaic construction in its sentence structure. This suggests that Mark may have used an early Aramaic document as a source. Aramaic was the spoken tongue of the lower classes in Palestine, and the earliest traditions must have been recorded in that language. Another plausible explanation is the assumption that Mark was a Jew accustomed to Hebrew writing in Greek.

Perhaps too much concern has been shown in the past over date and location of authorship. Even the most extensive research can produce little more than an educated guess in these matters. Probably Mark was a Roman Christian, living in Rome at the time of his writing. Whether this assumption is true does not make or break the Gospel itself. Let the text stand on its own; in this area the student can proceed on much firmer ground. Is not the description given by Papias sound? Although he indicates the originality of Mark, his statements concerning the organization of the material are misleading. For years the apparent lack of order in chronology and geographical sequence has been taken for granted. Although the continuity may at first be questioned, an analysis of the work reveals that Mark was concerned primarily with subject matter. He dealt with subjects that were of vital interest to the times, in a manner designed to serve those specific interests. Once this fact is understood the Gospel no longer shows poor organization, but demonstrates a carefully planned and purposeful design.

Purpose

The Gospel is not basically biographical. The foundation of both the structure and motivation for the narrative centers around one question: Why did Jesus Christ die on the cross? Secondary to this question and derived from it are two other expressions of the dilemma: Why was Jesus not recognized as the Messiah, and how could he have been executed by Rome and be the Messiah? These were questions the Christian convert might reasonably ask. How does Mark answer them? First he develops an understanding of the controversy between Jesus and the established authorities both religious and secular, and secondly he demonstrates a need for Jesus to die in order to fulfill a divinely appointed and preordained plan. In the first instance his approach is historical, while in the second it is theological.

Structure

The Gospel contains two main divisions. The first begins with the introduction of Jesus through John the Baptist and develops into the story of Jesus' teachings and activities associated with his message concerning the coming kingdom (the good news) which leads finally to Peter's recognition of him [Peter's confession 8:29] and the transfiguration story [9:1-13]. The second division [chs. 10-16] begins with the journey from the area of Caesarea Philippi which ends finally with the tragedy of Golgotha, followed by the glory of the empty tomb. The writing can be further divided into four main sections and an appended conclusion. After the introduction telling of John the Baptist and Jesus' baptism and temptation [1:1-13], follows a period of teaching confined for the most part to the area in the immediate vicinity of the Sea of Galilee. Within this section a short visit to Capernaum is described [1:14-45] during which Jesus calls his first disciples and performs mighty works of healing. A series of controversies heralds his second visit to Capernaum triggered by his mighty acts [2:1-12], his willingness to associate with people considered ceremonially unclean (Publicans and sinners) and his attitudes concerning fasting [2:13-20] and Sabbath observance [2:23-28]. In Chapter 3 Jesus heals a withered hand, appoints the twelve disciples and deals with further controversies. Here Mark is concerned with Jesus' source of power and authority. In all instances Mark demonstrates that Jesus is not guilty of the charges made against him while at the same time he reveals Jesus' new teachings and interpretations of the law [3:1-35]. Chapter 4:1-34 is a collection of parables which is followed by more mighty works. The description of these miracles concludes a subsection of the Gospel. Jesus now moves away from the area of his first ministry. He travels north toward Jerusalem [6:1-9:50]. Apparently two parallel accounts of the northern journey are included. The similarity between Chapters 6:30-7:37 and Chapter 8:1-16 is quite clear. Both include a feeding story, and although the statistics are different, the *modus operandi* in both cases is identical. The journey is followed by another series of controversies. Jesus crosses the strict legal boundaries of scribal tradition in respect to food regulations and defilement from contact with the unclean [7:1-23] and he criticizes the ancient belief in direct signs from heaven (God) [8:11-13]. Chapters 8 and 9 conclude the section with Peter's confession of faith that Jesus is the Messiah, Jesus' forecast of his own death, 'the transfiguration,' Jesus' denial of the expectation that Elias will return by indicating that such has already taken place, further healings, and finally admonitions to humility and tolerance.

Section three can be seen in Chapters 10-15 which begin with a description of Jesus' ministry in Jerusalem followed by another great section of controversies. Again the origin of his authority is questioned. He evades the issue with a clever gambit and turns the question back to the priests and scribes themselves [11:27-33]. He evades the charge of sedition by admitting the jurisidiction of secular authority in certain areas [12:13-17]; he makes his only pronouncement on the nature of heaven by stating that it is so unlike earth that no comparison is possible [12:18-27] and he interprets the law indirectly and irrefutably [12:28-34]. Chapter 13 is known as the Little Apocalypse. Mark's purpose is to make Jesus' Messianic character clear. Chapters 14-15 are the passion narrative and the Gospel concludes with section four, the story of the empty tomb [16:1-20].

A review of this simplified structure reveals how Mark accomplished his purpose. Nearly one-fifth of the total Gospel is devoted to reporting controversies in which Jesus always manages to exonerate himself from the charges while at the same time making clear the characteristics of the new covenant (kingdom of God). The issues under consideration were by no means dead in Mark's time. Sabbath observance, application of the law, the relation between internal feelings and outward manifestations, divorce, the love ethic, Jesus' power, authority and Messiahship—all were matters of hot conflict in the early church. Basically they involve the application of Judaism to the early Christian communities. Jesus emerges victorious and justified.

Secondly, Mark makes it quite clear that Christ's crucifixion was purposeful as part of the divine plan. Chapter 13 not only supports the viewpoint, but also seeks to explain to the early church why Christ had not yet returned [13:10]. Taken as a whole Mark makes his point well. Why was Jesus crucified? He was crucified because he was rejected by Judaism and its leaders. Mark makes their envy and hate abundantly clear by the series of controversies [15:10]. In the end he specifies their denial of his claim. Further, Jesus is crucified because he makes a free choice to be sacrificed in order to pay a price (ransom) for the sins of mankind [10:45, 14:24]. Lastly, and for Mark the most significant point, he is crucified because it is God's will (divine plan) [8:11; 10:33; 14:21, 36].

Grant points out that Mark also directed his Gospel toward certain controversies that existed within the church in

his time.[1] The question of authority and leadership was peren-
nial. Mark speaks directly to the point. Leadership in the early
church came from the original twelve [3:13-19]. Not only
does he state what authority these men were given, but he also
lists them by name. These are indications that Jesus' family was
the source of conflict among early Christian groups. They
questioned whether David's ancestry and blood relationship
was a source of authority. The problem of ancestry has been
discussed in early chapters and remains a matter of doubt.
Mark makes clear that the appointed disciples, not inadvertent
blood relationships, are the source of authority. He also
clarifies the position of John the Baptist.

Because John's followers continued to teach during
Christ's ministry and because the cult continued for many
years, Mark makes certain that John is understood to be nothing more than the means of announcing Jesus. John is a forerunner of the Messiah—never a rival. On the subject of
contemporary discipleship Mark speaks to an age that already
knew persecution. If martyrdom is required, then such is a
test of faithfulness and of discipleship itself, and martyrdom
must, therefore, be endured. Lastly, Mark comments on the
coming of the kingdom; God's rule was momentarily expected in early apostolic times. Although a misunderstanding,
early Christianity assumed that some overt action on God's
part was imminent. Mark affirms strongly that such things
will indeed take place in the appointed time [ch. 13].

OUTLINE OF MARK

Ch. 1 Title, 1:1

I. Introduction. Jesus and John the Baptizer, 1:2-13
    John the Baptizer, 1:2-6
    John's messianic preaching, 1:7, 8
    Jesus is baptized, 1:9-11
    Jesus is tempted, 1:12, 13

[1] Frederick C. Grant; *The Gospels, Their Origin and Their Growth*,
p. 84.

II. Jesus in Galilee, 1:14-9:50

A. *About the Sea of Galilee, 1:14-5:43*

Jesus begins his preachings of the kingdom of God, 1:14, 15
A day in Capernaum, 1:16-38
  a) Jesus calls his first disciples, 1:16-20
  b) Jesus heals a demoniac, 1:21-28
  c) Jesus heals Peter's wife's mother, 1:29-31
  d) Jesus heals the multitude at Capernaum, 1:32-34
  e) Jesus leaves Capernaum, 1:35-38
Jesus heals a leper, 1:39-45
Ch. 2 A series of controversies, 2:1-3:6
  a) Jesus heals a paralytic, 2:1-12
  b) Jesus calls Levi, 2:13, 14
  c) Jesus eats with publicans and sinners, 2:15-17
  d) The question about fasting, 2:18-20
  e) The new patch and the new wine, 2:21, 22
  f) The disciples pluck grain on the Sabbath, 2:23-28
Ch. 3   g) Jesus heals a withered hand, 3:1-6
Jesus' popularity and his cures, 3:7-12
Jesus appoints twelve apostles, 3:13-19a
Further controversies, 3:19b-30
  a) The charge of the scribes, 3:19b-22
  b) The Beelzebub controversy, 3:23-30
Jesus' true family, 3:31-35
Ch. 4 A collection of parables, 4:1-34
  a) The parable of the different soils, 4:1-9
  b) The purpose of parables, 4:10-12
  c) The meaning of the parable, 4:13-20
  d) The right use of parables, 4:21-25
  e) The parable of the seed growing secretly, 4:26-29
  f) The parable of the mustard seed, 4:30-32
  g) Jesus' use of parables, 4:33, 34
A group of miracle stories, 4:35-5:43
  a) Jesus quiets a storm, 4:35-41
Ch. 5   b) Jesus cures a maniac, 5:1-20
  c) Jesus is called to heal Jairus' daughter, 5:21-24
  d) Jesus heals a woman who touches his garment, 5:25-34
  e) Jesus restores Jairus' daughter, 5:35-43

B. *More distant journeys, 6:1-9:50*

Ch. 6 Jesus visits Nazareth, 6:1-6a
The mission of the disciples, 6:6b-29
  a) Jesus sends out his disciples, 6:6b-13

B. *Jesus in Jerusalem, 11:1-12:44*

Ch. 11 Jesus enters Jerusalem, 11:1-10
Jesus returns to Bethany, 11:11
Jesus curses a fig tree, 11:12-14
Jesus cleanses the temple, 11:15-19
The lesson of the withered fig tree, 11:20-26
A second series of controversies, 11:27-12:34
    a) Jesus' authority is challenged, 11:27-33
Ch. 12 *b*) The parable of the wicked vineyard tenants, 12:1-12
    c) The question about tribute to Caesar, 12:13-17
    d) The question about the resurrection, 12:18-27
    e) The question about the great commandment, 12:28-34
Jesus questions the scribes, 12:35-37a
Jesus warns against the scribes, 12:37b-40
Jesus praises a widow's offering, 12:41-44

C. *The discourse on the last things, 13:1-37*

Ch. 13 Jesus predicts the destruction of the temple, 13:1-2
The signs of the Parousia, 13:3-8
The disciple will be persecuted, 13:9-13
The "abomination of desolation," 13:14-20
False Messiahs and false prophets will appear, 13:21-23
The Parousia of the Son of Man, 13:24-27
The date of the Parousia, 13:28-37

D. *The Passion Narrative, 14:1-15:47*

Ch. 14 The plot against Jesus, 14:1, 2
Jesus is anointed at Bethany, 14:3-9
Judas agrees to betray Jesus, 14:10, 11
The disciples prepare for the Passover, 14:12-16
Jesus foretells the betrayal, 14:17-21
The Last Supper, 14:22-25
Jesus foretells Peter's denials, 14:26-31
Jesus in Gethsemane, 14:32-42
Jesus is arrested, 14:43-52
Jesus is examined before the high priest, 14:53-65
Peter denies that he knows Jesus, 14:66-72
Ch. 15 Jesus is tried by Pilate, 15:1-5
Jesus is condemned to be crucified, 15:6-15
Jesus is mocked by the soldiers, 15:16-20
Jesus is crucified, 15:21-32
Jesus dies on the cross, 15:33-41
The burial of Jesus, 15:42-47

IV. The finding of the empty tomb, 16:1-8

Ch. 16 [The longer conclusion of Mark, 16:9-20]
  [Another ending.]

Frederick C. Grant, *The Gospels, Their Origin and Their Growth.*

MATTHEW'S GOSPEL

Background

Scholarship is generally agreed that Matthew's Gospel is thoroughly Jewish in character. The slant and type of writing are what might be expected from a converted rabbi, still faithful to the religious traditions of Israel. Unlike Mark the language is polished Greek, well written by one who understood Christ's teaching. The work, systematic and carefully organized, has a strong Jewish flavor.[2] For the most part the writings deal with Christ's relationship to Judaism and come from a different era than Mark.

The Temple was finally destroyed in 70 A.D. by Titus, acting for his father, the Emperor Vespasian. With the fall of Jerusalem and the complete destruction of all things Jewish, Sadduceeism received its death blow. Even the corpse was destroyed. Jerusalem and the Temple lay in ashes. The cult was no more. Judaism could never again be the same. With the right wing of Sadduceeism gone, Pharasaism and the scribal school rose to power. Judaism became a matter of synagogue school with intense legalism as its first loyalty. At the same time, the ashes of Jewish Apocalyptism found fuel for a new flame in early Christian tradition. The fire thus started was dangerous to both Christian and Jew alike because Roman authority saw in it the torch of sedition. Twice it had brought destruction to the Jews. This inheritance of doubtful worth

---

[2] Note for example, kingdom of heaven for kingdom of God; Son of David for Messiah; Holy City for Jerusalem.

may certainly have contributed to the intensity of Roman persecution.

Purpose

Matthew,[3] a Jew writing to Jews sometime after the year 70 A.D. and probably before the turn of the century from Antioch or the region nearby, created a Gospel that fitted the times. Strongly apocalyptic and eschatological in general outlook, he broke with the current political views of his countrymen, while at the same time, if not actually defending the religious law, he certainly shows a strong allegiance to it [5:18]. Thus the Jewish convert might find in his writing an answer to apocalyptic hopes lost to the orthodox and, by discovering a new interpretation of the law, justify his apostasy. The writing constitutes a compendium of what could be known about Christ and his teachings. Not only are those filed quite systematically, but also frequent evidence is included to demonstrate that the ancient Messianic prophecies had been fulfilled. Such evidence was intended, no doubt, to strengthen Christian belief as well as to act as an apologia for the faith among the unconverted.

Structure

Even less a biography than Mark, Matthew is nevertheless more historical in his approach. He incorporates Mark almost in toto (about 90%), but adds many teachings that were apparently not available to his predecessor. The introduction, more extensive than Mark, contains a genealogy of Jesus and detailed acounts of the miraculous aspects of his birth. The Story of the Magi, the Star of Bethlehem, the Slaughter of the

[3] Not to be identified with one of the original twelve. The fact that he is so dependent on Mark substantiates this assumption. Mark was a second generation Christian, probably having known Peter in the latter's old age. If Matthew had been one of the original group, his sources and understanding would certainly have taken precedence over Mark's and he would not have been dependent on him.

Innocents by Herod, and the Flight through Egypt are not found in Mark. Matthew introduces the Galilean ministry with three explicit temptations in the wilderness rather than Mark's simple statement of Christ's retreat. In later chapters he adds the Sermon on the Mount, many long parables, some apocalyptic writing, and finally an account of the resurrection experiences in Galilee.

Like the usual scribal approach to teaching, the Gospel consists of five main divisions or discourses, each introduced by a suitable narrative section from Mark, the last of which contains a conclusion. Matthew's arrangement is suitable either to memorize or to act as divisions for public reading and instruction. The first section extending from the beginning to chapter 8 tells of Jesus' origin, preparation, the Galilean ministry, discipleship, teachings (The Sermon on the Mount) and the kingdom of heaven. The second, chapters 8-10, deals with apostleship and the method of spreading the new teaching. The material consists of case histories which can be applied to contemporary experience. The last part contains specific instructions concerning the pitfalls which may trap the disciple. The third section, chapters 11:1-13:52 opens with Jesus' ministry in Galilee and his interrogation by John the Baptist. General narrative follows telling of healing, controversies over the law, the question of signs and Jesus' true family [11:1-12:50 . The section concludes with a long discourse on the kingdom of Heaven couched in parables [13:1-52].

The fourth section, chapters 13:53-18:35 concerns the nature of faith and the means of its nurture within the church. Specific and typical examples of its application to life situations are given. The narrative tells of Jesus' visit to Nazareth, and the death of John the Baptist which is followed by a series of mighty works [13:53-15:39]. Chapters 16 and 17 recount Jesus' answer when the Pharisees demand a sign, Peter's confession of faith, the transfiguration, the coming of Elijah, healings, and a second passion announcement. The section ends with a series of parables which interpret the faith [18:1-35].

The fifth section, chapters 19:1-25:46 tells of judgment which the new Covenant places upon the old and predicts the final overthrow of the Old and the ultimate victory of the new Covenant which shall be heralded with signs and omens. The narrative includes a judgment on the subject of divorce and remarriage, the blessing of children and the liabilities imposed on godly character by wealth [19:1-30]. A long section of healings, judgments and parables follows [20:1-22:46]. Chapters 23-25 are concerned with interpretation of doctrine and signs of the kingdom to come. The section concludes with the passion, crucifixion, burial and resurrection [26:1-28:20].

Matthew's Gospel includes material from Mark, Q and some large sections of unclear origin probably from traditions peculiar to the area in which Matthew lived. Much of his material is clearly legendary, perhaps derived from apocryphal writings[4] as well as from the traditions of both Midrash and Haggadah which he fits into a Christian frame.[5] The nativity narratives [Ch. 1-2], Peter's Walking on Water [14:28-31], Peter's Commission [16:17-19], the Money in the Fish's Mouth [17:24-27] and Judas' death [27:3-10] are all of this type. Clearly apocryphal are the stories which tell that Pilate's wife sent a message for him to have nothing to do with Jesus [27:19], the statement which indicts the Jews for the crucifixion and the question, why Pilate permitted it [27:24-25], the accounts of the earthquakes immediately after Christ's death, the descriptions of the saints leaving their graves and walking about Jerusalem [27:51-53], the account of the guard at the door of the tomb [27:62-66], and finally, the Jewish explanation of the resurrection [28:11-15].

Many quotations from the Old Testament are written

---

[4] The Parable of the Tares 13:24-30; The Parable of the Unwilling Guest, 22:1-24; The Parable of the Householder, 20:1-16; The Parable of the Virgins, Ch. 25 ff.

[5] Apocrypha—noncanonical writings of questionable integrity,

Midrash—an ancient Jewish or Rabbinical exposition of a passage from the Scripture (O.T.).

Haggadah—explanatory anecdote from Rabbinical literature usually taken from the Talmud.

into the text as if contemporary to the period. Such additions are quite to be expected under the circumstances of early Christian writing. What other language and literature could the Jewish convert use for self-expression? It is impossible to create a religious expression that is divorced from the times. Were such a thing done the results would be irrelevant and meaningless. Although all the Gospels make use of Jewish religious literature, Matthew is particularly derivative, probably because of his cultural background and the location from which his writings came. A few examples from Matthew and the Old Testament suffice to demonstrate the point: "That it might be fulfilled which was spoken of the Lord by the prophet, saying, out of Egypt have I called my son" [Mt. 2:15]; "When Israel was a child, then I loved him, and called my son out of Egypt." [Hosea 11:1]. "Then was fulfilled that which was spoken by Jeremy the prophet, saying, In Rama was there a voice heard, lamentation and weeping, and great mourning, Rachel weeping for her children, and would not be comforted, because they are not" [Mt. 2:17-18]; "Thus saith the Lord; a voice was heard in Ramah, lamentation, and bitter weeping; Rachel weeping for her children refused to be comforted for her children, because they were not." [Jeremiah 31:15]. Perhaps most striking of all is the description of the triumphal entry in Zechariah 9:9: "Rejoice greatly, O daughter of Zion; shout, O daughter of Jerusalem; behold, thy King cometh unto thee; he is just, and having salvation; lowly, and riding upon an ass, and upon a colt the foal of an ass" which Matthew faithfully reproduces in his description of Christ's entry into Jerusalem even to the point of describing Jesus as having ridden upon both animals, a physical impossibility [21:7].

Lastly, Matthew seems to have included Christian interpretation and practice in his descriptions and accounts of Christ's teachings at periods when such practice could not as yet have been established. The explanations of John's baptism [3:14, 15] reflect an understanding of Jesus that must have come from much later than the event. The same is also true of

Chapter 12:5-7 in which Jesus makes a hidden statement of Messiahship or Chapter 13:36-43 which is an allegorical interpretation of the Parable of the Tares, presupposing Messiahship and judgment. The reference to self-castration in 19:12 ("There be eunuchs, which have made themselves eunuchs for the kingdom of heaven's sake.") speaks of a practice that did not take place until well into the Christian era. Lastly, Chapter 23:10 "Neither be ye called masters; for one is your Master, even Christ" speaks of a theology and title that clearly originated after the resurrection.

OUTLINE OF MATTHEW

Ch. 1 The infancy narrative, 1:1-2:23
      The genealogy of the Messiah, 1:1-17
      The birth of Jesus, 1:18-25
Ch. 2   The visit of the Magi, 2:1-12
      The flight into Egypt, 2:13-15
      The death of the innocents, 2:16-18
      The return from Egypt, 2:19-23

I. Discipleship, 3:1-7:29

    A. *Narrative, 3:1-4:25*

Ch. 3 The mission of John the Baptist, 3:1-12
      a) John's appearance and message, 3:1-6
      b) John's preaching of repentance, 3:7-10
      c) John's messianic preaching, 3:11-12
      The baptism of Jesus, 3:13-17
Ch. 4 The temptation of Jesus, 4:1-11
      The beginning of Jesus' ministry, 4:12-25
      a) Jesus begins preaching in Galilee, 4:12-17
      b) Jesus calls his first disciples, 4:18-22
      c) A preaching tour through Galilee, 4:23-25

    B. *Discourse, 5:1-7:29. The Sermon on the Mount*

Ch. 5 Introduction, 5:1, 2
      The Beatitudes, 5:3-12
      Salt and light, 5:13-16
      The reinterpretation of the ancient Law, 5:17-48
      a) Jesus' attitude toward the Law, 5:17-20
      b) The law forbidding murder, 5:21, 22

c) On reconciliation with friends, 5:23, 24, and enemies, 5:25, 26

d) The law forbidding adultery, 5:27-30

e) The law about divorce, 5:31, 32

f) The law about oaths, 5:33-37

g) The law about revenge, 5:38-42

h) On love for one's enemies, 5:43-48

Ch. 6 The true practice of pious works, 6:1-18

    a) Almsgiving, 6:1-4

    b) Prayer, 6:5-15

        The Lord's Prayer, 6:7-15

    c) Fasting, 6:16-18

The requirement of singlehearted devotion, 6:19-24, and trust in God, 6:25-34

    a) On true treasure, 6:19-21

    b) On seeing clearly, 6:22, 23

    c) On undivided loyalty, 6:24

    d) On trust in God: against anxiety, 6:25-34

Ch. 7 On judging others: against censoriousness, 7:1-5

On prudence in presenting the gospel, 7:6

The assurance of answer to prayer, 7:7-11

The Golden Rule, 7:12

The test of true discipleship, 7:13-27

    a) The narrow way, 7:13, 14

    b) The test of goodness, 7:15-20

    c) The criterion at the judgment, 7:21-23

    d) Hearers and doers of the word, 7:24-27

Jesus astonishes his hearers, 7:28, 29

II. Apostleship, 8:1-10:42

A. *Narrative, 8:1-9:34*

Ch. 8 Jesus' ministry of healing, 8:1-17

    a) Jesus heals a leper, 8:1-4

    b) Jesus heals a centurion's slave, 8:5-13

    c) Jesus heals Peter's wife's mother, 8:14, 15

    d) Jesus heals the sick at evening, 8:16, 17

The tests of discipleship, 18:13-22

Further miracles and healings, 8:23-9:8

    a) Jesus calms a tempest, 8:23-27

    b) Jesus cures two demoniacs at Gergesa, 8:28-34

Ch. 9 The call of Levi (Matthew), 9:9-13

The question about fasting, 9:14-17

The climax of Jesus' healing ministry, 9:18-34
  a) Jesus raises a ruler's daughter and heals a woman who
        touches the hem of his garment, 9:18-26
  b) Jesus heals two blind men, 9:27-31
  c) Jesus heals a dumb demoniac, 9:32-34

B. *Discourse, 9:35-10:42. The mission of the disciples*

Jesus has compassion on the multitudes, 9:35-38
Ch. 10 Jesus sends out his disciples to preach and to heal, 10:1-15
The disciples will be persecuted, 10:16-25
They must be fearless in confessing Christ, 10:26-33
Divisions in families will result from persecution, 10:34-39
The reward for receiving the missionaries, 10:40-42

III. The hidden revelation, 11:1-13:52

A. *Narrative, 11:1-12:50*

Ch. 11 Jesus goes about Galilee preaching, 11:1
The question of John the Baptist: Are you the Messiah?
    11:2-6
Jesus' words about John, 11:7-15
Jesus' view of his own mission, 11:16-30
  a) Jesus' criticism of his contemporaries, 11:16-19
  b) Jesus pronounces woes on the Galilean cities, 11:20-24
  c) Jesus' thanksgiving and invitation, 11:25-30
Ch. 12 Jesus and the law of the Sabbath, 12:1-14
  a) The disciples pick grain on the Sabbath, 12:1-8
  b) Jesus heals a withered hand on the Sabbath, 12:9-14
Jesus heals the multitudes, 12:15-21
The Pharisees' charge against Jesus, and his refutation of it,
    12:22-37
  a) Jesus heals a blind and dumb demoniac, 12:22, 23
  b) The charge of collusion with Beelzebul, and Jesus'
        reply, 12:24-30
  c) On blasphemy against the Holy Spirit, 12:31, 32
  d) The tests of goodness, 12:33-35
  e) On responsibility for idle words, 12:36, 37
The Pharisees demand a sign from Jesus, 12:38-45
  a) The sign of Jonah, 12:38-40
  b) Jesus criticizes his contemporaries, 12:41, 42
  c) The return of an evil spirit: the lapsed demoniac, 12:43-
        45
Jesus' true family, 12:46-50

B. *Discourse, 13:1-52. The hidden teaching of the parables*

Ch. 13 The parable of the different soils, 13:1-9
The reason for teaching in parables, 13:10-15
The disciples' blessings, 13:16, 17
The meaning of the parable of the soils, 13:18-23
The parable of the tares, 13:24-30
The parable of the mustard seed, 13:31, 32
The parable of the leaven, 13:33
Jesus teaches publicly by parables, 13:34, 35
The meaning of the parable of the tares, 13:36-43
The parable of the hidden treasure, 13:44
The parable of the costly pearl, 13:45, 46
The parable of the dragnet, 13:47-50
The instructed scribe or teacher, 13:51, 52

IV. The church, 13:53-18:35

A. *Narrative, 13:53-17:23*

Jesus visits Nazareth, 13:53-58
Ch. 14 The death of John the Baptist, 14:1-12
    a) Herod Antipas' opinion of Jesus, 14:1, 2
    b) Herod's murder of John, 14:3-12
Jesus feeds the multitude (5,000), 14:13-21
Jesus walks on the water, 14:22-33
Jesus heals the multitude at Gennesaret, 14:34-36
Ch. 15 Jesus rejects the tradition of the elders, 15:1-20
Jesus heals a demoniac girl in Phoenicia, 15:21-28
Jesus heals a multitude on a mountain, 15:29-31
Jesus feeds the multitude (4,000), 15:32-39
Ch. 16 The Pharisees demand a sign, 16:1-4
The discourse on leaven, 16:5-12
Peter's confession of faith and the transfiguration of Jesus, 16:13-17:13
    a) Peter confesses his faith that Jesus is the Messiah, 16:13-20
        The future founding of the church, 16:17-19
    b) The first passion announcement, 16:21-23
    c) The disciple's pathway of suffering, 16:24-28
Ch. 17 *d*) The transfiguration of Jesus, 17:1-8
    e) The coming of Elijah, 17:9-13
Jesus heals an epileptic boy, 17:14-21
The second passion announcement, 17:22, 23

B. *Discourse, 17:24-18:35. On church administration*

The temple tax, 17:24-27

Ch. 18 The question of greatness: rank in the kingdom, 18:1-5

Responsibility for leading others to sin, 18:6-10

The parable of the lost sheep, 18:11-14

On rebukes and reconciliation, 18:15-20

The rule of unlimited forgiveness, 18:21, 22

The parable of the unmerciful creditor, 18:23-35

V. The judgment, 19:1-28:20

A. *Narrative, 19:1-22:46*

Ch. 19 Jesus in Peraea, 19:1, 2

The question about divorce and remarriage, 19:3-9

Renunciation of marriage for the sake of the kingdom of God, 19:10-12

Jesus blesses the children, 19:13-15

Renunciation of wealth for the sake of the kingdom of God, 19:16-30

    a) Jesus and the rich young man, 19:16-22

    b) The hindrance of riches, 19:23-26

    c) The reward of complete renunciation, 19:27-30

Ch. 20 The parable of the day laborers in the vineyard, 20:1-16

The third passion announcement, 20:17-19

Jesus and the two sons of Zebedee, 20:20-28

Jesus heals two blind men, 20:29-34

Ch. 21 Jesus enters Jerusalem and cleanses the temple, 21:1-22

    a) Jesus enters Jerusalem, 21:1-11

    b) Jesus cleanses the temple, 21:12-16

    c) Jesus curses a fig tree, 21:17-22

Controversies in the temple court, 21:23-22:46

    a) Jesus' authority is challenged, 21:23-27

    b) The parable of the two sons, 21:28-32

    c) The parable of the wicked husbandmen, 21:33-46

Ch. 22   *d*) The parable of the marriage feast, 22:1-14

    e) The question about tribute to Caesar, 22:15-22

    f) The question about the resurrection, 22:23-33

    g) The question about the great commandment, 22:34-40

    h) The question about the Son of David, 22:41-46

B. *Discourse, 23:1-25:46. The doctrine of the judgment and the parousia*

1. The discourse against the scribes and Pharisees, 23:1-39

Ch. 23   *a*) Their hypocrisy, heartlessness, and ostentation, 23:1-12

  b) The risen Jesus appears to the two Marys, 28:9, 10
  c) The bribing of the guard, 28:11-15
  d) The risen Jesus appears to the eleven disciples, 28:16, 17
  e) The great commission, 28:18-20

Frederick C. Grant, *The Gospels, Their Origin and Their Growth.*

LUKE'S GOSPEL

Background

The Gospel according to Luke and the Book of the Acts of the Apostles share common authorship. The first is an introduction to the second or may more properly be considered the first section of two works that are part of the whole. The writings differ from Mark and Matthew in style and purpose as well as in the character of authorship. Luke was clearly a man of great education and high status. He wrote in polished literary Greek, sometimes from sources of his own, sometimes directly from Mark and Q, and sometimes from firsthand experience. Although Mark constructs Greek in Hebrew form, Luke speaks his mother tongue. Paul calls him a Gentile, but Luke was strongly influenced by Judaism, if not actually a Gentile follower of the Jewish God. Traditionally he is thought to have been a physician, and Paul actually refers to him as such. Much of his writing shows the sympathy and understanding one might expect from a medical doctor. Certainly his character fits the position. He was a second generation Christian writing after the fall of Jerusalem, probably in the last quarter of the first century.

Purpose

Unlike either Mark or Matthew, Luke writes biographically. The first section of his work (the Gospel) is largely biographical, while the second (Acts) is basically a condensed

summary of the early Christian movement. As such it is historical. Luke is a good reporter writing with meticulous care. He
states his primary purpose in the opening verses of his work.
"It seemed good to me also having a perfect understanding of
all things from the very first, to write to thee, most excellent
Theophilus, that thou mightest know of a certainty of those
things, wherein thou hast been instructed" [1:2-3]. The
second section is also directed to Theophilus who may have
been a Roman official. Actually there is no way of determining the exact character of Theophilus except that Luke's work
had as one of its chief purposes the justification, through careful presentation of its historical background, of the Christian
position as being other than seditious. If Theophilus were
other than Roman, the very point of the writing would be to
a large degree lost. The preface on the other hand may simply
be a concession to the accepted literary form of the period,
but in either case the purpose of the writing remains clear.

Rome was moving rapidly toward a policy of intolerance
and suppression. Luke attempted to demonstrate that such activity resulted from an unjust evaluation of the Christian movement, that no need existed to suppress Christianity, and that
the Christian should be given the same rights and privileges
afforded the Jew from whom he was not far removed. The
Gospel tried to relieve the mounting presure from Rome by
enlightening its readers concerning the nature of Christianity.
Luke points out that the established secular authorities could
find no fault with Jesus at the time of his trial. Both Herod
and Pilate were willing to release him. "Ye have brought this
man unto me, as one that perverteth the people; and behold,
I, having examined him before you, have found no fault in
this man touching those things whereof ye accuse him; nor
yet Herod: for I sent you to him; and, lo, nothing worthy of
death is done unto him" [23:14-15]. "Then said Pilate to the
chief priests and to the people, I find no fault in this man"
[23:4]. The work continues throughout to enumerate the
characteristics of Christian teaching against the background
of possible accusations from the State. From this perspective

it is also an apologia, and like many early historical writings, a polemic.

Structure

The Gospel incorporates more than half of Mark, but not as much as Matthew. Besides Mark, Luke used Q and some sources of his own. Whereas Matthew used Q in sections to form discourses, Luke breaks the material up and distributes it in small portions. His special sources add large descriptive and poetic passages to the nativity stories. The births of both John the Baptist and Jesus are described in romantic and legendary language with a continuity that is peculiar to Luke. Furthermore, several of the most familiar parables are unique to his writing: the story of the Good Samaritan, the Prodigal Son, the Rich Man and Lazarus, the Pharisee and the Publican, the Unfaithful Steward, the Unjust Judge, and in the early part of the book the story of Jesus teaching in the temple during childhood. Unlike Matthew, which uses a more typical organizational pattern, the Gospel depends upon historical sequence for its continuity.

Luke omits one long section of Mark [6:45-8:26], but includes a large descriptive portion of his own [9:51-18:14] which is written into the frame of Jesus' journey from Galilee to Jerusalem. Probably Proto-Luke was used as an outline and Mark was added afterwards in the following sections:[6] 4:31-44, 5:12-6:19, 8:4-9:50, 18:15-43, 19:28-36, 19:45-21:33, 21:37-22:13. Later additions relate to the nativity story, the passion, and the resurrection narratives.

The Gospel may be divided into six main sections. The first which includes the prologue ch.1:1-4 tells of Jesus' birth and early years (nativity stories) and the mission of John the Baptist, chs. 1-4:13 . The second section concerns Jesus' early ministry in Galilee ch.4:14-9:50. Included therein are parables, mighty works and the calling of the disciples, material already

[6] Frederick C. Grant, *The Gospels, Their Origin and Their Growth,* p. 118.

familiar to the reader of Mark and Matthew. Section three describes Jesus' ministry on the way to Jerusalem, chs. 9: 51 - 19: 27. Section four is limited to the Jerusalem ministry, chs. 19:28-21:38. Section five follows the established pattern of the passion, trial and crucifixion, chs. 22:1-23:56 and Section six contains narratives of the empty tomb and the resurrection appearances, ch. 24:1-53.

OUTLINE OF LUKE

The Prologue to Luke—1:1-4

I. The birth and early years of Jesus, his preparation and divine commission, 1:5-4:13

Ch. 1 The infancy and childhood of John the Baptist and Jesus, 1:5-2:52

    a) John's birth foretold, 1·5-25
    b) Jesus' birth foretold, 1:26-38
    c) Mary visits Elizabeth, 1:39-56
    d) The birth of John, 1:57-80

Ch. 2   *e*) The birth of Jesus, 2:1-20
    f) The naming of Jesus and his presentation in the temple, 2:21-40
      Simeon's thanksgiving, 2:25-35
      Anna's thanksgiving, 2:36-38
    g) The boy Jesus in the temple, 2:41-52

Ch. 3 The mission of John the Baptist, 3:1-20
    a) John's call and message, 3:1-6
    b) John's preaching of repentance, 3:7-9
    c) John's message to special groups, 3:10-14
    d) John's messianic announcement, 3:15-18
    e) John imprisoned by Herod Antipas, 3:19, 20
  The baptism and temptation of Jesus, 3:21-4:13
    a) The baptism of Jesus, 3:21, 22
    b) The genealogy of Jesus, 3:23-38

Ch. 4   *c*) The temptation of Jesus, 4:1-13

II. The ministry of Jesus in Galilee, 4:14-9:50

The beginning of Jesus' ministry, 4:14-44
    a) Jesus teaches in the synagogues of Galilee, 4:14, 15
    b) Jesus visits the synagogue at Nazareth and is rejected, 4:16-30

Ch. 9 Jesus and the twelve disciples, 9:1-50.

    a) Jesus sends out his twelve disciples, 9:1-6

    b) Herod Antipas' opinion of Jesus, 9:7-9

    c) Jesus feeds the multitude, 9:10-17

    d) Peter confesses his faith in Jesus the Messiah, 9:18-22

        Jesus foretells his own death, 9:21, 22

    e) The conditions of discipleship, 9:23-27

    f) Jesus is transfigured, 9:28-36

    g) Jesus heals an epileptic boy, 9:37-43a

    h) Jesus again foretells his own sufferings, 9:43b-45

    i) The disciples' question: Who is greatest? 9:46-48

    j) The strange exorcist, 9:49, 50

III. Jesus on the way to Jerusalem, 9:51-19:27

Jesus in Samaria, 9:51-10:37

    a) The Samaritan villagers reject Jesus, 9:51-56

    b) Three tests of discipleship, 9:57-62

Ch. 10 *c*) The mission of the Seventy, 10:1-24

        Jesus sends out seventy disciples, 10:1-16

        Woes pronounced on the Galilean cities, 10:13-15

        The seventy disciples return, 10:17-20

        Jesus' exultation and thanksgiving, 10:21, 22

        A blessing pronounced upon the disciples, 10:23 f

    d) The lawyer's questions, 10:25-28, and the story of the Good Samaritan, 10:29-37

Jesus' teaching on prayer, 10:38-11:13

    a) Mary and Martha, 10:38-42

Ch. 11 *b*) The Lord's Prayer, 11:1-4

    c) The parable of the friend at midnight, 11:5-8

    d) The certainty of answer to prayer, 11:9-13

Jesus is criticized by the Pharisees—and his criticism of them, 11:14-54

    a) Jesus is accused of collusion with Beelzebul, 11:14-23

    b) The lapsed demoniac, 11:24-26

    c) A blessing is pronounced upon Jesus' mother, 11:27, 28

    d) No sign shall be given but that of Jonah, 11:29, 30

    e) Jesus' criticism of his contemporaries, 11:31, 32

    f) Jesus' sayings about light, 11:33-36

    g) Jesus' criticism of the Pharisees, 11:37-44

    h) Jesus' criticism of the lawyers, 11:45-54

Ch. 12 Jesus and his disciples, 12:1-48

    a) Jesus warns his disciples against hypocrisy, 12:1

    b) Jesus exhorts his disciples to fearless proclamation of the gospel, 12:2-7, and to fearless confession of the Christian faith, 12:8-12

c) Jesus warns his disciples against covetousness, 12:13-21
  The parable of the rich fool, 12:16-21
d) Jesus exhorts his disciples to trust in God, 12:22-34
e) Jesus exhorts his disciples to be vigilant, 12:35-40, and to be faithful, 12:41-46
f) Different degrees of responsibility, 12:47, 48
The seriousness of the time, 12:49-13:9
a) The tragic aspect of Jesus' mission, 12:49, 50, and its consequences in family life, 12:51-53
b) Signs of the time, 12:54-56
c) Prudence in litigation, 12:57-59
Ch. 13 d) Tragic warnings seen in current events, and the call to repent, 13:1-5
e) The parable of the unfruitful fig tree, 13:6-9
The end of the Galilean ministry, 13:10-35
a) Jesus heals a crippled woman on the Sabbath, 13:10-17
b) The parables of the mustard seed and the leaven, 13:18-21
c) Few will be saved, 13:22-24
d) Casual acquaintance with Christ will not avail in the Judgment, 13:25-27
e) Reversals of fortune in the Kingdom of God, 13:28-30
f) Jesus leaves Galilee, deliberately, for Jerusalem, 13:31-33, whose tragic fate he foresees, 13:34, 35
Ch. 14 Jesus' table talk, 14:1-35
a) Jesus heals a man with dropsy, on the Sabbath, 14:1-6
b) Jesus teaches humility, 14:7-11
c) Jesus teaches charity, 14:12-14
d) The parable of the Great Supper, 14:15-24
e) The cost of discipleship, 14:25-33
f) The saying about salt, 14:34, 35
Ch. 15 Jesus and the outcast, 15:1-32
a) Jesus is criticized for mingling with sinners, 15:1, 2
b) The parable of the lost sheep, 15:3-7
c) The parable of the lost coin, 15:8-10
d) The parable of the lost son, 15:11-32
Ch. 16 Jesus' teaching about wealth, 16:1-31
a) The parable of the clever steward, 16:1-13
b) Jesus' criticism of the Pharisees, 16:14-18
c) The story of the rich man and Lazarus, 16:19-31
Ch. 17 The duties of the disciples, 17:1-10
a) The seriousness of causing others to sin, 17:1, 2
b) Jesus' saying about forgiveness, 17:3, 4
c) Jesus' saying about faith, 17:5, 6
d) Slaves do not claim either thanks or wages, 17:7-10

a) The preparation for the Passover meal, 22:7-13
b) The Last Supper, 22:14-20
c) Jesus foretells the betrayal, 22:21-23
d) The question of greatness, 22:24-30
e) Jesus foretells Peter's denial, 22:31-34
f) The two swords, 22:35-38
The arrest and trial of Jesus, 22:39-23:25
    a) Jesus in Gethsemane, 22:39-46
    b) Jesus is arrested, 22:47-53
    c) Peter denies that he knows Jesus, 22:54-62
    d) Jesus is mocked by his captors, 22:63-65
    e) Jesus before the Sanhedrin, 22:66-71
Ch. 23 *f*) Jesus before Pilate, 23:1-7
    g) Jesus before Herod Antipas, 23:8-12
    h) Jesus is sentenced to die, 23:13-25
The crucifixion of Jesus, 23:26-49
    a) Jesus is led to Calvary, 23:26-32
    b) Jesus is crucified, 23:33-38
    c) The penitent robber, 23:39-43
    d) Jesus dies on the cross, 23:44-49
The burial of Jesus, 23:50-56

VI. The Resurrection of Jesus, 24:1-53

Ch. 24 The empty tomb, 24:1-12
Jesus appears to his disciples, 24:13-49
    a) The appearance of the risen Jesus at Emmaus, 24:13-35
    b) The appearance to the disciples at Jerusalem, 24:36-49
The ascension of the risen Christ, 24:50-53

Frederick C. Grant, *The Gospels, Their Origin and Their Growth.*

JOHN'S GOSPEL

Background

Even the critical novice will be struck at once with the similarity of Matthew, Mark and Luke. The name Synoptic is properly applied to them because they share a common viewpoint and for the most part a common design. On the other hand, John clearly is not part of the family. His very first verse establishes the difference, and the student already familiar with the Synoptics finds himself lost and bewildered. The introduction is, at first reading, theological double talk. What possible connection can exist between this and the nativity stories in Matthew and Luke? Furthermore, the familiar baptism and temptation narratives are missing. The parables are not to be found.

The order of events so firmly established in the Synoptics is changed in John, as is the general locale of Jesus' teaching activity. The Synoptics depict his ministry for the most part in Galilee and then briefly describe the events in Jerusalem before the passion; the entire activity spans only a year. John reverses the order. He describes the ministry as taking place almost entirely in Jerusalem on the occasion of the great feasts, with only a few incidents in Galilee; the time extends over at least three Passovers. By synoptic tradition the disciples are called from their fishing activity on the Sea of Galilee, while the fourth Gospel tells that they were called from the followers of John, the Baptizer, beside the Jordan. John places the "cleansing of the temple" at the beginning of Jesus' ministry. The Synoptics put it at the end. The "last supper" is a Passover repast in the synoptic writers, but in John it takes place before the feast.

Not only is the subject matter treated differently, but the main theme itself is also different. The Synoptics see Jesus' preaching concerning the kingdom of God as central. John's entire Gospel has as its end the need to demonstrate that Jesus was the Christ—the Son of God. Whose reporting is to be followed? The answer may seem paradoxical, but it is not a true paradox. Both may be accepted. Once the purpose and historical perspective of John's Gospel is understood, the points of difference between his Gospel and the Synoptics are resolved.

The consensus is that John feels the order of thought to be more important than the order of events. The Synoptics interpret theology in the framework of history, whereas John places historical events in the framework of the Christian theological position. This type of reporting is foreign to the twentieth century where truth, physical fact, and split-second chronological accuracy are considered synonomous. Moderns tend to forget the frequency with which facts and statistics may lie. An unemployment figure of ten million is terrible to contemplate alone, but coupled with the statement that it is half that of ten years past it becomes a symbol of progress. The report that a man has beaten a dog to death appears at first to be a tale of incredible, sadistic brutality until the second line tells that he did so in order to save a playground of school children from a rabid animal. The ancient historian searched for the truth behind the physical fact, and once he had determined this, he felt free to rewrite the facts where necessary to reinforce and substantiate that truth, without further concern for what today would be considered the historicity of the narrative. John's last words might well have opened his Gospel: "and many signs and wonders did Jesus in the presence of his disciples, which are not written in this book: but these are written, that ye might believe that Jesus is the Christ, the Son of God; and that believing ye might have life through his name" [20:31].

Who was John to take such a mission upon himself? How close was he to the events? What did he know about Christian orthodoxy in the first century? Volumes expounding widely divergent theories have been written on these questions. In past years John's Gospel has been dated as late as the middle of the second century, but evidence now available from papyrus texts recently discovered in Egypt indicates that it was probably written as much as fifty years earlier, around 100 A.D.[7] This date places the Gospel close to apostolic tradition. The identity of the author remains a matter of dispute. From the earliest times Christians have assumed the author to have been an eyewitness of the events described, and they give the accolade to John, the younger son of Zebedee—therefore, not only an eyewitness, but one of the twelve, "the beloved disciple" himself. John is believed to have reached a great age and

[7] *St. John's Gospel, a Commentary* by R. H. Lightfoot, Oxford at the Clarendon Press, 1956.

to have been a man of authority in Ephesus. Although his authorship is still accepted by many, the time span required for his life presents difficulties. If the Gospel were written in the second century or later, John would have been in his nineties or even older at the time.

Under the circumstances of the era in which he lived, he would have been a remarkable man indeed simply to have survived, without then producing in his dotage such a magnificent work. Secondly, what little is known of John does not serve to identify him as the author. The Synoptics give him a high position which is certainly an acceptable credential, but he is also depicted in Galatians [2:9] as one of the three major authorities of the Church who gave Paul authority to carry his ministry to the Gentiles with "the right hand of fellowship," but who himself continued a mission to the Jews. The Gospel might reasonably be expected, therefore, to have a predominently Jewish slant, but it does not.

Another answer to this question of authorship comes from a theory advanced by T. W. Manson. It is likely that a Gospel tradition of both fact and interpretation evolved in the early Christian community of Jerusalem, the first seat of Christian authority. The original source of the tradition may also have been an anonymous disciple of Christ. In the natural course of Christian expansion the tradition would have moved to Antioch in Syria, the second great center of Christian activity and then later to the more advanced bases, one of the most prominent of which was Ephesus. Furthermore, it would have been edited as well as embellished along the way. This Ephesus tradition may be John's Gospel.

Streeter concludes that the conditions which convince scholars to attribute the Gospel to John, the Son of Zebedee, are equally applicable to John, the Elder. It may be that the name of this John, writing from Ephesus, was given to the tradition which originated anonymously in Jerusalem and traveled the editorial path through Antioch to Ephesus. Exactly who wrote the Gospel is unimportant. In his evident desire to remain anonymous he was successful, but no matter who wrote it, the Gospel is clearly authoritative and very close to its sources.

A matter no less controversial is the question of the sources themselves. Are Q, Ur-Marcus, proto-Luke, L and M to be found in John? The Gospel cannot be harmonized with the Synoptics and the designations of source material applicable to them have no relevence to John. The question remains whether John knew the Synoptics or their sources when he wrote his Gospel. In the first half of this century, scholarship was generally agreed that the author knew the other three Gospels and that he edited them, adding material unfamiliar to them from primitive sources of his own.

Dr. Gardiner-Smith has suggested a radically different possibility. The term "fourth Gospel" may be a misnomer. The difference in its tone suggests a source which represents a more rapid development of Christianity than the Synoptics and which may be in its origin contemporary to their sources or may even antidate them.[8] John may have known from independent sources the stories which are common to both his Gospel and the Synoptics. If this is true the Gospel has tremendous historical significance, but it is more commonly valued for its exposition of theological truth.

Although Gardiner-Smith's theory is an interesting possibility, it seems hardly possible for a Christian to have lived through this early apostolic period and to have reached the position of an elder in Ephesus and still remain ignorant of the Synoptics. Furthermore, John's obvious familiarity with the teachings of the faith both historical and theological seems to preclude the possibility of such ignorance.

Structure

John's introduction is couched in terms of Greek philosophy. The doctrine of the logos can be traced back to the very beginnings as a logical development from Heraclitus

<hr>

[8] *Saint John and the Synoptics,* p. 92, Dr. P. Gardiner-Smith, 1938.

(6th c.) who broke away from a purely physical understanding of the universe by positing a principle of reason at work beside matter. Plato and Aristotle developed theories that ideas possess reality in themselves, separate from the physical. Later the Stoics went back to Heraclitus and sought to connect Plato's world of ideas with the world of physical existence. They saw the universe as pervaded everywhere by eternal reason—the logos. Philo took the Stoic position and combined it with Plato. His great addition, however, was the subsequent combination of this conception of reason with the Old Testament understanding of God. The Old Testament God had become so transcendent after the Exile that he was absolutely separated from the world. By identifying the logos with the Old Testament conception of the word of God, Philo connected the deity with the world once again. Although this conception underlies the first eighteen verses of John's Gospel, John does not stop there. His primary concern is not with the word of God, but with the Word made flesh—the theme of the main body of his work.

Throughout the Gospel John's entire concern is to make the fact known that Jesus was the incarnate Word of God. So heavily is the point emphasized that he is in danger of forgetting Christ's humanity. To John, Christ's life is that of a heavenly being from first to last. Moral struggle is no longer an issue. The temptation and agony are not reported. The kingdom of God is no longer central. Only the nature of the incarnate Word and man's rejection of it are of importance. Secondly, the phraseology is not familiar to Hebrew thought. Although from a Jewish background, John writes for the Greek in the popular (Koine) Greek language of the day. Thus, a secondary purpose of the Gospel is an effort to give an acceptable understanding of Christ to the Greek world. The best summary of purpose comes from John himself. In a verse already mentioned [20:31] he refers to Jesus as both the Christ and the Son of God. The first is clearly a categorization from Jewish religious history identifying Jesus with the Messiah while the second—Son of God—fits the Greek understanding of the logos.

The Gospel has been broken down and outlined innumerable times in innumerable ways. Certain main divisions, however, are generally agreed upon. Clearly the introduction is a part unto itself [1:1-18]. Equally clear is the fact that Chapter 21 is an addition or appendix. Lastly, the work can be divided into almost equal parts, the first of which consists of Jesus' public ministry [2:12-12:50] and the second of which is made up of the final events in Jerusalem immediately before the arrest, trial, crucifixion, and resurrection [13:1-20:31], and an appendix [ch. 21]. Further the text itself indicates the possibility that some of the sections may appear in the wrong order. Many feel that 7:15-24 should be placed at the end of ch. 5. Also nine verses [22-30] of Chapter 3 may properly follow Chapter 2:11, and eleven verses [19-29] of Chapter 10 might better follow ch. 9:41.

The Gospel can be divided into eight sections, the first of which is an introduction followed by six sections comprising various phases of Jesus' public ministry and the eighth which makes up the remaining half of the book. A pattern of works followed by exposition is established in the first sections and continues through with slight divergences in sections five and six. Teaching passages seek to explain the inward and true meaning of the works; and the works are shown to be outward and visible signs of internal and invisible meaning. The various feasts of the Jewish religious calendar serve as frames for the established pattern. In the second part works and exposition are again linked together, but in the reverse order. Exposition explains the action which follows.

PART ONE

The Gospel opens with an introduction [1:1-18] which establishes the doctrinal position of the book followed by a narrative telling of John the Baptist's witness to Jesus and the conversion of the first disciples [1:19-2:11].

In the second section [2:12-4:54] Jesus begins his public ministry, by moving to Capernaum and thence to Jerusalem where he cleanses the temple [2:13-22]. When attacked by the Jews for this action, he makes a mysterious statement about destroying and raising the temple which, to the initiated, reveals his nature. The record then tells that many are converted by his mighty acts, but denies that this is the proper motivation for conversion [2:23-25]. Two conversations follow, one with Nicodemus [3:1-21], followed by a supplementary section of testimony by John, the Baptist, which probably belongs in ch. 2 and the second with a Samaritan woman [4:1-26]. Between is a commentary concerning God's light in this world, its nature and the terms upon which it is presented to man [3:31-36]. The conversations are with two entirely different people. Nicodemus is a teacher of Jews and, therefore, not only represents orthodoxy, but is also a symbol of respectability; the Samaritan woman is his opposite, for the Samaritans were from the point of orthodox Jewry pariahs in Palestine. The second main division ends with another of Jesus' overt acts—the healing of the nobleman's son [4:46b-54].

The third section continues the public ministry at the Feast of Pentecost (possibly Passover) and begins with a healing at the Pool of Bethesda [5:1-9a]. The immediate result of the Sabbath day miracle is a controversy with the Jews [5:9b-18], who seek Jesus in order to kill him. Already the beginning of the end is clear. The last part of this action consists of a monologue in which Jesus teaches that the Son has the power to give life [5:21]. At the outset he speaks in the third person, but in the last portion he reverts to the first [5:24] and points out that evidence (witness) is given everywhere of his incarnation, evidence which the Jews do not accept.

In the fourth section Jesus is seen for the last time in Galilee. He teaches the disciples and the multitude beside the Sea and performs the"miracle of the loaves"feeding the five thousand [6:1-15]. So impressed are the people by his leadership and mighty acts that they seek to make him king (probably they thought in terms of Jewish Messianic expectation), but Jesus departs to high ground. Later the disciples leave the area by water and are caught in a squall. After they have traveled about half way (25 or 30 furlongs = 3 or 4 miles), Jesus approaches them over the water, calms their fears at his unexpected appearance, and enters the boat. The next day the multitude, who themselves traveled to Capernaum by boat, cannot understand how Jesus made the trip since he embarked neither with the disciples at the outset, nor with the multitude later [6:16-25]. Jesus does not answer their questions directly, but in the preaching that follows teaches concerning the truth of his nature which the apostles have already recognized. The multitude seek him for the wrong reason [6:26]. Jesus is the source of life, but the people neither understand nor believe. At this point in the narrative John introduces the subject of another scholarly controversy, focusing the action on the Jews [6:41].

This is the only time the Jews appear in Galilee. Their first argument against Jesus' divinity is based on their claim of knowing his earthly origin [6:42]. His answer uses the metaphor given to the multitude—he is the bread of life which contains a spiritual and life-giving nourishment that even manna from heaven could not supply. The reference also concerns his eventual sacrifice and death. The skeptical Jews do not understand [6:52]. Jesus then reiterates his statement even more forcibly, not only in reference to his flesh, but also in reference to his blood [6:53-58]. At the end even some of the disciples seem unable to accept all that has been said [6:60], and Jesus faces a crisis in his teaching. A cleavage is taking place among the faithful [6:43]. Jesus predicts his betrayal and finally Simon Peter confesses the faith that Jesus is the Christ, the Son of the living God, thus reconciling Hebrew and Greek theology.

The fifth section uses the Feast of Tabernacles as its frame. Jesus is found teaching in the temple after the feast has begun. The controversy which ensues becomes violent; that the Jewish coterie's resolve to do away with him is made clear [7:25]. The general public is not, however, aware of the fact [7:20]. The crowds are evidently half-convinced of his Messiahship, but the Jews continue the controversy where it was broken at ch.5:27. The main argument centers around the issue of his origin. They know where he came from [7:27]. Furthermore, he is not from Bethlehem [7:42], but from Galilee [7:41] from whence surely no prophet was likely to arise [7:52]; nor are they capable of understanding his end [7:35, 8:22]. Jesus continues, nevertheless, to claim divine origin and authority.

The next morning Jesus returns to the temple and after making judgment concerning the woman taken in adultery [8:1-11] speaks again concerning his nature (origin and authority). Although he warns of judgment to come, the Jews refuse to accept his teaching and the multitude is uncertain. Although there are indications that some of the Jews may have been converted [8:31], the controversy continues.

Chapter 9 tells of the last great public controversy with the Jews. After Christ heals a blind man, the man is carefully cross-examined by the Jews and Pharisees. Then Jesus teaches concerning spiritual blindness [9:35-41] and tells the story of the Good Shepherd [10:1-10]. It is another prediction of things to come and indicates Jesus' will to die for mankind. The Gospel clarifies that such action is voluntary [10:11-18]. The last controversy, which takes place at the Feast of Dedication, may be misplaced [10:19-29]; it is better integrated into the text if it comes after Chapter 9:41. The section ends with Jesus' last appeal for faith and the account of his escape from the Jews who have become violent [10:30-39].

The sixth section tells briefly of Jesus' journey to Peraea and his return to Bethany near Jerusalem where he raises Lazarus from the dead [10:40-11:44]. Lightfoot sees the latter as a similitude and cause for the atonement implied in Christ's death.[9] In order to raise Lazarus Jesus must go into the place of departed spirits [11:11]. Thus, he must experience death in

[9] R. H. Lightfoot, *St. John's Gospel, a Commentary*, pp. 17 and 217 ff.

order to save Lazarus. Furthermore, the life and resurrection which Jesus offers comes through the gateway of death. The story here can be seen to parallel the crucifixion, death, and resurrection of Jesus in the last half of the Gospel. He even cries out immediately before Lazarus is raised [11:43] in much the same way that the other Gospels let him cry on the cross as he gives his life to atone for the sin of mankind. Thus, with his cry to Lazarus he can also be seen in the act of dying in order to bring about Lazarus' resurrection. The tomb from which Lazarus subsequently emerges is identical in description to that from which Jesus' resurrection took place.

If this view is taken John's Gospel might end properly with the last words of the story, the Lord's death having taken place when he gave life to Lazarus. The seventh section [11:54-12:50] of the Gospel would then be a sequel showing how external events work out as a result of what has passed. Jesus withdraws, but returns again at Passover time. He is now in constant danger. Even the anointment of Mary suggests death; the process is similar to that used in embalming bodies. The removal of the ointment with her hair may indicate that death has no lasting dominion over him [12:1-11]. Symbolic interpretation of the story reveals that Jesus has died, has now arisen and enters Jerusalem in triumph [12:12-19]. The account that some Greeks are evangelized may serve to indicate the universalization of Judaism. Lastly, in his teaching, Jesus summarizes the atoning process of sacrifice, pain, death, and resurrection [12:20-36]. In the final verses the author uses prophecy to indicate divine action. He makes plain that Jewish inability to believe is as much the result of God's will as is the conversion of the disciples.

PART TWO

Part two of the Gospel is the familiar story of the last days: the arrest, trial, crucifixion, and resurrection. Taken as a whole it is the same story which each one of the sections has already told. John presents Jesus as the incarnate Word of God, voluntarily giving his life on the cross. The reader will remember that in the first part of the Gospel, action precedes teaching and in the second teaching is given first and substantiating action follows. In broad outline, Chapters 13 through 17 can be read as an explanation to the disciples of the action told in Chapters 18 through 20. The first verse of Chapter 13 predicts the events which are to follow: "Now before the Feast of the Passover, when Jesus knew that his hour was come and that he should depart out of this world, having loved his own which were in the world, He loved them unto the end." The last line reveals that his final teaching is for them. Jesus then washes the disciples' feet, an act reminiscent of baptism (symbolic cleansing) and Judas Iscariot is at last openly marked as the traitor so often predicted in earlier sections of the Gospel. The first half of part two is almost entirely devoted to teachings which are divided into three parts, Chapters 13:31–14:31, Chapters 15:1–16:33, Chapter 17:1–26. The word here is not easily identified with the action to follow, and the chronology is also confusing. Crucifixion, death, and resurrection are referred to as departure and return, and although this action lies in the future, it is described as either having already taken place [16:23, 17:4] or as being in the process of accomplishment [14:31, 16:5].

The first teaching section is concerned for the most part with Jesus' departure and return [13:33, 14:18], with the coming of the Holy Spirit [14:16, 17:26], and with the future relationship of the disciples to the Lord [14:22, 21, 23]. The disciples interrupt the discourse with questions, whereas in the two following sections they remain still, except in the second part where they question his teaching briefly among themselves [18:29, 30].

The second section enlarges the first. The first seven verses of Chapter 15 with Verses 26 and 27 continue to explain the relationship of Jesus to his disciples and enlarge on his promise to return to them; these verses expand the explanation of the disciples' relationship to the Father through him and through the Holy Spirit which began in Chapter 14:16–21. The theme hence follows the basic teaching of the entire Gospel. The treatment the Church may expect from the world [15:18-16:24] is picked up word for word from 14:19 ff. and is followed by the metaphor of a woman in travail. Pain, sacrifice, and sorrow are necessary precedents for the joy which comes [16:16-21]. So also is sacrifice necessary for rebirth and salvation, death, and resurrection; Jesus spells the point out with multiple repetition, and after his statement [16: 28], the disciples understand at last. As a result, they make a confession of faith [16:30]. Jesus then predicts his abandonment by all and his ultimate victory over the world.

The third and last teaching section consists of three prayers through which the disciples actually witness the union that exists between the Father and the Son. Through Jesus they enter into the presence of the Father. The first prayer [17:1-8] concerns Jesus' mission on earth and his fulfillment of it, the second [17:9-19] concerns the disciples who are to be his representatives on earth, and the third [17:20-26] is a supplication for future disciples who will receive their faith from those Jesus leaves behind.

The second half of part two opens with the scene from the Garden of Gethsemane where Jesus is arrested. The action which follows is all clearly representative of prior exposition. John makes the issues clear. The rulers of the world (worldly authority and values) stand against the divine word. Judas vho throughout has represented an evil force, the chief priests, and the Pharisees, all come to arrest Jesus [18:3]. Even Peter runs true to form, impetuous and violent to the end. Jesus is taken and bound, but the disciples are not molested [18:1-12]. Peter's denial of his Lord at the preliminary hearing follows [18:13-27]. Unlike the Synoptics, John writes that Jesus admits both his teaching and his Messiahship. These admissions bring violence from the officers.

After Jesus receives a preliminary hearing before Pilate, the stage is set for the final curtain [18:28-32]. Although previously the cleavage between the world and the word of God has been made clear in terms of the Jews and Jesus, now the conflict is brought into sharp focus in the person of Pilate, the representative of the Roman Empire. Jesus cannot avoid the judgment and be the Christ. Johannine theology makes the outcome inevitable.

When Pilate asks what the charge is [18:29], the Jews have nothing to offer except their antagonism [18:30]. Pilate offers to let the Jews make their own judgment, but they decline to do so. Pilate then examines Jesus privately [18:33-38a] and, still unable to find any fault in him, attempts a compromise [18:38b-40], which is rejected by the Jews. The soldiers scourge and ridicule Jesus. Although such humiliations should prove that Christ is not King of the Jews and hence that the charges are pointless, the Jews still cry for his life, saying that Jesus has claimed to be the Son of God [19:1-7]. Since this is a charge worthy of death by Jewish religious law (blasphemy), Pilate may have felt some need to uphold it in order to keep the precarious peace which existed between Roman authority and the revolutionary religious element in Palestine. In any case he retired again to examine Jesus privately [19:8-11]. The issue now centers around Pilate's need to be just as an officer of the state. By speaking no words of defense Jesus leaves the decision entirely in Pilate's hands. He merely reminds Pilate of his obligations. When Pilate makes his decision [19:12], the Jews play their trump—the charge of sedition. Pilate must decide between God and the world. In a rage born of frustration and fear he throws this charge back in their faces, but Jesus is condemned [19:15-16]. The Jewish statement that they know no king other than Caesar repudiates all they have stood for as a religious nation. In their hatred of Jesus they have pawned their integrity.

In reporting the crucifixion John's Gospel does not differ in any important respect from the Synoptics. John states that Jesus bore his cross and makes no mention of Simon the Cyrene [Mk. 15:21, Lk. 23:26]. Only John records the fact that Jesus wore a seamless garment [19:23]. He borrows Verse 24 from Ps. 22:18. "They parted my garments among them, and upon my vesture did they cast lots." It is possible that the reference which follows to Jesus' mother and the beloved disci-

ple who will henceforth care for her may be an allegory referring to the Church and its members, who are now under
the protection of the Holy Spirit, or it may be that John is
demonstrating the fulfillment of Scripture in the whole section
beginning with the mother story and ending with the vinegar
[19:28-29], part of which is a quotation from Ps. 69:21.
Concerning v. 29, the question arises as to whether it points
back to the mother story or forward to the vinegar.

The Jews enter the picture again to dispose of what is left
of Jesus' earthly body. John understands the piercing of
Christ's side and the extravasation of water and blood as a sort
of baptism for the new Church. Its power flows from Jesus.
The help offered by Nicodemus is an account unique to John;
the Synoptics agree on Joseph of Arimathea [19:38]. Like the
others John writes that Jesus' body is embalmed and laid to rest
in a tomb in a garden [19:38-42].

The last part of this Gospel describes the resurrection.
This, rather than the crucifixion, is the real climax. Here proof
of all that has been taught is revealed. Jesus returns as he has
promised, not only in the flesh, but also in precisely the same
flesh with which he departed—the crucified body—and he
continues unchanged the relationship with those who were
intimate with him before his death on the cross. In both appearances Jesus makes clear the point concerning his body. In
the first instance he shows his hands and side which have been
pierced [20:20], and in the second he even invites Thomas to
thrust his hand into his side [20:27]. John, no doubt, feels that
his point has been made. The cycle is complete, and his last
words summarize the purpose of the work [20:31].

The appendix contains two main scenes and four divisions.
The first scene shows the disciples once again at their original
occupation, fishing in Galilee at the Sea of Tiberius. Seven,
with Peter as the leader, are mentioned. The expedition is unsuccessful, but upon the appearance of Jesus, who at first is not
recognized, their luck changes. The feeding story which follows, closely resembles the feeding of the multitude in Chapter
6:1-14, and the fishing episode is reminiscent of the Synoptic account of Christ's first call to be followed.

The second scene is the occasion of conversation between Jesus and Peter in which Peter is again commissioned to do the Lord's work [21:15-19]. A conversation with the beloved disciple, who may have shared authorship of the Gospel, follows [21:20-23]. The last lines of the book return to the first person and imply that no one is able to record all the great events of Christ's life on earth [21:24-25].

The exact reasons for the addition of the appendix remain obscure. Agreement is general that Chapter 21 is part of the original work. It appears in all but one of the earliest manuscripts. The author may have felt the need of tying the fourth Gospel more closely into the geographical locale of the Synoptics. Until this point Jesus' ministry has been almost entirely in Jerusalem; the synoptic tradition favors Galilee until the last days. Lightfoot suggests that the chapter has as its purpose clarification of the relationship between Peter and the beloved disciple for apostolic Christianity. Peter emerges as the administrator of the early Christian organization, while the beloved disciple is the repository of spiritual insight and the guardian of the revealed truth.

OUTLINE OF JOHN

Part One

I. Introduction and events leading up to the public ministry of Jesus, 1:1-2:11.

Ch. 1 A. *Theology and John the Baptist, 1:1-:18*

    a) God is the beginning of all things, is self contained and in existence before the world, 1:1-2

    b) God created all things, 1:3

    c) God created life in man and illuminated him, 1:4

    d) Man rejected God's illumination, 1:5

    e) John the Baptist was not part of the divine world, but merely gave testimony concerning it, 1:6-8

    f) The illumination of man was universal, but was not universally received. Some rejected God, 1:9-11

    g) Some received him and inherited the status of God's children, 1:12

   h) The contrast between spiritual and natural birth (may
       also refer to V.B.), 1:13
   i) A statement of the incarnation, 1:14
   j) The theme [1:6-8] is continued, 1:15
   k) The author has received illumination, 1:16
   l) Jesus Christ's revelation goes beyond this law and only
       through him is this full truth revealed, 1:17, 18

B. *Preparation for the ministry to come 1:19-2:11.*

John the Baptist's testimony, 1:19–34

   a) John states that he is not the Christ (Messiah), 1:19, 20
       John states that he is not Elias [Mal. 4:5], 1:21a
       John states that he is not the prophet [Deut. 18:15],
       1:21b
   b) John describes himself in the words of Deut. [18:15],
       1:22-23
   c) John states that his baptism is only a purification cere-
       mony preparatory to the greater spiritual baptism of
       Jesus, 1:24-27
   d) The event is reported in Bethabara, 1:28
   e) John tells of the sacrificial death to come, 1:29-31
   f) John tells of the spirit's descent upon Jesus on the oc-
       casion of his being baptized, 1:32-34

The first disciples are called, 1:35-51

   a) Two of John's disciples are converted, one of whom is
       Andrew, Simon Peter's brother, 1:35-40
   b) Simon and Philip are called, 1:41-44
   c) Nathanial (Bartholomew) is called and Jesus shows in-
       sight concerning the hidden thoughts of men, 1:45-49
   d) Jesus deprecates a faith based on the assumption that he
       has supernatural powers, 1:50
   e) Jesus refers to Gen. 28:12 in his prediction of mighty
       events to come, 1:51

Ch. 2   *f*) Jesus performs his first miracle in Cana of Galilee by
       turning water to wine at a wedding feast, 2:1-11

II. Jesus' public ministry begins, 2:12-4:54

A. *Jesus at the Feast of the Passover and a commentary,*
2:12-3:36

   a) Jesus goes to Capernaum, 2:12
   b) Jesus goes to Jerusalem and cleanses the temple, 2:13-22
   c) Jesus is in Jerusalem for the Feast of the Passover where
       many are converted by his mighty acts, 2:23

d) Jesus does not trust this type of conversion, 2:24-25

Ch. 3 <i>e</i>) Nicodemus is interviewed, 3:1-21

Another testimony by John the Baptist concerning Jesus may properly follow (2:11), 3:22-30

f) The author comments on the relation of heavenly sources for revelation to earthly ones. The acceptance or rejection of such can determine man's destiny, 3:31-36

Ch. 4 B. *Jesus leaves Judea and teaches in Galilee, 4:1-54*

a) Jesus leaves Judea for Galilee and the story of the Samaritan woman, 4:1-26

b) The disciples return and are taught by Jesus, 4:27-38

c) Samaritans are converted and Jesus arrives in Galilee, 4:39-46a

d) Jesus heals the nobleman's son, 4:46b-54

III. Jesus' public ministry continues, and the controversies begin, 5:1-47

Ch. 5 A. *Jesus attends the feast and breaks the Sabbath, 5:1-18*

a) Jesus attends the Feast of Pentecost (possibly Passover) and heals a man at the pool of Bethesda, 5:1-9a

b) The Jews create a controversy regarding the Sabbath, 5:9b-18

B. *Jesus preaches on his relation to God and the Jews become violently antagonistic, 5:19-47*

a) The relation of the Father to the Son, 5:19-29

b) The Son gives testimony concerning the Father and judges Jewish unbelief, 5:30-47

IV. Jesus' public ministry in Galilee and the contrast between public ignorance and the disciples' acceptance, 6:1-71

Ch. 6 A. *Jesus teaches his disciples and the multitude, 6:1-40*

a) The feeding of the five thousand, 6:1-15

b) Jesus walks on water, 6:16-25

c) Jesus preaches on the truth of his revelation, 6:26-40

B. *The Jews create a controversy concerning Messiahship and revelation, 6:41-59*

a) Controversy with the Jews, 6:41-51a

b) Jesus preaches on the Eucharist, 6:51b-59

c. *A crisis in Galilee, 6:60-71*
  a) Some of the disciples desert Jesus, 6:60-66
  b) Peter's confession, 6:67-69
  c) Jesus predicts Judas Iscariot's betrayal, 6:70-71

V. Jesus' public ministry continues; controversy with the Jews continues; the origin, destiny, and nature of Jesus made clear, 7:1-10:39

Ch. 7 A. *Jesus' ministry in Galilee and controversy with the Jews,*
  7:1-53
  a) Jesus teaches in the temple at the Feast of Tabernacles, 7:1-14
  b) Controversy with the Jews continues, 7:15-24 (5:47)
  c) Controversy at the feast, 7:25-36
  d) Jesus preaches concerning his revelation and the lines are drawn between himself and the Jews, 7:37-53

Ch. 8 B. *Jesus teaches in the Temple, 8:1-59*
  a) The woman caught in adultery, 8:1-11
  b) Jesus declares himself the light of the world, 8:12-20
  c) Jesus warns of judgment and reiterates his claim to be divine revelation, 8:21-30
  d) Controversy with the Jews, some of whom had believed, 8:31-47
  e) Controversy continues to confirmed opponents, 8:48-59

Ch. 9 C. *Jesus' ministry continues and last controversy with the Jews takes place, 9:1-10:39*
  a) A blind man is healed, 9:1-12
  b) The Pharisees and Jews cross-examine the man healed by Jesus, 9:13-34
  c) Jesus teaches concerning spiritual blindness, 9:35-41
Ch. 10 d) The story of the Good Shepherd, 10:1-18
    (The last controversy with the Jews on the occasion of the Feast of Dedication, 10:19-29 properly follows, 9:41)
  e) Jesus makes a last appeal for faith and escapes the ensuing wrath of the Jews, 10:30-39 (may properly follow, 10:17)

VI. Jesus journeys to Peraea and thence to Bethany, 10:40-
11:53

    a) Jesus escapes to Peraea, 10:40-42
Ch. 11 *b*) Jesus raises Lazarus in Bethany, 11:1-44
    c) Some are converted, but the Jews resolve to kill Jesus,
       11:45-53

VII. Jesus flees to Ephraim shortly before the Feast of the
Passover, returns to Bethany, and concludes his ministry at Jerusalem, 11:54-12:50

    a) Jesus at Ephraim before the feast, 11:54-57
Ch. 12 *b*) Jesus is anointed at Bethany, 12:1-11
    c) The triumphal entry in Jerusalem, 12:12-19
    d) Jesus preaches to the Greeks, 12:20-36
    e) The failure of Jesus' mission is explained by ancient
       prophecy (Isa. 53.1), 12:37 43
    f) Jesus' last public teaching, belief in him is belief in
       God, 12:44-50

Part Two

VIII. The last days, trial, crucifixion, resurrection, and
appendix, chs. 13-21

Ch. 13 I. A. *Events before the trial, 13:1-14:31*

    a) A pre-Passover meal (The Last Supper), 13:1-2
    b) Jesus washes the disciples' feet, 13:3-20
    c) Judas Iscariot is marked a traitor, 13:21-30
    d) Jesus gives the commandment of love, 13:31-35
    e) Peter's denial foretold, 13:36-38
Ch. 14 *f*) Jesus teaches the disciples for the last time concerning
    eternal life, and foretells the coming of the Holy Spirit,
    14:1-31

Ch. 15 B. *Events before the trial continued, 15:1-16:33*

    a) The allegory of the vine, 15:1-17
Ch. 16 *b*) Jesus again promises that the Holy Spirit will come and
    tells of the world's hatred, 15:18-16:4
    c) Jesus speaks to his disciples of his departure, 16:5-24
    d) Jesus finishes his teaching and the disciples profess to
    understand him at last, 16:25-33

Ch. 17 C. *Jesus prays to his Father in heaven, 17:1-26*

    a) Jesus prays for strength, 17:1-8
    b) Jesus prays for the disciples, 17:9-19
    c) Jesus prays for future disciples, 17:20-26

  II. A. *The arrest, trial and,crucifixion, 18:1-19:42*

Ch. 18 *a*) Jesus is arrested, 18:1-12
    b) The hearing before the Jews and Peter's denial, 18:13-27
    c) Jesus receives a preliminary hearing before Pilate, 18:28-32
    d) Jesus is examined privately by Pilate, 18:33-38a
    e) Pilate attempts a compromise, 18:38b-40
Ch. 19 *f*) Jesus is scourged and mocked; the Jews cry for his life, 19:1-7
    g) Jesus is examined privately a second time, 19:8-11
    h) Jesus is condemned, 19:12-16
    i) Jesus is crucified, 19:17-37
    j) Joseph of Arimathea and Nicodemus, 19:38-42

  B. *Events after the crucifixion, chs. 20-21*

Ch. 20 *a*) Mary Magdalene discovers the empty tomb, 20:1-10
    b) Jesus appears to Mary, but remains unknown, 20:11-18
    c) Jesus appcars to the disciples, 20:19-23
    d) Jesus appears again eight days later, 20:24-29
    e) John concludes the Gospel, 20:30-31

Ch. 21 C. *An appendix, ch. 21*

    a) Jesus appears at the Sea of Galilee, 21:1-14
    b) Jesus converses with Peter, 21:15-19
    c) Jesus and the beloved disciple, 21:20-23
    d) A remark by the editor concerning authorship and the end, 21:24-25

Part II

VII

The Resurrection

Not until after the resurrection can the early apostolic faith be properly termed Christian. Jesus himself was a Jew practicing his religion within Judaism. Although his early followers perhaps sensed the beginning of a new religious age, this was an age within the ancient faith, fulfilling ancient prophecy. To be sure, Jesus called for a new life because of this new age, but only after the resurrection could the new faith be a Christ-made or Christian thing. For this reason the break-off point between the first and second sections of this book has been placed before the resurrection narratives. Jesus died on the cross, a discredited and forsaken Jew. In his resurrection he became the Christ.

The earliest accounts of the resurrection do not come from the Gospels, but from Paul's first Epistle to the Corinthians.

"And he rose again the third day according to the Scriptures; and was seen of Cephas, then of the twelve: after that, he was seen of above five thousand brethren at once; of whom the greater part remain unto this present, but some are fallen asleep. After that he was seen of James; then of all the apostles. And last of all he was seen of me also, as one born out of due time." [I Cor. 15:4b-8.]

Considerable variation occurs among the Gospel accounts. Mark tells briefly of an appearance before Mary Magdalene

[16:9] and of a second appearance before two unnamed followers [16:12]. As in the other Gospels the report of these occurrences was not at first accepted by the majority. But the description of a third appearance before the eleven disciples leaves no doubt. In this instance Christ first upbraids them for their unbelief and then charges them with his ministry. "Go ye unto all the world and preach the gospel to every living creature" [16:14-15].

Matthew's account follows the same form, but uses far more apocalyptic language. Jesus is heralded by an angel of the Lord that appears accompanied by wondrous signs [28:2-3], and when Christ appears he foretells a tryst with his brethren in Galilee [28:10]. Matthew further includes the story of bribery by the chief priests in their effort to discredit the resurrection [28:13] and adds a Christian baptismal formula to Christ's commands [28:19].

Luke replaces the single angel with two. All three Gospels agree that Mary and Christ's intimates first experienced the predictions of the resurrection on going to the tomb. Luke pinpoints the first appearance at the village of Emmaus, a short distance from Jerusalem [24:13]. He follows this occasion with a long description of an appearance in Jerusalem during which Christ eats broiled fish and honey and which ends with his assumption into heaven [24:36-51]. Without specifying the exact location of the event Luke also describes a period of forty days in which Jesus appeared and taught the disciples. This description also ends with Christ's assumption into a cloud [Acts 1:3-9].

Although John omits the appearance of the angels at first, he agrees that Mary Magdalene found the tomb empty [20:2]. The angels appear on the occasion of her second visit to the tomb. Jesus appears to her immediately thereafter, but is not recognized [20:14]. He then appears to the disciples behind closed doors [20:19] where he charges them with his ministry and gives them power of the Holy Ghost (Spirit) [20:22]. Unique to John is the story of doubting Thomas which includes another resurrection appearance. In his last chapter

John tells of Christ's appearance to the disciples at the Sea of Tiberias [21:1] with a detailed summary of those who were present. Next comes a story of an appearance while the disciples are fishing which is paralleled in the Synoptics by a similar occurrence during the life of Jesus. In the end Jesus charges them with his ministry.

As in the case of the mighty works which Jesus performed during his lifetime, it is impossible to appraise the resurrection stories on the basis of the modern news story. Clearly, much of the material was already legendary at the time it was written. Further, the evangelists or some earlier source put into Christ's mouth words than can hardly be attributed to him. The Trinitarian baptismal formula which is found in Matthew clearly comes from a much later period, and John has made use of early accounts for his own particular purposes without regard to chronology.

Legends have, however, facts of some sort as their source. Even if the intricacies of critical comparison and investigation of sources are examined until all possibilities are exhausted, one central fact continues to emerge. All the persons most intimately associated with the early Christian movement were convinced beyond doubt that Jesus Christ rose from the dead. The exact nature of the experiences themselves can never be known. Were they subjective or objective? Exactly how many times and under what precise circumstances did they take place? A historical approach to the subject cannot answer these questions, but the shadow of uncertainty in this area is more than cleared by the light of certainty in the basic conviction which the appearances proclaimed. From that time on the men of Palestine who had been Christ's followers never wavered from the faith. They were totally convinced that Jesus Christ was the Messiah and that he had indeed cheated death itself to sit on the right hand of God. Off they went with burning urgency to tell the news to all the world. The Messiah had come. Truly the kingdom of God was at hand. Their lives were led for that end, and for that end alone. No amount of persecution could stop them. Neither the wiles of the Sanhedrin, nor the heavy hand of Rome made any difference to them. Many were to find crosses of their own on which to hang. Some were torn apart by wild beasts in the arena. Other were burned alive, but the basic conviction remained unchanged. History turned in a new direction, and the world itself was changed by what happened at Golgotha and in the days following. Herein is proof of the resurrection for those who seek it. Many carpenters have died and many criminals have been executed, but none has changed the life of man as did the simple carpenter from Nazareth, who was executed between two malefactors by a Roman court.

VIII

The Book of Acts

Background

The Book of Acts undoubtedly shares authorship with Luke's Gospel. Style, structure, orientation and theology are the same. Acts continues the Christian story into the first century. Although a Gentile, Luke writes from the Jewish viewpoint. In the beginning Christianity is pictured as a sect within Judaism which would, therefore, be afforded the same rights and privileges by the Roman government. In the Judaism of apostolic times, the high priest, priests and Levites were no longer very important. The real rulers and guardians of the faith were the elders, some of whom were to be found in every sizable community. Such a group was the Sanhedrin in Jerusalem. (Sanhedrin is a word derived from Aramaic. The corresponding Greek derivation is the more familiar presbytery.) In Acts the apostolic group of Christians is depicted as constituting a sort of congress which made decisions concerning the application of the new faith to specific life situations in much the same way as the Sanhedrin acted for the old religion. They even acted as a religious legislature for questions which came from outside the immediate area [15:2]. This similarity to the traditional, accepted system supposedly lent legitimacy to Christian procedure. Even the famous liberal scribe Gamaliel is reported to have suggested that Christians should not be molested [5:33-40].

Luke's understanding of "elders" is made clear in the text. The Jerusalem group are the most important and commissioned the others [6:2-6]. They send Peter and John to Samaria [8: 14]; they receive Paul after his conversion upon Barnabas' introduction [9:27]; and they even contend with Peter on matters of faith and practice [11:1, 2]. The group is clearly recognized as authoritative; the actual word elder is used in reference to them when relief is sent to Judea [11:30]. Paul follows the same line in the polity of his early churches [14:23]. Luke indicates that Antioch was a Christian center [13:1], although secondary to Jerusalem.

Purpose

The purpose of the book, which follows a fourfold theme, stands out clearly in its organization, background and slant. First, the writing is primarily an effort on Luke's part to put Christianity in such a light that it can be viewed with favor and accepted by the Roman authorities as a licit religion. In accomplishing this end Luke makes secondary points which clarify many aspects of early Christianity. Secondly, the Gospel writer enlarges his work in terms of revelation born of the resurrection experiences. Third, Luke makes the nature of Jesus Christ clear, and lastly, he outlines the development of the Christian movement. Furthermore, Acts was not written solely for the edification of Theophilus and the Roman official mind. It was also written to instruct Christians. The writing is oriented both for educated groups and for the lower classes. Continuing the theme of his Gospel, Luke is clear to the point that Christianity is a form of Judaism and as such should be accepted as a *religio licita*. Over and over again he cites precedents which reveal that men of authority accept the Christian position. Sergius Paulus is converted after observing a punitive miracle [13:10-12]; the Roman officials in Philippi gave Paul protection [16:37-39]; in Thessalonica Christians are released on bail [17:9]; Gallio, the proconsul, actually drives the Jews out of his court on Paul's behalf [18:16]; when the silversmiths try to make trouble in Ephesus, Paul and his followers are guaranteed full protection of the law [19:36-40]; Felix, the procurator of Judea, finds Paul not guilty of any crime against the state [23:29]; and although the charges made by the Jews are more incriminating, they nevertheless only accuse him of acting amongst Jews [24:5]; later Felix himself is almost converted [24:23-27]; Festus, the new procurator, can find nothing against Paul worthy of sentence and acknowledges his right to be heard before Caesar [25:25]; likewise Agrippa sees Paul as within the law [26:32]; and lastly even in Rome Paul is allowed to practice his religion [28:30-31].

When Stephen defends his position, Luke records statements which link him intimately with Jewish tradition: "our fathers" [7:11b, 39]. The phrase binds him to the orthodoxy of the past; Paul uses the same phraseology when he speaks in Pisidian, Antioch [13:17]. Christianity is to be seen not only as Judaism, but also as the only true Judaism. Certainly Christians considered themselves Jews at the outset; they adhered to the new aspects of their faith while continuing to worship in the temple [2:46, 3:1, 5:12, 5:20]. Even after years of missionary activity Paul made a point of observing the temple rites whenever possible [21:23-27].

More significant is Luke's treatment of Paul's missionary activity. He is never a free agent, but must report back to headquarters periodically. Jerusalem is the source of authority whose arm stretches even to far away lands, "and as they went through the cities, they delivered them the decrees for to keep, that were ordained of the apostles and elders which were at Jerusalem" [16:4]. The picture Luke draws of Paul is independent of and somewhat different from that which can be seen through the Epistles. In Luke he remains subordinate to the governing body of early converts who hold the status of ruling elders already mentioned as a Christian parallel to the Sanhedrin. In the list of leaders in the Antiochene community, Paul's name is last [13:1]. He is given authority but not equality by the group [13:3]. The background to Paul's growth is always Jerusalem. His ministry is described in a Jerusalem frame. As has already been mentioned Barnabas took him there at the outset [9:27]. Both Paul and Barnabas were sent there with relief for the needy [11:30]. Paul returned there to hear the decrees of the Jerusalem conference on the Gentile question [15:2]; he went back for a religious feast [18:21], and his free activity ended there [21:17].

Luke makes it quite clear that Paul always remained faithful to Jewish custom and authority. He never leaves the context of Judaism. His exhortations to faith could as well be those of a devout rabbi [14:22-23]; Timothy is made to undergo the rite of circumcision [16:3], and late in his ministry Paul took a Nazarite vow [18:18] and attended the temple feasts until the end of his freedom [20:16]. (See also Paul's own references to his Jewish background in his life, this work p. 157.)

Structure

The plan of the book is easy to follow. It shows the progress of the Christian movement step by step around the Mediterranean coast beginning with Jerusalem and ending in Rome. Six geographical divisions lie in between: Jerusalem [6:7]; Judea, Galilee and Samaria [9:31]; Antioch [13:1]; the Island of Cyprus [13:4]; Asia Minor [16:5]; Macedonia, Achaia and Asia [19:1]; and Rome [28:31]. It is generally agreed that sources for the first portion came from the area of Jerusalem, Caesarea, and Antioch, some of which may be of Petrine origin. A portion also apparently comes from a strong Jewish source [1:12-5:32, 9:31-11:18, 12:1-23]. Chapter 6:1-8 plus Stephen's speech [7:2-53] comprise material which is notably different in form and language from the rest and probably represents an insertion from a Hellenist and anti-Jewish tradition.

Chapter 8:5-40 which is Caesarean gives the story of Philip's ministry centering around his work in Samaria. The passage is of particular importance because of its references to the Holy Spirit and the new rite of the laying on of hands. Chapters 11:19-30, 12:24-14:28, some of 15:1-16:3 and all of

16:6-28:31 are Pauline material. Here also is the only place where a gospel tradition breaks into the first person; although some consider the use of the personal pronoun an editorial device, the we-sections of Acts are generally felt to be first hand reporting [16:10-17, 20:5-15, 21:1-18, 27:1-28:16]. Chapters 16:25-31 and 20:18-35 are clearly legendary while Chapter 17:22-32 is almost certainly not Pauline.

Besides its geographical plan Acts contains considerable biography which serves not only to establish chronological continuity, but also creates a frame for teaching sections which take the form of speeches. These are summaries of material Luke feels should be included and are not concise reporting of actual speeches. The time sequences, when specified, are confusing. A time table of Acts cannot be reconstructed from them. Luke tells that Paul was in Corinth a year and six months (18:11), in Achaia or Greece three months [20:3], in Caesarea two years [24:27], in Malta three months [28:11], and in Rome two years [28:30]. Added together these periods add to less than half the time of Paul's total known ministry, and do not correspond with other time intervals that can be fixed with some accuracy from outside sources or which are specified by the apostle himself. Biographically Paul is dominant, but Peter's early ministry is described and is linked to Paul by Stephen and Philip. Stephen's short life serves to show the futility of preaching to Jews with the hope of converting them in the early days, whereas Philip's ministry introduces the type of missionary activity which is to be the norm for Paul.

Like the Gospels, Acts seems to have been designed as a vehicle for the teaching techniques of the times. It can be read in sections which are adaptable to short periods of instruction, and it is repetitious. The decrees of the elder Christians (apostolic decrees) concerning sexual morality and ritual foods are repeated almost word for word twice. Compare 15:29 and 21:25. The story of Paul's conversion is told three times and both Chs. 9 and 26 tell of the journey to Damascus and the events on the road.

Easton points out that some of the speeches form groupings which balance the beginning and end of the work.[1] The first Christian sermon which is preached by Peter [2:14-36], his address in Solomon's portico [3:11-26] (and before the high priest [4:5-12]) and Stephen's defense [7:2-53] can be roughly matched by three long speeches at the end: Paul's first defense when he returns to Jerusalem for the last time [22:1-21], his address before the Council at his hearing [22:30-23:10] and his defense before Festus and Agrippa [26:1-29]. In between the trials are five speeches, each for a different type of audience and each of which speaks to a specific recurring problem of the early Christian mission. Peter's address in the house of Cornelius [10:34-43] is for God-fearers [10:1-2]; Paul's sermon in Pisidian Antioch is for a synagogue audience [13:16-41]. In Chapter 14 Paul turns to the Gentiles of Iconium and Lystra, while in Athens he pitches his speech to the most sophisticated Greek mind [17:16-34]. Peter's short address [15:7-11] clears up the Gentile question once and for all. Lastly, Paul's address to the Ephesian elders is for a Christian group [20:18-35]. Taken as a whole the speeches form a summary of the Christian position as Luke understands it.

Lastly, Luke substantiates the faith not by logic and legality alone, but by ample references to miraculous acts, which are spread throughout the entire book, beginning with Christ's ascension [1:6-11] and ending with Paul's healing the sick on the island of Malta [28:8-9]. Between the speeches and journeys are parallel records of various healings by both Peter and Paul. In Jerusalem Peter heals persons ill from unclean spirits [demon possession 5:15,16]. Paul accomplishes the same thing in Philippi and matches the mass cure in Malta as well [28:9]. Peter heals a cripple in Jerusalem [3:7]; Paul matches the act in Lystra [14:8]. Peter succeeds in raising Dorcas (Tabitha) from the dead at Joppa [9:36-41], Paul accomplishes as much with Eutychus at Troas [20:9-12]. Peter cures a man sick of the palsy at Lydda [9:32-34]; Paul cures the father of Publius on Malta of a fever and bloody flux [28:7, 8]. Both Peter and

---

[1] Burton Scott Easton, *Early Christianity: The Purpose of Acts and Other Papers.*

Paul are freed from prison by miraculous means—Peter from Herod [12:10], Paul in Philippi [16:26].

Further, throughout there are generous descriptions of mighty acts. The apostles are released from prison [5:19], Paul's sight is restored [9:18], Stephen possesses great powers of faith [6:8]; likewise Philip is capable of mighty acts [8:13], Paul recovers from snake bite [28:5], and the apostles in general are possessed of great powers [2:43].

Lastly, Luke records many miracles of direct revelation. Early Christians are given power to speak by the Holy Spirit [2:4, 4:31]. In Antioch Agabus predicts the future [11:28]. In Damascus the Lord appears to Ananias in a vision [9:10], to Paul at Corinth [18:9-10], and again to Paul in the last days of Jerusalem [23:11], and on the occasion of his shipwreck. On the occasion of Christ's ascension angels are seen [1:10], one appears to Cornelius in Caesarea [10:3], an angel directs Philip's ministry [8:26], Stephen too is guided by an angel [7:55]; Paul experiences an apparition [9:5-7], and the story of his conversion is charged with supernatural activity.

Luke's work comprises by far the largest portion of the New Testament—over a quarter of the whole. His sources are close to firsthand as the we-sections indicate. Of all the evangelists he perhaps comes closest to capturing for our times the feeling of apostolic Christianity.

OUTLINE OF
THE ACTS OF THE APOSTLES

I. The early church in Jerusalem, 1:1-5:42

Ch. 1 Introduction, 1:1-5
    The disciples in Jerusalem, 1:6-26
        a) The Ascension, 1:6-11
        b) The upper room, 1:12-14
        c) The speech of Peter and the election of Matthias, 1:15-26
Ch. 2 The coming of the Spirit on the day of Pentecost, 2:1-42
        a) The coming of the Spirit, 2:1-4
        b) The impression on the multitude, 2:5-13

IV. Christianity is carried to Macedonia and Achaia (Paul's Second Missionary Journey), 15:36-18:22

V. Christianity in the province of Asia (Paul's Third Missionary Journey), 18:23-21:16

VI. Paul in Jerusalem, Caesarea, and Rome, 21:17-28:31

Paul in Jerusalem, 21:17-23:35
- *a*) Paul's report to James and the elders, and their proposal, 21:17-26
- *b*) Paul is arrested in the temple, 21:27-36
- *c*) Paul is permitted to address the mob, 21:37-40

Ch. 22 *d*) Paul's address, 22:1-21 [cf. 9:1-31]
- *e*) Paul is threatened with scourging, but claims Roman citizenship, 22:22-29

Ch. 23 *f*) Paul's address before the council, 22:30-23:10
- *g*) Paul's encouraging vision, 23:11
- *h*) The plot against Paul's life, 23:12-22
- *i*) Paul is transferred to Caesarea, 23:23-35

Paul in Caesarea, 24:1-26:32

Ch. 24 *a*) The case against Paul, 24:1-9
- *b*) Paul's defense before Felix, 24:10-21
- *c*) Paul's trial is postponed, 24:22-27

Ch. 25 *d*) Paul's trial is taken up by Festus, 25:1-12
- *e*) A special hearing before Agrippa II, 25:13-27

Ch. 26 *f*) Paul's defense before Festus and Agrippa, 26:1-23 [cf 9:1-31]
- *g*) The end of the hearing, 26:24-32

Paul in Rome, 27:1-28:31

Ch. 27 *a*) The journey by sea and shipwreck, 27:1-44

Ch. 28 *b*) Paul is safe on Malta, 28:1-10
- *c*) The final stage of the journey, 28:11-16
- *d*) Paul meets with the Jewish leaders in Rome, 28:17-29
- *e*) Paul preaches in Rome for two years, 28:30, 31

[2] Frederick C. Grant, *The Gospels: Their Origin and Their Growth.*

IX

Paul of Tarsus

Ancient history has produced only three people whose lives have been so well documented that it is possible to know them in a personal sense. Two wrote nothing themselves. The third was a great writer of letters. Jesus of Nazareth was unique and, as a theological being, cannot properly be grouped with the others. Socrates of Athens and Paul of Tarsus remain. The first, a great philosopher, found immortal fame through the tremendous scope of his intellect; his honesty, simplicity and humility made him beloved by his followers. The description of his death in Plato's "Phaedo" reveals a character that has transcended the world while still living in it. The second, Paul of Tarsus, was also greatly loved, but for a different reason. His personality was too brittle, his wit too sharp to be endearing. Despite his personality, Paul was loved because of his compelling faith and faithfulness, but for those who were not converted to the faith, Paul was the object of intense hatred.

Place of Birth

As in the case of Jesus of Nazareth, the exact place and date of Paul's birth remain uncertain. The limits, however, can be narrowed with some accuracy. Certainly this is true in respect to the location. Although other material exists such as an early work titled, "The Acts of Paul," two chief sources exist from which Paul's life can be reconstructed: the accounts in Acts and the Epistles written by the Apostle himself. The material in "The Acts of Paul" is too legendary to be of value. The Acts of the Apostles reports that Paul was born in Tarsus, the most important city of Cilicia, a center of Greek culture and home of a famous university [Acts 9:11]. Likewise Paul makes the claim for himself: "I am a man which am a Jew of Tarsus, a city in Cilicia" [Acts 21:39, 22:3]. He was also undoubtedly a Jew, "circumcised the eighth day, of the stock of Israel, of the tribe of Benjamin, a Hebrew of the Hebrews; as touching the law, a Pharisee" [Phil. 3:5]. The assumption that Paul changed his name from Saul to Paul after his conversion has been popular in the past, but no sound basis can be found to substantiate the position. The shift does not take place until Paul and Barnabas have reached the Isle of Cyprus, years after the conversion experience. Nor can it be assumed that he took the name from Sergius Paulus of Cyprus, because the name change occurs before the meeting and conversion of Sergius. True, it may be significant that at this point in the narrative he is given status over Barnabas, but the best modern scholarship now assumes that Paul possessed both names from birth and might quite properly be referred to as Saul-Paul (Saul was the ancient king of the tribe of Benjamin).

Date of Birth and Death

At best, Paul's dates cannot be narrowed to limits of less than five years, except in the case of his contact with Gallio, Proconsul of Achaia and brother of the philosopher Seneca [18:12]. Here the archeologist Adolf Deissman has been able to supplement the information which comes from early literature. From the Delphian inscription he has fixed the date of Gallio's proconsulship to 51-52 A.D. Other identifiable dates are the death of King Aretas, 40 A.D.; the death of Herod, Agrippa, 44 A.D. [12:23]; famine under Claudius [11:28];

Festus' arrival in Judea, 59 A.D. [24:27], and the Neronian persecution of the Jews, 64 A.D.

Using the only accurate date as a pivot, it is possible to work back to Paul's birth and forward to his death, but with almost insurmountable difficulties in reconciling some of the data. Paul was brought before Gallio to be judged after he had been in Corinth for eighteen months [Acts 18:12]; hence Paul must have arrived in the city sometime near 51 A.D. If the Jerusalem Conference followed this trip, it would fall within a year or two of his departure 51-52 A.D. Paul dates his conversion fourteen years earlier [Gal. 2:1], thus around 36-37 A.D.[1] In II Corinthians Chapter 11:32 he makes reference to his escape from Damascus and to King Aretas, who died in 40 A.D. These data suggest that Paul's conversion was prior to the year 40. Luke reports that Paul was a young man at the time Stephen was stoned [Acts 7:58]. If he were between twenty and twenty-five, his birth date falls about twenty years before the conclusion of Christ's ministry, sometime near 5–10 A.D.

Working forward, the date of Festus is helpful. A new coinage was recorded in Palestine around 59 A.D.; if it is assumed that this took place as a result of the new proconsul's governorship, Paul's trial took place during that year. Allowing a year for his journey to Rome and adding the two years Paul spent there suggests that Paul lived near the time of the Neronian persecution in which the tradition of Rome has long held that he died 64 A.D. He would have been about fifty-five or sixty at the time, by ancient standard an old man.

Education and Background

Although the location of Paul's birth was a center of Greek learning, this fact alone does not mean that he was of necessity brought up as a cultivated Greek. Over the years, however, Paul has always been viewed as a man of learning and status. He himself admits to being a Pharisee [Acts 23:6,

---

[1] This figure is by some considered 14 plus 3, others feel that ancient methods of chronology would have included the first 3 years with the 14.

26:5], who studied under Gamaliel [Acts 22:3]. Furthermore that Paul was a Roman citizen is a factor of tremendous importance to his ministry [Acts 22:25 ff].

Little can be said of Paul's appearance, but he must have had great fortitude. He was able to travel extensively on foot, enduring the greatest physical hardships. He also survived at least one stoning, in which he was left for dead, and countless beatings and imprisonments. Even in his advanced years when taken a prisoner to Rome he survived starvation, shipwreck, and the bite of a venomous snake.

He did suffer, however, from a chronic ailment, the exact nature of which cannot be diagnosed. Occasionally he was taken with some sort of seizure, but it may be that this was not a symptom of his habitual malaise. The former has been thought by some to have been epilepsy, but a history of epilepsy seems incongruous, considering his great strength, and powerful intellect [II Cor. 11:6, Gal. 4:13-15].

Paul probably never formally became a rabbi, but there is much to indicate that he studied for the rabbinate. It was customary for those who planned such a career to learn a trade as well. He was a tentmaker (or leather worker). By this trade he frequently supported himself during the course of his missionary journeys.

Career

No doubt exists that Paul was violently opposed to the early Christian Church, "And Saul, yet breathing out threatenings and slaughter against the disciples of the Lord" [Acts 9:1].[2] The story of his conversion is psychologically ambivalent. Paul, a man of tremendous intellect, turned all his emotional energy toward destroying that which challenged the faith of his fathers. The fact that he was a man near the rabbinate may have contributed to his violence. Some time in this early period a spark of doubt must have begun to smoulder in his mind and with it, a conflict. Either the Christian or the

[2] Also Acts 7:58, 8:1, 26:10, 11; I Cor. 15:9; Phil. 3:6; Gal. 1:13, 23.

orthodox interpretation was right, but not both. When persecution of the unorthdox failed to resolve the conflict, Paul tried frantically and overtly to put down the faith which was turning his doubt to conviction. In rage, he obtained a letter of authority to carry his persecution to Damascus [Acts 9:2], but while on the road, the spark of doubt burst into a burning flame of conviction that he was no longer able to resist.

What follows is exactly what might be expected. Paul suffered a severe mental shock. His dilemma was suddenly resolved. Hate became love. His faith was changed in an instant. Perhaps conversion is not the right word to describe his intellectual change. Paul's understanding changed, but it was simply a new understanding of the basic position of Judaism. From a religion of legal righteousness he moved to a religion whose primary concern was the sinner and his redemption through faith. He shifted from the ancient way of honoring God, the creation of a right relationship by deeds of sacrifice and strict adherence to the law, to salvation by the grace of God. The physiological reaction to this sort of mental strain is well known. Blind and shaken [9:8] he was led to Damascus where he started a new life. If the law was fulfilled in Christ and salvation came by grace, it followed that Gentiles and God-fearers,[3] who were not within the law were no longer excluded. Paul, a product of Greek Judaism and, therefore, a man who could understand the great world, as well as the heart of Jewish orthodoxy, could speak with authority even in Jerusalem. This combination gave him as well the perfect qualifications for a missionary.[4]

Apparently he went to work at once. With zeal equal to that revealed in his persecutions, he set about preaching the

[3] God-fearers and semi-proselytes: In the Greek-Jewish communities there were those who were not followers of Judaism by birth and inheritance, but who followed the true God, by conviction. These people recognized the Jewish God as supreme and practiced Judaism.
[4] It is at this point in the narrative that Paul's theology breaks with the author of Acts. Luke's position is clear to the point that Christians were a sect within Judaism while Paul in his Epistles is equally clear to the effect that Christianity was Judaism's successor—a fulfillment of the past.

gospel. His defection angered the Jews. They looked on him as a traitor and acted accordingly. The persecutor became the persecuted. The Jews lay in wait at the gates of the city to kill him [9:24], but their plans were thwarted by the Christian underground. Paul was lowered over the wall elsewhere and thus escaped [9:25]. He worked first in Arabia [Gal. 1:15-17]. After three years he returned to Jerusalem for a two-week visit with Peter. He did not return again for fourteen years [Gal. 2:1]. During the intervening period Paul was occupied with his first and second great missionary journeys, described in Acts.

The First Missionary Journey

The first journey begins with his trip from Antioch to Cyprus [Acts 13:1-3]. Traveling by foot to Seleucia, the harbour for the city on the Mediterranean, he embarked with his beloved companion Barnabas and his nephew or perhaps his cousin John Mark for the island. The exact reason for this itinerary is not clear although the area may have been chosen because Barnabas had property interests there. Landing at Salamis, they began preaching in the synagogues [13:5]. From Salamis they moved overland to Paphos at the opposite end of the island. Here a miraculous incident resulted in the conversion of Sergius Paulus. It is at this point that Acts shifts its usage from Saul to Paul [13:9]. Here also Paul becomes the dominant character of the narrative.

It may be assumed that the Cyprus ministry was not a great success. Acts makes no reference to any large following. From Paphos the little group sailed to the coast of Asia Minor landing at Perga in Pamphylia. Although the young John Mark deserted and returned to Jerusalem [13:13], Paul and Barnabas moved inland to Pisidian Antioch where a church was founded from a portion of the synagogue congregation. Under these circumstances it is not surprising that Paul continued to be the object of orthodox persecution. The address which Acts reports in the synagogue is so strongly Lucan that many scholars attribute the words to the author of Acts rather than to Paul himself. The opposition to Paul's preaching became so great that he was forced to turn toward the Gentiles, but the shift came too late, and the missionaries were violently expelled from the city [13:50-52]. Paul was almost always on the run from then on. The party traveled to Iconium, but were soon forced onward to Lystra and Derbe, cities in Lycaonia [14:1-6]. Here Acts describes an amazing incident. Because of healings the two missionaries were actually taken for gods of the Greek pantheon. So well convinced were the people that they prepared to do sacrifice for them [14:11-13]. This misapprehension perhaps resulted from a genuine healing miracle of some kind [14:8-9]. All of the journey was not, however, happy. Paul was stoned in Lystra and left for dead [14:19], but as his followers stood about lamenting, he regained consciousness and on the next day was able to travel on to Derbe, which marks the limit of his first journey. Paul then turned back, perhaps because of the Taurus Mountains, perhaps because he feared that he might prove ineffective in the area. In any case he returned to Pamphylia, taught briefly in Perga and sailed from Attalia back to Antioch in Syria [14:20-28]. The total distance covered was about fourteen hundred miles and the period of time was around three years.

Apparently Paul remained in Antioch for a prolonged period [Acts 14:28, 15:35; Gal. 2:11-12]. In describing the Antiochene sojourn Luke insists that the Gentile question is settled, but it must be noted that Paul's own description in Galatians places the occasion fourteen years after his conversion, not three, thus dating the visit at the end of his second missionary journey (or a break in it). Luke tells that the conference took place on his third visit to Jerusalem [Acts 9:26, 11:27-30, 12:25, 15:2]. Paul mentions only one prior visit in Galatians. Agreement is general that the first visits mentioned in each case report the same occasion. In the case of the others considerable difference of opinion still exists. Some hold that the second visit referred to in Galatians [2:1] is identical to the Jerusalem Conference of Acts 15:2. Others feel that the second Galatian visit is the same as the famine visit of Acts 11. Such scholars date the Galatian Epistle as having been written before the Jerusalem Conference; they believe that the Gentile question which it mentions must refer to a private conference. This chronology places the Epistle to the Galatians at a much earlier date. An evaluation might point out that Paul is probably a more reliable source of information for his visits than Luke and that he describes only two visits. The chronology which relates Gal. 2:1 and Acts 15:2 seems valid, for the conference is described as decidedly more than a private meeting, the details of which probably would not have been familiar to Luke. Considering the total length of Acts, Luke devotes a large portion to the conference. Furthermore, it is possible that Paul made the second visit mentioned by Luke but didn't consider it sufficiently important to mention when he wrote the Galatian Epistle.

The Second Missionary Journey

Paul's second journey began in sadness. He quarreled with his old friend Barnabas over John Mark. Barnabas wanted John to go on the trip. Paul would not have him. Paul was never to see Barnabas again. Taking Silas instead he traveled over the mountain region of his first trip through Syria and Cilicia to Derbe and Lystra, while Barnabas sailed with John once again to Cyprus [15:36-16:1a]. In Lystra a second companion was added to Paul's company—Timothy who was circumcised to appease the Jews. After visiting Paul's old communities where there were now many Christians, the party traveled through Phrygia and the region of Galatia (central Asia Minor), probably preaching in the towns of Amorium, Pessinus, Orcistus, and Nacolia. (At this time the North Galatian churches may have been founded.) Apparently Paul was taken ill and remained in the area longer than he had intended [Gal. 4:13].

Luke wants to make it quite clear that the Holy Spirit guided the little band of missionaries. They were barred by the Spirit from Asia and Bithynia [16:6-7] and moved instead to the coastal town of Troas. There Paul was guided by a vision to the greatest conquests of his missionary career. Luke again makes plain what he feels to be a divine plan [16:9-10]. Paul was given direct marching orders. He moved accordingly to Greece by way of Samothrace, the port of Neapolis (Kowalla), and Philippi [16:11-12]. In Philippi he baptized Lydia, a dye merchant [16:14-15]. Thence the party moved through Amphibolis and Apollonia to Thessalonica (Salonica); on the trip Paul continued to teach first in the synagogues [17:1-2]. The inevitable antagonism from unconverted Jews was violent. Paul fled at night to Berea (Verria) [17:10]. There the party split. Paul went on to Athens where on Mars Hill he suffered his worst humiliation and only real defeat. The Greeks did not ridicule or persecute him; instead they were almost totally indifferent to his teaching. The story of Christ's resurrection was not acceptable to the Athenian mind; only a few were converted [17:32-34].

At last Paul reached Corinth [18:1] where failure was exchanged for success. There he made lasting friends and founded churches which were to bring about the creation of some of his greatest Epistles. There he converted Priscilla and Aquila, who had recently migrated from Italy because of the Emperor Claudius' Jewish persecution in Rome. Not only were the family sympathetic Jews, but also they were, like Paul, tentmakers. When trouble developed again from synagogue people, Paul was forced to take refuge in the home of one Justus. He converted many, however, including the ruler of the synagogue, a man whose name was Crispus [18:8], to whom Paul administered the sacrament of baptism. During this period the incident concerning Gallio, so important to establishing the dates of Paul's life, took place. As a result of the religious riots his presence caused, Paul was taken before the Proconsul to be judged. The complaint of the Jews [18:11-17] was fortunate because it produced inadvertently the most reliable point of chronological identification in Paul's career.

After a long period, Paul left Corinth for Syria, accompanied by his new friends, Priscilla and Aquila [18:18]. Apparently sometime prior to this he had taken some sort of vow involving religious discipline, possibly the Nazarite vow [Numbers 6:1 ff]. Such a vow might only be ended with a suitable sacrifice at Jeruslaem. Paul stayed briefly in Ephesus and then made a quick trip to Jerusalem [18:21]. It may be that at this time he took a collection to help the Jerusalem church and that he sought advice on the Gentile question (Gal. 2:10; Acts 11:27-30, 15:2; see pages 162, 163 on chronology of the Jerusalem Conference).

The Third Missionary Journey

Once again Antioch served as a base for Paul's missionary expedition. Luke does not say how long he remained there— probably long enough to rest, see old friends and make contact with the elders of the Christian movement, then he was off again. With endless energy he worked his way through Cilicia by way of the Galatian churches [18:23]. There Apollos entered the scene [18:24-28]. From Nacolia Paul traveled through Phrygia by way of Metropolis to Ephesus [19:1] where he settled down to a long and fruitful ministry [19:10]. As usual he spoke in the synagogue until opposition developed sufficiently to make progress impossible. After the inevitable took place, Paul continued to teach in the off hours of a school which belonged to Tyrannus [19:9].

In this period even disciples of John the Baptist were converted, and Paul's ministry follows much the same pattern as that described in the Gospels themselves [19:3-5]. Many healings are reported. In one instance the narrative approaches humor when it describes an attempt by a group of charlatans to emulate Paul's mighty acts. They are roundly trounced by the infuriated madman whose devil they had attemped to exorcise [19:11-16]. Paul's ministry is successful in vanquishing current superstitions. Even the soothsayers and men possessed of curious learning burned their talismans and manuals [19:17-20], but there were times of great tribulation as well. Whether Paul's reference to the "beasts of Ephesus" [I Cor. 15:32] refers to an episode involving games similar to those practiced in the Roman arena, or whether the reference is simply figurative language, the point is quite clear that he was at some time in danger of life and limb. Perhaps the incident took place when he was imprisoned in Ephesus [II Cor. 1:8,9].

In Ephesus Paul was opposed by a new group; quite naturally the craftsmen and jewelers who made icons were not pleased with a religion that could ruin their business. Acts relates that a man named Demetrius, a silversmith, who made silver shrines for the goddess Diana claimed that Paul's teaching had hurt the trade. He incited his fellow workers to riot. Some of Paul's friends were caught, but Paul himself escaped and the disturbance was quelled without harm having been done [19:24-41]. (Probably sometime during this period Paul wrote Philippians, Corinthians, and possibly Romans, although the latter is usually attributed to Corinth.)

From Ephesus Paul went into Macedonia and Greece for approximately three months, during the first part of which he met Titus [20:1-3]. Hearing from him that all was well in Corinth, he went back to his old church for a personal visit (see pp. 201 ff. on the chronology of the Corinthian Epistles). While there he planned further conquests. He wanted to preach in Rome itself and Spain (see Epistle to the Romans 15:28), but he could not effect even his immediate plans. Although he hoped to travel by sea back to Syria [20:3], the Jews were after him again. Hearing that they lay in wait for him either at the port or even in the ship itself, he was forced to delay his departure and eventually sailed from Philippi where he was joined by Luke and a delegation from the Asian church [20:4]. In Troas Paul worked a healing "miracle" made necessary by his preaching. Paul's sermons were too lengthy for some, and a young man fell asleep during one of them. Losing his balance he slipped out of a third-story window and was taken for dead until Paul revived him [20:9].

After a time in Troas, Luke traveled south to Assos by ship while Paul made the journey on foot. From Assos they went to Mitylene on the island of Testos together. From there passing quickly by Chios, Samos and Trogyllium, they came to

Miletus [20:15]. There Paul, with a presentiment of ill to come, left the elders who had probably come from Ephesus. Then he went on with Luke by ship through Coos and Rhodes to Patara [21:1] where they embarked for Tyre.

In Tyre Paul was warned again not to go on to Jerusalem, but undaunted, he continued the journey by way of Ptolemais where he laid over for a day and then continued on to Caesarea where he stayed with Philip for a short time before going on to Jerusalem.

Paul's Last Visit to Jerusalem

Paul's free missionary activity was soon to end. He was to travel again, but as a captive to Rome for trial and martyrdom. Already a controversial figure, he was immediately attacked in Jerusalem. He was mobbed by the Jews and would probably have been beaten to death had it not been for the timely arrival of the Captain of the Guard and a contingent of Roman soldiers. Paul's obvious status saved him; he was given permission to address the crowd while under protection. He spoke in Hebrew instead of Greek. Apparently order was preserved for a time. Then, when rioting broke out anew, the guard took Paul away to be beaten officially, but his citizenship saved him from this indignity and he was held to be brought before the Sanhedrin for a hearing [ch. 22].

During the hearing Paul defied the High Priest Ananias whom he addressed as "whited wall," and saved himself by a clever gambit. Knowing that the Pharisees and Sadducees differed violently on the subject of the resurrection after death, he mentioned his Pharisaical background and brought up the question of immortality. In the dissension that followed within the body, the main issue was forgotten. The group became violent, and the Roman authority was forced to give Paul protective custody. As a result a band of forty or more swore to murder Paul. With the cooperation of the chief priest and elders a plot was laid to that end, but Paul's nephew overheard the intriguers and subsequently reported to him. Paul summoned the Captain of the Guard who took immediate action.

The large force which the Captain deemed necessary to assure safe conduct indicates that the disturbance was extensive. Even the guard was not sufficient in itself, because Paul was taken to Antipastris by night. On the next day he was bound over to the Roman governor, Felix in Caesarea [chs. 23-24].

Felix would not hear the case unless the plaintiffs presented themselves in court. Paul was held for five days until the chief priests came to the city with elders of the Jewish community, including Tertullus who acted as prosecutor. The complaint was the usual one of sedition, revolutionary religious activity, and profanation of the temple, but Paul pleaded his case so well that Felix not only appeared sympathetic, but seems also to have been on the point of conversion. Nevertheless, he did not release Paul, but, to placate the Jews, made no immediate decision. Acts does not make Paul's exact status clear. Probably he was under house arrest with limited freedom. This situation continued for two years, at the end of which time Festus succeeded Felix and the case was reopened.

Once again the Jews brought false accusations against Paul. Festus was anxious to please them [25:9], but dared not contravene the rights of a Roman citizen. Paul appealed for a hearing before Caesar (Augustus) which was his right. At this juncture, Acts reports that Agrippa visited Palestine with his sister, Bernice, who was also sister of Felix's wife, Drusilla. Paul's hearing before Agrippa served as an excuse to create an occasion of much pomp and circumstance [ch. 25]. Once again Paul defended himself so well that he was found guilty of nothing worthy of the death penalty. The procedure on the two occasions of Paul's trial is strongly reminiscent of the procedure by which the Jews accomplished the crucifixion of Jesus. Paul's citizenship threw the balance in his favor.

Paul's Last Journey

Although the trip to Rome which followed Paul's appeal has frequently been listed as a fourth missionary journey, it cannot properly be so named. Paul may indeed have carried out some successful evangelism on the way. To be in his presence was to be subjected to tremendously strong and persuasive Christian witness, but he was a prisoner on the trip, traveling under orders rather than under his own volition. The journey was the last lap of a race which he had run well, but which had as its prize martyrdom and for its trophy, the grave.

The pattern of conflict and trial continued to mark Paul's life. He traveled under guard embarking at Adramyttium to sail up the coast of Asia Minor. The vessel touched at Sidon where Paul was permitted to visit his friends. From Sidon they sailed past Cyprus, because of unfavorable winds, over the sea of Cilicia and Pamphylia to Myra, a city of Lycia. There the officer in charge transferred Paul and his party to a ship sailing from Alexandria bound for Italy carrying a large number of passengers and a cargo of grain. Unfavorable weather continued to plague the expedition. The ships of the day could not sail into a head wind. Progress was slow. The vessel struggled westward along the coast to Cnidus on the southwest corner of Asia where the course was changed southerly toward the island of Crete. Even so, the winds were unfavorable. The ship finally reached a placed called Fair Havens near the city of Lasea on the south coast of Crete, but there the voyage came to a standstill. By then it must have been October, for the season of Yom Kippur had come and gone. From early fall until spring sea travel in the area was so hazardous that shipping trade became impossible for ancient vessels. Paul advised the men in charge that further progress could be made only with great risk. Both master and owner of the ship opposed his advice, and the vessel put out to sea. Perhaps they felt that the sheltered harbour of Phenice (Phoenix) would make a better place to weather the winter storms. At first they found smooth sailing with fair southerly winds. Sailing close to the coast of Crete, they must have thought all was well. No doubt officers and men believed Paul's reluctance to be the natural result of his unwillingness to go to Italy and to face the reception which they thought waited him there. The soft winds proved to be a weather breeder, however, and Paul was soon vindicated. The wind shifted northerly and came up with gale force (tempest). The unwieldy vessel was forced to sail before the wind in a desperate effort to avoid the battering of giant seas. Actually there was no other choice. (A heavy cargo vessel designed in the first century could not have been held into the wind by any helm). Driving before the storm, they sailed into the lee of a small island, Clauda, which lies twenty miles south of the Cape of Matala, the uppermost tip of Crete. In the shelter thus offered the crew took emergency measures to save the vessel. The small boat which was customarily strapped to the stern was taken inboard and lashings were passed under the keel of the ship itself to support the ribs and planking. So great was the wind that the crew feared she might be driven all the way across the Mediterranean to the dreaded sandbar shoals of Africa. The tremendous surf of that region promised only one end. Canvas was reduced to the barest of storm sails and a sea anchor was rigged, but even so the ship was on the verge of foundering. Taking water badly she wallowed on through three days of terror. With neither sun nor stars to be seen, with Africa at an uncertain, but diminishing distance, and with a ship growing ever more water-logged, it is small wonder the crew became desperate. Loose gear and cargo were jettisoned. Luke records that Paul experienced a vision in which he was told that all property would be lost, but that the ship's company would survive, and that he would surely be tried before Caesar. Nevertheless, the storm continued for two weeks before blowing itself out. The hardship on the vessel by that time must have been almost unbearable. Tired beyond human endurance with no respite from wind and wave, cold, hungry, and lost, all hands must have seen a watery grave as proximate and inevitable.

Finally, in the middle of the night, they saw land. Soundings showed a depth of twenty fathoms decreasing rapidly. Four anchors were cast off the stern in a desperate effort to keep the ship from being driven ashore. Some of the crew, seeking to save themselves, put the small boat over the side under the pretext of attending to the moorings and the soldiers acting under Paul's orders cut them loose. Apparently those in command occasionally deferred to Paul, because when he suggested that a meal be eaten in preparation for the certain rigors of the day to come, this was done. The crew then lightened the ship by throwing over what remained of the cargo.

When dawn came, no one recognized the shoreline, but they saw an inlet into which they hoped the ship might be sailed. The venture was unsuccessful. A tide rip and hidden reef succeeded where storm had failed. The ship grounded violently and the stern was torn away by the heavy surf. The soldiers were on the point of executing all prisoners rather than run the risk of their escape, but the officer in charge refused permission. Paul's vision proved an accurate forecast. All hands were able to make their way to shore through the surf either unassisted or by clinging to bits of wreckage [ch. 27].

The island turned out to be Melita (Malta) which lies nearly a hundred miles south of Sicily. Because they were not Greek, the people are referred to by Acts as barbarians, but they seem to have been kind to the survivors. Paul set about making a fire at once and was bitten by a snake which the people took to be an omen of guilt. When he survived the venom, however, as in Lystra, they assumed him to be a god. Acts goes on to assert that, after this incident, Paul worked several miracles which no doubt confirmed the assumption. The party was forced to remain on Melita for three months before a ship which had wintered there sailed to Syracuse on the southeast coast of Sicily. After a short three-day layover, the journey continued to Rome without further difficulty by way of Puteoli and Appiiforum where Paul once again met with old friends.

Paul in Rome

Once in Rome, the prisoners were taken to jail, but Paul was left under house arrest with a specially assigned guard. He was able to preach in the dwelling and even made an appeal to the Jews, some of whom were converted. This ministry continued for two years. Then Paul disappears from history. Although some scholars have tried to show that he left Rome and traveled westward to the limits of Spain, the evidence is unconvincing. He may certainly have intended to do so (Romans), but an historical approach must let the curtain fall as Paul teaches under guard in his Roman home, journey's end for the long trail leading from the Damascus road.

X

The Greek World
of Apostolic Christianity

The Land

Before the Pauline Epistles can be understood, the New Testament student must know something of the world in which the apostles lived. He must study the type of life, the cities, the modes of travel, the people and their religious outlook, as well as their fears and joys, their complaints, their calls to worship, and their marching orders. In fact without insight into Greek culture the Epistles cannot be properly interpreted. Lastly, Pauline language is a hazard. Until recently the student has been burdened with the necessity of interpreting English of centuries past in terms of modern vernacular as well as of evaluating the translations themselves.

Paul walked onto the stage of history through the gateway of Christ's exit. Stephen was stoned on the outskirts of Jerusalem, and it was there that the young Saul stood by and watched. Jerusalem today lies on the edge of Israel in a small section of land encroaching into Jordan. These lands, with Lebanon and the Syrian portion of the United Arab Republic, back the eastern shores of the Mediterranean Sea. Paul turned to the Christian God on the road to Damascus, which is today a Syrian city in the U.A.R.

Antioch, the second great center of the early Christian movement, is now Antakya in the southernmost section of Turkey, a narrow strip of land extending about one-fifth of the way down the eastern coast of the Mediterranean. Westward the island of Cyprus remains unchanged. Asia Minor, now under Turkish rule, forms the northern coast of the Mediterranean, extending from Syria to the Aegean Sea. This is the ancient land where Paul first traveled with the Christian message. It comprises what was then known as the Kingdoms of Antiachus, Pisidia, Lycia, Phrygia, Galatia, and, northwest to Asia, Bithynia and Pontus, the latter of which borders the Black Sea. The ancient city of Ephesus no longer exists; its life was destroyed by silt which filled its harbour.

Thrace, Macedonia and Achaia are today the westernmost portion of Turkey, lying to the west of the Dardanelles, the Sea of Marmara and the Bosporus which joins modern Greece on its western border and Bulgaria on the north. Stretching to the westward Achaia and Macedonia comprised not only all of the modern Greece, but also Albania and the southern section of Yugoslavia. What remains of the ancient world west of Asia Minor is familiar in the form of Sicily and the Italian boot.

Travel and Communication

Travel and communication were extremely difficult. Man moved for the most part by foot in constant danger of assault by bandits or peoples from unfriendly states. Letters were sent by carriers who took weeks or even months to deliver them over what would today be considered short distances. The apostolic world was connected, however, by well-established lines of commercial travel by land and by sea. From Rome to Palestine a constant stream of commerce and the logistics of military liaison charted within close limits the paths followed by Christian expansion. Paul followed the most direct route on his last, captive journey. Without shipwreck and unfavorable wind, his party would have traveled up the eastern Mediterranean coast to Antakya (Antioch), thence westward skirting the coast of Turkey (southern Asia Minor) to the island of Rodhos (Rhodes). Here the usual course turned south to Crete after which followed a long and dangerous sea passage northwest to Italy's toe, through the strait of Messina along the western coast to the Bay of Naples and the port of Pozzooli (Puteoli). In favorable weather the journey took from two to three months and from the middle of November to the middle of March, the trip was impossible. From Naples the last lap could be completed either by land along the Appian Way to Rome or by ship up the coast to Ostia.

A variation of the sea route included land portage in Greece. Instead of heading south at Rodhos, shipping continued up the Turkish coast through the Sea of Crete and the Aegean to Korinthos (Corinth) where small ships were sometimes dragged across the isthmus. The sea journey continued through the Gulf of Patrai northward along the western coast of Greece and Albania until a point opposite the Italian coastal town of Brundisi (Brundisium) was reached. The ships then sailed westward to the eastern coast of Italy where the journey to Rome was finished on land.

Sometimes the first section of the trip from Palestine was made by land route which roughly approximates a major portion of Paul's first missionary journeys in Asia Minor. It was possible to travel westward through Syria and Turkey to the west coast where the ancient city of Ephesus stood and there embark to finish the journey by either one of the customary sea routes. Lastly, the trip could be made almost entirely by land. Instead of embarking at Ephesus, the traveler could make the short trip either across the Bosporus or the Dardanelles, continue on to the west coast of Greece by land, and then cross to Brindisi and Rome.

The Way of Life

Aside from difficulties of communication and travel, the ancient world was not very different from our own. Moderns tend to make two common mistakes in point of view: first, they assume that the ancient world was entirely primitive and secondly, they assume that the early Christians were advocates of twentieth-century Protestant morality. The world of apostolic Christianity was not a Christian world in the present day sense of the word. In Paul's time Christians did not even use the word in connection with themselves extensively. In fact Paul does not use the word at all, and Luke uses it only twice [Acts 11:26, 26:28]. The only other New Testament reference is found in the First Epistle General of Peter, 4:16. The word is probably of Antiochene origin. Coming from a city known for its nicknames, its first connotations were derisive rather than respectful. The word "Christ" to the Jew was a Messianic title which could not be applied to Jesus of Nazareth. To apply the term to him would be to admit his Messiahship. To the unconverted Jew, the followers of Jesus must have remained Nazarenes. *Christian* was a label acceptable only to pagans who had taken a title and turned it first into a proper name and then into an adjective.

The apostolic world in which Paul lived was strikingly similar to our own, comprising much the same way of life beset by the same tensions. The Romans ruled the world, but the Roman peace was kept by the Roman sword. Cold war with great sections of the ancient world was constant, and brush fires in the form of local revolts were frequent. Troop movements were a familiar sight. Roman regulars as well as native troops were used. Customs, furniture, food, superstitions, and the religious practice of foreign peoples traveled to Rome with the soldiers,[1] and Roman law followed their footsteps into distant lands.

Although the world was ruled by Rome, the language of the Empire was for the most part Greek. It was to remain the language of both the gospel and the liturgy for two hundred years. Greek culture continued to be a tremendous influence. Art, literature, and science were born in Greece and,

---

[1] See ancient religions and philosophies, p. 8.

although orphaned through war and conquest, were adopted by Rome.

In spite of difficulties in transport, the world into which the apostles literally walked was a world of great commerce. Commerce wooed wealth, and wealth begot inequality. The peace which Rome forced on the world made trade possible. Cities grew at the ports of call on the trade routes; slaves were a by-product of conquest; and as might be expected, there was considerable disparity in the distribution of wealth. The tremendously rich minority felt no concern for the vast and very poor majority. The mixture of many cultures, economic expansion, increased travel, large and small states, jealousies and rivalries—these things brought civil strife in Roman times as they do today, and the world found itself incapable of dealing adequately with the tensions and divisions which were inherent in the nature of the Roman state.

The upper classes living in extravagant luxury followed the way of a cafe society that sought to outdo itself in entertainment and riotous living. The women used cosmetics, affected extravagant hair styling, and modeled the most lavish attire. Banquets, theatres, and games were a round of activity broken by trips to country resorts. The Mediterranean cruise was not begun by the Cunard Line, nor were British men-of-war the first to patrol the Suez. Roman ladies traveled to Ephesus, and Roman triremes carried troops to trouble spots across the sea.

The Cities

Ephesus was not only a trade terminal for land and sea transport, it was also the seat of the Roman administration for the province of Asia Minor (Turkey). It was a city boasting a theatre that could dwarf many a modern stadium with its seating capacity of twenty-five thousand. The streets were paved and lighted with arcades to provide shade from the sun and protection during inclement weather. A great public library was available to its citizens. A city of rare beauty, it became a Mecca for the traveler. People came from far and wide to attend the festival days and to worship its ancient gods, the chief of whom was Artemis (Diana).

Another city that grew because of its strategic location on a trade route was Corinth. Like Ephesus, it was also a government center, and even more than Ephesus, it was a resort town. Of its many ruins which remain today, one of the most beautiful is the temple of Apollo, splendid testimony to the city's exquisite beauty. Life in Corinth was a cross between Paris and Las Vegas. The town was a play place whose women were famous for their charms and their availability.

Rome was the world's center. There politicians could change the map or assassinate the Emperor with equal ease. Games provided entertainment for the aristocracy and death for the participants. Baths and banquets kept aristocratic Roman bodies soft and fat. Ambitious generals, hard from foreign campaigns, paid suit to ladies whose charms were enhanced by the political favors their husbands could command. Slaves, who were both gentlemen and scholars before conquest, served the households of the rich, acting as tutors, artists, entertainers or servants, as their talent might prescribe. Rome, the capital city, was a place of unrivaled beauty, power, and corruption.

The Emperor

The emperor was god. The first to be given the title of Divus was Julius Caesar. The tradition became established as a matter of policy in the provinces although in Rome proper, emphasis fluctuated with the political tenor of the times. Thus in occupied territories to deny the emperor's divinity was tantamount to sedition. Actually emperor worship was more a form of nationalism than religion. He was never worshipped in the manner associated with contemporary church ritual. Such rites as were carried out in his name did not require congregational participation. Rather, he was the object of public veneration expressed in patriotic activity. As the head of the empire, he represented the glory of Rome. He was the symbol for empire at the festival triumphs. His birthday and the anniversary of his accession to power were celebrated as public holidays and festival occasions. The Fourth of July, Washington's birthday and V-day are perhaps less religious in character, but represent much the same sort of thing. The people of ancient times were polytheists used to many gods, some of whom were little more than names given to superstitions, but it was to these that they turned in times of spiritual need and not to the emperor.

Unlike twentieth century Christian America, the Roman world saw no relationship between religion and moral conduct. The gods of the Greek pantheon frequently indulged in irregular sexual activity, not only among themselves, but with mortals. They were not above malice, deceit, and revenge. Nevertheless, their advice and help were sought. The shrine of Esculapius, the god of medicine, was a place where miraculous healings took place. Oracles gave advice that was understood as authoritative, not without good reason. The oracle at Delphi spoke to the ancients only after deliberation and her forecasts and advice were remakably accurate and germane to the needs of the supplicant. Perhaps the riddles in terms of which the oracle spoke were sufficiently ambiguous to guarantee fulfillment, but the fact remains that oracles were sought and respected. Oracles gave advice to the love-lorn, found lost wallets, picked winners, and even spoke for the shades (the dead).

XI

The Pauline Letters

General Background

A fine line can be drawn between an epistle and a letter. The former is usually a communication written for general reading, whereas the latter is a personal communication. Although Paul's Epistles were undoubtedly read to congregations of Christians and although they deal with general problems, they have the personal touch of letters and can best be described as such. They were written about specific situations in different cities, and each must be read in the light of the particular problem and locale to which it was directed. Furthermore, the mood of the author is a factor to be considered. Paul's temper was often sorely tried by his young churches. He spoke through his letters to his people with pride in their loyalty, with sadness at their weakness, with righteous anger over their failures, with exhortation, with supplication, and with the authority of a saint.

Authorship

Not all the letters are Paul's. Scholarship is in agreement that Romans, First and Second Corinthians, and Galatians are definitely Pauline, while general agreement considers Hebrews and the three Pastorals (First and Second Timothy, and Titus) to be of different authorship. Ephesians, Philippians, Colossians, and Philemon are questionable. In the case of Ephesians some of the earliest manuscripts do not contain the reference, "at Ephesus" (Eph. 1:1). Second Thessalonians is almost certainly a forged copy of the first letter which is itself of questionable authorship. These facts should not be shocking, nor should they detract to any large degree from the letters themselves. The ancients frequently signed the names of well-known persons to their works in order to gain authority and acceptance, particularly for religious literature. The questionable letters have tremendous value and speak with clarity and insight that approximates Paul's authorship. Although the critical aspects of each work will be considered with the letter itself, some of the methods used to determine authenticity might well be mentioned here.

The letters can be appraised quite easily on the basis of style and vocabulary. Paul used, for the most part, certain well-recognized personal mannerisms. Where these suddenly change or do not appear, the wary scholar is likely to question the material. Even where the letters are deliberate imitations, as in the case of the Pastorals, the critical scholar has little difficulty in detecting the differences. Lastly, the content is important. Some of the letters appear to be Pauline in style, but do not speak from a Pauline environment and so do not seem to represent his period.

Chronology

Pauline chronology continues to be one of the most controversial New Testament subjects. It has already been noted that only one or two anchor points in his life (the proconsulship of Gallio, Festus' accession in Palestine) are established without doubt. The exact spot from which each letter was written is also uncertain. Some of the letters place themselves within general areas and periods; others present possible alternatives, either of which fits the known facts. A jigsaw puzzle is difficult enough when the picture is seen on the outside of the box and none of the pieces occur in duplicate, but with Paul's letters the picture must be reconstructed from matching and interchangeable evidence and the final picture remains incomplete in spite of the best efforts of scholarship and theology.

Two types of evidence are available for chronological appraisal: internal evidence coming from the subject matter of the letter itself—specific dates or occurrences—and external evidence, relating letters to a known context or showing marked similarity to other letters whose dates are known. Although some of Paul's letters clearly identify their points of origin, their exact dates remain debatable. The Thessalonian letters were probably written from Corinth (if both are accepted as authentic) not long after the Thessalonian church was founded before the end of Paul's second missionary journey. Galatians was probably written from Antioch. General agreement places Romans in Corinth shortly before Paul's last trip to Jerusalem. The Corinthian letters were certainly from Ephesus. Philippians, Colossians, Ephesians (if authentic), and Philemon probably originated in Ephesus although strong evidence also points to Rome.

The letters are arranged in modern Bibles according to a custom which originated in the fourth century when Christian literature was transferred from papyrus to vellum. The letters were arranged according to length rather than in chronological order. Today either Thessalonians or Galatians is considered the earliest. Thessalonians held primacy for many years. Recently Galatians has been given priority by some scholars.[1] The letter in general has, however, much in common with Romans, and if similar letters come from similar times and places, it belongs near the end not the beginning of Paul's career. On the other hand, some internal evidence points strongly to an early date.

[1] Hebert Newell Bate, *A Guide to the Epistles of St. Paul*, p. 50.

XII

The Galatian Letter

Background

Internal evidence for an early date is strong. What does Paul say? "I marvel that ye are *so soon removed* from him that called you into the grace of Christ unto another Gospel" [1:6]. The phrase *so soon removed* indicates clearly that Paul had not been away from the Galatian community for a long period. On the other hand Chapter 4:13 suggests that he had made more than one personal visit to the churches and hence points toward a much later date. Lastly, in Chapter 2 he specifies the number of years which had elapsed since his first and second visit to Jerusalem, so that the letter must have been written after the second visit.

External evidence complicates the analysis further. The letter does not indicate that Paul was aware of the decrees set forth by the Jerusalem Conference. If this is taken as evidence, Paul's second visit to Jerusalem was not, as many assume, the occasion of the Jerusalem Conference. Not only is the early date of the letter now in question, but also the date of the Jerusalem Conference is no longer certain. Scholars offer various solutions to the dilemma. It may be that some sort of conference did take place on Paul's second visit (mentioned in Galatians) but that it took the form of a caucus among a few leaders to clear up administrative difficulties and was not a full-fledged council on matters of doctrine. The Epistle mentions three specific results of the meeting: it accepts Paul and Barnabas as apostles with status similar to that of the original twelve; it separates Paul's area of activity from Peter's; and it adds a plea to remember the poor [2:1-10]. Advice concerning circumcision is only implicit in the passage. The description of Paul's visit fits what Acts describes as the famine visit [Acts 11:27-30]. Both Bate and Barnett conclude that Paul wrote Galatians prior to the Jerusalem Conference of Acts 15 and accept the earlier date, before 49-50 A.D., for the letter.[1] The value of the letter does not rest, however, on the date. It may have been written from Antioch, Ephesus or Corinth depending on which date is accepted. If the early date is taken, the letter probably originated in Syrian Antioch.

Paul's first visit to Galatia was prolonged by illness. "Ye know that through infirmity of the flesh I preached the gospel unto you at first" [4:13]. Originally he probably did not anticipate staying so long in the area, but as a result of the circumstances he undoubtedly felt a great affection for the people and they also were united closely to him. Although the church was strong in the faith, something went wrong, for Paul's letter shows his surprise and hurt. Apparently, after Paul established the mission, a group of Judaizers descended on the new church quick to cast doubts on Paul's authority and the validity of his message. The problem was essentially the same as that which beset his entire ministry and its resolution produced the formal doctrinal position of the new faith. At the time the Galatian letter was written, however, the matter was far from settled.

Which was to take precedence, the ancient laws of Israel or the new revelation? Paul's message was clear on the point that salvation (justification) came only through Jesus Christ. Justification or a right relationship with God would no longer be created by simple adherence to the law of Moses. In fact, the words of Paul's sermon at Pisidian Antioch, whether

[1] See also Galatians, Prof. John Dow, *The Abingdon Bible Commentary*, Abingdon-Cokesbury Press.

Lucan or not, make clear that the new relationship with God was an addition that made possible something which had heretofore been impossible. "And by him all that believe are justified from all things, from which *ye could not* be justified by the law of Moses."

To the Jewish mind the fact that many accepted Jesus as the Messiah was indeed a bitter pill, but to this strong medicine Paul had added another, disloyalty to the law. Furthermore he preached this gospel in the synagogues with some success. Even orthodoxy was shaken, while the God-fearers who did not feel the traditional loyalties came easily into the Christian fold. Small wonder the synagogue authorities and intensely loyal Jews despised him. They expelled him from the synagogues and pursued him from one community to another. These people visited the Galatian communities, instigating the inevitable conflict. The question of Gentile independence from the law was only one symptom of the illness. Because the Jews saw the disease as a malignancy that could kill Judaism, they felt free to practice radical surgery.

The early church had not yet determined its position. Was Christianity a sect within Judaism demanding adherence to the law, or was it something which could stand in ancient tradition, but on its own authority? Was Judaism the only door through which a man could enter the sanctuary of the Christian faith? If such were the case, Jewish ceremonial and law held good for the Gentile convert as well as for the Jew. He must undergo the rite of circumcision, observe food taboos, eat with no ceremoniously unclean persons, and observe the religious holidays. Such questions as these were in the process of resolution when the Galatian churches were founded. Despite conflict with the conservative Christian group in Jerusalem, Paul was eventually to have his way. The Jerusalem court settled the matter in favor of Gentile independence.

Men who stood for the old faith had done their job well in the Galatian communities. Strong doubts assailed the new converts. The Judaizers had potent logical ammunition to attack Paul's message. (The line followed was not unlike the argument used by Luke to demonstrate the legitimacy of the Christian religion. Even the author of Acts took pains to demonstrate that the new faith was a thing within Judaism.) After all Jesus, by his own admission, came not to destroy the law but to fulfill it. The Christian church must then be a part of the Israelite tradition and not a thing opposed to or outside it. Logically, the first loyalty must be to Moses and the law. If Jesus set the law aside this was reason enough to repudiate his teaching, and show him to be a false prophet. A Christian then must accept the law or deny Jesus.

A second, no less logical, argument might have questioned the right of Christians to edit Jewish religious literature. It seemed inconsistent to accept the major prophets, yet repudiate Moses. The new sect should accept all or none. Lastly, the Jew who did not believe Jesus to be the Messiah must have seen him as a renegade Jew with no authority whatsoever. The adherence of large portions of orthodox congregations to his teachings must have been a terrible shock, and Paul himself must have seemed a gross religious traitor. It was to Galatian churches shaken by doubts such as these that Paul wrote his letter.

Structure and Content

The Galatian letter may be roughly divided into three sections. The first, consisting of Chapters 1 and 2, substantiates Paul's authority and defends his position; the second, Chapter 3:1 through Chapter 5:12, deals with the question of Christ's authority in relationship to Moses' authority; and the remaining portion seeks to inspire the Galatian mission and concludes with a direct appeal to the congregation.

The letter does not open with the usual greeting but is abrupt and direct. Who is it that writes? By what authority? "Paul, an apostle, (not of men, neither by man, but by Jesus Christ, and God, the Father, who raised him from the dead)." He immediately supplies an answer to those who might question his motivation. Only after having made his position plain does he write the salutation. He then states that only one true gospel can exist. By its nature it cannot be duplicated [1:1-9]. Point by point he moves to refute the opposition. He indicates that he is not concerned with the opinion of men, because to be so would show clearly that he is not God's servant. His teaching comes directly and independently from Jesus himself. Furthermore, Paul points out that he is familiar with the Jewish position. "After all I was at one time a Jew who persecuted Christians" [1:10-14]. But once having been converted he carried the new work successfully on his own. He saw Peter and James for only a short consultation and remained unknown to the elders in Judea. After fourteen years he returned and his Gentile gospel was accepted. Although uncircumcised, Titus was also accepted by the Jerusalem elders.[2] Thus, the questions the Galatians were debating had already been settled. Paul was seen by the elders as the missionary to the Gentile world, while Peter remained the great apostle to the Jews.

Paul then tells of his public dispute with Peter. Apparently the decision in Jerusalem concerning fellowship with Gentiles was not easily practiced in Antioch when Jew and Gentile mixed together. The gap between theory and practice was not bridged at once. Peter had at first been willing to eat with Gentiles, but under advice from James withdrew [2:11-12]. Apparently Barnabas did the same thing. Paul shows himself strong and consistent in the face of Peter's weakness and inconsistency [2:14]. Having told the story, he caps his argument by stressing that justification comes from Jesus and not from legalistic practice [2:16]. Paul then moves from his public condemnation of Peter into a confession of faith. The first section of the letter concludes with his reiteration that salvation is achieved through Christ's sacrificial death and with a final statement that salvation comes not through the law, but through Christ.

[2] Some scholarship feels that 2:3-5 indicates that Paul suffered Titus to be circumcised as a compromise measure and that the event is mentioned to indicate Paul's broadmindedness.

The second section of the letter begins with a strong rebuke. Paul asks how is it possible for anyone, having once
accepted Jesus, to reverse things and go back to the law. Once
having received the Spirit, one is foolish to return to affairs of
the flesh. Paul asks if wondrous works are accomplished by
the law or by faith in Jesus [3:1-5]. Going back to Abraham,
a symbol all Jews must accept, he points out that a patriarch's
fame rested primarily on his tremendous faith. Strict legalism
brings a curse upon those who cannot conform in every way
[Deut. 27:26], and no man can find true salvation through
such conformity alone. Faith is the way to salvation. True
blessedness comes through Christ by his sacrifice. The blessing
once for Jews alone now comes also to Gentiles.

The Jewish religion began a long time before Moses,
whereas the law began with Abraham's great faith and the
covenant relationship with God. The law developed later and
was a guide to the righteousness now fulfilled in Christ. The
law then is not final; Christ is [3:15-22]. (The traditional belief that the law came by angelic mediation is seen in Deut.
33:2, Gal. 3:19, Acts 7:53, Heb. 2:2).

In the last part of Chapter 3 Paul uses the analogy of a
schoolmaster (tutor), who not only takes charge of a boy's
education, but also takes general care of him until manhood.
Once of age the boy is free from supervision and inherits the
full privileges to which he is due. In the case of the Christian,
he interprets the faith and promise of Abraham and all old
distinctions vanish in Jesus [3:23-29].

The analogy of the tutor continues in Chapter 4 in terms
of an heir who is no different from any other child, or servant,
until mature. Then he receives his inheritance. So also before
Christ, man had no freedom, but once Christ had come, man
received sonship, his full inheritance and was free from the law
[4:1-7].

Paul then chides the Galatians for their relapse to superstition. Has his work been in vain [4:8-11]? After Paul men-

tions his illness, the appeal which follows reveals a close personal relationship. For a few lines the Epistle softens [4:12-20]. He then moves into another analogous appeal using a scriptural frame that even the most orthodox Jew must accept. The analogy reiterates the sonship theme. What is the real significance of the story of Sarah and Hagar [Gen. 16-17]? Sarah was a free woman, Hagar a bondservant (maid) taken by Abraham because at the time Sarah seemed too old to produce an heir. Hagar gave birth to Ishmael and later to her utter astonishment, Sarah conceived a child, Isaac. The line of inheritance passed to Isaac, the legitimate heir, rather than to the elder Ishmael. Similarly spiritual descent follows the line of freedom, Sarah, Isaac, Christ and the spiritual home, the heavenly Jerusalem, while the other, the line of bondage, Hagar, Ishmael, Sinai (the law), and the earthly Jerusalem is not the Christian's true inheritance [4:21-5:1].

No compromise can be made. If one is concerned with outward manifestations of legalism, the spirit of Christ is not known, and all is lost. Paul asserts that only faith is ultimately effective. In the verses that follow, he seems carried away by emotion. Exulting in his freedom, he can't understand why anyone once free would go back to the law [5:2-6]. Apparently the Galatian group had done well [5:7] until outside influence had interfered. The problem of circumcision was infiltrating the whole chuch [5:9], but whoever was responsible for bringing the problem to Galatia would get the judgment he deserved [5:10]. Verse eleven which follows presents difficulties. Apparently Paul had been accused of advocating circumcision. If he had done so, he asks, why would he have been persecuted? Since he was persecuted, he must not have favored the rite for Gentile converts.

The last section of the letter, returning briefly to Paul's argument concerning the Spirit, asserts that the new liberty implies the practice of love theology. Those who possess the Spirit will live a certain type of life. Freedom doesn't mean moral license. Privilege implies responsibility. The Spirit constrains the flesh. Paul leaves no doubt about his reference.

Affairs of the flesh are enumerated in detail. These pagan vices, sexual offenses, heathen worship, factions, and licentious appetites cannot be tolerated. The fruit of the Spirit is, on the other hand, love, joy, and freedom. He pleads that there be no more factions and jealousies among the Galatians.

In the last chapter Paul makes a personal plea that his new churches live in brotherly love. The word *brethren* connotes the affection he felt for them [6:1-11]. That he was in the habit of using a secretary and probably dictated his letters at night, weary after a long day in the mission field, accounts for the occasional lack of continuity in his letters [5:7-12]. At the end of the Galatian letter he adds a postscript in his own hand, directed at first against the Judaizers who have caused so much trouble and reiterating in the end that Christ is above the law. The letter concludes with an affectionate blessing.

OUTLINE OF THE GALATIAN LETTER

I. Paul's defense against the Judaizers, 1:1-2:21

Ch. 1 A. *Introduction, 1:1-10*

    a) An immediate statement of authority, 1:1
    b) Salutation, 1:2-5
    c) Only one true gospel, 1:6-9
    d) Paul does not preach for the sake of popularity, 1:10

    B. *Paul tells of his days following conversion, 1:11-24*

    a) His gospel is from Jesus Christ, 1:11-12
    b) Paul's conversion and independence, 1:13-17
    c) Paul's first visit to Jerusalem, 1:18-20
    d) Paul indicates his freedom from Jerusalem authority, 1:21-24

    C. *The days after his second visit to Jerusalem, 2:1-21*

Ch. 2   *a*) Paul visits Jerusalem a second time, 2:1-2
    b) Titus is accepted uncircumcised, 2:3-5
    c) Paul accepted as an apostle to the Gentiles as Peter was to the Jews, 2:6-10
    d) Paul tells of his public dispute with Peter, 2:11-15
    e) Paul completes his argument against Peter's position, 2:16-21

II. Jesus Christ ascendent over Moses (the law), 3:1-5:12

Ch. 3 A. *Faith and the Law, 3:1-29*

> *a*) Paul rebukes the Galatian church for its lapse, 3:1-5
> *b*) Abraham was a man of faith, 3:6-9
> *c*) The law brings a curse; faith produces blessing, 3:10-14
> *d*) The law acts as a guide, but is not final, 3:15-22
> *e*) Faith releases all men from subjection to the law, 3:23-29

B. *Spiritual inheritance, 4:1-5:12*

Ch. 4   *a*) An heir is nothing until his majority is reached, 4:1-7
> *b*) Paul reproaches the Galatians, 4:8-11
> *c*) Paul makes a personal appeal mentioning his illness, 4:12-20

Ch. 5   *d*) Paul turns to an analogy in Jewish religious literature, 4:21-5:1
> *e*) Paul strikes at the law again, 5:2-6
> *f*) Paul digresses through emotion, 5:7,8
> *g*) Concerning circumcision, 5:9-12

III. Exhortation to faith and a direct appeal, 5:13-6:18

A. *The implications and fruits of the Spirit, 5:13-26*

> *a*) Paul speaks against bickering, 5:13-15
> *b*) Tension between spirit and flesh, 5:16-18
> *c*) A list of pagan vices, 5:19-21
> *d*) Fruits of the Spirit, 5:22-23
> *e*) Fulfilment in Christ, 5:24-26

Ch. 6   *f*) A final exhortation to right conduct, 6:1-10

B. *Paul's postscript written in his own hand, 6:11-18*

> *a*) Paul castigates the Judaizers, 6:11-17
> *b*) The blessing, 6:18

XIII

The First and Second Thessalonian Letters

THE FIRST THESSALONIAN LETTER

Background

Unless the early date for Galatians is accepted, Paul's letter to the Thessalonians is by far the earliest of his writings and antedates the Gospels. He had crossed into Europe on his second missionary journey, traveled to Philippi and thence by way of Amphipolis and Apollonia to Thessalonica where he remained about three weeks [Acts 17:1-2]. From Thessalonica Paul had moved on to Berea where he left Timothy and Silas while he continued to Athens where they joined him again. Sometime in this period word must have come that all was not well with the Thessalonian mission, for Timothy was dispatched to investigate. Paul went on to Corinth [Acts 18:1-5; I Thess. 3:1-5]. When Timothy joined him in Corinth, he brought specific details of the difficulties in Thessalonica. It is to these that Paul's first letter is addressed. Paul remained in Corinth eighteen months [Acts 18:1, 11] and the letter was probably written in the first part of his visit. The Corinthian visit is accurately fixed by Gallio's preconsulship, which places the Thessalonian letter sometime early in the year 50 A.D.

Thessalonica, named after Alexander the Great's sister, and known in modern times as Salonika, is one of the few cities of the ancient world whose prominence has not dwindled. Situated on the northwest corner of the Aegean Sea, it was the provincial capital of Macedonia and an important trade junction on the Ignatian way. Unlike Philippi or Corinth, Thessalonica was a free city ruled by its own officials without deference to Rome. Already four hundred years old in Paul's time, it is today not only the oldest Christian city in Europe, but also one of the oldest cities in the world. Acts describes Paul's residency there as a brief three weeks, but it seems doubtful that he could have made so many warm friendships and established so strong a church in that length of time. Furthermore, he was gainfully occupied at his trade and evidenced complete familiarity with the area and the people of the outlying districts. Lastly, he received help from Philippi [Phil. 4:16]. All of this data points toward a prolonged visit. Unlike the smaller cities of Macedonia, Thessalonica was a center of Jewry with a large synagogue in which Paul probably began his teaching. Acceptance was, as usual, quick with the Gentile element (God-fearers) who lingered on the fringes of Jewry. Then trouble arose with the Jews, and Paul moved on leaving, however, a well-established Christian group. Then in his absence questions arose concerning his teaching, questions no doubt instigated by the Jews or aroused by outsiders from Philippi. Dissensions arose in the new church.

Apparently Paul was charged with disloyalty to his Gentile converts. Why had he not returned to them? On top of this, the application of the Christian gospel to life was in question. Theory and practice needed to be reconciled. Like ancient cities in general and seaports in particular, Thessalonica was teeming with sexual promiscuity. Unlike the Hebrew, the Greek mind saw no relation between religion and sexual behavior except where a cult might actually incorporate sexual activity in its ritual. The people in Paul's new church felt free to criticize Paul, as well as to judge one another. In the absence of long work hours they became preoccupied with one another's affairs, particularly the sexual mores. Individual freedom challenged authority. Paul's teaching concerning the kingdom of God which he regarded as imminent at the time was foreign to the Greek mind and caused much perplexity and misunderstanding with serious consequences for the peace and welfare of the community. Some people had actually ceased work altogether in view of the fact that the world was about to end. Others looking forward to the benefits of the kingdom were worried about friends and relatives who had died before its arrival. What was to become of them? Had they lost their chance? These are the questions Paul's letter seeks to answer.

Structure and Content

The letter consists of two main sections, the first of which deals with the charges against Paul and gives thanks for the continued steadfastness of the community, and the second of which is concerned with the weaknesses of the people in their understanding and practice of the faith. The first section can be subdivided into the salutation, thanksgivings, and a defense, and the second into instruction against specific weaknesses, a few general admonitions, and the benediction.

After a short salutation in which Paul links himself with Silvanus and Timothy, a surprisingly large section, considering the brevity of the letter, is devoted entirely to thanksgiving. (This seems only tenuously related and provides a transition. Joint authorship was not unusual in ancient times. Occasionally communication passed between several members of a family at once. Silvanus is undoubtedly properly identified with Silas of Acts. Acts 18:5, II Cor. 1:19, I Pet. 5:12). It may be that Paul was anxious to assure the church of his warmth and love for them in spite of the admonition which must follow and of the doubts they now felt toward him. He congratulates the Thessalonian church on being an example to all Macedonia and Achaia. Apparently it was already a recognized center of missionary activity for the area. Furthermore, Paul says that the Holy Spirit was clearly manifest in the work there [1:1-10].

The first part of Chapter 2 (V.1-12) defends the apostles' conduct while in Thessalonia. He reminds the church that he came from Philippi harried and in danger, but in spite of this preached no watered gospel. He made no compromise with the truth for the sake of popularity and acceptance. Furthermore, unlike some evangelists they had asked for no support from the community; instead, to avoid becoming a burden, they had worked night and day in order to care for themselves and to preach the gospel at the same time. Proof that the approach was sound could be seen in the success of the ministry. Paul thanks God that the word had been well-received [2:13-16].

Paul points out to those who may have accused him of desertion that his heart and spirit have always been with his new converts, but Jewish pressure is so great that he cannot return safely. He says that he is prevented from coming although he wishes he could. Verses 15-16 speak with great feeling against the troublemakers. Even so, Paul reminds the the congregation that Timothy was sent to encourage the group and to relieve Paul's anxiety. The letter assures them that they had not been forgotten [3:1-5], and that the news which Timothy brought back concerning the church's loyalty was joyful. Paul gives thanks again and ends the section with prayer for the mission before turning to the weaknesses which have developed in the community through misunderstanding and improper interpretation of the Christian message.

Paul had difficulty in reconciling Hebrew sexual codes with the Greek way of life. In respect to sex the implications of the Christian faith were not understood by his converts. On this matter the letter speaks quite clearly [4:4-5]: the Christian can no longer follow the conduct of his unconverted brother in sexual matters. While on the subject of behavior, Paul speaks briefly concerning the love relationship basic to Christian living [4:9-10], and passes on to a main disorder peculiar to Christian teaching. If the kingdom of God was at hand and a new world order was imminent, many reasoned that the affairs of this world were no longer important. Idle hands are likely to find trouble. Idle people were a source of agitation in the community. Paul's advice is short and to the point: he tells them to mind their own business and get to work [4:11-12].

In the last part of Chapter 4 Paul answers questions concerning the second coming of Christ. There is no need to worry. Those who have died will rise at the time of judgment and receive benefits equal to those who have remained alive.

In the first part of Chapter 5 Paul continues his teaching on the resurrection. Going to the Scripture he uses Christ's own words. No one will know when the kingdom of God will come, but the day of judgment will come as a thief in the night [5:1-2]. Fortunately for the Thessalonians, however, they are not in darkness. No need exists to fear the occurrence. Paul tells his flock the Christian has been saved in Christ, before moving on to matters of church discipline. Apparently the church already recognized certain persons, probably elders of the community following the Jerusalem tradition, as leaders. Paul exhorts the community to acknowledge the leadership of these people [5:12-13]. The reference to "disorderly, fainthearted, and weak" may apply to those groups he has already admonished at length: those who had ceased to work, those who were concerned with the consequences of the second coming, and those who were undisciplined in sexual matters. The whole is an exhortation to Christian understanding of human frailty. Paul does not condone vengeance or judgment under any circumstances [5:15]. After a listing of suitable Christian activities, the letter concludes with an exhortation to prayer and brotherly love, a charge that it be read to all, and a benediction [5:25-28].

OUTLINE OF
THE FIRST THESSALONIAN LETTER

I. Salutation, thanksgiving, defense, and prayer, 1:1-3:13

Ch. 1 A. *Salutation and thanksgiving for the Thessalonian Church,*
1:1-10

   a) Salutation, 1:1
   b) Thanksgiving, 1:2-4
   c) The Holy Spirit active through Paul, 1:5-7
   d) Thessalonica a Christian center, 1:8-10

Ch. 2 B. *Defense and thanksgiving, 2:1-3:13*

   a) Further thanksgiving, 2:1-16
   b) Paul hindered by outside powers, 2:17-20
Ch. 3   *c*) Timothy sent to the Thessalonians, 3:1-5
   d) Paul's joy at good news from Thessalonica, 3:6-8
   e) Thanksgiving and prayer, 3:9-13

II. Instruction directed at weaknesses within the church
and conclusion, 4:1-5:28

Ch. 4 A. *Christian conduct, 4:1-5:11*

   a) Sex morality, 4:1-8
   b) Exhortation to Christian love, 4:9-10
   c) Paul speaks against disorder, 4:11-12
   d) Paul speaks on resurrection and judgment, 4:13-18
Ch. 5   *e*) The time of the second coming, 5:1-11

   B. *Church discipline, conclusion, and benediction, 5:12-28*

   a) Church discipline, 5:12-24
   b) Conclusion, 5:25-27
   c) Benediction, 5:28

THE SECOND THESSALONIAN LETTER

Background

The authenticity of the second letter to the Thessalonians
is open to question. Even a cursory reading reveals it to be in

many sections nearly identical to the first letter (I Thess. 1:2 f = II Thess. 2:13 = 3:11 f = 2:16 f, 4:1 f = 3:1 f, 5:24 = 3:3, 5:23 = 3:16). This in itself is suspicious. Why would Paul copy his own letter? Is he simply adding emphasis to the first? The letter contains no evidence for such a view. Secondly the tone of the second letter is formal whereas the first manifests a feeling of close fellowship. More important is the contradiction in section 2:1–12 which deals with the second coming of Christ. In the first letter [4:11–5:13] the Lord will come as a thief in the night, while in the second the Messianic age will be heralded by definite signs of disintegration in the present era. Why should Paul change his theology within the space of a few weeks?

Various explanations have been offered to reconcile the the differences. Morton Enslin[1] suggests that the letter may come from a later period in which it was becoming apparent that the Messianic age as understood by early Christianity was not nearly as imminent as had been supposed. Thus,the writer assures the Christian community that the age will indeed come, but not right away. Before it does break into history, warnings will be clearly discernible.

Other solutions suggest that both letters are authentic, but written to two different communities, one Gentile and the other Jewish, which would account for the difference in tone, if not entirely for the changed theology. No strong evidence can be found to substantiate this theory.

If the letter is assumed to be authentic, it was probably written shortly after the first, as a follow up to lend emphasis. It may be that Paul received a second report from Thessalonica to the effect that some of the troubles about which he wrote at first had been corrected, while others remained. He doesn't mention the "weak," but does refer to disorderly conduct. Everyone in the community had not gone back to work. Accordingly Paul deals with the Messianic age again, but in dif-

---

[1] Morton Scott Enslin, *Christian Beginnings,* p. 242.

ferent terms. This explanation is not entirely satisfactory, for the first letter is more emphatic in reference to the Messianic age than the second, whereas the reverse should be the case to substantiate the theory.

Structure and Content

As in the first letter, the salutation is followed by thanksgiving, prayer, and encouragement in the face of persecution [1:1-12].[3] The main point of the letter is contained in Chapter 2:1-12. The section deals with the Messianic age and the signs which will portend its arrival. Then the letter returns to further thanksgiving and prayer [2:13-3:5]. The last portion is a strong castigation of those who have continued in idleness [3:6-16]. The final lines are an attempt at authentication and a blessing.

OUTLINE OF

THE SECOND THESSALONIAN LETTER

I. Salutation, thanksgiving, prayer, and encouragement, 1:1-12

Ch. 1   a) Salutation, 1:1-2
         b) Thanksgiving and prayer, 1:3-4
         c) Encouragement and vindication, 1:5-12

II. The Messianic age, thanksgiving, prayer, admonition, and blessing, 2:1-3:18

Ch. 2   a) The second coming, 2:1-12
         b) Thanksgiving and prayer, 2:13-17
Ch. 3   c) Paul prays that the Church may be free from persecution, 3:1-2
         d) Paul prays that the Thessalonians will be inspired, 3:3-5
         e) Paul castigates the disorderly, 3:6-16
         f) Signature and blessing, 3:17-18

³ 1:6-10 possibly an interpolation.

XIV

The Corinthian Correspondence

THE FIRST EPISTLE OF PAUL THE APOSTLE TO THE CORINTHIANS

Background

Unlike Thessalonica which was one of the oldest cities on the European continent, Corinth was a comparatively new town which had been founded by Julius Caesar as a military colony in the year 46 B.C. The old city had been destroyed by the Roman Consul Lucius Mummius Achaicus a century before. Its culture was, however, predominantly Greek. Greek was the spoken language. Licentious excesses encouraged by the worship of Astarte-Aphrodite were rampant. Also well known to the Corinthians were the mystery cults. Corinth was something of a boom town with boom town license.

Paul arrived there from Thessalonica and Athens. Apparently he had hoped to return to Macedonia from Athens and may not have included Corinth in his original itinerary. Opposition prevented his proposed return. In Corinth he fell in with the family of Aquila and Priscilla, who had recently left Rome because of Jewish persecution there. Although Acts tells that he remained in town for eighteen months, he probably did not devote all this period entirely to the Corinthian mission. As in Thessalonica and Galatia he undoubtedly moved about the surrounding country founding many small Christian cells [I Cor. 1:2, II Cor. 1:1]. When eventually trouble arose with the Jewish element, Paul was protected by the long arm of Roman law in the person of Gallio the Proconsul. The Corinthian church was accordingly assured freedom from persecution. Paul might well have expected the new mission to grow strong in such fertile ground, but freedom bred license and its outgrowth was disorder and dissension far worse than in any of his other churches.

From Corinth, Paul traveled on, teaching at Ephesus and then continuing to Jerusalem by way of Caesarea (see p. 164). After the Jerusalem Conference he returned to Ephesus where he remained for two or three years [Acts 18:18-19:1, 19:8-10]. The Corinthian correspondence indicates that during the Ephesian visit he made a quick trip to Corinth which is not recorded in Acts. Later he left Ephesus and traveled by way of Troas to Macedonia and the Thessalonian churches to pay his last visit to the Corinthians.

All indications suggest that the Corinthian letters with the exception of the last were written from Ephesus during the period of his stay there. The last comes from a slightly later time when Paul was traveling through Macedonia on the journey which preceded his last visit to Corinth. The letters themselves substantiate Ephesian origin [I Cor. 16:8, 16:19] and Acts corroborates the evidence [Acts 18:19, 19:26]. Paul arrived in Corinth for the first time in the spring of 50 A.D. and left in the fall of 51 A.D. Allowing two or three months for his Jerusalem trip, we can date his Ephesian visit between the last of 51 A.D. and the spring of 54 A.D. The date of the Corinthian letters, with the exception of the last which falls slightly later, must be within this period.

The church, despite every advantage, did not blossom or come quickly to maturity. Evidently soon after Paul left it became filled with dissension, disloyalty, and disorder. The freedom assured by Gallio's decision bred a lack of discipline which extended into all divisions of church activity. Contact with pagan cults and the heathen life of the city produced temptations the new church was not strong enough to resist. The inspiration of the spirit (gifts of the Spirit) degenerated into manifestations of hysteria and subsequent disorders in worship. Finally, the church developed a strong parochialism coupled with internal party loyalty.

Structure and Content

Apparently the lines of communication between Ephesus and Corinth were good. Paul received not only letters, but also word of mouth reports concerning the bad situation which had developed in his young church. Undoubtedly many letters were written back and forth and what the Bible records as 1st and 2nd Corinthians is only part of the whole. Furthermore, it is quite clear that the letters as presently recorded represent not two, but certainly three and probably four pieces of correspondence with interspersed fragments of others.

1st Corinthians is not the first letter that Paul wrote to this young church. Evidently word had come to him of sexual excesses always shocking to his Jewish mind, and he had written to the Christian group that they should part company with those who were wanton in this respect. "I wrote you an epistle not to company with fornicators" [I Cor. 5:9]. A portion of this letter may be incorporated into II Corinthians [II Cor. 6:14-7:1, I Cor. 6:12-20, 10:1-22]. If verses 6:14-7:1 are removed, II Cor. 6:11-13 is properly followed by 7:2 and the continuity of thought is preserved. Furthermore, the reference in I Cor. 5:10-13 applies very well to the theme of the passage deleted from II Corinthians.

If the deletion is accepted as representing a fragment of Paul's first letter, three letters are immediately identifiable: the first letter referred to in I Corinthians and contained in II Corinthians, I Corinthians and II Corinthians. The material is valuable not only because of subject matter, but also because of the doubt it casts on the integrity of II Corinthians. Neither Epistle can be considered as an integrated whole. The Corinthians probably wrote considerable material between Paul's first letter and his second letter which is I Corinthians and which is a reply to that writing brought to Paul by the hands of Stephanus, Fortunatus, and Achaicus [I Cor. 16:17].

Paul's reply [I Cor.] speaks about the problems which have risen in respect to marriage, platonic relationship between the sexes, eating meat offered to idols, the use and abuse of spiritual gifts, the collection for the poor in Jerusalem, immortality, and possibly also the status of women in the church. After word was brought by the Stephanus group [16:17], further news came from the house of Chloe telling not only of confusion in matters of doctrine, but also of the division of the churches into factions [I Cor. 1:11-12]. Paul answers the questions that have been raised with specific references, "now concerning" [I Cor. 7:1, 8:1, 12:1, 16:1] and says that he will send Timothy [I Cor. 4:17, 16:10] and that he will follow himself when he can [I Cor. 4:19, 16:2, 5-7].

Timothy left with Erastus to go to Corinth by way of Macedonia, but if he actually reached Corinth, he was unable to cope with the situation there, and Paul made a quick trip, probably by sea for an on the spot inspection. The visit was heartbreaking and trouble-filled (not recorded in Acts, but seen in II Cor. 2:1, 12:14, 13:1). On his return to Ephesus he wrote a severe letter which is incorporated into II Corinthians [2:3, 9, 7:8-12]. Many feel that Chapters 10–13 are also part of this letter sent by the hand of Titus. After a period of illness [II Cor. 1:8, 9], Paul set out by the land route to visit the church [II Cor. 1:15, 16, 23]. Sometime, probably in Macedonia, when he received word from Titus that all was now well [7:15–16], Paul wrote the fourth and affectionate letter contained in II Cor. 1–9.

The subject matter of the Corinthian letters as they appear in the Bible can be studied without further breakdown. Fortunately the material is valuable as it stands and the chro-

CORINTHIAN CORRESPONDENCE

Ephesus   Corinth

I. Paul's first letter on fornication

⎯⎯⎯⎯⎯⎯⎯⎯⎯⎯⎯⎯⎯⎯⎯⎯⎯⎯⎯⎯⎯⎯⎯⎯⎯⟶

I Cor. 5:9
II Cor. 6:14-7:1
I Cor. 6:12-20
I Cor. 10:1-22

Letters to Paul raising many questions

⟵⎯⎯⎯⎯⎯⎯⎯⎯⎯⎯⎯⎯⎯⎯⎯⎯⎯⎯⎯⎯⎯⎯⎯⎯⎯
⟵⎯⎯⎯⎯⎯⎯⎯⎯⎯⎯⎯⎯⎯⎯⎯⎯⎯⎯⎯⎯⎯⎯⎯⎯⎯

News from Fortunatus, Stephanus,and Achaicus by word of mouth [I Cor. 16:17]

News from the house of Chloe by word of mouth [I Cor. 1:11-12]

II. Paul's second letter concerning problems

⎯⎯⎯⎯⎯⎯⎯⎯⎯⎯⎯⎯⎯⎯⎯⎯⎯⎯⎯⎯⎯⎯⎯⎯⎯⟶

I Cor.

Timothy and Erastus [Acts 19:22]

⎯⎯⎯⎯⎯⎯⎯⎯⎯⎯⎯⎯⎯⎯⎯⎯⟶

Paul's quick trip to Corinth by sea.

[II Cor. 2:1, 12:14, 13:1]   ⎞
⟵⎯⎯⎯⎯⎯⎯⎯⎯⎯⎯⎯⎯⎯⎯⎯⎯⎯⎯⎯⎯ ⎠

III. Paul's third and severe letter

⎯⎯⎯⎯⎯⎯⎯⎯⎯⎯⎯⎯⎯⎯⎯⎯⎯⎯⎯⎯⎯⎯⎯⎯⎯⟶

[II Cor. 2:3, 9, 7:8-12, cs 10-13]

Titus

⎯⎯⎯⎯⎯⎯⎯⎯⎯⎯⎯⎯⎯⎯⎯⎯⎯⎯⎯⎯⎯⎯⎯⎯⎯⟶

Paul enroute to Corinth by way of Macedonia

⎯⎯⎯⎯⎯⎯⎯⎯⎯⎯⎯⎯⎯⎯⎯⎯⎯⎯⎯⎯⎯⎯⎯⎯⎯⟶

News from Titus

⟵⎯⎯⎯⎯⎯⎯⎯⎯⎯⎯⎯⎯⎯⎯⎯

[II Cor. 7:13-16)

IV. Paul's fourth and affectionate letter

⎯⎯⎯⎯⎯⎯⎯⎯⎯⎯⎯⎯⎯⎯⎯⎯⎯⎯⎯⎯⎯⎯⎯⎯⎯⟶

II Cor. 1-9

nology of the letters only serves to clarify the judgments which Paul makes. The two letters can, therefore, be read as such, and for the sake of simplicity they will be so treated rather than in fragmentary form.

The First Epistle of Paul the Apostle to the Corinthians opens in the customary manner with a salutation and greeting which is immediately followed by thanksgiving for the Corinthian church. The letter then turns to the problem of factions within the Christian group which are the cause of division and bitterness. Apparently the matters were brought to Paul's attention by word of mouth reports from Chloe [1:11]. Some of the Corinthians were boasting about their baptism; there were rival leaders. Paul writes vehemently that Christ isn't divided [1:13]; Christ was crucified for everyone and everyone is the same before him. Even the leaders are only Christ's servants [1:14–17].

Paul reminds the Corinthians that they are no longer to seek salvation through philosophy and intellectualism as in the past, any more than the Jews who expected to find it in signs from God. Such means are no longer proper. Christ is these things and much more: he is the power of God (source of signs) and the wisdom of God (Logos) together [1:18-25]. The language which Paul uses comes out of his Jewish background [v.20] and is reminiscent of Isa. 19:11,12; 33:18; 44:25.

Paul continues shrewdly. After all, he asks, by what power are the leaders in Corinth made important? They were not of any consequence until they became Christ's followers. That is the significant fact. God works through humble people so that the important people cannot glory in him falsely [1:26-31]. The letter is nearly sarcastic. Paul speaks strongly to gain a sober bearing, but for fear he may engender ill feeling and lose his authority, he softens the impact by assigning himself to the ranks and reminding them that he came there with simple words and actually was ill at the time. Nevertheless, he asserts that he spoke only of Christ and did not use worldly methods to promulgate the gospel [2:1-5].

Paul turns to theology in an effort to stabilize the Corinthian church. He says that God's wisdom is above all and existed before the world. Obviously if this very wisdom had been understood before, Christ would not have been crucified [2:6-8]. Paul's teaching is new to man's understanding [2:9], and God's Spirit pierces the depths of man's mind, but as a man's thoughts cannot be seen by others and are known only to him, so God's wisdom can be known only to God [2:11]. The Spirit of God, not the wisdom of this world, is, however, what has illuminated the Christian [2:12-13].

The humanist cannot understand spiritual things because he doesn't have the necessary spiritual insight. The spiritual man can, on the other hand, understand, and those who have been so enlightened serve as the media of God's revelation [2:14-15]. Paul's concluding verse (16) is a quotation from Isa. 40:13.

The Epistle returns in Chapter 3 to the matter of Paul's own humility, mentioned at the beginning of Chapter 2. A man who is spiritual is controlled by the spirit, whereas the carnal man is controlled by carnality. In such a man, the flesh predominates. Paul points out that at the time of his arrival and immediately thereafter Christianity in Corinth belonged to neophytes with only an elementary understanding of the faith. Accordingly he fed them spiritual pap until they were able to digest the full implications of the faith. Even after all they had learned, they remained unable to assimilate an adult diet [3:1-3]. They continued to behave as unregenerate human beings, ordinary men, as evidenced by their boasting of party loyalty, which is clear indication that they have misunderstood the gospel [3:4]. No room exists for jealousy among Christians. No one is important in himself. All are servants of the Master [3:5-9].

The metaphor now shifts from field to building, from cultivation to construction. Christ is the foundation of faith. Not only must the foundation be solid, and undoubted, but also the building must be properly constructed. In language the artisan class can understand, Paul outlines the need to build

well. Otherwise in the time of judgment the poorly constructed faith will not be strong enough [3:10-13]. If the
foundation is right, however, a man can be saved even though
he must suffer great tribulation [3:14-15]. Paul again places
the obligation upon the Corinthians. They have a trust; they
are God's building. He warns that if the trust is not kept, terrible consequences will ensue [3:16-17].

Following the theme which centers around the difference
between worldly and spiritual values, Paul becomes poetic in
an effort to inspire the young church. He says that man's wisdom is foolishness before the greatness of God. The only important things are God and Christ. Everything belongs to
Christ and Christ belongs to God [3:19-23].

Paul asserts that it is not wise to be preoccupied with man-
made standards of judgment. Man is, at best, simply a steward
(a man who holds something in trust for another) whose obligation is to be faithful to God rather than to judge others. As
faithfulness is the chief virtue of a steward, the standard for
judgment rests with God, not man. Paul is not, therefore, concerned with what people may think of him with particular reference to the Corinthians who are as yet not spiritual. Theirs
is, after all, worldly judgment, whereas he stands under God's
judgment [4:1-5].

Paul turns next to the prideful boasting of the Corinthians.
Having spoken to them in metaphor [4:6], he shows that they
have no reason to be puffed up. Why should they think of
themselves as such very important people? They are no different from anyone else. Although everything which they possess is a gift, they act as if they have accomplished something
[4:7]. Paul tries to elicit sympathy, heaping coals of fire on
the Corinthian mission. The lines which follow become lyric
as Paul contrasts Corinthian behavior and his own conduct as
the humble and true disciple [4:8-13].

Paul goes on to assert that, although the Corinthians may
have had many instructors, when all is said and done he is the
one person responsible for their faith [4:14-15] and he, Paul,
is their father in Christ, the only real authority. Paul then says

that he will send Timothy to instruct and remind them of the true teaching [4:16-17]. Lastly, he strikes at those who may have accused him of deserting the church. He can come to Corinth with either chastisement or with love.

The next item concerns the shocking moral disorders within the church. In the first instance Paul speaks not only about general sexual promiscuity, but also about a specific case of incest. Although the reference to a man living with his father's wife is probably to a man living with his stepmother, the interpretation has been debated. In any case Paul is clear concerning the action he feels must be taken. The Corinthians had done nothing about the situation. They showed no deep concern. Paul says that the church must be assembled and the offending party formally excommunicated [5:1-5]. Using the familiar metaphor, Paul shows how this sort of conduct can corrupt the whole church. The church must continue purified and clear.

Verse nine which follows is clear indication that a letter had been written prior to the material above. "I wrote unto you an epistle." Apparently either the content of the former letter had been misunderstood or the Corinthians had found themselves incapable of following its dictates. The warning not to have anything to do with fornicators and men of bad moral character did not mean that all communication and relationship to the heathen world must cease [5:9-10]. Probably the Corinthians had attempted complete isolation and, failing in this, had given up all restraint. Paul says that he cannot and shall not judge those outside the Christian group. That is up to God, but for Christians, the situation is quite different. Paul makes it clear that immoral conduct is not to be tolerated. The wicked (Christian) must be expelled [5:9-13].

Apparently the Christian community continued to use secular courts. Although Paul was shaken by the fact that Christians should find need of litigation in the first place, he felt that, if judgment were necessary, it should come from within the community. Christians stood on a plane above the unjust heathen. Someday Christians would judge the world, the saints and even the angels. Men with this inheritance certainly should not go to the heathen for judgments. The worst of the situation, writes Paul, is the need for such judgments against fellow Christians [6:5]. This in itself shows something to be amiss [6:7]. It would be better to suffer an injustice than to admit such antagonism. Paul asserts furthermore that it is foolish to think that people of bad moral conduct can enter the kingdom of God. He is specific and detailed in giving a list of sexual aberrations and other moral deviations [6:8-10]. He reminds the church that some of them fell into these categories, but that they were cleansed through baptism and are now justified in Jesus [6:1-11].

The section which follows may be a fragment from an earlier correspondence. It deals almost entirely with the relationship between body and spirit, and between the physical and the inner life. With a line of reasoning typical of Greek philosophy and wisdom, the Corinthians had taken two positions: first, that they were above the law, and therefore free, and second, that the body had certain legitimate functions which were outside moral judgment [6:12-13]. Food, they thought, was to be eaten and sex was to be enjoyed. But, says Paul, although these things may appear to be in the same category at first, such is not the case. Our bodies have another inheritance, eternal life. Furthermore, the body is a part of a continuity at the head of which is the Spirit. Lastly, Christians form the body of Christ on earth. Sin against the body is also, therefore, sin against the Spirit. The body is for the service of the Lord. The last verse of the section speaks of Christ's sacrifice for mankind. It is taken from a simile which depicts mankind buying freedom from the law just as a slave might buy his freedom with his savings through the mediation of a priest.

First Corinthians turns next to a group of problems arising from sex, social relationships with pagans and pagan ways of worship. The fact that Paul expected the second coming to be soon, probably within his lifetime and certainly not long after, must be kept in mind. His ethic is an interim ethic. His advice is always in the perspective of a sudden change to a new era which quite naturally makes it different in many respects from that which might have been given for a long term situation.

In the first place it is best to be absolutely continent [7:1]. Paul is concerned with the Jewish understanding of sex and the belief that Adam's sin was transmitted to subsequent generations by the sex act. A realist, he knew that such an order would not and possibly could not be followed. Sexual union is to take place only within the context of marriage. Each party must consider the needs of the other. The wife is not to refuse her body to the husband, nor the husband his body to the wife. Abstinence is justifiable only by mutual consent, for the purpose of self discipline [7:2-6]. Although Paul was apparently celibate [7:7], he did not then feel that the condition was necearily right for everyone. He may have seen complete discipline as a matter of vocation.

Chapter 7:8-11 is strongly colored by Paul's understanding that the end of the old order was in sight. The unmarried will do well to remain single so as not to be encumbered at the time of judgment [7:8], but if sexual desire cannot be contained, it must be satisfied within marriage, and continence is not as desirable as marriage [7:9]. On the subject of divorce Paul follows the line set forth in Mark's Gospel [10:11,12]. Marriage bonds are not to be dissolved. Separation can only be followed by reunion with each other, not by another marriage [7:10-11].

The problems arising from mixed marriages are not unique to our time. Paul speaks clearly on this subject and on his own authority [7:12] with no precedent in the gospel. If either husband or wife remains pagan the bonds shall not be broken by the Christian party. Even as the children of Christian parents are sanctified by their parents' relationship, so the pagan partner in marriage may be consecrated by union with a Christian, but if a separation should take place, it is perhaps best to end the marriage [7:13-16].

On the subject of status, Paul feels that the Corinthian Christians should continue as they were at the time of conversion. They should not hide circumcision, nor should the operation be done over to attempt to remove its effects [7:17-18]. External appearances are not important. Loyalty to Christian morals and ethics is the important thing (note that 7:23 repeats 6:20). God is above earthly affairs and man is beyond these things. Man is united in his common loyalty to Christ [7:19-24].

Paul goes on to state that he speaks on his own authority and not on Christ's. He makes the obvious judgment which his position demands. If a person is single, marriage and its inevitable encumbrance are best avoided in light of what is to come, but marriage is, in itself, not a dishonorable estate. The obligation which it involves may, however, prove detrimental [7:25-35].

The reference "his own virgin" [7:36] may apply to a man and his daughter or ward, but is more likely a reference to spiritual or platonic marriage in which the partners do not indulge in sexual congress. In this case, Paul feels that it is wise to remain aloof, but if one of the partners should yield to sexual union (marriage) with another Paul would not denounce the actions as sinful. Furthermore, he does not feel that continence between parties to the spiritual union should continue in the event that sexual desire becomes uncontrollable [7:37-38]. At the end of the passage Paul reiterates the teaching of the beginning. Death alone dissolves marriage.

The Epistle now returns to the subject of sacrificial food, but Paul prefaces the passage with a strong warning against spiritual conceit. Converted people know that idols mean nothing. Only one God exists. But this fact isn't understood by everyone. Besides, some people can't shake off their old associations. They know about idol meat and feel themselves to be defiled when they eat it. Whether to eat or not is not of vital importance. It makes no difference which portion is taken [8:8]. The important thing is not to let your action be a stumbling block for others who have less acute understanding of the situation. If another should fall as a result of your example, you are responsible for his fall. Under these circumstances it is best to abstain from eating meat that has been sacrificed to idols. Rather than lead his brother astray, Paul would become a vegetarian for life [8:1-13].

Paul now digresses from the discussion of idol meat to which he returns in Chapter 10. The opening of Chapter 9 appears to be a manifestation of conceit, as does a great deal of the Pauline literature which deals with his devotion, steadfastness and call. The language of the time must, however, be remembered as well as the fact that Paul gave his life to the Christian cause. Paul's mission is always his first thought, and references to himself must always be understood in the light of that fact. In many instances they are simply means of establishing his authority; eventually the statements usually turn to humility for the Lord's sake and a desperate effort to humble his readers. "If I, with my background, think nothing of myself, then why do you, with your limited understanding, think so much of yourselves" [9:22].

Chapter 9 opens with a statement of apostleship. Paul says his authority comes from Jesus Christ. Furthermore he has cultivated and cut a path for the Lord and should be responsible for reaping the harvest. Other apostles evidently took their families with them on missionary excursions. Paul has not done so. Both he and Barnabas have supported themselves. (In Chapter 9:14 Paul points out that this is not really necessary, because the Lord hath said that those who preach the gospel should live by it, that is, be supported by it, and there are good precedents in the Old Testament to substantiate this as well.) In Verse 15 he points out further that he has not taken advantage of this custom or right. His reward is in the preaching he does. In the verses that follow, Paul casts back their conceit. He has the authority of Jesus. He has not asked for help, yet he considers himself the servant and slave of all. In what sort of position does this leave the Corinthians? The implication is obvious [9:19]. Paul has done all for the sake of the gospel, adapting himself to all conditions for the faith [9:20-22]. Lastly, Paul insists that this work cannot be accomplished without discipline. Even as the athlete schools his muscles for the race, so has Paul trained his mind and body to win for Christ's sake [9:23–27].

Paul moves again to the Old Testament for a precedent and authority. Self-confidence is a thing to watch carefully. Salvation is not automatic for those who have been converted. They can lapse. He cites as an example what happened to the children of Israel that were led out of captivity by Moses. Some of them fell by the wayside. Verse 4 refers to the rocks from which, by Jewish tradition, Moses drew water [Ex. 7:17, numbers 20:1-13]. Verse 5 says that many suffered death because of their return to idolatry and warns the Corinthians not to let this happen to them [10:1-13].

The passage which follows speaks from a philosophical position foreign to modern times but familiar to the ancients in its acceptance of primitive Greek cosmology. To participate in any activity of worship that involves a god creates some sort of permanent relationship with that god. Although Paul had no belief in pagan gods, he undoubtedly believed in demons and felt them to be associated with pagan places of worship. To be present at idol sacrifices, he felt, might contaminate a person in an unavoidable mechanical or sacramental fashion quite independent of belief. No matter how clear a man's conscience might be on the subject, harm might ensue. Therefore, Paul urges the Corinthians to stay away from idol feasts.

Paul next returns to the matter of meat sacrificed to idols. Such meat was sold in the market place, and when a man went out to dine, he could not always be sure of the origin of the meat served. Although certain acts may be perfectly permissible from a strictly legal point of view, they may create misunderstanding and possible harmful consequences; they may not be expedient. Paul warns his congregation to be careful that they don't offend another person's conscience and to act in the best interest of God's glory lest they be misunderstood. It is not the individual that is finally important, but the consequences for the group. Paul urges the Corinthians to follow Christ's example (10:14–11:1).

The next section deals with various types of disorder which had occurred in church gatherings. The first passage, concerned with the need for women to be veiled in church, is meaningful only when seen in the era from which it comes. His advice comes from the Greek need to comply with Greek custom. In Paul's time an unveiled woman was one whose moral life was open to question. Such people entered into irregular marriages and were not classified as respectable matrons. A woman whose head was shaven was an adulteress [11:2-16]. Verse 2 indicates that Paul had spoken on the subject before and that some of what he had said had been accepted, but further explanation was needed. Paul indicates that a woman is subordinate to her husband in the same way that man is subordinate to Christ, but subordination is not necessarily dishonorable. The head of Christ is God. Clearly then subordination does not imply dishonor. According to Jewish custom it was not acceptable for a man to pray with his head uncovered. In a Christian circle such action dishonored God. Similarly for a woman to do so was a dishonor to her husband. Verses 8-12 refer to the creation myth in Genesis [Chs. 1-2]. Paul then states that women have been given a natural veil, long hair, and ends with a direct assertion of authority [11:16].

The true sacramental aspect of the Lord's Supper seems to have been obscured by the activities within the Corinthian church. Not only were cliques in evidence at the communal meal, but also table manners were atrocious. Some came to the feast drunk; others pushed forward and served themselves from the choice dishes leaving nothing for those who were late. Paul feels that divisions within the church have served only one good purpose; the righteous and approved in doctrine can be easily discerned [v.19], but for the unrighteous only severe condemnation is in order. Paul asks his readers to compare the present activity with the origin of the Feast [11:23-26]. The picture isn't the same. Furthermore, a person can take the sacrament to his damnation as well as his salvation [11:27-29]. Already the consequences of bad behavior can be seen in the poor health of some and the death of others [11:30]. But if the Corinthians had used restraint and appraised themselves, things would be different. God's judgment has, however, the advantage of saving one from the world's doom. Lastly, such trouble can be avoided by waiting until all have arrived and by eating together with decency and order[11:33-34].

Paul's next three chapters should be considered as a single unit. Unfortunately Chapter 13 is often read as a simple treatise on love, but its proper implication can be understood only within the context of Chapters 11 and 14. The primary subject is not love, but a particular type of disorder in assemblies, resulting from hysteria. In early apostolic times Christian gatherings often became so inspired that many members gave way to hysterical manifestations of faith. The most familiar example comes from Pentecost when the disciples and their companions poured into the street from the upper room and were thought to be drunk [Acts 2:1-13, 10:46]. Hysterical babbling certainly conveys a message everyone can understand. It betokens intense excitement and enthusiasm. Modern medicine calls it glossolalia. Sometimes it may be true hysteria; at others it may be affectation. The holiness churches of our time frequently display the phenomenon in their worship services, and recently it has occurred in some of the orthodox denominations.[1] To Paul two issues were at stake, the genuineness of the occurrence and the frequency with which it took place. Paul points out that the phenomenon takes place not only with Christians, but also with pagans, and in that case by idol inspiration rather than by the Holy Spirit. In instances such as these, the experience means nothing whereas when inspiration comes from the Holy Spirit, the phenomenon is genuine. One method of determining the difference is by interpretating the message. If a man curses God, the source is not genuine; if he praises God, he speaks for the Holy Spirit [12:1-3]. The Holy Spirit can inspire people in many different ways. Some become philosophical, others have

---

[1] Some claim the language spoken in our time is Kioné (Greek).

insight into truth, others have great faith, others can heal the sick, others perform mighty works, others prophesy, others can discern good and evil spirits, others speak with tongues (glossolalia), others can interpret the words so spoken, but all receive their ability from the same source, and all represent a unity in diversity [12:4-11].

Paul then moves to a metaphor: the body has many members all of which are dependent but each of which has a particular function; even so is the body of Christ on earth. He enlarges the illustration with a parable which uses the same framework [12:12-27]. The last four verses of the passage act as a summary. Apostleship, the art of prophecy-teaching, possession of unique power, healing, acts of charity, administrative ability, glossolalia, and interpretation, all these things cannot belong to one person. Furthermore, they must occur in combination with something else. They are, in fact, part of something more which is the right motivation for all things and without which these talents are meaningless [12:28-31].

Love is the motivation which alone gives meaning to all these things. (Note the Latin *caritas* is best translated *love*.) Without love the most lyric speech in heaven or on earth is nothing more than the hollow clang of cymbals used in pagan worship (Paul probably refers to the use of cymbals by the Cybelene priesthood) [13:1]. The ability to foretell the future, insight into the human affairs, even the knowledge of godly things coupled with a faith strong enough to move mountains [Mt. 17:20], all are nothing without love [13:2]. Though a man were to sell all that he possessed to feed the poor and even give his body for a burnt sacrifice, the achievement would be nothing without love [13:3].

Next, Paul enumerates love's characteristics. Love is patient and kind. Love is not jealous, is not boastful and conceited, is well behaved, is not selfish, is not irritable, does not keep a reckoning of evil or find pleasure in the evil doings of others, but, on the contrary, finds joy in truth. Love's endurance has no limit. Love is completely trustful. Love's hope does not fade. Love carries on to the end although everything else does, in fact, fail eventually [13:4-8].

The contrast between love and prophecy and knowledge is made clear. Once a prophecy has been fulfilled it is valueless. The need to inspire by "speaking in tongues" will grow less important and eventually will be entirely unnecessary. Once special insight has been proven by truth it is no longer of consequence. When all are enlightened, partial knowledge is no longer significant. Present knowledge and prophecy are always incomplete, but once complete understanding comes, the incomplete exists no longer; in the same way, once a child has reached adulthood, his childish mental processes are superseded [13:9-11]. Lastly, Paul shows that the knowledge of the present time will be superseded by the new order [13:12]. Faith, hope, and love all have a lasting place in life, but the greatest of the three is love.

After his introduction and explanation concerning "tongues" and love in chapters 12 and 13, in chapter 14 Paul makes his point directly. He sets the record straight. Although he has nothing against tongues and apparently spoke in tongues at times himself [14:18], he feels that prophecy is more important. The man who speaks in an unknown tongue edifies himself alone, whereas the prophet can be understood by all [14:1-12].

But, Paul continues, if a person does speak in "tongues," pray that the language may be interpreted. The Spirit speaks through the man, but the mind does not understand what is being said. Pray that both mind and body may understand. Unless a person can be understood, how can the novice be expected to chorus *Amen*? A few well chosen words that can be understood are far better than a long and meaningless oration [14:13-19].

After suggesting that the Corinthians are childish in their emphasis on "tongues," Paul fortifies his argument with a reference to Isaiah [28:11, 12]: tongues are for unbelievers. Pauline logic here is based on his rabbinical background and is obscure.

Tongues are for unbelievers, prophecy for believers [14:20-25].

Paul's attitude is related to the special problems of the Corinthians. Apparently, the meetings in Corinth were next to bedlam. In one corner " speaking in tongues" and interpretation might hold the floor; in another psalms were read. Here doctrine was expounded. There men with insight spoke prophetic words, others sang, others prayed, and perhaps in the midst of all the communal meal of communion might take place. Paul insists that this sort of behavior must stop and that the Corinthians use self control. He says to let two or three speak in succession, no more. Take turns. If a man speaks in tongues be sure somebody is there who can interpret what is being said. Without an interpreter, the inspired person should remain quiet [14:26-33].

Verses 34-35 are generally accepted as a gloss. Paul does not express the sentiment in his earlier section on women where it might be expected [11:5]. The lines also interrupt the continuity and do not appear in some major manuscripts.

At the end of the chapter Paul points once again to Corinthian conceit and asks whether Corinthians originated the word. Paul asserts that anyone with real insight will know that he speaks the truth in his admonitions. He tells the congregation to go ahead and speak in "tongues," but to do so decently and in order [14:34-40].

Chapter 15, perhaps even better known than Chapter 13, concerns the resurrection of the dead. Not only was the old question concerning the time of the resurrection bothersome to the Corinthians, but also a more profound difficulty confronted the Greek mind. The conception of a bodily resurrection was not congenial to Greek thought. Immortality, if it existed at all, was a matter which concerned the soul. The body at best was considered the soul's prison (cf. Pythagoreanism and the Orphic cults). Contempt for the body had already caused trouble in respect to sex morality. Furthermore the Greek failed to comprehend the full implication of Christian doctrine in respect to the resurrection of the dead. Probably many in Paul's new church denied the resurrection of the dead altogether. Obviously a body once decomposed in the grave could not be expected to rise as such. This point of view could not be reconciled with a mechanistic concept of heaven and made belief even in the resurrection of a spiritual body impossible, for only a natural body could ascend to a natural heaven. Paul directs himself to these problems.

First, he summarizes the Christian position. He notes that he has already preached the most important part of the gospel to the Corinthians [15:1-3]. A summary of the events surrounding Christ's death and resurrection follow with ample witness cited as proof of the facts. The summary is close to a statement of creed and bears marked similarity to the official position of Christendom taken centuries later at the great councils. The fact of the resurrection cannot be denied. What about the empty tomb? If it is granted that Christ rose from the dead, resurrection is possible. Unless this fact is accepted the entire basis for the Christian faith is destroyed [15:12-19].

But Christ is risen indeed and this resurrection is part of an age-old evolutionary process by which the failings of man are overcome. Adam represents carnal mankind (see p. 210). All men share in both sin and death through his inheritance. Christ, on the other hand, is the spiritual source of new life [15:20-22]. Apparently Paul felt that the resurrection of mankind, as in the case of the new age, was a progressive affair. First, Christ had risen, then those close to him, then his followers at his second coming. Meanwhile Christ's rule must be in effect until he has vanquished all evil in due succession. The last and worst to be conquered by him is death itself, and when Christ is finally triumphant, God will reign [15:20-28].

Apparently early Christians baptized living persons as proxies for those who had died [15:29]. What would be the point of doing this if the dead didn't rise? The fact that the Corinthians indulged in the practice indicated that they secretly believed in the resurrection. Paul shows life to be pointless without the ultimate meaning which immortality implies. Why run great risks? Why not live the Epicurean life [15:29-34]? (V. 33 is a quote from Thais of Meander.)

Paul then seeks to explain the bodily resurrection by removing the materialistic understanding which was the stumbling block for the Greeks [15:35]. He uses a parable concerning the obvious difference between a seed and the plant it produces. Just as the seed dies to produce the plant, so the present body must perish in the creation of a new one. All seeds do not bear wheat. God gives to each a new body as he may will [15:35-38].

On earth all bodies are not the same; they differ according to the need of their environments [15:39]. Such is also true in other regions of existence [15:40-41]. The analogy is clear. "So also is the resurrection of the dead" [42a]. Life on earth is similar to the seed. Its characteristics are insubstantiality, dishonour, and weakness, but even as the seed is transformed in dying, so is the body changed to a state of subtantiality, glory and power. Two kinds of body exist [15:42b-44]. The first fulfills the needs of the soul in physical existence on this earth; the second fulfills the life of the spirit (soul) which comes through Christ [15:45]. The first body is made for life on this earth; the second comes from heaven and is suited to a heavenly existence. As we have borne the first type of body, let us also bear the second [15:40-49].

Paul evidently feels that flesh and blood ultimately perish, but that a moment will come when all men will be changed whether they have died or not. That which is subject to decay will change to that which is forever substantial. The perishable body cannot inherit eternal life. Only the spiritual body does this, and when the change takes place Christ will be finally victorious [15:50-54] (v.55 is strongly reminiscent of Hosea 13:14). Christ accepts death's challenge and defeats death. Sin makes death terrible and the law gives power to sin by specification [15:56], but death and sin are abolished through the power of Christ. Therefore, Paul insists that his readers stand firm and remain steadfast. If they work with conviction they will not, he says, be frustrated in the end; their labours will not be in vain [15:57-58].

The last chapter treats with the collection to be raised for Jerusalem, mentions the possibility of a visit from Timothy, excuses Apollos,and closes with four exhortations, greetings and a blessing. Paul asks that a portion of each week's earnings be set aside and suggests that the Corinthians choose their own representatives to bring the largess to Jerusalem [16:1-3]. He then tells of his plans to visit the church after traveling once again through Macedonia [16:4-9]. He foretells Timothy's visit and excuses Apollos [16:10-12]. The final section asks the church to be steadfast and strong and to behave like men. Also it asks that they love one another [16:13-20]. The Epistle ends with a greeting, salutation, and blessing [16:21-24].

OUTLINE OF
THE FIRST EPISTLE OF PAUL THE APOSTLE
TO THE CORINTHIANS

I. Salutation, greeting, and thanksgiving, 1:1-9

Ch. 1   a) Salutation and greeting, 1:1-3
b) Thanksgiving, 1:4-9

II. Concerning parochialism, Christian revelation, and internal party loyalty, 1:10-4:21

A. *Factions, the cross, humility, and revelation, 1:10-2:16*

a) Factions within the church, 1:10-17
b) The cross is central, 1:18-25
c) A reminder of their calling, 1:26-31
Ch. 2   d) Paul cites his own humility, 2:1-5
e) Paul speaks to the profundity of God's revelation, 2:6-16

Ch. 3 B. *Sectionalism, judgment, and a preachment, 3:1-23*

a) Paul returns to problems of sectionalism, 3:1-9
b) Paul continues with a new metaphor, 3:10-15
c) Christian obligation and judgment, 3:16-18
d) Paul preaches with emotion, 3:19-23

Ch. 4 c. *Standards and discipline, 4:1-21*

    a) By what standard are men evaluated, 4:1-5
    b) Paul castigates the Corinthians for their pride, 4:6-13
    c) Who brought their faith and by what authority, 4:14-21

III. Disorders from bad moral conduct, 5:1-6:20

Ch. 5 A. *a*) Fornication, incest, and the church's judgment, 5:1-8
    b) Relationships with the heathen world, 5:9-13
Ch. 6 B. *a*) Christians should settle their differences out of court, 6:1-11
    b) Concerning the body's relationship to the spirit, 6:12-20

IV. Paul's reply to the Corinthian church on questions concerning sex, food offered for sacrifice, and social intercourse with pagans, 7:1-11:1

Ch. 7 A. *a*) Marriage obligations, 7:1-7
    b) Marriage, divorce, morality and circumcision, 7:8-24
    c) Marriage and Virginity, 7:25-40
Ch. 8   *d*) Concerning meat offered to idols, 8:1-13

Ch. 9 B. *Paul's example and defense, 9:1-27*

    a) Example and authority, 9:1-3
    b) Paul's example, 9:4-6
    c) Old Testament precedent, 9:7-14
    d) Paul has followed a straight line, 9:15-22
    e) Paul has been a disciplined man for Christ's sake, 9:23-27

    c. *Social intercourse, freedom, and idol feasts, 10:1-11:1*

Ch. 10   *a*) Too much self confidence can be destructive, 10:1-13
    b) Idol feasts and the Eucharist incompatible, 10:14-22
Ch. 11 *c*) Sacrificed meat, 10:23-11:1

V. Disorders in Church, 11:2-14:40

    A. *Women's headdress, and the Lord's Supper, 11:2-34*

    a) Women to be veiled, 11:2-16
    b) Concerning the Lord's Supper, 11:17-34

    B. *Inspiration by the Holy Spirit, 12:1-14:40*

Ch. 12 I. Types of inspiration, 12:1-31
    a) Standards for spiritual inspiration, 12:1-3
    b) Differences, 12:4-11

THE SECOND EPISTLE OF PAUL THE APOSTLE TO THE CORINTHIANS

Background and Content

The background to the Second Epistle has already been considered under the section on the Corinthian letters. Chapters 1-9 probably constitute a single piece of correspondence with the exception of the section 6:14-7:1 which is generally felt to be a fragment of Paul's first letter. The main body of the Epistle is the joyous letter inspired by Paul's receiving news that the church was responding to his previous instructions. The last four chapters (10-13) are probably the "Severe" letter which brought about the conditions for which the first nine chapters give thanks and which was the third major letter written to the Corinthian church.

Structure

The letter opens with the customary salutation and greeting. Timothy replaces Sosthenes of First Corinthians and Paul mentions the Christians in Achaia [1:1-2]. Paul had evidently undergone some frightful ordeal, either illness or persecution, from which he felt that he had been saved by God's hand, [1:8-10] for he includes the account in his thanksgiving [1:3-11].

A rather long section devoted to his defense and justification follows. In the first place, he says his message is inspired by God and is not a matter of worldly wisdom and expediency. His message has already been accepted by the Corinthians which in itself is noteworthy and a precedent for authority [1:12-14]. Verses 15-16 mention a visit to the church which evidently did not materialize. His "Severe" letter was probably a substitute for the proposed expedition. Although the reason for abandoning the plan is obscure, Paul says that the proposal was not simply worldly doubletalk. He insists that he is not one who says yes and no at the same time; this isn't his way of dealing. He calls God as witness to that [1:17-18]. Christian teaching doesn't follow such lines. God's promises are all affirmed in Christ [1:19-22].

Paul says that his proposed visit was cancelled because he feared the pain it might cause. For him to come again in controversy might well destroy his effectiveness as an apostle. The purpose of his previous writing was not to cause pain, but to demonstrate his deep concern for their welfare [1:23-2:4].

Apparently some person in the community had caused trouble in connection with Paul and had been punished by the

church, for Paul pleads that the man be forgiven and rein-
stated. If they will forgive him, Paul will accept the judgment.
Paul forgives him in Christ. The subtlety of the devil must not
be given an opportunity to make gain [2:5-11].

The next two verses return to the narrative which was
broken at 1:10a, but give way immediately to a passage devoted to praise. It seems that Paul had hoped to meet Titus in
Troas, but, failing in this, had moved on anxiously to Macedonia where he received good news about the Corinthian church.
His words of praise thank God, who always gives victory to
Christians and whose sweet incense of understanding permeates
the world through apostleship [2:14]. That the scent of salvation is with all Christians can be discerned by all, whether they
are to be saved or are headed toward doom. To the former,
salvation is the fragrance of life; to the latter, the scent of
death. Paul asks who is big enough for the task [2:15-16]. He
says that we are not like those who corrupt God's word; we
speak under God's authority as Christ's ministers [2:17].

The old questions of Judaism and ancient authority in
respect to Christians seem to have been a problem for the
Corinthians as well. Paul asks whether testimonial letters are
necessary to establish authority [3:1]. The Corinthian church
by the fact of its existence is a testimonial for all to see [3:2].
This is a letter not written with ink, but by the Spirit of God,
not engraved on tablets of stone, but in people [3:3]. Paul
includes himself and his congregation in saying that our confidence is in God through Christ, not in ourselves. We are
ministers of the new contract, not concerned with the letter
of the law, but with the Spirit [3:4-6]. Paul shows that adherence to the letter of the law leads to death of the soul,
whereas the contract with the Spirit produces life. The old
law which is death was so glorious that the Israelites couldn't
look directly at Moses' face after he received it. If the old was
so glorious, how much more the new? If the old which brought
condemnation and death was glorious, how much more so that
which brings life and salvation [3:7-11]?

Paul then enlarges on the characteristics of the Spirit. The

Spirit's inspiration gives hopes to the apostles. Moses veiled his face so the people wouldn't see his glory fading away, but their minds were blinded because even today they do not, says Paul, understand. Yet if a man turns to the Lord, the veil is removed and liberty from the law ensues. Paul says that we who are Christian are not veiled. We are transfigured by the glory of the Lord [3:12-18].

This then is the new ministry which God in his mercy has given, and Paul is resolved to press on with vigor in this cause [4:1]. He next makes a short summary of questionable practices. Paul defends his actions. He says he never used subterfuge. If his words are not understood, it is the result of spiritual blindness [4:2-4]. Paul says he does not preach his own ideas, but only the Christian message. God, who first made light [Gen.], has illuminated the apostles' hearts so that they can give the knowledge of God's glory to man as it is revealed in Jesus Christ [4:5-6].

Paul points to the contrast between the glorious message and the means chosen for its promulgation, a great treasure contained in earthenware jars. The power of the Spirit is a sustaining force in the midst of despair and perplexity. The apostle is, therefore, never alone in persecution and, although he may be thrown down, he is never finally vanquished [4:7-9]. Everyday they (Paul and his companions) share some of Christ's death, but as a result, the power of his life is in their bodies. In constantly facing death, they are able to make Christ manifest to the Corinthians in their lives [4:10-12]. Paul says his faith is Scriptural. He speaks from the certain belief that the power which raised Jesus from the dead shall also through him (Jesus) raise the Christians. All these things are done for the sake of the Corinthian church to reflect the glory of God [4:13-15].

Paul writes that the power of grace is a sustaining force in his life. Although the outward man suffers wear and may collapse, the inward is constantly sustained. The small troubles work toward a permanent and great reward. Paul says his life is measured by invisible things which are eternal rather than visible, and temporal affairs [4:16-18].

Having introduced the question of relationship between eternal and temporal affairs, Paul moves on to questions pertaining to the soul. The passage which follows represents a later attitude than that in I Cor. 15, which deals with the same subject. Paul no longer feels that judgment and general resurrection will take place within his life span on earth. He now considers what happens to the soul in the interim between death and judgment. We know that if our earthly body is taken away, God will give us a permanent heavenly body [5:1]. Paul mixes the metaphors of housing and clothing. We are not happy in our present clothing, because we long for the permanent dress of immortality which will not leave us naked when the old is destroyed. As long as we are clothed with mortality, we shall have a painful longing for our immortal house. This is God's plan promised by the Spirit [5:2-5]. Being at home in the body means, therefore, that we are away from the Lord, while being close to him is more desirable. Nevertheless we try to please him either way, for we shall sometime appear before him to be judged according to our actions, whether good or bad [5:6-10].

In the light of these circumstances of life, Paul tries to show the purpose and method of his ministry. Judgment is a fearful thing to contemplate. Accordingly, Paul says his methods are certainly honorable to men and clear to God. Although further recommendation isn't needed, if the Corinthians want to answer those who are concerned with outward things, Paul and his companions can give them reason for pride [5:11-12]. Paul goes on to show that his ecstatic (hysterical) manifestations of faith were for the glory of God, while his dealings with the Church were always strictly down to earth. He asserts that his motivation has not been selfish, but comes from love of Christ. Christ died for everyone and everyone must now live in Christ. Therefore pride or privilege can no longer be a concern of the ministry. Even though we knew Christ in the flesh once, we don't know him in that way now. Once a man becomes a part of the Christian fellowship, he is brought into a new world [5:13-17]. Paul says that all these new relationships are the work of God. He then outlines God's methods and the purpose of the ministry. God has reconciled himself to the apostles through Christ and has commanded them likewise to reconcile others to him. The apostles, Paul says, are ambassadors in Christ. Paul closes with a plea that the church be reconciled to God, because God gave Christ to sin to redeem the world [5:18-20].

The section which follows is an appeal and a statement of the contradictions the Christian ministry creates. The opening line asks that the grace of God not be wasted, for the time which was predicted is at hand [Isa. 49:8]. Paul wants to make certain that no obstacles are placed in the way of his converts. Under no circumstances should his ministry be discredited or blamed for Corinthian failure to accept God. Paul then summarizes the characteristics associated with a genuine ambassador of Christ. Being patient, enduring hardship and disasters, being beaten, imprisoned, or mobbed, working hard, standing watch without food and sleep, all these requirements combine with sincerity, insight, patience, kindness, the power of the Holy Spirit, and genuine love and honesty. The apostle exemplifies the power of God and righteousness in every quarter. In every situation Paul shows that the Christian minister must hew to the line. Righteousness and integrity are his weapons everywhere whether they be against honour or dishonour, praise or blame.

Paul's next lines have been variously interpreted. They attempt to explain the paradox of Christian service. Men may call the apostles impostors although they speak the truth. The missionary must be humble, yet he will be well known to the public. He dies daily by earthly standards, yet in doing so he finds true life. He suffers, but his spirit is never completely killed. His work is sorrowful and painful, yet it is the source of the greatest happiness. Although he is poor in this world's goods, he is able to make others rich in the Spirit. A minister of Christ has nothing in this world, yet he possesses things which are of unbounded value because he is not of this world [6:1-10].

The lines which follow are filled with warmth and affection. Paul writes with utter frankness, opening his heart to the Corinthian church. If any contention exists, it is on their part, not his. He asks no reward other than that they treat him with the same frankness [6:11-13].

The letter now digresses in a warning to avoid pagan contacts. The continuity breaks so obviously that many critics believe the section to be a fragment from another writing. Paul speaks against mixed marriages and makes a strong comparison between Christ and the devil, and between idol worship and the opposite Hebrew tradition. Paul asks that the church remember the promises God has given and pleads that the community keep itself clean in flesh and spirit by giving itself completely to God [6:14-7:1].

After the digression the letter returns to his affectionate theme, again asking for acceptance and reiterating that his conscience is clear. Paul also writes of his pride in the Corinthian church. The letter then mentions his deep emotion on receiving news from Titus and, in doing so, picks up the narrative which he left at 2:13. When in Macedonia he traveled in deep unhappiness. The church was troubled by Jewish pressure without and by disloyalty from within. He had sent a severe letter to the Corinthians. What was their reaction? Now God had given him comfort by means of Titus' news that the church was loyal. Although his harsh letter was still a painful memory, it was a source of joy because of the results it achieved [7:2-9]. It was not written to punish, but to clarify their thinking; it had apparently accomplished its purpose. Paul rejoices in the change that has come over the church. Even the relationships between the Corinthians and Titus is much happier. Paul feels that his confidence in the church is completely vindicated [7:10-16].

Apparently the Macedonian churches, although very poor themselves, had been moved to give generously to the collec-

tion being raised for the needy in Jerusalem [8:1-5]. Paul
asked Titus to finish the work which he had begun among the
Corinthians, by arranging an offering there [8:6]. As the
church abounds in faith and other manifestations of the Spirit,
it should also abound in generosity. This is not, writes Paul, an
order, but a suggestion prompted by the Macedonian example.
It is a good way to prove the church's love. In Verse 9 Paul
turns to Christ as an example: Christ possessed everything yet
became poor that others might be made rich. The letter then
returns to the main point under discussion. Paul's advice follows. As the first to do so, the church began a collection a
year ago; he asks them to follow through with the offering
[8:10-15].

Continuing with plans for the collection, Paul commends
Titus and two others for the task. He clarifies the purpose for
sending them. He insists that there be no grounds for scandal
in the administration of the collection [8:16-22]. The last part
of the passage commends Titus and the other messengers and
challenges the church to demonstrate its love and vindicate
Paul's boast of its loyalty [8:23-24].

Paul then tactfully explains the need for sending Titus
and the others. He knows that it isn't really necessary to remind the Corinthians, but in light of the fact that he boasted
about them as much as a year ago, he wants to make sure they
will be ready when the time comes to deliver. It would
look bad if the Macedonians were to find them unprepared
[9:1-5].

Paul concludes with an exhortation to give generously:
"He who sows sparingly will reap sparingly" (V.6). The
words which follow are reminiscent of Prov. [22:8-9]: "He
that soweth iniquity shall reap vanity: and the rod of his anger
shall fail, He that hath a bountiful eye shall be blessed; for he
giveth of his bread to the poor." Paul goes on to demonstrate
that God will supply all needs and enough surplus to make
generosity possible. He tells them that they will be like the man
the Psalmist extolled [Ps. 112:9]: "He hath given to the poor;
his righteousness endureth forever." The God who makes the

the seed grow will also make their gifts fruitful [9:10]. They will be enriched in giving. Thus, Paul urges that they be generous and their generosity will evoke thanksgiving to God. The collection will not only supply the needs of the people in Jerusalem, but will also inspire much thanksgiving from them [9:11-12]. This giving will demonstrate devotion to Christ, and men will thank God for the givers' loyalty. Furthermore men will pray for them and will be brought close to them because of the grace of God in them [9:13-14]. The passage closes with thanks to God for such a great gift [9:15].

The last four chapters of the Epistle are generally considered to be a portion of the "Severe" letter. The tone changes abruptly as Paul defends himself and castigates the Corinthians for their attitudes and actions. He opens with an appeal to the church for the forbearance and gentleness of Christ and asks that he not be put to the need of being outspoken and harsh in their presence. He doesn't want to deal with those who insist that the tenets of his work are worldly. After all, the battle is on a spiritual plane even if life is lived on a worldly level [10:1-3]. His weapons are all powerful spiritual tools that cannot be resisted by the defenses of men. Once the church is generally obedient, the disobedient will be disciplined [10:4-6].

Paul seems to think that he has been charged with being a mighty man with the pen, but unattractive in person and poor as a speaker [10:10]. Paul writes directly to the point. He says he is a Christian of equal status with other Christians [10:7]. His authority was given to build a church, not destroy one [10:8]. Paul challenges those who doubt his ability. What he has written in letters, he can support in person [10:7-11].

Paul's authority, as well as his jurisdiction in reference to others who set themselves up as leaders in the Christian movement, seems to have been questioned. He separates himself from those whose standards are worldly and selfish. Paul keeps within legitimate claims the lines drawn by God [10:12-13]. It is legitimate for him to work among the Corinthians, for it was he who first came there to preach the gospel. He doesn't boast of work done by others or work outside his jurisdiction, but hopes that the growing fate will make expanded activity possible [10:14-16]. But he reminds them of Jeremiah [9:24]: "Let him who glory, glory in the Lord." Self-commendation is not important, whereas God's commendation is [10:17-18].

Paul moves next to the authority of ministers. From the beginning the church was plagued by "false prophets." As Christianity spread, many made a good thing for themselves by preaching the gospel, but the message was not always the true faith. Paul exposes false preachers, who had apparently influenced the Corinthian church, for what they are. He asks that the Corinthians bear with him in his enthusiasm which is a godly thing. He uses Old Testament imagery describing the relationship between God and Israel (God and the Church) as conjugal [11:1-2]. He fears that they may be seduced by apostolic charlatans in the same way that Eve was corrupted by the serpent. Evidently the young church was quick to accept preaching that was not true to the party line—such as a different picture of Jesus or a different gospel message. Paul shows how different his approach has been. He doesn't consider himself inferior to these glib salesmen. Although his preaching may not be as good, his insight is true. His humility has been a mistake. While he has cost the Corinthians nothing, he has maintained himself on what he received from the other churches [11:5-10]. Such behavior should indicate that he loves the Corinthians greatly. He writes that he intends to continue this policy in order to expose the false apostles, whom he castigates strongly as fakes, like Satan, pretending to be objects of light. Satan's ministers may appear to be righteous for the time being, but they will receive their just deserts in the end [11:11-15].

In the following verses Paul turns to his own witness. He tells the Corinthians not to think him a fool, but to listen to what he can boast about, even though such speaking is not godly, but foolish. The letter becomes intensely bitter and sarcastic. Paul accuses the church of haughtiness in its presumption to wisdom; he says ironically that it can well tolerate his foolish remarks. His irony becomes knife-edged when he says that their tolerance certainly is great. "Why they actually don't object to tyrannical actions, to being fleeced, even to being slapped in the face." Making clear that this is fool's language, he lists the attributes that have at once been both the source of tribulation and talent: he is a Jew, an Israelite, a descendant of Abraham, and a minister of Christ, who has worked hard, been in prison often, been beaten innumerable times, faced death frequently, been beaten the regulation thirty-nine stripes by the Jews five times, been beaten with rods, been shipwrecked, and so on. The passage ends with Verse 31, a testimonial to the truth of his words. The next two verses describing his escape from Damascus appear to be a postscript.

Having told of his trials, Paul then tells of his spiritual inspiration and of his sickness. He also tells of a vision which the Lord gave him to make him humble. In the end he asserts that he finds strength through enduring his weakness and trials [12:1-10].

The letter then turns back to the matter of apostolic support. Paul says that true apostles don't try to make a good thing for themselves out of the ministry. Paul apologizes for his boasting, but says that it is forced upon him by the actions of the church, for he isn't inferior to the other ministers. He asks whether the Corinthians think they are inferior to the other churches because he has not been a burden to them; then he adds that he will not burden them on his third visit either. He wants the Corinthians for Christ, not for their money [12:11-14]. Lastly, Paul reminds them that when Titus came, he acted as Paul has acted [12:18].

The chapter closes with a statement of his hopes for the Corinthian church, but makes it plain that he really doesn't need to apologize. In the end the Corinthians will be held accountable. God is the ultimate judge [12:19]. He suggests that, if things don't change in Corinth, his next visit may not be pleasant. Paul next lists Christian vices which he hoped might not be in evidence when he arrived [12:20-21].

In the next section he continues the same theme. He predicts his visit again and quotes from the book of Deut. [19:15b]: "At the mouth of two witnesses, or at the mouth of three witnesses shall the matter be established." He has already told them once and he repeats that when he comes again, he won't be lenient with offenders; his firmness is a proof that he speaks with the authority of Christ, who is a tremendous inward resource [13:1-4]. He asks that the Corinthians examine themselves to make sure whose side they are on and whether they have real faith or are reprobates. Apostles work, writes Paul, for truth no matter what the consequences. If their weakness proves the Corinthians strong, they are glad to be weak. Paul ends by stating that these things were written then so that when he came in person he would not need to use his authority in Christ [13:5-10]. The letter concludes with admonitions concerning Christian behavior and a blessing [13:11-14].

OUTLINE OF

THE SECOND EPISTLE OF

PAUL THE APOSTLE

TO THE CORINTHIANS

I. Salutation, greeting, and thanksgiving, 1:1-11

Ch. 1   *a*) Salutation and greeting, 1:1-2
         b) Thanksgiving, 1:3-11

II. Paul and the Corinthian church, 1:12-7:16

A. *Defense against unworthiness and lack of feeling, 1:12-2:17*

         a) Paul's message inspired by God, 1:12-14
         b) A proposed visit, 1:15-16
         c) God as good as his word, 1:17-22
Ch. 2   *d*) An explanation, 1:23-2:4
         e) Disciplinary problems with the church, 2:5-11
         f. The Macedonian trip, 2:12-13
         g) Praise and exaltation, 2:14-17

B. *Apostleship, 3:1-6:10*

Ch. 3   *a*) The new ministry, 3:1-11
      b) Concerning the Spirit, 3:12-18
Ch. 4   *c*) Paul's gospel is clear, 4:1-6
      d) The incongruities within apostleship, 4:7-15
      e) Temporal and eternal values, 4:16-18
Ch. 5   *f*) Body and soul, 5:1-10
      g) The purpose of the ministry, 5:11-20
Ch. 6   *h*) Characteristics of the ministry, 6:1-10

    C. *Paul and the Corinthian church, 6:11-7:16*

      a) An affectionate appeal, 6:11-13
Ch. 7   *b*) Avoid pagan contacts, 6:14-7:1
      c) Affectionate appeal continued, 7:2-4
      d) Reaction on news from Titus, 7:5-16

III. Collection for the church in Jerusalem, 8:1-9:15

Ch. 8   *a*) The collection in Macedonia an example, 8:1-15
      b) Titus and two other treasurers commended, 8:16-24
Ch. 9   *c*) Why sent, 9:1-5
      d) The basis for the appeal, 9:6-15

IV. Paul's defense and castigation of the Corinthian church, 10:1-13:10

Ch. 10   *a*) The accusation of cowardice answered, 10:1-6
      b) The accusation of weakness answered, 10:7-11
      c) Authority and jurisdiction, 10:12-18
Ch. 11   *d*) Spurious apostles, 11:1-15
      e) Paul's credentials, 11:16-33
Ch. 12   *f*) A vision and Paul's infirmity, 12:1-10
      g) The test of apostleship, 12:11-19
      h) Paul's fears concerning the Corinthians, 12:20-21
Ch. 13   *i*) Warning and admonition, 13:1-10

V. Admonition and benediction, 13:11-14

      a) Admonition, 13:11-13
      b) Benediction, 13:14

XV

The Roman Letter

Background

After his return to Corinth for the last time, Paul was ready to turn his face westward. He had already brought the word of God to the lands surrounding the Mediterranean which lay east of the Italian boot. The Church was well established in Galatia, Macedonia, and Achaia. The time had come to move on. Only one piece of business remained unfinished. The collection which had been raised for Jerusalem relief waited to be delivered [15:25-28]. Paul lingered in Corinth for three months and decided to make the trip to Jerusalem with the collection before moving on to new fields [Acts 20:2-3]. By then he was an old hand at missionary activity. The days were growing shorter and his remaining years were numbered. Still, with inexhaustible zeal, he contemplated the entire world for Christ. Besides evangelism in lands that had not yet heard the word, he felt that he had something spiritually unique to offer the Roman church [1:13]. As Antioch had given way to Ephesus as an advanced base for his sallies against paganism, so now Ephesus was to give way to Rome, and Rome was to be a staging area for an expedition to Spain and the ends of the known world. The letter to the Romans may have been written to prepare the way for establishing a new base of operations and to instruct the existing church concerning the faith.

It seems certain that Paul's visit to Corinth took place after II Cor. 1-9 was written, because the collection wasn't ready at that time (p. 203). The visit was sometime around the early part of 55 A.D. which places the Roman letter in that year.[1]

Authorship

No doubt exists concerning the letter's main body, and even the small sections which present critical problems are so typically Pauline that they are generally accepted as authentic. Unlike the Corinthian letters, the vocabulary, style, and religious slant are all Pauline. Questions concerning the letter center around the authenticity of Chapters 15 and 16 as part of the original letter and the direction of the letter to the Romans.

Clear evidence exists that some early recensions omitted Chs. 15 and 16 and that no mention was made of Rome as it now appears in 1:7 and 1:15. Some writings substitute "in love" for "in Rome" [1:7] and omit the word with no substitution in 1:15. The subject matter in Ch. 16 includes several statements difficult to reconcile with the situation known to exist in Rome at the time it was written and clearly unsuitable were the letter directed there.

First, the chapter includes a long list of greetings to Paul's friends. The question immediately comes to mind whether Paul would have had many close friends in a city he had never visited. The list of salutations is reminiscent of Paul's letters to churches where he had labored hard and tarried long. Furthermore, Epaenetus is specifically identified with Achaia, while Priscilla and Aquila at this period were in Ephesus. It may, of course, be possible for them to have removed to Rome from which they came originally, but Paul makes no mention of such change.

Secondly, the section 16:17-20 refers to teachings which can be assumed to be Pauline. Otherwise how could he speak with such authority concerning them or even know what they

---

[1] By Phillips, 57 A.D., Barnett 56 A.D.

were? The arguments within the letter are typical of the approach Paul uses to churches he founded rather than what might be expected for a group of people for the most part unknown to him. If the letter in the last part were used to introduce Phoebe [16:1] to the Ephesian church, the picture would be immediately clarified. Not only do the greetings fall into place, but the tone makes more sense.

Several theories have been advanced to reconcile the difficulties. None changes the value of the letter as far as the subject matter is concerned. Enslin suggests that Chs. 1-14 comprise a general letter intended for all the churches in Asia Minor.[2] In the draft sent to Ephesus Paul might have appended Phoebe's introduction and the special salutation to his friends there. In view of the fact that he contemplated a visit to Rome, he may also have directed his scribe, Tertius, [16:22] to draft another copy with specific directions to the Roman church, with some special comments regarding Christian responsibility and with a statement concerning the purpose of his proposed visit [Ch. 15].

Structure and Content

The letter does not contain so much of the personal touch as those already reviewed. Both Galatians and Corinthians deal with specific questions to be found among newly formed Christian groups. The latter is also highly emotional. On the other hand, Romans, while remaining a letter in form, is far more carefully organized and is generally subdued. Although directed to both Jews and Gentiles, it is probably more a Gentile letter in tone. The opening follows the familiar pattern of salutation, credential, and thanksgiving [1:1-15]. The main body consists of two sections, the first of which is an apologia and exposition of the Christian doctrine of salvation [1:16-11:36], and the second of which seeks to relate the doctrine to life [12:1-15:33]. The first section can be subdivided into two parts. Paul clarifies his argument that the gos-

[2] Enslin, p. 268.

pel is the fulfillment of a divine plan [Chs. 1-8]; next he seeks
to explain the situation in which the Jews presently find themselves [Chs. 9-11]. Chapter 16 has the characteristics of a postscript.

Vs.16-17 of Chapter 1 are a precise title and summary of
the material which is to follow. Paul writes that the ospel is
God's saving power received by faith. Although God has
made his will quite clear to man from the beginning of the
world, man has refused to acknowledge his sovereignty. In
his profession of wisdom, man was a fool who exchanged the
image of the uncorruptible God for the false image of mortal
man and even other worldly creatures down to creeping things
[1:18-23].

Having deliberately given up God's truth, man was
handed over to disgraceful passions [1:24-25]. A list of terrible judgments, the result of this situation, follows: women
lost normal sexual desire and sought satisfaction in perversion;
men likewise became sexually perverted [1:26-27]. As men
would not acknowledge God, He let them be filled with unrighteousness. Worse than the unmentionable things to which
man degenerated was the fact that he not only was a part of
low activity, but also approved these things in others, even
knowing that such actions left the perpetrator worthy of death
[1:28-32].

No one who follows such practices is beyond God's judgment, [2:1]. Paul turns the fire of his invective on the orthodox who stands in judgment on others. In V.9 he makes plain
that his reference is to the Jew as well as the Gentile. God's
judgment is impartial. No one can escape it [2:2-3]. God's forbearance and kindness are a means of leading man to repentance, but if man refuses God, the wrath of God accumulates in
righteous judgment which will come to each according to his
deeds [2:4-8]. God will judge Jew and Gentile alike [2:9-16].

Paul then attacks the Jew for his failure to keep the law.
The Jew is proud of his God and rests secure in the law. He
knows the difference between right and wrong through the
law and can confidently guide those who cannot see and who

are spiritual babies [2:17-20]; but although he may have the ability to guide others, he hasn't guided himself [2:21]. A list of failures follows and V.26 suggests that some men outside Jewry may be closer to proper observance of the law than those within. The outward sign of circumcision means nothing if it doesn't betoken inward conformity. A Jew must be a Jew at heart with a life lived for God and not for man [2:22-29].

Next the letter counters charges which may come from the Jews. Paul says that a logical question concerning the ultimate value of the old covenant would be whether a Jew has any advantage as a result of this relationship. The answer is a clear yes. The Jew profits in every way, for God committed his decrees to the Jews and he remains faithful in spite of Jewish unfaithfulness [3:1-3]. God remains true no matter how badly men may fail him. Paul quotes from scripture in (3:4). He asserts that, sophistry typical of the Greek mind, the Jews might further argue that God used their wickedness to make goodness apparent and that it would, therefore, be unjust for God to punish them for their actions. Some might even suggest that evil be done deliberately so that God's goodness might result. Paul considers the suggestion slanderous [3:5-8].

Paul now summarizes his argument. After a brief statement that all mankind stands under the same judgment, he quotes at length from scripture [3:10-18]. The law makes sin recognizable, but no man can expect to justify himself before God simply by adhering to it [3:19-21]. The theme turns to the second point of 1:16-17: "The just shall live by faith." The righteousness of God comes to all who have faith in Jesus Christ. All have sinned and are in need of this redemption. God has made appeasement possible through the act of Christ's crucifixion, a propitiation which is received and made effective through faith. The sins of the past are thereby remitted and those who believe in Jesus are thus justified. The crucifixion demonstrates God's righteousness [3:22-26]. By reiteration Paul makes his point perfectly clear. God is the same both for

Jews and Gentiles. Men should have no pride in the law and in works. Redemption is on a different plane. Man is justified by faith, not by deeds. These facts do not invalidate the law, but establish it at the proper level [3:27-31].

In the next chapter Paul seeks to forestall any possible rebuttal. Abraham might be cited as an example of justification by works. Paul shows the fallacy of the position. Abraham did much for which he might indeed be proud, but not proud before God. God considered Abraham righteous because of his belief. Man's faith is considered as righteousness and is God's gift [4:1-6]. Paul follows with a quotation from Psalm 32:1-2. The point is then clarified. Abraham's faith, which places him among the righteous before God, was a fact before his circumcision. Legal conformity to circumcision did not make him righteous. Circumcision was simply a sign of his righteousness. The uncircumcised Abraham can be seen as a spiritual father to those who are righteous without the act, as well as to those who have conformed [4:7-12]. Paul enlarges the argument for emphasis. Abraham is the spiritual father of all, both Jew and Gentile [4:17] (quoted from Gen. 17:5). The promise made to Abraham was not given because of his conformity to the law, but because of his righteousness which came by faith. If, on the other hand, conformity to the law alone brings salvation, faith is no longer of value and God's promise is meaningless. The law is only a means of measuring sin. (Only when there is a law, can a law be contravened.) God's promise is to all men, those under the law and those who have lived by faith [4:13-17]. The last part of the chapter refers to Abraham's acceptance of God's promise that he should be the father of many nations at a time when he was aged beyond potency and his wife Sarah was barren. Nonetheless Abraham's faith did not waver. The fact that this faith was counted as righteousness was not recorded for Abraham's credit alone, but is a principle applicable to man today if he believes in God who raised Christ, the Lord from the dead that he (man) might be justified [14:18-25].

Chapter 5 turns to the joyful aspects of this new under-

standing. As man is justified by faith, he achieves peace with
God through Christ. The Christian lives in happy anticipation
of glorious things to come. Not only is his faith a source of
hope for the future, but it is also a source of power for the
present [5:1-5]. Before Christ died for man, he had no
strength. Action such as Christ's doesn't occur often among
men, but God's love was so great that he let Christ die for
man, although he is a sinner. This atoning act is ground for
rejoicing [5:6-11].

The Jew felt that Adam's sin was passed to all mankind
as a matter of inevitable inheritance. Paul now shows that
Christ has changed the situation. Sin came into the world by
one man (Adam) and as a result of sin death also came. Sin
was in the world, therefore, before the law (Moses), [5:12-
14]. As one man (Adam) brought sin and death, now one
man (Christ) brings righteousness and life. As one act of sin
brought God's condemnation on all men, so one man's act
brings man's acquittal. The law points out the extent of sin,
but God's grace is even more extensive. Where sin once ruled,
now grace abounds to bring eternal life to all believers [5:12-
21].

In Chapter 6 Paul continues to outline the relationship between sin and grace. Should man sin in order to make grace
more plentiful? Paul answers emphatically in the negative.
Man is dead to sin. He has in his baptism shared Christ's death
and burial and so also he shares in the new life. Life is now
lived on a new level [6:1-5]. The lines which follow repeat
the theme: death to the old, life in the new through Christ.
Sin must no longer have any power over man's body, so man
shouldn't let his bodily parts be instruments of unrighteousness.
Sin is no longer man's master. Man doesn't live under the law,
but under grace [6:6-14].

Although the cleavage between the old and the new is
complete, this doesn't imply that without law sin is meaningless. Man is as he lives. What he follows in life indicates
whether he is motivated by sin or righteousness [6:15-16].
Fortunately where once man was the servant of sin, now by an

act of obedience he is the servant of righteousness; where once his body was given to vice for the purpose of being wicked, now it is given to righteousness as a means of becoming good. The results of the former could only mean death, of the latter, eternal life. The result of sin is death. God's gift is eternal life through Jesus Christ, the Lord [6:17-23].

Paul turns to marriage as an illustration. A man is subject to law only as long as he is alive. For example, a woman is bound to her husband only as long as he lives. Once he is dead, she is no longer bound [7:1-3]. Christians are dead to the law through Christ's death on the cross. Henceforth they are married to another relationship established through Christ [7:4]. When man lives in the flesh, the law made sin apparent and made him produce death, but now man is free from the law and free to serve God in the Spirit [7:4-6].

In the next section Paul enlarges on the relationship between sin and the law. Sin and the law are not the same thing, although the law may act to specify what sin is. Furthermore, sin then finds a way of making itself manifest through legal specifications. Outside the law man was spiritually alive, but once within, spiritually dead [7:7-11]. Paul faces a severe difficulty in his need to reconcile the evil results of the law with his respect for the traditions of Judaism of which he was a part. The passage is difficult to follow. In Verses 12 and 13 he shows the law to be holy and good. How can it bring death? Sin is made manifest by the law. The law specifies what sin is, and thereby creates it and this process is a means to death [7:12-13].

Paul follows with a description of the tension within himself. The law is concerned with the spiritual; it is he who is carnal. The essential nature of man is outlined. The good that he would like to do, he does not do. The evil that he doesn't want to do, he does. How can this paradoxical behavior be explained? It is not he who acts in this manner; the sin within him supplies the motivation [7:14-20]. Two conflicting principles are at work, the reason of the conscious mind and the dictates of the flesh. What can free him from the conflict within his sinful nature? Paul thanks God that a way out exists through Jesus Christ, the Lord (7:21-25).

Paul now outlines the basic tenets of Christianity. A long passage follows explaining the means whereby God released man from the dictates of the carnal. Christ is victorious over the flesh. For the first time the phrase "in Christ" is used. It has two connotations. First, the phrase seems to imply the existence of an aura or atmosphere which is spiritual and other worldly and in which man may live. Secondly, it refers to the body of Christ on earth which is synonymous with the Church or the body of Christians on earth.

Those who live "in Christ" are free from sin's condemnation. They walk in a different circle. The law failed because of human nature, but God sent Christ to live in the flesh (nature) and condemned sin which Christ took upon himself. Now man through Christ's victory is able to live by the Spirit and can actually fulfill what the law demanded. Flesh and spirit are in tension. The carnal cannot please God, but man is no longer carnal if the Spirit is in him. If Christ is in man, his sinful nature is dead, but his spiritual nature lives. Furthermore, not only does the spirit live, but also man's mortal body lives as a spiritual body in the resurrection [8:1-11]. Paul outlines the core of Christian belief. Now man need no longer live by the dictates of the flesh (carnal standards). That way of life leads to death; the new way leads to life. Man is free at last. Referring to the Old Testament and the story of Hagar and Sarah [Gen. 16], Paul demonstrates that Christians enjoy a relation to God that is similar to sonship. Man shares Christ's inheritance by sharing his sufferings. Man will also share in his glory. Sonship not only implies a glorious inheritance, but also implies brotherhood [8:12-17].

Present sufferings are nothing in comparison to future glory. All creation awaits the ultimate revelation belonging to the sons of God. Creation cannot as yet understand reality, but God has given hope by which to live. In the end the created world will be released from corruption and given the glorious liberty which belongs to the children of God [8:18-21].

Plainly up until now the whole world throbbed in pain (the word *hope* implies lack of immediate fulfillment). Also, ever within converted man a tension remains while he waits for the redemption of full sonship. The Spirit of God is a sustaining power both for hope and for man's weakness. Man doesn't know how to pray properly, but the Spirit prays from within, creating an expression that goes beyond words, and God, who sees into mind and Spirit, knows the Spirit's intention [8:22-27].

Paul continues to enlarge on the implications of Christian hope. If a man accepts God's love, he will also love God and all things will work for his welfare. God chose certain men to share brotherhood with Christ. The chosen were made righteous and glorified [8:28-30]. As Paul's theme now approaches its climax, his words pour out his burning conviction of Christ's victory over evil and man's redemption through his atoning act on the cross. With God on the Christian's side, who can stand in opposition? God gave his Son. Cannot a God who does this be trusted to give man everything else? Who dares to challenge those chosen by God? None other than Christ has the right to condemn, and rather than condemn him, he gave his life for the Christian. Paul becomes lyrical in his impassioned expression. Nothing can separate man from victory through Christ. Pain, persecution, poverty, danger, force or arms, none of these things is enough. V.36 is a quotation from Ps. 44:22. In the end Paul touches all mankind's fears and tribulations. The section ends in a crescendo of questions to which only one answer can be given. Nothing, absolutely nothing can change the fact that the Christian conquers all of life through Christ [8:31-39].

The letter might now properly turn to some of the more obvious applications of the doctrines outlined in the first portion, but instead Paul turns for three chapters to what must have been, in his mind, a bitter question. Why had God's chosen people, the Jews, repudiated their Lord? What was to become of them? Perhaps it was that God had rejected Israel. These questions were a source of pain and anxiety to Paul. In answering them he laid the foundation for the doctrine of election which was to be basic to much of Protestant thought in the Reformation as well as to Christian orthodoxy as understood by St. Augustine. Paul opens chapter nine with a statement of his deep concern. He asks God to witness to the fact that he speaks the truth. The condition of his fellow Israelites is a source of pain, and he would even be willing to sever himself from Christ if such an act would win them over. Paul surveys what God has given the Jews, everything: adoption as sons, the insight to his glory, the covenants, the law, true worship, promises fulfilled, the patriarchs, and even Christ by descent [9:1-5]. This doesn't mean, however, that in the end God's promises have failed. Not all who are of actual physical descent are necessarily true (spiritual) Israelites [9:6]. Paul now develops an argument from scriptual history to demonstrate how God's selection has operated throughout the ages from Abraham to Esau. V.13 is quoted from Mal. 1:2,3.

Paul asks whether God's selection is unfair, and answers that it is not. God predicted such selection according to his sovereign will [Ex. 33:19]. For an example Paul points to the case of Pharaoh whose heart was hardened by God [9:14-18]. Paul next seeks to forestall a logical objection to his argument. If God's will is irresistible, how can man possess responsibility? Paul evades the question with a statement that it is not man's province to question God's action. He uses an analogy to back his point. A potter can make what he wishes with his clay without being questioned. The clay certainly doesn't have any ability to say what sort of vessel will be made. The analogy is of scriptural origin, taken from Isa. 45:9 and Jer. 18:6. The children of Israel are the clay which God molds. God has perhaps in the past allowed things to endure which should have been destroyed, in order to demonstrate the great resources of his glory to those whom he considered fit to receive his message—his chosen people, the elect, both Jew and Gentile. Quotations from Hosea and Isaiah follow: Hos. 2:23, 1:10, Isa. 10: 22, 1:9, [9:20-29]. Both Hosea's prediction of a people called and Isaiah's doctrine of the remnant demonstrate the principle of selection. Lastly, Paul points out that certain people (Gentiles) did not meet the law's standard of righteousness, but accepted that which the Jew refused and attained righteousness by faith, while the Jews following the law lost the right of the proper motivation and tripped on the stumbling block predicted by Isaiah 8:14 and 28:16 [9:30-33].

Paul shows where the Jews failed, but the passage leaves hope for those who have as yet not turned to God through Christ. He prays that the Jews will turn. Their great zeal for righteousness is misdirected through ignorance. They need only accept Christ in whom the search for righteousness through the law terminated [10:1-4].

Moses' teaching that man finds life through perfect adherence to the law is right in theory, but impossible in practice. That kind of righteousness cannot be achieved. Righteousness by faith answers many questions. There is no need to ask who is going up to see Christ in heaven, or who is going down to him where the dead are. A man doesn't need to go to these places to find Christ. The answer is near at hand, actually in man's spoken word and in his heart. The answer is heartfelt faith, confessed by word of mouth. The Scripture says whosoever believeth in him shall not be disappointed. This applies to everyone without distinction, both Jew and Gentile [10:5-13].

A list of hypothetical excuses for not having understood God's word follows. The Jews might plead ignorance through lack of instruction [10:14]. Paul answers them summarily with a quotation from Isaiah 52:7. The gospel has indeed been preached abroad. The Jews have had ample opportunity to hear the message, but all have not accepted it [Isa. 53:1]. Faith comes by hearing the message about Christ. If asked whether they have heard, they must answer yes. The word of God has gone out to all the earth as Psalm 19:4 describes. If asked then whether Israel knew, the answer must again be yes; they knew because as far back as Moses' time the warning was given [Deut. 23:22], and the prediction was pointedly made that God would be manifest among those who did not seek him [Isa. 65:1]. Isaiah says God continually reaches out to disobedient and gainsaying people [Isa. 65:2], [10:15-21].

Paul does not close the door on the Jews. In the next chapter he holds out hope for a consecrated remnant. Has God repudiated all those who were originally his chosen people? Paul answers strongly in the negative. For one, Paul himself is an Israelite whom God has not cast away. What does the scripture say? A quotation from Elijah follows [I Kings 19:10] in which the prophet claims that he alone remained faithful, but the facts proved that he was one of seven thousand who remained loyal [11:1-4]. Likewise, says Paul, a remnant remains loyal today. They are chosen by grace and, therefore, not because of their actions, [11:5-6]. Thus,Israel as a whole did not come through, but a few have succeeded. The rest were blind, as the scripture bears out (Isa. 29:10, Deut. 29:4 and Ps. 69:22, 23). The course of events does not demonstrate a complete loss. As a result of Israel's failure, salvation has come to the Gentile, and this fact acts as a stimulus to the Jews. If Jewish failure has accomplished so much, how much more were they to fulfill God's plan [11:7-12].

Paul now turns his pen to the Gentiles. They are not to assume that as the emphasis of his ministry is on them, the Jew has been excluded. Rather, the Gentile ministry may serve as a means of saving the Jew [11:13-14]. V. 15 refers to the Old Testament understanding of ritual offering which specified that when a portion of the whole was offered to God, the remainder was also consecrated by the act [Num. 15:20]. Paul uses the simile to introduce a longer one beginning with V.17, pertaining to wild and cultivated olive trees. The olive tree is God's grace. Some of the branches, the Jews, have been broken off and wild branches, the Gentiles, were grafted on in their place. Paul tells his readers not to boast about this. Remember that the tree, God's grace, supports the branches, not the branches the tree. Paul warns his readers not to say that the branches were broken off to make room for the Gentiles, but rather that the Jews lost their place because they didn't believe, and the Gentiles have theirs because they did. The situation is, however, not entirely secure. God could remove the wild branches as quickly as he removed the natural ones. The Jews experienced his justice; the Gentiles, his kindness. If the Gentiles abuse their privilege they also can be cut off. The Jew can more easily be restored than the Gentile, because of what he is, and such restoration is not beyond God's power [11:15-24].

In the last part of the section, Paul makes clear that in the end salvation will come to the Jew as well as the Gentile. The blindness of Israel is part of God's plan and will continue only until the appointed number of Gentiles have been saved. When the number is reached all Israel will be saved [11:25-26a]. Paul uses passages from Isaiah and Jeremiah as illustrations [Isa. 59: 20, 21, 27:9; Jer. 31:33] [11:26b-27]. Paul says that at the moment the Jews are enemies of God to bring about Gentile conversion, but that in the end they will be among the elect. God does not withdraw his gifts once he has given them. Paul's argument is devious. As the Gentiles found mercy which would have belonged to the Jews except for their disobedience, so the Jews will eventually share the mercy extended to the Gentiles! God permits all men unbelief so that he can have mercy on all [11:28-32]. Paul concludes with an exclamation of God's inscrutable goodness and with quotations from Isaiah 40:13,14 and Job 35:7, 41:11 which follow the same theme [11:33-36].

The letter now turns to the application of Christian principles to life. As a result of the teachings Paul has summarized in the first eight chapters, certain conduct can be expected on the part of Christians. All earthly activities should be for the glory of God. He warns his congregation not to conform to worldly standards, but to live by God's plan [12:1-2]; then he lists Christian precepts. He commands that the Christian not be conceited but try to understand life in terms of the faith God has given to everyone who will receive it. From such understanding life results in which each person has a proper function. The analogy of the body, reminiscent of the Corinthian letter, indicates that each person is given a particular gift by grace and that each gift should be used to advantage. If the gift is preaching, the recipient should preach faithfully. If it is ministering to others, the recipient should concentrate on that. If teaching, then he should devote himself

to that. If exhorting others to faith, he should concentrate on
that. If he gives to the poor, he should do it without ostentation. The executive should work hard, and the man filled with
compassion should be cheerful. Love should be sincere. All
should break with evil and follow that which is good [12:3-9].

From describing the gifts of grace Paul moves to a detailed
summary of Christian attitudes and behavior. The passage
which follows is strictly similar to the opening section of
Christ's Sermon on the Mount [Mt. 5] and V.14,15 are
nearly exact reproductions of the Beatitudes. V.20 is a quotation from Proverbs 5:21, 22. At the last, Paul exhorts the
church to overcome evil with the forces of good which are at its
command [12:10-21].

Paul now speaks on the relation of the Christian to civil
authority. His position is basically the same as that taken by
Christ. "Render unto Caesar the things which are Caesar's, and
unto God the things which are God's" [Matt. 22:21, Mk. 12:
17, Lk. 20:25]. The church had not at this time been the object of persecution and enjoyed the same protection afforded
the Jew. Roman administration was for the most part wise and
just. Although the situation was to change radically under
Nero a few years later, Paul's point of view is conditioned by
a period of peace in which he was frequently afforded protection under the law. He says to obey civil authority because all
authority comes from God. Thus, to oppose recognized authority is to oppose God, and to do so will result in punishment
[13:1-2]. Magistrates are only feared by the dishonest. The
law-abiding citizen receives commendation. The magistrate
serves God for man's good, but the evil-doer has good reason
to be alarmed. The power of the civil law is not a hollow conception. The magistrate is the instrument of God's judgment
on evil-doers. Civil authorities should be obeyed because they
are God's ministers in the context of civil life. It is right to pay
taxes for the support of the public welfare. The Christian
should give to everyone his just due [13:1-7].

Paul commands the Christian not to be in debt except in
respect to love which forms a perpetual obligation. The man

who loves his neighbor has fulfilled the law. Paul's statement is in accord with the second condition in Christ's summary of the law [Mt. 22:37-40]. In V. 11 he points out that the time for judgment is near: "It is later than you think"; therefore act accordingly. Follow Christ rather than the dictates of man's base nature [13:8-14].

Apparently legalists existed among the Christians who made a fetish of observing certain fasts. Paul says that Christians of strong faith should be free from this sort of semisuperstitious discipline. Therefore, observance of these disciplines might be a symptom of weakness in faith. Paul's first reference [14:1-2] is probably a delineation between vegetarians and those who feel free to eat anything. Each in his own way may be understood, however, as following godly practice. The strong should be tolerant of the weak. A man shouldn't criticize others who are Christ's servants and who are responsible only to him [14:3-4].

Paul takes a second example from those who were preoccupied in observing days made special by Jewish festivals or the superstitions of astrology. His response to them follows the same line as that given for fasts. He urges every man to be true to his convictions, but to remember that no man is self contained. Man lives and dies in Christ. In life and death each belongs to God. Christ lived and died that he might be lord of both realms. Paul asks, Why criticize others, since all men will someday be judged by God's standard [14:5-12]?

Paul admonishes his flock not to become preoccupied in judging others. The strong should not act as a stumbling block for the weak. Nothing is unclean in itself, but if a man understands it as unclean, then as far as he is concerned the thing is unclean. A person who deliberately upsets another over the matters of diet is not acting with Christian love. The question of food should not be a destructive one to a man for whom Christ died [14:13-16]. The passage is paralleled in I Cor. 8:7-13. The kingdom of God is not a matter of food and drink, but righteousness, peace, and joy in the Holy Spirit. Men should follow those things which contribute to God's kingdom [14:17-19]. Paul clearly feels that Christian faith is above ritual observance. Nothing is any longer unclean for the faithful, but a bad conscience can be harmful if a person feels that a ceremonial law is broken. Paul urges that no one cause another to stumble in this respect. Some are free by faith, and a man is happy who has no restrictions on what he permits himself in regard to food, but whoever has restrictions is wrong if he doesn't follow them. His action in this respect is not the result of faith and is, therefore, sinful [14:20–23].

Chapter 15 contains a summary of what Paul has already set forth. The strong in faith must tolerate the weak rather than try to please themselves. One should conform to his neighbor's standard rather than cause him to fall. Even Jesus didn't do what he wanted to do [15:1-3]. The words of Scripture were written long ago to teach us today and through their teaching of patience and comfort, man finds hope. Paul asks that the God who gives patience and consolation may unite man through Jesus Christ, and then may man glorify God, the father of the Lord, Jesus Christ. He hopes that man's heart may be opened as Christ opened his heart to man for the glory of God [15:1-7].

Many scholars feel that the next six verses (8-13) are out of place. They fall more properly into the subject matter of chapters 9-11. Jesus Christ fulfilled God's promise made to the early patriarchs by coming to the Jews, and yet the Gentiles also were taught to glorify God. After a series of quotations from Scripture [Deut. 32:43, 15:11; Ps. 117:1], the passage ends with a benediction [15:8-13].

The letter now turns toward matters of particular concern for the Roman church. The opening lines commend the group for their character and background. Clearly they are a mature community capable of spiritual self-determination. Nevertheless, because of the grace of God which is his authority, Paul ventures to remind them of the things they have been taught. His constant endeavor is to bring the Gentiles to God. Paul evidently feels that he has unique gifts of the Spirit to bestow on the Roman church [15:14-18]. Further, he hopes to preach where the word of Christ has not yet been heard and to build where others have not been. The passage ends with a quotation from Isaiah [52:15].

The last part of the letter outlines Paul's plans for the future. Until now he has been involved with work in the area stretching from Jerusalem to Ulyricum, but now since this work is finished, he is to realize an old ambition. He will visit the Romans on the way to Spain. First, he'll travel to Jerusalem to take the collection from Macedonia and Achaia, which was a fair thing for the Gentiles to give. In this fashion they returned something to the Jews in the form of this world's goods for what they had received from them spiritually [15:22-28]. Paul says that when he finally comes, he will bring the full blessing of Christ's gospel. He concludes by asking for prayers that he may escape from the unbelievers in Judea and that the relief may be safely delivered. The letter ends with a blessing [15:29-33].

The last chapter seems to be a postscript and is unsuitable for a Roman community. The problems surrounding the passage have already been discussed in the early part of the chapter (p. 237). The first two verses are a commendation for Phoebe [16:1-2]. A long list of greetings follows [16:3-16] interrupted by a warning against party spirit and false teachers [16:17-20]. After a list of greetings from Paul's companions [16:21-24] the chapter concludes with a doxology [16:25-27].

OUTLINE OF THE ROMAN LETTER

Ch. 1 Salutation, credentials, and thanksgiving, 1:1-15
    a) Salutation and credentials, 1:1-7
    b) Thanksgiving and mission, 1:8-15

I. Argument and exposition, 1:16-11:36

  A. *Paul's Interpretation of the Christian faith, 1:16-8:39*
    a) The gospel is God's saving power received by faith, 1:16-17
    b) Man's repudiation and God's penalties, 1:18-32

XVI

The Philippian Letter

Background

The City of Philippi lay eight miles inland from the port town of Neapolis and was the first city in Europe to which Paul brought his ministry. Originally known as Krenides, named for the springs which abound in the area, it was conquered and renamed by King Philip of Macedon in the middle of the fourth century B.C. In Philippi the republican forces of Brutus and Cassius were defeated by Anthony and Octavian in 42 B.C. Made a Roman colony by Caesar Augustus, it took on the characteristics of a garrison town, but was also granted the "Italic right," which meant that it enjoyed the rights and privileges associated with Italy itself. Not only prominent because of its military connections, it lay on the Ignatian Way, the great Roman trade route which stretched from Dyrahachium on the Adriatic to Byzantium on the Hellespont. Philippi was perhaps more inclined to pagan religions than the other cities which Paul visited. A famous shrine to Dionysus was on nearby Mount Pangaeus, while Judaism was not even represented by a synagogue.

Paul visited Philippi for the first time when he crossed from Asia Minor to the continent on his second missionary journey, and it was probably from Philippi that he wrote his last and joyous letter to the Corinthians after he heard news of their reaction to his severe letter. The church there was particularly dear to him. It was one of the few from which he was willing to receive financial help [Phil. 4:15, II Cor. 11:9] and apparently the community had helped at the time of his captivity [Phil. 4:10]. The church was not filled with the dissension and theological questioning so familiar in the others. The tone of his letter for the most part reflects this circumstance. It is a softer letter than those in which Paul's pen must mend fences broken by disloyalty, pressure from Judaizers, jealousy, and factionalism. Only one section is devoted to each of these things respectively, and in the second instance the matter appears to have been completely settled in Paul's mind.

The letter is not, however, without critical problems. Question has been cast on the authenticity of authorship, and a strong case can be made for each of three different points of origin with corresponding differences in date. The reference to bishops and deacons [1:1] is felt by most to be an anachronism. The Church had not yet developed in Paul's time to the point where orders of the clergy were delineated. Some feel that the Clement to whom the letter refers [4:3] must be Clement of Rome who lived considerably later than Paul. Other objections to authenticity arise from the style and doctrine which are felt to be off key. None of these objections are finally determinative. The references to bishops and deacons may be titles of authority without the significance later attached to them or, what is even m re likely, the line may be a gloss. Clement may not be Clement of Rome, but as easily may be a prominent Christian in Philippi of Caesarea. Lastly, the style and tone are certainly sufficiently Pauline to be his own writing simply in a different key as a result of the letter's theme and the circumstances of its writing. The consensus gives the letter Pauline authorship.

Questions concerning origin and date are not so easily settled. The letter is probably known as one of the captivity letters.[1] No doubt exists that it was written while Paul was a

---

[1] Four letters of the New Testament were ostensibly written by Paul while in jail: Philippians, Colossians, Ephesians, and Philemon.

prisoner. Not only does the main body signify captivity, but also the fact is made clear by Paul's words "so that my bonds become manifest in Christ throughout the whole praetorian guard" [Phil. 1:13]. Which period of Paul's captivity best fits the letter's requirements? Acts describes two prolonged periods of imprisonment: two years in Caesarea while he awaited trial in Rome and two years or more in Rome. Paul was undoubtedly held for frequent short periods while waiting for a hearing, as in the case of his arrest before he faced Gallio in Achaia. A third and long period of imprisonment in Ephesus seems highly probable. Although Acts makes no mention of it, considerable evidence exists to substantiate the assumption. II Cor. 1:8 refers to desperate trouble in Asia which was nearly beyond the Apostle's endurance; I Cor. 4:11 describes persecution and hardship; II Cor. 1:9 talks of circumstances which made death imminent; a similar story is told in II Cor. 6:9; and Paul's Roman letter makes direct reference to prison [Rom. 16:7]. Paul was, it seems, almost in constant trouble with the authorities [II Cor. 6:5, 11:23], and he even mentions an ordeal with beasts in Ephesus. Acts tells of a major dispute with the silversmiths there. It must be remembered that prison was not a means of punishment for the ancients, and a person could be held for indefinite periods while waiting trial and sentence. As Paul used Ephesus as his general headquarters for a longer time than any place else, it is quite likely that his terms of confinement there were also longer. The question then is from which of three places the Philippian letter was written—Ephesus, Caesarea, or Rome.

Opinion is divided on the subject. References to Roman government in the letter might apply equally well to all three locations. To be sure, Rome was the capital, but a garrison and governor were located in both Ephesus and Caesarea. The letter proposes a visit to Philippi [2:24] which would hardly apply to the case were Paul imprisoned at Caesarea. At that time he had appealed to Caesar as a Roman citizen and knew that he would be sent to Rome for a trial which would preclude the possibility of an immediate visit to Macedonia. If, on the other hand, Rome is taken as the location for his writing, one must suppose that Paul had abandoned his plans for visiting Spain. Furthermore, the distance between Rome and Philippi would have made frequent passage of messengers very difficult. The journey was approximately four hundred miles on foot, broken by two days at sea. Ephesus was only ten days to two weeks by sea from Neapolis. The distance is short enough for messengers to pass back and forth with some facility. While in Ephesus, Paul contemplated a trip to Macedonia and, indeed, later went there. Lastly, Paul seems to have been more intimate with the Philippian church than the long period of absence required by Roman origin permits. Although many scholars still favor Rome, Ephesus seems to fit all circumstances a little better. If Ephesus is accepted as the letter's point of origin, the date lies sometime in Paul's sojourn there, probably in the spring of 54 A.D. and about the same time as his third letter to the Corinthians. Barnett suggests that the letter actually comprises two letters,[1] 1:1-3:1 being the first and 3:2-4:23 the second. The similarity of 3:2-4:23 in tone to second Corinthians might place it in the Corinthian period, while the first part might be a later letter written from Rome. Although the letter has several logical ending places and although a clear line can be drawn in the middle between both subject matter and tone, other equally acceptable explanations of these facts can be given. First, if two letters, they might have been written from the same location, either Rome or Ephesus, and secondly the break might simply result from the letter's having been started at one time and finished after an interruption later.

The Philippian church had given Paul help in the past [4:15]. Now Paul languished in jail, and the loving Philippians, on hearing the news, sent Epaphroditus to give succor and report concerning his situation. While with Paul, Epaphroditus had become ill. The people at home heard of his illness and were much concerned. Evidently news had traveled back and forth several times [2:25-28]. Meanwhile Epaphroditus had recovered and was ready for the trip home. Paul probably sent the Philippian letter with him on the occasion of his return.

[1] Albert E. Barnett, *The New Testament, Its Making and Meaning*.

Structure and Content

The letter contains two main sections, the first of which is a highly personal answer to inquiries concerning Paul's situation and his ministry, followed by an exhortation to humility in the face of opposition, an exhortation to humility and unity, a Christological statement, and personalia concerning himself, Timothy, and Epaphroditus.

The second section is far more vehement and, at the outset, is strongly reminiscent of the Corinthian correspondence. It begins with a vituperative castigation of Judaizers, leading into a section deploring lawlessness and describing its evil results. This part is followed by an exhortation to unity in respect to two factions within the church, and concludes with a long thanksgiving for the aid sent from Philippi, a doxology, a closing salutation and benediction.

The opening salutation is brief and direct. The line referring to bishops and deacons may be either retranslated as the single word "overseers" or dropped as a gloss [1:1-2]. The prayers and thanksgivings which follow set the tone of the letter. Paul's joy and fellowship with the church are clearly manifest [1:3-11].

Paul follows immediately with a statement concerning his bondage which is known to everyone in the area. Apparently he is giving a direct answer to inquiries from Philippi [1:12-14]. The letter gives evidence of rivalry between Paul and others who also proclaimed the gospel. He deplores the situation but feels that the first priority is the gospel's proclamation no matter who does the work [1:15-18]. Paul feels that the prayers of the Philippians and the Holy Spirit will sustain him in his hour of need as he faces trial which may end with the death sentence [1:19-20]. Faced with the choice of life on this earth or death, he is torn between the possibility of knowing the glory of union with Christ through death or the service of Christ on earth. As he is needed to promulgate the gospel, he feels that life on earth is the proper choice for the time being [1:21-26]. The chapter ends with an exhortation to humility that the Philippians may be worthy of the gospel which he preaches on their behalf and encouragement in their contest against paganism in the community. The passage may refer to the strong Dionysian cult whose center was nearby. In this contest the Philippians not only have an opportunity to serve Christ, but also to suffer for him as Paul has done [1:27-30].

Chapter 2 opens with a strong exhortation to humility, unselfishness and unity in the faith [2:1-4]. The letter then turns to a Christological statement: Let Christ be an example. Christ was God by nature and yet was willing to give up everything to be a servant in the likeness of man and was obedient even up to his death. As a result God exalted him and gave him the name of Greatest of All. Everyone and everything should bow down to Christ the Lord to the glory of God the Father [2:5-11]. The verses present a problem in interpretation. The early Christians felt that Paul's reference is to the pre-existent Christ (V.6) while modern scholarship is inclined to understand the lines as expressing the attitudes of Christ's manhood.

Paul draws a logical conclusion for the church from the Christology he has outlined. So now as the Philippians have always been faithful to Paul's teachings whether he was absent or present, they shall continue to work out their salvation, anxious to do God's will for he works in man to give him both volition and the power of achievement [2:12-13]. The Philippians must stand as a beacon light for Christ in the darkness of a perverse generation that Paul may be proud of them in the day of judgment. He will know then that his time wasn't wasted. If he is to die (as a result of some judgment not yet pronounced), he wants to be happy in the knowledge of their faith. Let them also rejoice in him [2:14-18].

The first section of the letter concludes with personal remarks concerning Paul's relationship to the church and to Timothy, the situation in respect to Epaphroditus, and a short exhortation. Paul hopes soon to send Timothy, who will bring back first hand news from Philippi. Timothy is unequaled in his devotion to Christ and has worked for the gospel with

Paul as a child might serve his father. Others are self-seeking. Timothy will be sent as soon as Paul finds out what his future is to be, and by God's grace it may well turn out that Paul himself may soon come [2:19-24]. In the meantime Paul sends Epaphroditus, their messenger and minister because of his desperate homesickness and serious illness from which he has recovered by God's mercy. Thus, Paul is saved from a double sorrow. The Philippian welcome of Epaphroditus will make Paul joyful. Epaphroditus should be greatly honored by them for he nearly gave his life in God's service. Lastly, Paul asks the church to rejoice in God's service and ends with a statement that he isn't bored by constant repetition of this theme [2:25-3:1]. The lines may indicate that Paul had written other similar letters to the Philippian church.

The second section of the letter begins with a warning against Judaizers. The tone changes completely and one can almost hear Paul's voice rise in ire. He warns his readers to beware of the dogs, wicked workers and unbelievers who would mutilate the body by physical circumcision. The truly circumcised are circumcised in spirit [3:2-3]. Paul then outlines his own claims which are equal to or above anything anyone else can produce in the same line. He has been properly circumcised, is of the tribe of Benjamin, a true hereditary Jew, a Pharisee, one time persecutor of Christians, yet all these things he willingly threw away for the greater advantage of finding salvation in Christ through faith [3:4-8]. The next three verses speak in mystical terms of spiritual union with Christ. Paul seeks to become so identified with Jesus that he may die as he died with the hope of finding thereby the same resurrection [3:9-11]. The lines are perhaps an admonition to those who thought they had already achieved spiritual perfection, while Paul himself is still one who seeks. His only goal is to press forward to the future and escape the past [3:12-14]. He admonishes the spiritually mature to follow this example. What has functioned properly in the past will continue to do so. Unity of faith and conduct are the rule [3:15-16].

Paul then makes himself and his close followers an exam-

ple. Those who do not follow his line of conduct will be in
serious trouble that can only end in catastrophe. Such people
are lawless and care nothing for the sanctity of the body, but
glory in earthly things. Paul and the faithful are citizens in a
heavenly jurisdiction where earthly bodies will exist in a new
form. The transformation will be accomplished by the mighty
power through which all things shall finally be subject to
Christ [II Cor. 5:1-5, I Cor. 15:55-58]. The section ends with
an affectionate exhortation to stand steadfast in the faith [3:17-
4:1].

Apparently even the Philippian church was subject to
some discord. The passage which follows gives evidence to the
presence of factionalism, a thing Paul could not abide. Euodias
and Syntyche were evidently the center of party conflict. Paul
asks that they be reconciled and charges one of his loyal fellow
workers with the task of peacemaker [4:2-3]. An exhortation
to rejoice in the Lord, the dominant theme of the letter, fin-
ishes the order for reconciliation and is followed by an injunction that the disputing parties give themselves to prayer in order to find God's peace [4:4-7]. As an afterthought Paul
enlarges on the subject of Christian meditation. Truth, honor,
purity (justice), love, goodness are the things which Christians
should contemplate. The result of such activity can be seen in
his life [4:8-9].

Already the letter has come to two conclusions. The benediction in V.9 might be considered another. Some critics consider this evidence that the letter is a conglomerate of several
fragments. Instead of concluding, Paul now adds his thanks to
the church for its gracious provision of his needs. The lines
are like a postscript. Paul rejoices in Philippian thoughtfulness
over a long period, thoughtfulness which appeared again when
the need arose. He doesn't speak from desperate need because
he has learned to get along on little as well as when he had much
[4:10-12]. He can face anything through the strength God
gives him in Christ. Nevertheless the Philippians did well by
sharing his troubles. They alone have helped him in the past.
The tangible gift isn't as important, however, as the reward

they will receive for their Christian behavior [4:13-17]. Paul has all that he now needs. He is, in fact, rich as a result of the gifts brought by Epaphroditus. Philippian generosity is a sweet smelling thing to God. God will supply all Philippian needs through Jesus Christ [4:18-19]. The section closes with a doxology [4:20].

The last lines are a salutation to all in Philippi from all that are with Paul. Again the question of the Caesar's household arises. Is the reference to Rome or elsewhere? The letter ends with the customary benediction and a signature [4:21-23].

OUTLINE OF THE PHILIPPIAN LETTER

1. Salutation, thanksgiving, personalia, exhortations, Timothy, and Epaphroditus, 1:1-3:1

Ch. 1   a) Salutation, 1:1-2
        b) Thanksgiving and prayer, 1:3-11
        c) Paul's bondage and his present ministry, 1:12-26
        d) Exhortation to humility, unity and strength against paganism, 1:27-30
Ch. 2   e) Exhortation to unity and Christology, 2:1-11
        f) Christ's humility and exhaltation, a guide and encouragement, 2:12-18
Ch. 3   g) Personalia, Timothy and Epaphroditus, 2:19-3:1

II. Concerning Judaizers, pride, Christ, lawlessness, an exhortation to remain steadfast, thanksgiving and benediction, 3:2-4:21

        a) Against Judaizers and pride, 3:2-16
Ch. 4   b) The consequences of lawlessness and the body's true home, 3:17-4:1
        c) Further exhortations, 4:2-9
        d) Thanksgiving for Philippian aid, 4:10-20
        e) Closing salutation and benediction, 4:21-23

XVII

The Letters to Philemon, Colossae, and Ephesus

Background

The letters to Philemon, Colossae, and Ephesus are so closely related and present problems whose resolution, if possible, is so dependent upon the interrelationship, that they can best be studied together. Opinion remains divided on place of origin, destination, and authorship. On only one point is scholarship in accord. Paul is generally accepted as the author of Philemon. Some doubt exists concerning the authorship of Colossians, and Ephesians is thought by many to be spurious.

Colossae, Laodicea, and Hierapolis were three small cities in Phrygia, located in the Lycus valley five or six days inland from Ephesus. Laodicea was founded by Antiochus, the Great, and named after his wife Laodice. Colossae, a town in decline, lay on the south bank of the Lycus River, a tributary of the Meander which poured into the Mediterranean near Miletus. Hierapolis was famous because of its baths, but none of the three could be considered important.

In the case of the Pauline letters already discussed, differences of opinion concerning direction and readership made no difference to the understanding of content. Such is not true with the three letters under consideration. In the case of Philemon, two schools of thought present two very different interpretations of content as a direct result of questions arising from the direction of the letter.

Since the second century Philemon has been commonly accepted as a simple private letter to one Philemon, dealing with the matter of his runaway slave, Onesimus. The salutation also mentions Apphia and Archippus, who were assumed to be Philemon's wife and son. At first glance the occasion for writing seems quite plain. Onesimus has run away taking with him some of his master's belongings. Either he has been arrested and shares Paul's confinement or has come to him for help. In any case a deep and affectionate relationship has grown up between the two men. Onesimus has come to be a strong Christian. Now he is to return to his master. Paul will pay for whatever he has taken. Paul writes asking that he may be received with Christian love and forgiveness. Philemon is evidently an inhabitant of Colossae for Paul refers to his slave as being a Colossian [Col. 4:9]. He must also have been a close friend or Paul would not have so freely requested the guest room [Philem. 1:22].

More recent scholarship understands the letter very differently. John Knox and others[1] feel that the letter was written to Archippus, who was, rather than Philemon, the master of Onesimus. Philemon is thought to be a man of influence among the churches in the Lycus valley area and probably according to this theory, resided in Laodicea and not Colossae. He was to exert his influence on Archippus. The purpose of the letter is to obtain Onesimus' freedom that he may return and serve Paul in the Christian cause. The "Christian ministry" to which reference is made in Colossians [Col. 4:17] is to make possible further Christian service through the work which Onesimus will do once he is free to return to Paul's service.

It is felt that Paul wrote two letters to the area, Philemon and Colossians. A possible reconstruction of the events sees Epaphras as an important Christian in the churches of Laodicea,

---

[1] Philemon among the letters of Paul, Albert E. Barnett, *The New Testament, Its Making and Meaning*.

Colossae and Hierapolis [Col. 4:13]. He may even have been their founder. Apparently he met Paul in prison to seek advice on matters of theology and church administration, or a less likely possibility is that he may have been arrested and brought to Paul's prison. In any case his arrival made the matter of Onesimus' return an immediate concern. Paul sent Onesimus home with Tychicus [Col. 4:7-9], carrying two letters each of which was to be read in both Laodicea and Colossae [Col. 4:16]. The letter to Philemon is assumed to be the letter that was to come to Colossae from Laodicea.

The usually accepted place of origin, as with Philippians, is Rome, but for much the same reason that Philippians may more likely have been written in Ephesus so also Philemon, Colossians and Ephesians may have been written there (if Ephesians is accepted as Pauline, it nevertheless was almost certainly not written to the Ephesians). A few hold to Caesarea, but Paul's suggestion in Philemon that a guest room be kept ready for him hardly fits the place of a man in captivity waiting transportation to Rome for trial, nor does the remark fit particularly well into Paul's prospective future itinerary from Rome in the event of his acquittal [Philem. 1:22]. He had yet to visit Spain. Lastly, the twelve hundred mile trip to Rome is rather a long distance for a runaway slave, and the communication which both Philemon and Colossians hope to bring seems to suggest more immediate intercourse than the greater distance would make possible. Also to be noted are the greetings Paul sends from six companions [Philem. 1:1, 1:23,24], none of whom, with the exception of Luke, are mentioned elsewhere as having accompanied him to Rome. Ephesus fits the vacant spot in the puzzle better than either of the other two cities. It is only a hundred miles from Laodicea and Colossae. Communication would have been comparatively rapid. If it is accepted as the place of origin, the letters were probably written in 54 A.D. If they were written in Rome they are later—60-62 A.D.

The authenticity of the Colossian letter has sometimes been questioned on the basis of vocabulary, style, and general slant. The letter, is, however, included in the earliest collection of Pauline writing and was well known to the apostolic fathers. Further, the reconstruction of the events surrounding its composition in reference to the letter to Philemon (to Archippus) demand authenticity for the letter. Philemon is almost universally accepted as authentic. So also Colossians may be accepted.

Epaphras was evidently concerned with some sort of heretical teaching which had become popular in the area. The exact nature of the theological error is not clear. Perhaps some phase of gnosticism had become popular. Christ would have been depicted as only one of many stages of enlightenment to which man's mind might aspire in its ascent to God. Colossians speaks concerning two points: the case of Onesimus and the divinity of Christ. Perhaps also, as a result of the false teachings, moral problems had arisen in the communities.

The question of the Ephesian letter remains. Although the letter shares prominence with the main body of Paul's writings from the first century, Paul's authorship is generally denied. If Paul wrote the letter, both its purpose and impersonal tone are difficult to explain. The greetings are short and hardly what might be expected for a letter addressed to a community where he had spent nearly three years. The theory that it may have been a circular letter does not fit with its inclusion in the Philemon, Colossian, Ephesian triad. The area to which Philemon and Colossians are addressed was comparatively limited and was covered by the first two letters. Because some early writings omit the word Ephesus entirely, it seems clear that the letter wasn't addressed to that community. In the second century Marcion thought the letter to have been originally addressed to the Laodicean church, but Colossians already includes that community.

Although on first reading, the letter appears to be an almost exact reproduction of Colossians with the omission of those elements which make it personal and applicable to a specific situation, and with two additions, an exhortation to cooperation and spirituality [4:1-16, 6:10-20], further analysis suggests that someone other than Paul tried to copy the letter.

The style and vocabulary are questionable. It is difficult to find any reason for Paul's having written the letter. Its similarity to Colossians is, therefore, a point against, rather than for Pauline authorship. Although Ephesians has value and insight in its portrayal of the early Christian point of view, the weight of evidence clearly places it outside the Pauline circle. The subject matter indicates a later date than its companions. Christ is no longer the lone foundation of the Church. The apostles have taken his place [2:20-22], heretical sects have had time to make their appearance [4:14], and the church itself is now regarded as a means of revelation. Barnett advances the interesting hypothesis that Onesimus prospered so well in Christian service that he later became Bishop of Ephesus and that it was he who penned the letter.[2] It has already been seen that on the earliest copies no address is given. The letter may well be an encyclical from Ephesus on the subject of the heresies prevalent at the turn of the century.

THE LETTER TO PHILEMON

Structure and Content

The letter of Philemon is perhaps the most personal of all Paul's writings. The salutation is warm and personal. The inclusion of Timothy's name is odd if the first interpretation of the letter is accepted [1:1-3]. A thanksgiving follows immediately after the opening. Paul thanks God, mentioning the addressee in his prayers for he has heard of his great love and faith [1:4-7]. The main point of the letter follows. Paul makes a plea on behalf of Onesimus. Although Paul, being now both an ambassador[3] and prisoner for Christ, has the prerogative to

---

[2] Barnett, p. 185.
[3] Dodd and others prefer the word "ambassador" rather than "aged" of the RV, V.8.

tell what one's Christian duty is, he now asks a favor for Onesimus, who became a son to him while he was in prison. Onesimus may formerly have been of no value to his master, but now he can be valuable to both Paul and his master [1:8-11]. That Paul is sending Onesimus back is a heart-rending experience. Paul would like to keep Onesimus so that he might continue to work for the gospel in Ephesus even as his master would do. But without permission Paul would not keep him. He doesn't want to force good deeds. They must come through free choice to be of value. Perhaps the real reason for separation is that now Onesimus' master can have him in a new relationship, not as a servant, but as a brother in Christ's service, dear to Paul, but dearer to his master because he is bound to him both in flesh and spirit [1:12-16]. If the addressee really feels himself to be a partner of Paul's in Christian service, then he must receive Onesimus as a Christian partner. If Onesimus has stolen, Paul will repay the debt. Paul tells the recipient of the letter to remember that he owes all he is in Christian service to Paul [1:17-19]. Paul asks that he be made joyful and happy through the good actions to come. He writes knowing, he says, that more will be done than he asks [1:20-21].

Paul concludes by asserting that he will soon visit the community and asking that a guest room be kept ready for him [1:22]. Greetings from a list of five companions follow after which the letter ends with a blessing [1:23-25].

OUTLINE OF THE LETTER TO PHILEMON

Salutation, thanksgiving, concerning Onesimus, personalia, greeting and benediction, 1:1-25

Ch. 1 a) Salutation, 1:1-3
      b) Thanksgiving, 1:4-7
      c) Concerning Onesimus, 1:8-21
      d) Personalia, 1:22
      e) Greeting from five companions, 1:23-24
      f) The blessing, 1:25

THE COLOSSIAN LETTER

Structure and Content

The letter contains two main sections, one theological [1:3-3:4] and one dealing with the practical applications of theology [3:5-4:18].[4] The first can be subdivided into five parts: salutation, thanksgiving, and prayer (1:1-14); a part dealing with theology (1:15-23); a personal statement of vocation (1:24-2:7); a polemic against false teachings (2:8-19); and a statement concerning the basis of Christian understanding [2:20-3:4]. The second contains four main subdivisions: Christian behavior [3:5-17]; domestic relations [3:18-4:1]; exhortation to prayer and circumspect behavior [4:2-6]; and lastly, a section dealing with recommendations for Tychicus and Onesimus concluding with greetings and the autograph [4:7-18].

The letter opens with the customary salutation [1:1-2] in which Paul links himself with Timothy. This is followed by thanksgiving and prayer. In the thanksgiving Paul tells that Epaphras was the founder of the church in Colossae and that it was he who brought Paul news of the community [1:3-8]. V.6 indicates the universality of the gospel. The prayer which follows effects a transition to the theological statements concerning the nature of Christ. Paul prays that the Colossians will continue to be filled with a true understanding of God's will and that they may act accordingly [1:9-10]. Paul prays that the Colossians will be strengthened by God; that they will be able to endure any tribulation while giving thanks to God who made them capable of sharing saintly inheritance. God has saved man from the power of darkness. By God's action man now lives in the kingdom of his Son and is thereby saved from sin [1:9-14].

---

[4] C. H. Dodd. Abingdon Bible Cm.

THE LETTERS TO PHILEMON, COLOSSAE, AND EPHESUS

The significance of living under Christ's jurisdiction depends upon a form of Christological understanding. Paul devotes the next six verses to the nature of Christ. By making the finality of salvation through Christ quite clear, the statement counters the Gnostic position that Christ might be simply one stage of enlightenment. Christ visibly expresses the invisible God. He existed before creation and it was through him that everything is made [1:15-16a]. A series of qualifying phrases follow which demonstrate the absolute universality of Christ's rule [1:16b-17]. Christ is the head of the body which is the Church. All life both from the beginning of life at its first inception and rebirth from the dead begins in him. It is God's will that through Christ's divinity and sacrifice on the cross everything in heaven and earth should be reconciled [1:18-20].

The letter says the Colossians live under this Christian economy, and although they have in the past been alienated and antagonized by evil actions, they are now reconciled through Christ's death on the cross. This reconciliation is, however, dependent upon continued faith. The Colossians must not allow themselves to lose the hope which the gospel supplies; Paul is a minister of such universal hope [1:21-23].

In the next section Paul digresses to outline the consequences of conversion in terms of his own vocation. Paul rejoices in suffering for the Colossians because it gives him an opportunity to share in the sufferings which Christ bears for his body which is the Church. Paul is a minister by God's commission to preach his word [1:24-25]. In the past this was a mystery, hidden throughout the ages, but now made known to those who believe and made known by them to the Gentiles. The secret is that Christ in man brings the hope of glory. So the news is proclaimed to all that everyone may be made perfect in Christ. For this reason Paul works as hard as he can with God-given strength [1:26-29].

Paul now refers directly to himself in relation to the Colossian Church. He wants the congregation to know how deeply he cares for them and for the Laodiceans, even though he doesn't know them personally. He wants them to be joined together in Christian love and to be completely enlightened concerning the revelation of God through Christ. All wisdom and knowledge are contained in Christ [2:1-3]. Paul doesn't want the Colossians to be fooled by the persuasive speech of Gnostic teachers. Although he is not present in person, he is with them in spirit, seeing with pleasure the community's solidarity of faith. Having received Christ, they must act accordingly. Their faith should continue to be cultivated along the lines which they were taught and they should be very thankful [2:4-7].

In the section which follows Paul returns to theology to clarify the Christian position in reference to Gnostic heresies. Paul warns the Colossians against the assumption that intellectualism rather than Christ, can be a means of salvation. God is revealed through Christ alone, and man can be fulfilled only through him who is the head of all things [2:8-10]. The next five verses are typically Pauline. The Colossians were circumcised in the circumcision of Christ, having shared in Christ's death. Through baptism, they are now dead to sin and likewise share in resurrection to a new life. Having once been dead because of their sinfulness and their uncircumcised state (being outside the law), they have been given a new life by God's forgiveness. The law was obliterated by Christ's action on the cross. Christ thereby triumphed over all powers [2:11-15].

Paul believes he has shown that Christ is above all powers that might conceivably exist. The Gnostics believed revelation was experienced in degrees mediated by different levels of spiritual beings. Further, they felt that certain ascetic practices made revelatory achievement possible by releasing the spirit from the bondage of the flesh. Paul now refutes the validity of these practices. He urges the Colossians not to be led by those who make a great issue out of food regulations, feast day observations, or special religious seasons, all of which are mere shadows of reality. The real thing is Christ. The Colossians are not to be deprived of the fruit of their faith by submitting to the worship of angels, the product of mistaken unspiritual understanding which doesn't recognize the "Head" [5] which unifies the body's growth [2:16-19].

Since the Colossians have died with Christ to this world's principles, why should they subject themselves to man-made ritual ordinances which will change in time? These things have some semblance of value in facilitating worship, humility and bodily asceticism, but are of no real worth against the dictates of the flesh [2:20-23].[6]

Because the Colossians share Christ's resurrection, they are to be motivated by values which come from God. Paul says that their minds should be directed toward heavenly, rather than worldly things to which they are dead. Although their true life is hidden for the present, when Christ appears again they will share in his glory [3:1-4].

Paul now turns to activities which can be expected to result from conversion. Certain worldly conduct is no longer permissible. Sexual immorality, lustful behavior, covetous actions, these things, forms of idolatry, can no longer be countenanced. This sort of behavior brings God's wrath on those who do not obey him. Once the Colossians were ruled by such things, which are now to be cast away. As they have put away their old nature and have assumed a new nature which seeks to emulate Christ, anger, malice, untruth, and scurrility can no longer be a part of Colossian life. In this new life, Paul asserts, no distinction exists between men. Christ is the only important thing. The Colossians, who are now God's elect, must behave accordingly. A list of virtuous actions follows and culminates in an exhortation to love one another [3:5-13]. Peace must rule among the Colossians as it rules in the body of Christ, of which they are a part. Christ's teaching is to live in their hearts to make them wise, and they should teach one another with psalms and hymns singing praise to God. All actions, both of word and deed, should bear Christ's stamp and

---

[5] Christ the Head of the Body of the Church.

[6] The sentence V.23 has been translated and interpreted in many different ways. The line as it appears in the text is senseless and is probably the result of an early corruption.

should be transacted with thanksgiving to God through Christ [3:14-17].

Paul now applies Christian ethics to domestic relationships. Wives are to show their husbands proper respect and husbands are to love their wives with sympathetic understanding. Children are to be obedient, for authority has a place in God's plan, but parents are not to be over-authoritative. Slaves are to obey their masters in this world, not simply to curry favor, but because authority is part of God's order. Paul urges his readers to work hard, for in the last analysis faithful service is service to God and men will be judged accordingly. Man's final reward is heavenly, rather than mundane. Status makes no difference to God's judgments. Masters must treat their slaves fairly. Masters as well as slaves are subject to God [3:18-4:1].

Lastly Paul exhorts the Colossians to pray persistently and especially for him so that he may be given the opportunity to continue his ministry the pursuit of which has presently placed him in jail. The request for special intercession on his behalf is parenthetical. In the next verse Paul completes his list of Christian activity. He urges discretion in dealings with non-Christians. He tells Christians to make every minute count, be courteous, and to season speech to the taste of those to whom it is spoken [4:2-6].

The letter concludes with the statement that Tychicus will bring news with Onesimus and recommends both messengers highly [4:7-8]. A long list of personal greetings follows [4:10-15]. Verse 16 asks that the letter be read in Laodicea and suggests that the Colossians also read the Laodicean letter. In the end Paul appeals to Archippus that he may live up to the imperatives of his faith [4:17]. The last verse is an autograph.

OUTLINE OF THE COLOSSIAN LETTER

I. Theology, Christian understanding of life, and answers to false teachings, 1:1-3:4

Ch. 1 A. Salutation, thanksgiving, and prayer, 1:1-14
  a) Salutation, 1:1-2

THE EPHESIAN LETTER

Like the Colossian letter, Ephesians contains two main divisions: the first is concerned for the most part with theology [1:1-3:21], while the second deals with various applications of Christianity to specific life situations [4:1-6:24]. The first section can be subdivided into four smaller divisions: the first deals with God's election and thanksgiving; the second concerns redemption through Christ [2:1-10]; the third asserts that the Gentiles are unified in Christ [2:11-22]; the fourth explains "Paul's" mission and includes a prayer [3:1-21]. The second main section contains six divisions, the first of which is concerned with Christian unity [4:1-16]; the second outlines the consequences of Christian belief [4:17-32]; the third lists certain types of Christian conduct [5:1-21]; the fourth lists the duties of husbands and wives in respect to each other [5:22-6:9]; the fifth is an impassioned exhortation to Christian action [6:10-20]; and the last speaks of Tychicus and ends with a blessing [6:21-24].

The letter opens with an unusually brief salutation. Many early manuscripts omit the phrase "at Ephesus" and Marcion in the second century referred to the letter as being addressed to the Laodiceans [1:1-2]. "Paul" says God has blessed the Ephesians (Christians), choosing them even before creation to share the relation of sonship through the action of Christ [1:3-5]. This was accomplished by God's grace freely given through Christ's sacrifice which brought forgiveness [1:6-7]. God has made his will known. Everything in creation should be unified in Christ [1:8-10]. The Ephesians are part of God's heritage for the purpose of acting to his glory. In receiving the gospel and in believing it, they are guaranteed reception of their inheritance and a part in the final glory of God [1:11-15].

As in the corresponding portion of the Colossian letter [Col. 1:3-8], "Paul" now gives thanks to God for the Ephesian church [1:15-16]. The section is considerably shorter than in Colossians and moves immediately to intercession. "Paul" prays that God will reveal himself further to the Ephesians so that they may fully understand the greatness of their destiny in Christ, who was raised from the dead by God's power to sit in judgment over all powers. Christ is the head of the Church which embodies his Spirit [1:17-23].

As a result of these circumstances man lives in a new spiritual economy. The section is close to the thought expressed in Colossians 1:13-20, 2:20. Once the Ephesians were worldly and lived under the jurisdiction of evil powers. They were, therefore, in a state of death, but through Christ they have been made alive [2:1-3]. God, being merciful, raised man, even though he lived in a condition of sin, to a condition of heavenly existence through Christ [2:4-6]. Future generations will thereby be able to understand God's generosity and grace to man through Christ. Man is saved through faith by grace which is the result, not of man's activity but of God's free gift [2:7-9]. Man was in the first instance made by God, and then made complete in Christ. Good actions on man's part are the result of his relationship to Christ [2:10].

"Paul" now stresses the unity of all mankind through Christ. The Ephesians are to remember that they were once outside the law and were separated from Christ outside the community of Judaism without hope of salvation [2:11-12]. But Christ has superseded the old law, has broken down the barrier which existed between Jew and Gentile, and has made peace. From two he has made one new man [2:13-15]. Man is now unified by the cross. That enmity no longer exists is a fact preached far and wide. The Gentiles are no longer outsiders, but are part of the heavenly kingdom [2:16-19]. "Paul" now shifts from the metaphor of body to building: the Gentiles are now part of the building, God's holy temple, whose foundation is the apostles and prophets and whose cornerstone is Christ [2:20-22].

"Paul" tells in the next section of his calling and the special revelation made to him that Jew and Gentile are equal in God's purpose. "Paul" is Christ's prisoner for the Gentiles. God has given him unique insight by direct revelation. As "Paul" has already indicated by his writings, previous generations did not know that the Gentiles were to share equally in God's inheritance [3:1-6]. "Paul" was made a minister by God's grace to preach the good news to the Gentiles [3:7-9]. All men are to understand the mystery which was concealed in the past. All powers are now to know God's purpose in which Christ, who is the source of man's confidence, is central. Although "Paul" is imprisoned over these great issues, the Ephesians are not to be upset by his confinement which is to their honor [3:10-13].

"Paul" now turns to intercede with God, asking that he will grant the Ephesians such inward spiritual strength that Christ will enter their hearts by faith so that, being rooted in love, they may understand with the saints the full extent of Christ's love which goes beyond normal comprehension. In this way they will be filled with godliness [3:14-19]. The prayer ends with an ascription [3:20-21].

The second main section of the letter begins with an exhortation of Christian unity. "Paul" asks the Ephesians to live according to the demands of their inheritance. He asks them to be humble and patient with each other and to preserve unity by love [4:1-3]. All men are part of one body, the result of one Spirit. So all men share in a common calling, one God, one hope, one faith and one baptism, but each man also has a different function within the whole, according to the particular gifts Christ has given him [4:4-8]. V.8 is a quotation from Psalm 68:18. (If Christ ascended into a heavenly realm, he must have descended to the world. The ascended Christ is the same as he who came to earth.) "Paul" goes on to assert that various gifts were given to men. Some were made apostles, others prophets, some preachers, others teachers in order to consolidate the body of Christians into a single unified faith, aspiring toward the full maturity of Christ's stature [4:11-12]. No longer can Christians be like intellectual children, easily moved by every erroneous outside influence; now they must grow up to Christ, the Head. The body articulated by joints grows in love through the proper function of each part [4:13-16].

Christians can no longer behave like pagans who are motivated by intellectual conceit and blindness, alienated from God by ignorance, as a result, living a life of sensuality and vice [4:17-19]. Christians do not learn such things through Christ if they hear him properly. Christianity demands that such things be repudiated. The old way of life is to be abandoned. The Christian lives a new life of righteousness, holiness, and truth [4:20-24].

A list of Christian imperatives follows: speak truth; don't be controlled by anger; do not steal, but work for a living in order to be able to help others; do not use scurrilous language; do not offend the Holy Spirit, the source of redemption; put away all bitterness, anger, abusive behavior, and maliciousness. The Ephesians are to be kind, tender, and forgiving even as Christ was all these things to them [4:25-32].

The next section continues to specify Christian conduct. The lines have a familiar ring coming from the Colossian letter: be God-like as children who look to their father's example; love even as Christ loved to the point of sacrifice; do not tolerate sexual immorality and covetousness, vice, light conversation, and bad jokes. No person guilty of sexual immorality or covetousness, a form of idolatry, will be part of God's inheritance. Don't be deceived by those who sin. God's judgment comes to the disobedient because of these things. Have no part of them. The Ephesians were once in darkness, but now have become enlightened and must act accordingly having nothing to do with sinfulness. The sort of activity associated with sinful people cannot be tolerated. God's light makes sin recognizable [5:1-13]. V.41 is scriptural. Live circumspectly. Make every minute count. Abide by God's will. Don't become drunk with wine, but be filled with the Holy Spirit. Sing praises to God with hymns and psalms. Give thanks to God in Christ's name and be subservient to each other through reverence to Christ [5:14-21]. The passage parallels Colossians [3:14-17].

The sections 5:22-23 and 6:1-9 closely parallel Colossians 3:18-4:1 (see p. 274).

At the last, "Paul" exhorts the Ephesians to be prepared to fight against the forces of evil. Put on God's armour because the battle isn't simply against the flesh of this world, but is a fight against the powers of spiritual evil whose source is outside the world.[7] God's armour is made up of the belt of truth, the breastplate of righteousness, the shoes of the gospel, the shield of faith, the helmet of salvation, and the sword of God's word [6:10-17]. Lastly, "Paul" exhorts the Ephesians to

---

[7] Paul's cosmology evidently included fallen angels who were at war with righteousness.

prayer, to be alert and to pray that he may be made lyric in his proclamation of the gospel [6:18-20].

The letter concludes with a recommendation for Tychicus and a blessing [6:21-24].

OUTLINE OF THE EPHESIAN LETTER

I. God's election, redemption, Christology and "Paul's" mission, 1:1-3:21

Ch. 1 A. *Salutation, God's election, prayer, thanksgiving, and intercession, 1:1-23*

    a) Salutation, 1:1-2
    b) God's election, 1:3-5
    c) Redemption through Christ, 1:6-7
    d) The Ephesians to receive God's promise, 1:8-15
    e) Thanksgiving and prayer, 1:16-23

Ch. 2 B. *Redemption through Christ, 2:1-10*

    C. *Gentiles unified with Jews in Christ, 2:11-22*

    a) Gentiles once outside the law without hope of salvation, 2:11-12
    b) Jew and Gentile unified by Christ's action, 2:13-15
    c) Gentiles now share in the kingdom, 2:16-19
    d) Gentiles are now part of God's building, 2:20-22

Ch. 3 D. *"Paul's" mission and prayer, 3:1-21*

    a) "Paul's" mission, 3:1-13
    b) Prayer, 3:14-21

II. Christian unity, conduct, family relationships, exhortation, concerning Tychicus and benediction, 4:1-6:24

Ch. 4 A. *Christian unity through love, 4:1-16*

    a) An exhortation to unity, 4:1-3
    b) Unity and diversity of gifts, 4:4-9
    c) Divisity of functions to achieve unity of faith, 4:10-16

    B. *Consequences of Christian belief, 4:17-32*

    a) Difference between Christian and pagan living, 4:17-24
    b) Christian behavior, 4:25-32

Part III

XVIII

A New Era

The scope of this reference book covers three periods in the development of Christianity: the period of pre-Christian beginnings during the lifetime of Jesus before the faith was understood during which time it was embryonic within Judaism, the period immediately following the resurrection experiences when the faith came to birth and grew to adolescence, and the period following early apostolic times which saw Christianity grow to manhood with clear statements of doctrine, church organizations and a disciplined leadership. Although the early period is described by the Gospels and Acts, the writings themselves (with the exception of Mark), belong to the last. The times immediately following the resurrection which represent Christianity in its infancy come to the twentieth century through Paul's pen. Both Paul and Mark wrote before the fall of Jerusalem in 70 A.D. A time of darkness follows for which no literature gives light. Paul made the transition from Judaism to Gentile Christianity and gave the new faith to the world, but his illumination on the Damascus road was darkened forever by a Roman dungeon and Jerusalem lay dead before Titus' sword.

With the Jerusalem elders dead or dispersed and Paul lost to the world, the infant church was left without leadership. The army of the faithful marched without headquarters until new officers came up from the ranks. As the years passed, strag-

glers were brought into line, discipline returned, a marching
manual was developed, generals directed the leadership, and a
judge advocate corps came into being. A strong faith and a
definitive Christian position dealt with the philosophies and
religious conflicts of the time. Heresy became a possibility because orthodoxy was defined. Ecclesiastical organization appeared. Orders of the clergy were recognized. Bishops, priests
and deacons presided at church functions. Christianity emerged
to take its place in the big world of philosophy, geopolitical
tension, national conflict, councils, persecution, dissension, and
war. The writings which remain to be studied belong to this
period and represent new authorship and subject matter geared
to a new demand.

THE PASTORAL EPISTLES

Background

From the earliest times the first and second letter to Timothy and the letter to Titus have been attributed to Paul. For
over a century they have been commonly referred to as the
Pastoral Epistles, because at first glance they appear to be letters of instruction concerning pastoral functions. Neither assumption is correct. Although the length of this work does not
permit a full treatment of all the critical problems involved,
sufficient evidence can be given to point the way.

The subject matter of the three letters as well as the language almost certainly places them beyond Paul's time. During
his lifetime the kingdom of God was momentarily expected.
In later eras the expectation dimmed and was no longer fore-
most in Christian thought. The Pastorals are not concerned
with it as an immediate reference. Orders of the clergy did not
exist in Paul's time. The Pastorals accept them. Furthermore,
lines of orthodoxy were drawn against philosophies which
were not an issue in the first century. The writings are strongly
slanted against Gnostic practices. Lastly, Paul, throughout his

known letters, always sees salvation as the result of a changed inward man brought about through faith by grace, while in the Pastorals religion becomes the acceptance of dogma.

Furthermore, it is hard to visualize these writings as addressed to Timothy and Titus. Of all persons in the ancient world, they should have been most familiar with Paul's authority and devotion, as well as the proper way of managing Christian activities inside and outside the church. If all the evidence is considered, the critical student is forced to the conclusion that the writings are neither letters nor pastoral and that they were not written by Paul nor received by Timothy and Titus.

Rather than letters, the writings may more properly be described as manuals dealing for the most part with Christian behavior. The names of Timothy and Titus are simply a literary device, a frame for instruction which seeks Pauline authority for its sanction.

Opinion varies on the date and place of authorship. Agreement is general that the Epistles were written after the turn of the century. The exact time cannot be placed and has been variously fixed from 100-125 A.D. to as late as 180 A.D. Although the letters specify respective places of origin, this evidence cannot be accepted. A better clue is the style, which is clearly Roman. An educated guess, therefore, might fix Rome as the point of origin. The texts were probably directed toward general Christian leadership. Some scholars feel that the three Epistles were written as one. Certainly they can be so closely associated that the background for one speaks for them all.

FIRST TIMOTHY

Structure and Content

First Timothy can be divided into seven sections: a brief salutation [1:1-2] is followed by the problems and qualifications of the Christian teacher, a thanksgiving and a charge [1:3-20]; the second consists of an exhortation to prayer, Christological considerations, and a delineation of the status of women in church affairs [2:1-15]; the third concerns criteria for Christian leadership [3:1-13]; the fourth acts as a title which explains the letter's purpose [3:14-16]; the fifth urges zeal against false teaching [4:1-16]; the sixth specifies action for certain cases [5:1-6:2]; and the seventh is, for the most part, a continued exhortation to godly behavior, followed by a short final warning and a benediction [6:3-21].

After a very brief salutation from "Paul" to "Timothy" [1:1-2], the Epistle moves at once to consider some of the problems and qualifications of Christian teachers. Those who teach must not become involved with pagan doctrines, but bear in mind that they are in a position of stewardship in respect to God's word. The teacher's job is to train within the limits of Christian love, clear thinking, clear conscience and absolute loyalty to the faith [1:3-5]. Some have forsaken this line in favor of meaningless philosophical wanderings bolstered by quotations from the law [1:6-7]. The law is good when properly applied. Its greatest value, however, is not for the righteous, but for those without principle [1:8-9a]. A list of examples follows and the section ends with a summary stating that the law is against any teaching that is contrary to the gospel which was entrusted to "Paul."

In the next section "Paul" digresses to give thanks for his conversion. He was at one time a blasphemer and a persecutor, but having been these things through ignorance he cannot be blamed. Without any doubt, Christ came into the world to save sinners and "Paul" was among the worst. The example should be clear; if Christ were willing and able to save "Paul," he would do so for all believers that they too might inherit eternal life. The paragraph ends with an ascription [1:9b-17].

"Paul" now charges "Timothy" with the job of teaching the Christian way of life as he was ordained to do. "Timothy" is to hold to the faith with a clear conscience. Some have failed in this respect and have wrecked the faith. Hymenaeus and

Alexander were excommunicated for their behavior [1:18-20]. The charge acts as an introduction to the remaining portion of the letter. In Chapter 2 "Paul" exhorts Christians to indulge in all types of prayer for all types of people. Even kings and persons in authority are to be included in order to assure tranquillity and acceptance for Christians [2:1-2]. Such action is proper in God's sight. All men are to be brought to an understanding of the truth and will thereby be saved. Jesus Christ is God's only representative. Jesus gave himself as a ransom for man's sins, and Paul was appointed a missionary to the Gentiles in this connection [2:3-7].

In stressing the function of prayer in Christian life "Paul" makes his understanding of female status clear. Christian men are to pray at every opportunity in an atmosphere of peace. Women are to be unostentatious and quiet in public worship [2:8-10]. Women are to be subservient to men. "Paul" refers to the story of Adam and Eve to demonstrate woman's position, but follows with a statement of female mission. Women are saved through their proper function, motherhood [2:11-15].

The first part of Chapter 3 concerns church leadership and indicates a degree of ecclesiastical organization as yet undeveloped in Paul's time. It states that, without any doubt, a bishop must be a man beyond reproach [3:1-2a]. There follows a list of virtues which includes sexual morality, temperance, honesty, self control, generosity and the ability to command. A bishop must also be mature in the faith [3:2b-7]. The criteria for deacons are no less strict [3:8-13]. The chapter concludes with two verses, one of which explains why "Paul" has written and the second of which is probably a quotation from an early Christian hymn [3:14-15].

The next chapter goes on to say that the Spirit foretold the aberrations of faith which are presently manifest, false doctrine, hypocrisy, pagan ritual, and food regulations. Everything, however, that God has made is good if properly used [4:1-5]. A good minister will convey these facts to the Christian community holding Christ's ideals before them and refus-

ing to have any traffic with fictitious and profane teaching
[4:6-7a]. A minister must discipline himself in godliness.
Ascetic practices may help for a time, but spiritual discipline
involves both temporal and eternal life. Without any doubt
this is true. For this reason Christians labor and strive for godliness. These things are to be taught by good example which
every young man can give [4:7b-12]. Young ministers are not
to forget that they received the gift of proclaiming God's
word through the laying on of hands.[1] They must continue
to study and give themselves entirely to the job at hand. In
doing so they save themselves as well as those to whom they
minister [4:13-16].

For the most part, the remaining portion of the Epistle
deals with the type of action to be taken by Christian ministers
in specific cases. A rebuke to older people must be tempered by
consideration for age. Even younger people are to be shown
sympathetic understanding [5:1-2]. The passage which follows deals with the special case of widows who were usually
in need of help because, in the ancient world, a woman had
no means of support other than her family. First "Paul" suggests that it is the duty of the immediate family to care for
the widowed, but in the event that no family exists, the community must be responsible [5:3, 4, 8]. Widows over sixty
should certainly be cared for, but younger women had better
marry again and be about the proper business of womanhood,
housekeeping and raising children [5:5, 6, 7, 9-16].

The last part of Chapter 5 concerns church officials. An
official who teaches and acts in an administrative capacity is
worth double pay. To substantiate his claim "Paul" quotes
from Scripture [Deut. 25:4, Mt. 10:10, Lk. 10:7]. Accusation
against such people must be presented by two or three witnesses. If reproof is necessary, it should be public in order to
be an example to others. Above all things, impartiality must be
preserved [5:17-21]. The reference to "laying hands on a man"
refers to commissioning or instatement, not to violence [5:22].
V.23 perhaps refers to some disorder of Timothy's supposedly

[1] Acts 8:18.

known to Paul, but this can only be assumed if the authorship is genuine. Otherwise the verse becomes a directive concerning the moderate use of alcohol. The Epistle goes on to assert that some judgments are easily made whereas others require time. The same holds true for good works. Some are immediately discernible, but all inevitably become apparent in time [5:24-25].

Christian slaves are, the Epistle asserts, to serve their masters well and must not take advantage of Christian brotherhood [6:1-2].

"Paul" now turns back to his opening theme. False teachers can be detected by manifestations of improper values, conceit, ignorance, silly arguments, strife, innuendo, etc. In them piety is seen as a way of making money [6:3-5]. Godliness is gainful, but not in that fashion. Food and shelter are all a man really needs. Those who direct their energies otherwise become corrupt [6:6-11]. In the next seven verses "Paul" exhorts "Timothy" to avoid this sort of corrupting influence. Rather than worldly gain he is to be concerned with eternal life, and with fighting the good fight until the second coming of Christ [6:12-16].

The Epistle goes on to say that the rich must not be preoccupied with their wealth, but must trust in God, who indeed gives all things for man's pleasure. They are to find pleasure in good deeds and willingness to help others. In this way they prepare for eternal life [6:17-19].

At the close of the Epistle "Paul" entreats "Timothy" to guard the faith entrusted to him and not to be led astray by false teachings. The Epistle ends with a very brief grace [6:20-21].

OUTLINE OF FIRST TIMOTHY

I. Salutation, a teacher's qualifications and work, and a charge, 1:1-20

Ch. 1   a) Salutation, 1:1-2
         b) The teacher at work, 1:3-11

SECOND TIMOTHY

Structure

Second Timothy, which is only one third as long as the first letter, can be divided into five sections. The salutation is followed by a relatively long thanksgiving and commendation more reminiscent of Paul than anything in First Timothy. The section contains a brief parenthesis saying that Phygelus and Hermagenes were among a large group of defectors in Asia and mentioning the care Onesiphorus gave to Paul [1: 1-18]. The second section deals with the qualifications of Christian ministers [2:1-26]. The third continues advice to Timothy that was started in the second section and warns against false teachers [3:1-17]. The fourth consists of a final charge [4:1-18], and the fifth of last personal instructions, salutations, and a brief benediction [4:9-22].

Content

The salutation is nearly identical to the opening lines of the first letter [1:1-2]. "Paul" affectionately thanks God for "Timothy's" conversion [1:3-5]. He reminds "Timothy" of his ordination and beseeches him to continue his work with enthusiasm. "Timothy" must not be ashamed of his faith nor of the fact that "Paul" is presently a prisoner. "Timothy" is to remember that Christians are not saved by their own works, but by the grace of God. God's purpose is eternal and existed before creation and has been made manifest by Christ in the present [1:6-9]. Christ is victorious over death and brings man immortality through the gospel. Because "Paul" is an apostle of the gospel, he is imprisoned, but he is not ashamed, nor is he worried about the truth of the gospel. He knows Christ and is certain that he will be vindicated [1:10-12]. "Paul" entreats "Timothy" to hold to the party line. "Timothy" is to cherish the gospel through the Holy Spirit which dwells in men [1:13-14]. Three parenthetical verses interrupt the section. They explain that Phygelus and Hermogenes defected from the faith with many others in Asia and that Onesiphorus ministered to "Paul" while he was in prison [1:15-18].

The second section lacks continuity, but deals generally with the qualifications for Christian ministry in reference to "Timothy." "Paul" now beseeches "Timothy" to carry on the work which he (Paul) initiated. He asks that "Timothy" be strengthened by grace, that he continue to pass on "Paul's" teachings, and that he be willing to suffer the hardships "Paul" has endured. A series of metaphors follows "Paul's" entreaty: as a soldier is willing to suffer hardship for his cause, as an athlete trains in order to win, as a farmer works hard to obtain the harvest, so the Christian must also strive. "Timothy" is to bear in mind that Christ, the descendant of David, rose from the dead. Although "Paul" has been imprisoned like a common criminal for this gospel, God's word goes on. "Paul" is willing to endure anything so that God's elect may obtain salvation through Jesus Christ [2:1-10]. Without any doubt in suffering and dying with Christ, Christians also share his inheritance. If they deny him, they will be denied. Christ is always faithful; he cannot be other than what his nature prescribes [2.11-13].

In the next section, for a few verses, "Paul" digresses from direct reference to "Timothy" to give some general advice. Ministers are bound by certain specifications. They are to be reminded of the gospel's chief points as outlined by "Paul" and must avoid mere verbiage which can undermine faith. He exhorts "Timothy" to be a workman who has nothing of which to be ashamed [2:14-15]. He asserts that unchristian teaching spreads like an infection. Hymanaeus and Philetus, for example, made mistakes about the resurrection, saying that it had already occurred and hence undermining the faith of others. God's truth remains firm, however, and two things are apparent: God knows his own, and all true Christians must have no part in unrighteousness [2:16-19].

"Paul" then writes that in a large house many different types of vessels are used, each with a different value and function. God's household is the same. There if a man purges himself of evil, he makes himself a vessel of value and honor. The minister (Timothy) must flee from youthful desires and, in the company of the converted, must follow righteousness, faith, love, and peace. God's servant must not be a man of violence. He must be self-controlled and gentle. He must tactfully correct those who oppose him, with the knowledge that God may win them to truth. In this way they may see things properly and escape from the devil's snare [2:20-26].

In the next chapter "Paul" continues to direct "Timothy"

and warns of perilous times ahead. The chapter opens with a list of evils which the last days may produce. Every type of evil is defined. Although people who indulge in evil practices may even give the appearance of godliness, ultimately they won't manifest God's righteousness. "Timothy" is to have nothing to do with such people for whom silly, sinful women are an easy prey. As Jannes and Jambres withstood Moses, so will these corrupt men withstand the truth. In the end their folly will be recognized [3:1-9]. "Paul" asserts that "Timothy" has followed his teaching and example. "Timothy" knows how God saved "Paul" at Antioch, Iconium, and Lystra. All of Christ's followers can expect persecution, while evil people become increasingly bad. "Paul" admonishes "Timothy" to continue to abide by the things he has learned which he knows are true because of their source. He is to remember that his knowledge goes back to childhood and Scripture (O.T.) which can bring him to salvation through faith in Christ. All Scripture is inspired by God and has a proper teaching function [3:10-17].

In Chapter 4 "Paul" gives "Timothy" a last charge followed by personal instructions. The passage is strongly nostalgic. "Paul's" ministry is drawing to a close. In God's name he exhorts "Timothy" to preach the word. He must always bear in mind the urgency of his calling. The time will come when men will turn away from truth for easier teachings which suit their lusts. "Timothy" is to remain sober and strong in the faith. "Paul's" time is, however, at hand. He is ready to depart and does not regret the time spent in God's glorious service for he will be in the good company of all those who have loved God through the vision of Christ [4:1-8].

The Epistle closes with personal instructions and news. Demas has proved unreliable and has gone to Thessalonica. Crescens has gone to Galatia and Titus is in Dalmatia. Luke remains with "Paul." "Paul" asks that "Timothy" bring Mark with him for Mark is always useful. Tychicus has been sent to Ephesus. "Paul" asks that "Timothy" bring his cloak from Troas and warns against Alexander. He tells of his trials (possibly in an arena) and reiterates the fact that his mission is to the Gentiles. With a final statement of his trust in God and with personal salutations, "Paul" closes the Epistle [4:9-22].

OUTLINE OF SECOND TIMOTHY

I. Salutation, thanksgiving and commendation (1:1-18)

Ch. 1   a) Salutation, 1:1-2
        b) Thanksgiving, 1:3-9
        c) "Paul's" mission and "Timothy's" trust, 1:10-14
        d) Concerning Phygelus, Hermagenes, and Onesiphorus, 1:15-18

II. Qualifications for Christian ministers, 2:1-26

Ch. 2   a) A personal exhortation to Timothy, 2:1-13
        b) Counsel concerning Christian ministers, 2:14-19
        c) A metaphor and further advice, 2:20-26

III. Warning and advice continued, 3:1-17

Ch. 3   a) Warning, 3:1-9
        b) Advice continued, 3:10-17
Ch. 4

IV. A final charge, 4:1-8

V. Last personal instructions, salutations and benediction, 4:9-22

        a) Last personal instructions, 4:9-18
        b) Personal salutations, 4:19-21
        c) Benediction, 4:22

XIX

The Epistle to Titus

Structure

The Epistle to Titus opens with a comparatively long salutation [1:1-4] followed by four sections: The first concerns instruction for "Titus' " work in Crete with particular reference to qualifications for church officials and the unruliness of the Cretans [1:5-16], the second tells how the gospel should be applied to various classes of people [2:1-15] the third asks that Christian attitudes be maintained [3:1-11], the fourth concludes the Epistle with personal instructions, salutations, and a brief benediction [3:12-15].

Content

The salutation contains "Paul's" basic theology. "Paul" has been called into God's service and follows the faith of God's elect which promises eternal life. God, who cannot lie, promised this before creation. God has now, at his discretion, made the truth known through "Paul" [1:1-4].

In the second section "Paul" outlines qualifications for church leadership. Apparently "Titus" has been left in charge of the church in Crete. "Paul" says that leaders who are above reproach must be appointed. He then lists qualifications. Church leaders must have the ability both to win converts and to withstand the opposition [1:5-9]. Many unruly men, particularly among the Jews, must be silenced. These men work for money and teach false doctrine. Cretans have been described by one of their own number as liars, beasts, and idle gluttons. They must be severely warned against Jewish untruth. No longer are they to be permitted to emphasize Jewish fables and the legal technicalities of defilement. Defilement is actually a subjective matter. A clean mind assures complete cleanliness, but an unclean mind will defile everything. Ceremonies don't necessarily change a man's mental state. Although they claim to know God, these people show otherwise by their activities [1:10-16].

The third section gives advice concerning the application of the gospel to particular categories of people. The first nine verses ask that all classes of people put the gospel into practice. The old are to act as examples to the young, but youth is no excuse for irresponsibility. Young men and women are to behave with circumspection. By so doing they will show themselves examples of applied Christianity. They are to be above reproach and to leave no ground for criticism from the unconverted [2:1-8]. Likewise slaves can exemplify Christian doctrine by faithful behavior [2:9].

"Paul" ends the section with a brief doctrinal summary. Man has been brought into a state of salvation by God's grace. Worldly lusts are no longer a motivation. Man must live in the new economy of God's grace upheld by the constant hope of Christ's second coming. Christ gave himself on the cross to redeem mankind and to make all people like himself, clean and pure, with hearts set on good behavior. "Titus" is to teach these things. He is to let no one treat him with contempt [2:11-15].

In the fourth section "Paul" lists certain expedient Christian attitudes. Christians are to obey those who are in authority and work willingly when required to do so. They are not to be slanderous or argumentative, but gentle and well-behaved. Before Christ's love was made manifest, men were foolish, disobedient, and dishonest, living by worldly lusts and pleasures

and were filled with envy and hatred. Man wasn't changed by
his own action, but by God's merciful grace. Man was cleansed
and regenerated by the Holy Spirit which came through
Christ. Being saved by grace, man now can inherit eternal life.
"Paul" asserts that without any doubt these things are true.
Titus is to affirm the truth with utmost confidence so that those
who believe may make manifest their faith in good activities.
Such things are good for everyone. Preoccupation with foolish
speculation, genealogies, controversies, and arguments about
the law serve no good purpose. A man who persists in such
activity after two warnings should be expelled from the Christian community. He brings on his own condemnation by his
actions [3:1-11].

The Epistle concludes with instructions concerning
"Titus' " relief, Artemas or Tychicus. "Paul" says that "Titus"
should encourage Zenas and Apollos. He asserts that Christians
are to be self-supporting. The Epistle ends with a brief salutation and benediction [3:12-15].

OUTLINE OF THE EPISTLE TO TITUS

I. Salutation, 1:1-4
Ch. 1

II. Qualifications for church leadership, 1:5-16
    a) Qualifications for leaders, 1:5-9
    b) The unruliness of Cretans, 1:10-11
    c) Such people to be silenced, 1:12-16

III. Applied Christianity, 2:1-15
Ch. 2   *a*) Christianity applied to various classes of people, 2:1-10
    b) The heart of the gospel, 2:11-15

IV. Christian attitudes to be maintained, 3:1-11
Ch. 3

V. Instructions concerning "Titus' " relief, salutation, and
benediction, 3:12-15

XX

The Epistle to the Hebrews

Background

The Epistle to the Hebrews is one of the most uncertain of all New Testament writings in respect to authorship, date, and destination. Even the title seems to be a misnomer. The Epistle opens without salutation and greeting, and, although the last chapter which mentions Timothy is somewhat Pauline in style, it is generally considered to be of different authorship from the preceding twelve. The writing, therefore, gives no clue either at the beginning or end as to its point of origin or addressee. Modern scholarship denies Pauline authorship almost without exception. Furthermore, the Epistle offers no evidence for apostolic or near apostolic authorship. At one time or another scholars have suggested as author nearly all of the familiar New Testament names: Paul's companions, Silas, Barnabas, Timothy, Aquila, Priscilla, Luke, and even Clement of Rome. To attribute the Epistle to these or any particular name is little better than guesswork and serves neither to explain nor substantiate the writing.

The writing itself suggests authorship outside the Pauline era. Unlike Paul's letters which substantiate their authority by reference to his conversion and call, the writing in Hebrews indicates secondhand knowledge of Christianity originating in a later era [2:3]. Further the style and theology are clearly not Pauline. Not only is his personal touch absent from the Epistle, but his chief points are also lacking. Justification by faith, mystical union with Christ, dying and rising with Christ, these familiar themes do not appear. The second coming is not a great issue in Hebrews, and salvation is, unlike its counterpart in Pauline doctrine, a future event.

The author is evidently a second or third generation Christian. He writes by far the best Greek of the New Testament. Hebrew does not color his sentence structure. Theologically he is clearly a Platonist who accepts Philo's understanding of the Logos. Drawing heavily on Plato's world of ideals, heavenly archetypes, and the only true reality, he depicts earthly things as shadows or reflections of the true and real. Applied to Christology the philosophy is used to explain the significance of Christ's sacrifice on the cross. Hebrews draws, in respect to religion, a parallel to Platonic doctrine. The Old Testament represents the earthly shadow, whereas the New Testament is heavenly reality.[1] Christianity is the final and complete religion. Unlike the repetitive, earthly, Levitical sacrifice, Christ's sacrifice was single and final. As a result the opportunity for forgiveness comes only once. Sin after baptism and redemption cannot be removed. Relapse from faith is fatal. His cosmology accepts a heavenly hierarchy existing in a series of heavens (seven). If he were a Jew, he was clearly a Hellenist. He was also certainly a man of strong Christian conviction. To say more is to venture into uncertain speculation.

The Epistle evidently originated outside Italy and may have been directed to Roman Christians [13:24]. Agreement is general on the first point, but not on the second. Because the writings are known to have been popular in Alexandria, they might have originated there, but Ephesus fits almost as well. In fact any Christian center where Paul's works were known could form a background for the writing, because it was generally included in the early Pauline portfolio. Chapter 13 in which the Roman destination is implied is subject to serious doubt as part of the original. If it is deleted, the Epistle

[1] 8:2, 8:5, 9:23, 10:1.

has the characteristics of a general writing to all Christians who were suffering persecution and trials in the era. On the one hand the letter seeks to explain and prove Christ's divine mission and on the other it describes the terrible consequences of relapse from faith.

Granted the Epistle places itself outside the Pauline era because both its readers and its author admit to receiving Christianity secondhand, it was probably written after 70 A.D. [2:3]. The letter refers to persecutions [10:32 ff.] which may have been from Nero's era. Reference to immediate suffering [10:36, 11:35-39, 12:1-11, 13:7] may indicate the time of Domitian's disfavor. This assumption would place the letter around 95 A.D. The fact that Clement of Rome was familiar with the letter also points to the last decade of the first century.[2]

The purpose of the letter seems clear, although in the past its main emphasis was misunderstood. At first reading the Epistle may appear to be addressed to Jewish Christians who are on the point of returning to Judaism. The title was perhaps derived from this circumstance. More careful scrutiny indicates, however, a general audience. The letter is now accepted as an apologia to strengthen Christians against competitive religions and philosophical worldliness. It might further have been used to bolster Christian faith in the face of organized persecution.

Structure

The writings have been variously divided by theme and digression, by paragraph subject matter and by sectional subject matter. Any division is to some extent arbitrary because the subject matter overlaps the break-off points. For the purpose of simplification and study, five main divisions can be made: the first concerns the high priesthood of Christ [1:1-5:10], the second is an admonition warning against relapse

---

[2] Some scholarship places Clement as late as 120 A.D. which might make the Epistle later. Others consider it as early as 80 A.D.

from the faith [5:11-6:20], the third returns to the main theme, Christ's supremacy as high priest [7:1-10:18], the fourth is a history of faith and Christian obligations [11:1-12:29], and the fifth a postscript or later addition [13:1-25].

Content

The structure of the writing is more that of an early theological tome than of a letter. This fact is apparent from the outset. With no salutation or greeting, the work enters into the main theme at once. The opening is not unlike that in John's Gospel and the theology is similar. God, who spoke in the past through the prophets, has now revealed himself through Christ. Christ, superior to all angels, represents God (and represented God) in all things from the beginning and sits in final judgment on mankind [1:1-4]. The second part of the chapter amplifies the theme of the introduction. Christ's superiority to the angels is demonstrated by a series of Scriptural quotations [Ps. 2:7, II Sam. 7:14, LXX Deut. 32:43, Ps. 104:4, Ps. 45:6, 7, Ps. 102:25-27, Ps. 110:1].

At the outset Chapter 2 outlines briefly the logical consequences of Christ's superiority. Christians must not relapse into the old beliefs. If transgression against God's word when revealed through the angels brought judgment, how can one expect to escape from the consequences of disobedience to Christ's revelation. This word come through those who heard it spoken and has been confirmed by miraculous acts and by action of the Holy Spirit [2:1-4].

The next section returns to the theme of Christ's superiority. The future belongs to Christ, not the angels. The statement is substantiated by a quotation from Psalm 8:4-6. All things are under Christ's control even if his power cannot be seen for the present [2:5-8].

The second half of Chapter 2 explains the reason for Christ's death on the cross which might, if misunderstood, be an impediment to faith. Christ is seen as lower than the angels only as a temporary measure. Christ, the means of bringing perfection to all, must suffer like everyone in order to be complete. Christ is one with man whom he sanctifies. The point is demonstrated by quotations from Psalm 22:22 and Isaiah 8:17, 18 [2:7-14]. By his sacrifice Christ has delivered man from the fear of death. The point is reiterated in the closing lines of the chapter. By his suffering Christ was able to act as a propitiation for man's sin. By becoming man and suffering like as a man, he was able to redeem man. In his action he became the faithful high priest [2:15-18].

The opening paragraph of Chapter 3 makes Christ's superiority over Moses clear. The builder of a house is more important than the house, the creator more important than the created. Moses is a servant in God's house while Christ is a son in it with a son's authority. Man belongs to the new relationship if he remains strong in the faith and doesn't relapse [3:1-6].

The next section of the Epistle, beginning with 3:7 and running through the end of Chapter 4, forms a unit in itself and constitutes a practical appeal derived from the theology which it expounds. The passage opens with a text taken from Psalm 95:7-11 [3:8-11]. The lines which follow amplify the text. Christians must be careful not to repeat the errors of falling away from the faith which were committed in the past. Continued exhortation to faithfulness is required lest some relapse. Only faithfulness to the very end is sufficient [3:12-14]. The people with whom God was displeased were the people whom Moses led out of Egypt, not all of whom received the promise. Many were buried in the wilderness because of disbelief [3:15-19]. Because the original promise still holds good, Christians must not fall short of receiving it. They have the opportunity which the ancients lost because, although they heard, they did not believe. The opportunity has always existed, having been made at the time of creation. Those who believe partake of God's rest [4:1-3]. God rested on the seventh day and rest is part of God's plan for men. Although those who first heard God's word did not receive his rest because of disbelief, God has given man another opportunity

[4:4-7]. If Joshua had been successful in bringing the Jews to God, no mention of another day would have been made. A full rest is still available for God's people which will be similar to God's rest after his work of creation. Christians must strive to achieve God's rest and must not let disobedience be (as in the case of the ancients) a cause of failure. The word of God is alive and active. It is sharp enough to pierce man's innermost thoughts and motivations. God cannot be fooled. The passage implies that God's judgment is inevitable [4:11-13].

As Christ, the great high priest, has transcended the heavens, the Christian must be strong in his faith. But Christ is not simply transcendent, he is also imminent. He has shared in man's temptations, but resisted them all. Man should, therefore, in time of need feel free to approach God in the confidence of a merciful and graceful reception [4:14-16].

The first part of Chapter 5 amplifies the theme of the last part of Chapter 4. High priests are chosen from men to represent man to God. The high priest offers gifts and sacrifices to God for man's sins and is able to deal sympathetically with man's weakness because he knows it (within) himself. His offerings are, therefore, both for himself and for the people whom he represents. So Christ knows man's weakness having been tempted as a man is tempted [5:1-3]. As in Aaron's case, the high priest is not self-appointed, but is called by God. Christ did not choose the position, but as the Scripture proves [Psalm 2:7 and 110:4], was called by God [5:4-6].

When he was a man on earth, Christ in desperation asked God to save him from death. His prayers were heard because of his reverence. Although he was God's Son, he had to experience obedience through the things he suffered. Having been made perfect as a result of his suffering, he is able to bring salvation to all men who obey him. He is named by God a true high priest after the order of Melchizedek [5:7-10].

The second section of the Epistle digresses from the main theme to warn against the dangers of relapse from faith. Verse 11 introduces the digression. It asserts that although more should be said about the high priesthood, it is difficult to explain to those who are spiritual dullards. At a time when they ought to be teachers, they need to be taught the basic elements of the faith. They require a child's spiritual diet, being incapable of digesting solid, adult food. Solid food is for mature Christians who can discern good and evil instinctively [5:11-14]. Christians should move beyond the simple ABCs of Christian principle, repentance, faith, baptism, ordination, immortality, and judgment [6:1-3].

Those who have been enlightened, who have experienced salvation and have received the Holy Spirit, who have known God's word and understood something of the eternal and who have then relapsed cannot return to a state of salvation. In their failure they crucify Christ again and expose him to shame. Fertile ground should produce useful crops and receive God's blessing; but if it bears thorns, it is cursed and burns [6:4-8].

The next passage softens the message of damnation. Fortunately those to whom the letter is addressed are not in the position described. Surely the terrible fate of the relapsed will not fall upon them. God won't forget their good works and faithfulness in caring for his saints. They must be equally alert to the complete meaning of Christian hope and follow the example of those who through patient faith receive God's promises [6:9-12].

The Epistle now turns to the Old Testament to demonstrate God's absolute reliability. Genesis 22:16,17 records God's promise to Abraham. When God made a promise to Abraham, he swore an oath to himself because there was no one higher to whom he might refer. God promised Abraham great blessings and great increase in his family. Abraham waited patiently and the promise was eventually fulfilled. Men swear by something greater than themselves, and an oath is final. God made a double promise by swearing an oath to himself. Christian hope is doubly attested by God who cannot lie. Christians, refugees from this world, have great encouragement in the hope thus given, which acts as an anchor for their souls. The anchor is not in this world alone, but is grounded in the eternal. Christ has already passed into the eternal world having become, on man's behalf, a high priest forever after the order of Melchizedek [6:13-20].

In Chapter 7 the Epistle returns to the main theme, the high priesthood of Christ. The first three verses draw a picture of Melchizedek from the fourteenth chapter of Genesis. Melchizedek, king of righteousness, king of peace and priest of God most high, met Abraham on his return from battle and blessed him. Abraham gave him one tenth of the spoils of war. Melchizedek had no father or mother, nor was he born, nor did he suffer death; but like the Son of God he was not subject to time [7:1-3].

The section which follows demonstrates Melchizedek's superiority to Abraham. Consider how great this man was. Even the patriarch Abraham gave tithes to him. Furthermore, according to law, the descendants of Levi who became priest had the right to demand tithes from the people even though they be descendants of Abraham. But Melchizedek who was not in that line of descent not only took tithes from Abraham, but also blessed one who was in possession of God's promises. A benediction comes from a superior to an inferior [7:4-7]. The men of the Levitical priesthood who receive tithes are subject to death, but Melchizedek did not die. The tribe of Levi descended from Abraham. In the person of their forefathers they paid tribute, therefore, to Melchizedek [7:8-10]. (Logic indicates that Melchizedek, being superior to the fathers of the present Levitical priesthood, is also superior to the priesthood itself.)

The argument continues in the next section. The failure of the Levitical priesthood is demonstrated. If the Levitical priesthood, the source of the law, was able to bring man to perfection, why should another priest of the order of Melchizedek instead of Aaron be necessary? If the priesthood is changed, the law also is superseded. Christ, the high priest, belonged to another line which had nothing to do with previous priestly functions. Christ came from the tribe of Judah which Moses never mentioned in connection with the priesthood.

Words of scripture [Psalm 110:4] proclaim his priesthood which comes not from earthly law, but from the authority of an eternal life [7:11-17].

The next paragraph reiterates the argument. The old law no longer stands. It has been proven ineffectual by its inability to bring anyone to spiritual perfection. A new hope is now available. Christ's priesthood rests upon God's oath, whereas the Levitical priests have no such authority [7:18-22]. There are many Levitical priests because they die and must be replaced, but Christ, being immortal, provides an unchanging and continuously active priesthood which gives him the ability to save all who seek God through his mediation [7:23-25].

Finally, Chapter 7 summarizes Christ's qualifications. He is holy, guileless, undefiled, beyond sin and higher than the heavens. He doesn't need to offer daily sacrifices after the manner of the Levitical priesthood because he offered himself as a sacrifice once and for all. The law creates high priests who possess human weakness, but Christ, who is eternally perfect, received his authority by God's oath which came after the law [7:26-28].

Chapter 8 continues to enlarge the main theme. Christ is the "ideal" high priest whose "ideal" sanctuary is made by God and not by man. Since a high priest's function involves sacrifice, Christ also offers something. If Christ were on earth he would not be a high priest because there are others who are qualified to make offerings according to the law. These men are, however, only a copy of the genuine, heavenly priesthood. Moses was warned to follow the heavenly pattern in his construction of the sanctuary [Ex. 25:40], [8:1-5].

Christ's ministry is greater than anything the old relationship was able to produce. It is based upon higher promises. If the old relationship had proved sufficient, no need would have existed for a second one. The Old Testament tells that God was not satisfied [8:6-8a]. A long quotation from Jeremiah follows to prove the point; for the most part it follows the LXX, [Jer. 31:31-34]. The prophecy predicts the formation of a new relationship, citing God's dissatisfaction with the past

[8:8b–12]. By speaking of a new relationship, God outdates the old. A thing that grows old is in the process of deteriorating [8:13].

Having explained Christ's "ideal" priesthood in the "ideal" sanctuary, the Epistle turns in Chapter 9 to the matter of Christ's perfect sacrifice. The paragraph describes the earthly sanctuary. On entering the tent one came first to a room in which were candlesticks, a table and the sacred bread. This was known as the Holy Place. After passing a second curtain, he entered the Holy of Holies. In it were a golden incense brazier, the ark inlaid with gold which contained a golden jar of manna, Aaron's rod, and stone tablets inscribed with the law. In this room was the mercy seat over which cherubim stood in glory [9:1-5].

The Levitical priesthood used the Holy Place regularly for daily offices, but they entered the Holy of Holies only once a year to offer a blood sacrifice for the priest's sins and the sins of the people. The Holy Spirit signified by this arrangement that free access to the presence of God was not available as long as the first sanctuary still existed. The situation tells a story. The gifts, sacrifices, and ceremony do not touch the inner conscience to make the worshipper perfect. Their value is only temporary until the new revelation [9:6-10].

Christ, the high priest that was promised, now enters the "ideal" sanctuary which is not the product of human agency. By his single sacrifice he obtained man's redemption once and for all. Atonement is not accomplished by animal sacrifice. If animal sacrifice has value as an offering, how much more does Christ who offered himself a perfect sacrifice to God [9:11-14]?

As a result of his sacrifice, Christ created a new relationship. Through his death he achieved the ability to redeem sin committed under the old relationship and made it possible for those who hear God's call to receive his eternal inheritance. A will does not go into effect until the testator's death [9:15-18]. Even the old relationship was created by shedding blood [Ex.

24:3-11]. Sacrifice is necessary for the remission of sin [9:19-22].

Earthly copies of the heavenly sanctuary could be cleansed by earthly sacrifices, but an "ideal" sanctuary required an "ideal" sacrifice. Christ didn't enter into a man-made sanctuary, a pattern of the real thing; he entered heaven itself to appear before God on man's behalf [9:23-24]. Christ was not to offer himself repeatedly in the manner of the earthly high priests with another creature's blood, or he would have had to suffer continually from the beginning of the world to the present time. Rather than this, Christ suffered once at the end of the era to vanquish sin. As men die only once before judgment, so Christ made only one offering before his second appearance which will not take place to cope with sin, but to bring salvation to believers [9:25-28].

Chapter 10 reiterates the main theme. The old law is a shadow of reality and cannot by continual sacrifice bring its participants to perfection. Otherwise sacrifices would have been discontinued because those who worshipped by that means, having been cleansed, would no longer be conscious of sin. The old sacrifices only serve as reminders of sin. The point is confirmed by a quotation from the LXX, Ps. 40:6-8 [10:1-7].

God has no pleasure in animal sacrifices and burnt offerings made according to the law. Christ said that he came to do God's will. He changed the old order for the purpose of establishing a new one. Man has been sanctified once and for all in accordance with God's will by the offering of Christ's body [10:8-10].

The repetitive offerings of earthly priests are utterly futile, because they cannot remove sin. When he made one complete and final sacrifice, Christ on the other hand sat down at God's right hand to wait for his enemies to be made his footstool [Ps. 110:1]. In his single offering he made all men perfect who are sanctified. The Holy Spirit bears out the point when it says man's sin will be forgiven [Jer. 31:31-34]. Sin once forgiven does not require further atonement [10:11-18]. Christians now can know God because Christ by his sacrificial action passed through the veil which stood between God and man. Man now has a great high priest in God's house whom he should approach with sincerity, faith, clear conscience, and a clean body. Faith must not falter. God is true to his promises. Christians should be considerate and work in Christ's service. They should not, as some do, fail to attend church functions, but must encourage one another as the judgment day approaches [10:19-25].

Those who sin deliberately after having known the truth cannot be redeemed a second time, but can only expect to be destroyed by the fire of God's judgment. In Moses' time a man who showed contempt for the law was killed on the word of two or three witnesses without compassion [Deut. 17:2-7]. How much greater will be the punishment for one who has put the Son of God to scorn, profaned the sacrifice which created the new relationship, and has treated the Holy Spirit with contempt. Vengeance belongs to God [Deut. 32:35]. The Lord will judge his people [Deut. 32:36, Ps. 135:14]. It is a fearful thing to be the object of God's punishment [10:26-31].

Having depicted the terrible consequences of apostasy, the Epistle turns to offer hope to the faithful. Remembering how much they endured in the old days after their conversion, Christians are to remain strong. Christians were abused publicly. Trouble was shared by all. When some were imprisoned, they were not abandoned. Christians endured the confiscation of property in the knowledge that they possessed more valuable lasting spiritual endowments. They are not to lose their fortitude which has a great final reward. They are to be patient so that having followed God's will, they may receive his inheritance [LXX Hab. 2:3]. Christians are not to be like those who, shrinking from faith, fall into perdition. Christians belong with those whose souls are saved by faith [10:32-39].

The last two chapters of the Epistle turn from the theme of Christ's high priesthood to the subject of faith and the Christian life. The first lines of Chapter 11 define faith and the nature of creation. Faith is confidence that Christian hope will be fulfilled and the conviction that the unseen world is real.

The world was created by God's word and reality extends beyond observable matter [11:1-3].

Because of faith Abel possessed insight to make a better sacrifice than Cain and was shown to be righteous. His witness still speaks after his death. Because of faith Enoch passed directly to heaven without experiencing death. He was known to please God which is impossible without faith. A man must believe that God exists and that he rewards those who believe in him. Through faith Noah understood unseen things and built an ark to save his family. In so doing he left the world to condemnation and won for himself righteousness which comes from faith [1:4-7].

In blind faith Abraham journeyed to the promised land [Gen. 15:7]. Through faith in God's promise Sarah conceived a son when past normal childbearing age [Gen. 16:2, 21:1,2], so that from a man near the age of death an entire race was born [11:8-12]. These men died in faith, not having experienced the full promises, although they saw them in the distance. They admitted that they were strangers and pilgrims in this world. People who admitted this fact indicated that they sought another true country—not the place they left, for they could have returned there, but rather a heavenly realm. God accepted them and prepared a heavenly city for them [11:13-16]. Abraham's faith was so great that he was even willing to offer his son as a sacrifice [Gen. 22:1-18]. He believed God capable of raising his son from the dead which God did, figuratively speaking [11:17-19].

By faith Isaac and Jacob passed God's promises on to their descendants. By faith Joseph was certain that his body would be buried outside Egypt [Gen. 50:24-26] [11:20-22]. By faith Moses' parents saved the infant child from Pharaoh. Through faith the adult Moses renounced privilege and chose to share the burden of God's people rather than enjoy the temporary rewards of sinful associations. He felt Messianic service to be more valuable than all Egypt's treasures. His faith in the invisible God was greater than his fear of Pharaoh. By faith he passed through the Red Sea. The walls of Jericho collapsed before the faith of the Israelite forces. Rahab did not perish in disaster because of her faith [11:30-31].

The next eight verses summarize the many great works accomplished through faith, and the terrible trials endured by faith.[3] Nevertheless, although past generations saw their faith vindicated in part, they did not experience the Messianic age. God's plan includes the present; perfection cannot be achieved without the people of this time [11:32-40].

The last chapter of the original Epistle deals with various aspects of Christian living. The first two verses are an exhortation to Christian service based on the great examples of faith in the previous section. A metaphor from the Greek games explains that if one casts sin away, as people watch, he can move in patient hope and with inspiration toward Jesus, the originator and perfection of man's faith. In enduring the cross he understood the joy that follows suffering and was made equal to God. Bearing in mind what he endured, be courageous [12:1-3].

But man's fight against sin has not as yet reached the point of bloodshed. Has the exhortation in Prov. 3:11-12 been forgotten? Trials must be endured as God's correction measures. God treats man as a son. No son ever grew to maturity without correction. If man weren't corrected by God, he would not be a legitimate son. Earthly fathers punish their sons and are given reverence in return. How much more should be given to the heavenly father? Man may inherit eternal life. Earthly fathers use their own standards as a basis for correction, but God corrects man so that he may become holy. Correction is never pleasant at the time, but it is fruitful in producing righteousness afterwards [12:4-11].

Man must not move in fear and trembling. He must walk straight so that the weak will not fall, but will find strength. To find God man must search for peace and be consecrated. He must be sure to remain faithful to God's grace for without

[3] Dan. Chs. 3 and 6, I Kings 18:8-24, II Kings 4:18-37, II Macc. 6 and 7, II Chron. 24:20-22, Isa. 5:1-14.

it bitterness can cause trouble that results in the defilement of many who become fornicators or profane people, like Esau, who sold his birthright for a meal. He had no second chance no matter how hard he pleaded [12:12-17].

Christians today do not approach an earthly mountain that blazes with fire and is darkened by storm. They do not hear blaring trumpets and voices so awful that those who hear can not stand the sound. The mountain was so sacred that even a beast was stoned for touching it. So frightening was the sight that even Moses was desperately afraid [12:18-21]. Christians approach, however, Mt. Zion, God's eternal city, the heavenly Jerusalem, replete with angels, first born souls elected to heaven, God judge of all, the spirits of God, men made perfect, and Christ the mediator of the new relationship by a sacrifice better than Abel's patriarchal offering. Christians must not fail to hear the voice of God. If men who did not listen when his voice spoke on earth did not escape his wrath, what chance is there for those who turn away from his voice when it speaks from heaven? In the past his voice shook the earth; now he promises not only to shake the earth, but the heavens as well [Ex. 19:18, Hag. 2:6, 21]. At that time all material things will be destroyed. Only spiritual reality will remain. As the spiritual kingdom in which Christians live, therefore, will not be destroyed, they must serve God reverently and with awe. The Epistle ends with the assertion that God is indeed a consuming fire [12:18-29].

Although some assume Chapter 13 to be a postcript, it is generally assumed to be a later addition in Pauline style. The first section is a list of rules for Christian behavior. Love your Christian brothers. Do not fail to be hospitable to strangers; they might be angels [Gen. 18:2-19:3]. Think of the imprisoned as if you were imprisoned with them, of those who suffer as if it were your body that suffers. Keep marriage honorable and have no part in sexual immorality. God condemns those who are sexually loose. Don't be avaricious. Be content with what you have. God has said he will not fail or forsake you

[Deut. 31:6, Josh. 1:5]. The Christian can say with confidence that he fears no man because God is his strength [Ps. 118:6] [13:1-6].

The next section exhorts Christians to respect their preachers and follow their example, for Christ's word is eternal and unchanging [13:7-8].

A warning against misinterpretation and pagan sacramentalism follows. Christians are not to let themselves be enticed into false religious practices. The spirit is sustained by God's grace and not by dietary rules which haven't proved profitable for those who follow them. Those who still serve the earthly sanctuary have no right to share in the Christian sacrifice. The bodies of sacrificial animals are burned outside the camp. In his sacrifice Jesus also suffered outside the city. Christians should, therefore, share his disgrace outside the earthly city for they are not of this world, but should seek the world to come. To praise God by the spoken word of faith in Christ is Christian sacrifice. Nevertheless Christians must not forget good works for these things are also pleasing to God [13:9-16].

Christians must obey their leaders who stand guard over their spiritual lives. They should make them happy and not sad in their leadership. Insubordination is not profitable [13:17-19].

Prayer is requested for those who have written the letter. The chapter ends with a long doxology, news from Timothy, and a blessing [13:20-25].

OUTLINE OF THE EPISTLE TO THE HEBREWS

I. Christ the one true high priest, 1:1-5:10

A. *Christology, 1:1-2:18*
Ch. 1   *a*) Introduction, God's revelation complete in Christ, 1:1-4
         b) Christ superior to the angels, 1:5-14
Ch. 2   *c*) Implications of Christ's superiority, 2:1-4
         d) Further evidence of Christ's superiority, 2:5-8
         e) The purpose of Christ's death explained, 2:9-18

B. *Christ superior to Moses and an appeal, 3:1-4:16*

Ch. 3 a) Christ superior to Moses, 3:1-6
Ch. 4 b) An appeal, 3:7-4:16

Ch. 5 C. *Christ the true high priest, 5:1-10*

    a) Christ knew man's temptations, 5:1-3
    b) Christ's priesthood of divine origin, 5:4-6
    c) Christ's sonship, 5:7-10

II. An admonition, 5:11-6:20

Ch. 6 a) The dangers of lethargy, 5:11-6:3
    b) The danger of relapse, 6:4-8
    c) God cares for the righteous, 6:9-12
    d) An example from the Old Testament, 6:13-20

III. Supremacy of Christ as high priest, 7:1-10:39

Ch. 7 A. *Christ, the perfect high priest, 7:1-28*

    a) Melchizedek, 7:1-3
    b) Melchizedek superior to Abraham, 7:4-10
    c) The Levitical priesthood inferior to the order of Melchizedek, 7:11-17
    d) Christ supersedes the old priesthood, 7:18-25
    e) Christ, the high priest, 7:26-28

Ch. 8 B. *Christ, the "ideal" high priest in the "ideal" sanctuary, 8:1-13*

    a) The "ideal" sanctuary, 8:1-5
    b) The new relationship, 8:6-13

Ch. 9 C. *Christ offered the supreme sacrifice, 9:1-28*

    a) The earthly sanctuary, 9:1-5
    b) The sanctuary in use, 9:6-10
    c) Christ offered the "ideal" sacrifice, 9:11-14
    d) Christ's sacrifice was necessary, 9:15-22
    e) Christ, the "ideal" sacrifice also the final sacrifice, 9:23-28

Ch. 10 D. *Failure of the Jewish sacrificial system, 10:1-39*

    a) Levitical sacrifices inadequate, 10:1-10
    b) An emphatic reiteration, 10:11-25
    c) The terrible consequences of relapse, 10:26-31
    d) A message of hope, 10:32-39

IV. A History of faith and the Christian obligation, 11:1-12:29

Ch. 11 A. Various aspects of faith, 11:1-40

  a) Faith and creation, 11:1-3
  b) The faith of Abel, Enoch and Noah, 1:4-7
  c) Abraham's faith, 11:8-19
  d) The faith of other Patriarchs, 11:20-22
  e) Moses' faith, 11:23-29
  f) Israelite faith and Rahab's faith, 11:30-31
  g) A general statement concerning faithfulness, 11:32-40

Ch. 12 B. The Christian life, 12:1-29

  a) Exhortation to Christian living, 12:1-3
  b) The need for suffering, 12:4-11
  c) Suffering accepted with courage, 12:12-17
  d) The old relationship and the new, 12:18-29

V. Advice, exhortation, warning, doxology, salutation and blessing, 13:1-25

Ch. 13 a) Advice to Christians, 13:1-6
  b) Church leaders to be respected, 13:7-8
  c) Dangers of false teaching, 13:9-16
  d) Obedience to leaders and prayer, 13:17-19
  e) Doxology, salutation and blessing, 13:20-25

XXI

The Catholic Epistles

In early times fourteen Epistles were designated as Pauline literature—the thirteen which bear his name and the Epistle to the Hebrews. Today only four are granted unquestioned Pauline authorship—Romans, First and Second Corinthians, and Galatians, although, as has already been seen, evidence for authorship for some of the others is sufficiently clear to provide general acceptance. Besides the Pauline portfolio seven other letter-like writings were accepted in the canon: The Epistle of James; First and Second Peter; First, Second and Third John; and Jude. These were known as the Catholic Epistles, but, as in the case of the Pauline letters, the legitimacy of the title is debatable.

The word *catholic* in America has become identified with the Church of Rome. When properly understood the word means, however, *universal* from its Greek origin. In reference to the letters under consideration, scholars debate the application of the word, not its meaning. The question is whether the letters are catholic in their acceptance or catholic in their direction. The writings are probably encyclical, written with general readership in mind. Some scholars even suggest that they share common authorship. The western branch of the church held the letters to be generally accepted as canonical writing in which case the word *catholic* is interchangeable with the word *canonical*, whereas eastern usage seems to apply the adjective to the direction of the letters. In any case all the

Epistles were not immediately accepted as part of the canon. In the second century only First Peter and First John were generally recognized, and it was not until the fifth century that the entire group became canonical literature.

The writings are generally placed outside early apostolic times and the Pauline era. They are concerned with matters that were not an issue in the Church until ecclesiastical organization began to be recognized and until the time of organized persecution by Roman authorities. The Neronian persecution was concerned for the most part with Roman Christians (about 64 A.D.), and it was not until the last decade of the first century that, under Domitian, persecution became systematic and empire-wide.

THE FIRST EPISTLE OF PETER

Background

The letter is strongly Pauline. Not only is the style similar, but also much of its material can be traced to Ephesians and Romans. This fact at once suggests other than Petrine authorship. Other facts tend to substantiate the assumption. The Greek is not colored by Hebrew sentence structure and certainly isn't what might be expected from a simple Galilean fisherman. Furthermore, Peter was not primarily concerned with Gentile Christianity, whereas Paul's entire ministry was devoted to Gentile conversion. It is hard to visualize Peter's use of Pauline material even if he were familiar with it. That he knew it is doubtful by reason of his age and environment. The author recognizes, furthermore, a degree of church organization and corruption which could hardly have developed in Peter's time. Lastly, the main theme of the letter is to encourage Christians in the face of persecution. It urges Christians to remain steadfast and not to lose the final goal, loyalty to Christ and eternal life. By the example of love and purity they are to make the gospel a reality and in so doing are to excite the admiration of their enemies. The direction and attitude do not fit Peter's era. That Christ's life is not mentioned is incredible in a writing whose author was supposedly the big fisherman. The weight of the evidence clearly throws the balance away from Petrine authorship.

Since the author of the letter knew Paul's letters, it must have been written after 70 A.D., probably around 95 A.D. The letter was known to Polycarp. A likely time of origin which fits the internal and external evidence is between 95-117 A.D.[1] Its author was probably a Roman Christian who directed his writing to the general readers among Christians in Asia Minor.

Structure

The Epistle does not lend itself to division. The theme is generally consistent throughout. Analysis reveals six sections: the first, reminiscent of Paul, contains a salutation, greeting and praise [1:1-12]; the second indicates what Christian doctrine means to the life of man [1:13-2:10]; the third lists some practical applications of Christianity to life [2:11-3:12]; the fourth deals with the problems of suffering [3:13-4:6]; the fifth considers suffering in terms of final rewards [4:7-19]; the sixth contains an exhortation to leadership, a final greeting, and benediction [5:1-14].

Content

The salutation and greeting follow the traditional form. Authorship and direction of the Epistle are specified. The use of the word "dispersion" presents some difficulty, for normal usage would imply that the letter was addressed to Jews or Jewish Christians. The term, as used here, is undoubtedly enlarged to refer to all Christians. The Epistle jumps to a com-

---

[1] Benjamin W. Robinson suggests that the letter may have been dictated to Silvanus which might account for the non-Petrine Greek and that the persecutions which it considers were Neronian. Acceptance of these assumptions might justify an early date, about 64 A.D.

paratively long section of praise which serves to substantiate its Christology. God is praised for giving Christians a second birth of hope by raising Jesus from the dead. They now have a new inheritance in heaven, not subject to change and decay. God directs Christians through faith to salvation, prepared for the day of judgment. They can rejoice in this fact even in the face of present grievous trials which are, however, temporary. These things are to be endured to prove a faith which is far more valuable than perishable things. When Christ is finally revealed, the faith then proven will bring praise, glory and honour to Christians [1:4-7]. Although Christians have not actually seen Christ, nevertheless they love him and believe in him and know indescribable joy in the anticipation of salvation. The ancient prophets spoke of this salvation and searched hard for it. They foretold the grace which now comes to Christians and tried to determine the time of its arrival when they predicted Christ's suffering and the glories that would follow. Final revelation did not come to them, but to the present time by means of the gospel whose source is the Holy Spirit. Even angels are interested in such things as this [1:8-12].

The next section establishes the theme of the writing. Christians are to be alert and serious and should let Christ's revelation be the source of hope. Being now obedient to their new understanding, they cannot live by the lusts of their ignorant days. They are to follow Christ's example.[2] If Christians worship God as a father who judges man with utter impartiality, they should be aware of the possible consequences of the relationship [1:13-17]. Christians must bear in mind that they were redeemed from the futile life of past generations by the price of Christ's pure sacrificial blood and not by things of this world's transitory worth. Christ, who existed before creation, fulfilled himself in the present in order to bring Christians to faith in God. God raised him from the dead and glorified him to create Christian faith and hope [1:18-21]. As Christians have been made pure by obedience to God's truth to the point of under-

[2] Lev. 11:44, 19:2, 20:7.

standing true brotherly love, they must accordingly show heart-felt love toward each other, for they are reborn creatures begotten by God's eternal word, not creatures from a perishable earthly generation. As Isaiah has shown [Isa. 40:6] earthly things perish, but God's word is eternal. This is the gospel [1:22-25].

The first part of Chapter 2 describes man in terms of spiritual regeneration and applies the concept of the temple's place in the old relationship to man's position in the new. Christians can no longer have any part in evil, deceit, hypocrisy, jealousy, and slander. As men reborn in Christ, Christians should long for pure spiritual nourishment in order to grow to a state of salvation which will come about if they have tasted God's grace [2:1-3].

Christians come to God as precious, living stones, rejected by men, but chosen by God, to form a spiritual temple in which, like priests, they offer spiritual sacrifices which are acceptable to God through Christ. The fact is substantiated by scripture [Isa. 28:16]. Christians are precious in God's sight [Ps. 118:22], but God rejects those who do not believe [Isa. 8:14] [2:4-8]. They stumble on God's word and are not of the elect, but Christians are God's chosen people, his royal priesthood, his holy nation, God's own. In the past they were nothing and did not know of God's mercy, but now God has called them from darkness into light, and they have obtained God's mercy. Accordingly they must be a witness to show God's excellence [2:4-10].

The second half of the chapter begins section three which exhorts Christians to follow certain precepts of Christian life. As Christians are not permanent residents of this world, they must not be governed by lusts of the flesh which are at war with the soul. Although the people with whom Christians live may speak of them slanderously, their conduct must be such that in disastrous times they will bring men to God by their good example [2:11-12].

For the Lord's sake Christians are to obey secular authority whether it come from the king (emperor) or a governor appointed to punish law breakers and reward good citizenship. It is God's will that the ignorant criticism of foolish men should be silenced by good example. Freedom is not license to do evil, because man remains obligated to God. Christians should respect all men, love the Christian brotherhood, fear God, and honor the king [2:13-17].

Servants should honor not only good and gentle masters, but also those that are perverse. If a man endures pain through injustice, it means something to God. There is no particular merit in suffering patiently for afflictions which are justly deserved, but if a man suffers patiently for doing well, God sees this as meritorious behavior. Christians are called to such action by Christ's example. He wasn't guilty of any sin, deceit or trickery, yet when he was abused, he did not resist; when hurt he did not threaten, but committed himself to God's justice. He gave his body to be beaten and crucified to heal man and save him from sin. Man, like a sheep had gone astray, but has now returned to the shepherd and guardian of his soul [2:18-25].

The parallel between the acceptance of recognized secular authority and the duties of the Christian relationship is continued in Chapter 3. Wives are to be obedient to their husbands who may be brought to an understanding of God by good example, though they do not believe the word. Beauty is not to be dependent upon elaborate hair styling, clothes or jewelry, but rather is a matter of lasting purity of spirit which God values highly. Women who trusted in God and obeyed their husbands were adorned with the garment of purity of spirit in the patriarchal days. Sarah obeyed Abraham calling him lord. Christians stand in that lineage provided they live properly and do not let doubts lead them astray. Likewise, husbands are to live with their wives honouring them and knowing that, although they are physically weaker, they nevertheless share equality in God's grace. This way of life is necessary for a true prayer life [3:1-8].

Finally, all Christians should be of one mind living together with sympathy, love, and humility. Evil should not be returned for evil nor insult for insult. The writer asserts that Christians are called to this way of life and as a result they will inherit blessedness. A quotation from Ps. 34:12-16 follows to conclude the section [3:9-12].

Section four deals with the problem of suffering. It says that those who do good works will probably not be subject to harm, but if harm should befall them, Christians should be neither fearful nor troubled because they are blessed in their action. They are always to make Christ holy in their hearts. Christians are to be ready at all times to explain reverently the reason for their hope. Their conscience must be clear at all times so that those who revile Christian living will be put to shame. If it be God's will, suffering for good deeds is better than suffering for evil ones. Christ, the righteous, once suffered for the unrighteous to bring man to God. His body died, but he lived again in spirit [3:13-18].

The passage that follows accepts Old Testament cosmology. Apparently the author wishes to indicate that Christ descended into the place where departed spirits were thought to be held in bondage and preached to them [3:19]. The lines which follow refer to Gen. 6:1-4 and to traditions found in Enoch in which the offspring of the illicit union of the sons of God and the daughters of men felt divine wrath through the flood. Only eight souls survived. The belief that Christ's salvation was universal is indicated herein.

Similarly through Christ's resurrection, Christians have been cleansed in baptism, not simply of fleshly dirt, but of mental impurities. With clean minds they can approach God. Christ sits on the right hand of God in heaven. All authorities and powers are subservient to him [3:20-22]. Christians are to take Christ's sufferings in the flesh as an example and arm themselves with an attitude like his. Suffering for righteousness develops strength to resist evil. Christians are not to lead the rest of their lives in accordance with the dictates of fleshly lusts, but by God's will. Times past may have been good enough for pagan pastimes, satisfaction of all types of sensuous desires, orgiastic revelings, and idolatrous washings. As a result, old companions may speak evil of Christians, thinking it strange that they no longer take part in these things. Such people will stand under God's judgment which extends to both the living and the dead. The gospel was preached to departed spirits that they, through judgment, might inherit eternal life [4:1-6].

The fifth section deals with further implications of judgment. As the last days are approaching, Christians are to be self-controlled men of prayer. Most important, they must love each other deeply, because love can overcome many types of sin. Christians must be uncomplaining in their hospitality. Being good stewards of God's grace, they are to minister to each other, each with his own God-given talent. If a man preaches, he is to preach God's word truly; if he serves the church he is to do so with godly strength so that God may be glorified in all things through Jesus Christ. The passage closes with a doxology [4:7-11].

The letter now turns to the effects of persecution on Christian character. Christians are not to be surprised by the fiery trials they must face to prove their faith for they should not look on persecution as abnormal. They should rejoice in that they share Christ's sufferings. When Christ's glory is revealed, Christians will be filled with joy. If Christians suffer because of their faith, they are blessed because God's glorious spirit rests in them. They must not be in a position to suffer as a result of evil deeds. If a man suffers because of Christian belief, he need have no shame for in doing so he glorifies God in Christ's name. The time of God's judgment has arrived, and if it starts with Christians, what will happen to those who don't believe the gospel? If the righteous are barely saved, what will befall sinful people? Those who suffer for God's sake should commit their souls to their faithful creator and continue to lead a Christian life [4:12-19].

In the last section the letter ends with an exhortation to those who are in a position of leadership. The author, who is an elder and who saw Christ's suffering and who will share in the glory to come, asks that those who are in charge of Christian communities exercise oversight willingly, not with reluctance, in a godly manner, not for worldly gain, but from genuine concern. Leaders are to be exemplary rather than authoritative. When the chief Shepherd reveals himself, Christian leaders will receive an unfading accolade. Similarly younger people should recognize seniority. All Christians should wear the cloak of humility and serve each other willingly, because God does not favor pride, but always gives his grace to humble people. Christians should, therefore, be humble under God's mighty hand so that in due time they will be exalted. Knowing that God cares for them, they should commit themselves to his custody and not worry [5:1-7].

Christians must be self-controlled and alert at all times, because their enemy the devil stalks them like a lion seeking to destroy them. He is to be withstood with faith in the knowledge that all Christians suffer similarly, that in due time, after they have suffered a little while, the God of all grace, who called them to eternal glory through Christ, will make them strong and perfect. The passage concludes with a doxology [5:8-11].

The letter ends with a statement that it is brought by Silvanus (some say dictated to Silvanus). The reference to Babylon is thought by many to be a metaphorical reference to Rome. The last lines are a greeting from Mark, a salutation, and blessing [5:12-14].

OUTLINE OF THE FIRST EPISTLE OF PETER

I. Salutation, greeting, praise and encouragement, 1:1-12

Ch. 1 *a*) Salutation and greeting, 1:1-3
      b) Praise and encouragement, 1:4-12

II. Implications of Christian doctrine in man's life, 1:13-2:10

      a) Follow Christ's example, 1:13-25
Ch. 2 *b*) Man is God's temple, 2:1-10

III. Precepts for Christian living, 2:11-3:12

      a) Man's loyalty to God, 2:11-12
      b) Secular law to be obeyed for God's sake, 2:13-17
      c) The duty of slaves and the reward of suffering, 2:18-25
Ch. 3   *d*) Subjection of wives a godly example, 3:1-12

IV. Patient suffering a Christian virtue, 3:13-4:6

      a) Undeserved suffering, 3:13-18
      b) Christ and the departed spirits of men, 3:19-22
Ch. 4   *c*) Christ as an example, 4:1-6

V. The last days are approaching, 4:7-19

      a) Christian life in the last days, 4:7-11
      b) Persecution endured brings salvation, 4:12-19

VI. An exhortation to Christian leadership, God's protection, and conclusion, 5:1-14

Ch. 5   *a*) Exhortation, God's protection, 5:1-11
      b) Conclusion and benediction, 5:12-14

THE EPISTLE OF JAMES

Background

No New Testament writing is more difficult to place as to authorship, leadership, and date. Opinion on these matters remains divided except within very wide limits, and many do not even regard the Epistle as a letter. The author describes himself as "James, a servant of God and of the Lord Jesus Christ." In times past the accepted authorship, accordingly, was James, the brother of Jesus. Jewish authorship (a Jew converted to Christianity) fits the tone of the writing. The author makes no claim to be an apostle, yet seems to be a man of authority. The fact that he was sufficiently well known to require no further introduction coupled with the authoritative tone might well be construed to back James' authorship. The weight of evidence against such authorship, however, far out-balances any justification for its continued acceptance. Three points are clear: that the letter was not accepted as canonical literature until the last part of the fourth century makes it seem hardly likely that its author was a man as prominent in the Jerusalem church as James; that its Greek is nearly as polished as that of Hebrews makes it seem hardly likely that it could have been written by a Galilean peasant; that the style is clearly that of the Greek diatribe, a literary device James hardly could be expected to use.[3] No positive evidence can be found for attributing the writing to any of the other Jameses of the New Testament times, neither James the Son of Zebedee nor James the Son of Alpheus. It has been suggested that the writing is a piece of some longer Hebrew tome given Christian color by interpolation at 1:1 and 2:1. Only two conclusions can be drawn with any degree of certainty: the writing comes from the pen of a Jewish Christian who chose James' name to lend authority to the work, and the letter is pseudonymous work whose true author will remain unknown.

The writing is addressed to "the twelve tribes which are of the dispersion." In the early Christian age the phrase probably indicated general Christian readership rather than dispersed Jewry. Christians considered their earthly existence as pro tempore, their true home being heaven. They also followed the Jewish tradition and considered themselves God's chosen people.

The Epistle has been variously dated from as early as around 64 A.D. to as late as 150 A.D. depending on authorship. The extremes make it either one of the earliest or one of the latest New Testament writings. If the author was James, the brother of Jesus, it probably originated in Palestine sometime in the last decade prior to the fall of the temple (A.D. 70). As has been demonstrated, this date does not fit the other characteristics of the letter. The author's misuse of Paul probably places it after the Pauline letters' first flash of popularity

---

[3] Rather than the diatribe some see the writing as patterned after Hebrew wisdom literature.

(95 A.D.), hence in a period after the turn of the century. Origen, who knew the letter in the third century, thought it to be of early authorship and attributed it to James. The letter was also known to Clement of Rome. A date somewhere around 100-125 A.D. seems to satisfy more conditions than any other.

The Epistle is clearly not a true letter. The salutation is a bare formality and is not followed by a greeting or individual address. The writing ends abruptly. Rather than as a letter, the work can be described as a tract or written sermon with no clear-cut structure. Attempts to outline the subject matter reveal, instead of subject sections, a series of counsels for proper living connected by the phrase, "my brethren." Unlike the Pauline literature and the other Epistles, it is not written about any central problem. The general theme seems to be exhortation against hypocrisy and recommendation of straight conduct.

Structure

Any structural breakdown as a result of the Epistle's form must be to a large extent arbitrary. Following the "my brethren" delineations, ten sections can be outlined: the opening [1:1], temptation and reward [1:2-18], the gospel to be heard and acted upon [1:19-27], warning against being unduly impressed by status and acting in contempt for God's laws [2:1-13], the valuelessness of faith without works [2:14-26], a general warning against unchristian living [3:1-4:10], recommendation of forbearance and condemnation of the rich [4:11-5:6], exhortation to patience [5:7-11], condemnation of perjury and exhortation to prayer [5:12-18], the rewards of fruitful ministry [5:19-20].

Content

The Epistle opens with an extremely brief salutation and address. Many scholars see the section as a later addition to the original [1:1]. The writing jumps immediately into the first section which for the most part is concerned with the relationship between temptation and the rewards which result from resisting it successfully. Temptations endured produce spiritual stamina which is finally a pleasure not a trial. By proving their faith Christians work toward perfection and should continue to do so until they become spiritually mature [1:2-4].

If a man isn't wise enough to cope with his problems during spiritual growth, he may get enlightenment from God through prayer, for God gives liberally without reproach. Prayer must be offered without reservation. A doubtful man moves back and forth like a surging sea. Such a two-faced man cannot hope to obtain anything from God [1:5-8].

A poor man can find joy in the knowledge that he is spiritually wealthy; the rich man, in that he has understood his spiritual poverty in time to save himself, because worldly status eventually withers like grass in a hot sun and a scorching wind. Its beauty eventually perishes. Similarly a rich man's way of life will pass away [1:9-12].

Joy comes to the man who resists temptation for, once qualified, he will receive the crown of life which God promises to those who love him. God cannot be blamed for man's temptations. God cannot be tempted nor does he tempt others. Man is led into temptation by his own ravenous hungers. When these desires motivate his life, he is led into sin and the end of full-fledged sin is death. No mistake must be made about that. All good and perfect things come from God, who is immutable and consistent. By God's will Christians are, through the gospel, the first to be saved [1:13-18].

Christians must be ready to listen, slow to speak and self-controlled because anger doesn't produce righteousness. Impurity and evil must, therefore, be purged from their lives so that the gospel which saves their souls can be received. Not only must God's word be heard, but it must also be put into practice otherwise those who think they have heard are deluding themselves. A man who hears God's word and does not act accordingly is like a person who glances at himself in a mirror and immediately forgets what he saw. A man who hears God's word [4] and follows its teachings does not hear and forget, but practices his beliefs; such a man finds joy in his activity. If a man considers himself religious, but cannot control his speech, he is deceiving himself and his religion is pointless. Genuine religion in God's sight is manifest in such actions as caring for orphans and widows who are in need and by keeping oneself unsullied by worldly influences [1:19-27].

Christians must not confuse faith in Christ with worldly status. When a rich man wearing jewelry and fine clothes is given a high place in the synagogue while to a poor man with shabby clothes is given a low one, this is clear indication that worldly judgments are being made on the basis of class distinction. Character appraisal is not a man's province and is an evil activity [2:1-4]. Christians should note that God chose the poor of this world to inherit his kingdom. Isn't it true that rich people oppress Christians and drag them into court? Don't they slander Christ's name [2:5-7]? If a man lives up to the Scriptural law of free man, "Thou shalt love thy neighbor as thyself," he does well, but those who are impressed by personal status commit sin under God's law. A man who breaks one point of law is a lawbreaker even if he keeps all the rest. The one who said, "Thou shalt not commit adultery" also said, "Do not kill." If a man does not commit adultery, but kills, he has become a law-breaker. Christians are, therefore, to speak and act as men who are to be judged as free men. Those who show no mercy will not receive it. Mercy tempers judgment [2:8-13].

How can a faith that does not manifest itself in actions be of any value? Can that kind of faith save a man? What good is it to tell the naked and hungry to go their way in peace, to say be warm, be fed and not give them what they need? Similarly a faith that doesn't motivate action is dead. One man simply claims to have faith, another makes no such claim, but does good deeds. The first cannot make his faith visible in order to prove it, but the second, by his works, demonstrates

[4] Some scholars assume this to refer to the Sermon on the Mount.

that he has faith. To believe in one God and to stop there is not enough. Even demons go that far and tremble at the thought of that God.[5] Certainly faith without good actions is fruitless [2:14-20].

Wasn't Abraham, the ancestor of the faithful, justified before God by his actions in being willing to offer his son Isaac as a sacrifice? In his case faith motivated his actions and was fulfilled in them [Gen. 22:1-18].

The Scripture which said Abraham believed God was proved and it was reckoned unto him for righteousness; and he was called the friend of God [Isa. 41:8, II Chron. 20:7]. Clearly man is justified by good actions and not by faith alone. Similarly Rahab, the harlot, was justified by works in receiving Joshua's spies and showing them a different way back [Joshua 2]. Even as a body without breath[6] (spirit) is dead, so also faith without good actions is dead [2:21-26].

Be cautious about becoming a teacher; teachers stand under a stricter judgment than lay people [3:1]. Everyone makes mistakes. A man who never made a mistake while speaking would be perfect and could control himself in every other way as well. A big horse can be forced to obedience by a small bit. A huge ship driven by heavy winds can be steered by a little rudder. Although a man's tongue is small, it can accomplish great things. A small fire can spread to consume an entire forest. Man's tongue can be an evil fire which poisons the entire body and can cause the entire world to burn. Man has subdued all the animals, but he has not been able to tame the human tongue. It is always potentially evil. Its poison is deadly. Man's tongue blesses and curses men who are made in God's image. Blessings and curses come out of the same mouth. This situation should not exist. A fountain doesn't spout good and bad water from the same opening. A fig tree doesn't bear olives and vines don't produce figs. Salt water doesn't turn fresh [3:2-12].

The religiously wise and understanding Christian will be

[5] See Ch. II and p. 19 on heavenly hierarchy.
[6] See Ch. II and p. 23 on spirit and breath.

an example of proper living and humility, but jealousies and factionalism in man's heart must not be the source of pride or a reason to deny truth. The type of wisdom which produces these things is not godly, but sensual and devilishly earthly. Where jealousy and factionalism exist, there also is confusion and vile behavior. But God's wisdom which produces peace is pure, gentle, sympathetic, merciful, productive, consistent and honest. Those who make peace will harvest the reward of righteousness [3:13-18].

What is the source of dissension? Doesn't it arise from internal emotional conflict? A man's ravenous hungers are not satisfied and so he is filled with envy, the cause of strife. Man's petitions are not answered because they are not offered in the right spirit. He seeks only his personal satisfaction. Man who is unfaithful to God should know that worldly values are in conflict with God. Anyone motivated by such values is God's enemy. Does man suppose that Scripture means nothing? Is man's God-given natural desire simply a matter of envy? God also gives grace to those who are disposed to receive it. As the Scripture points out, "God resists the proud, but gives grace to the humble" [Prov. 3:34]. If man approaches God humbly, he will be received. Man must be both inwardly and outwardly clean. He must be honest. He must suffer hardship for his faith and give up pleasures that cause strife. His merry laughter must change to lament; his light-heartedness to a serious mien. If a man is humble before God, he will eventually be raised to great heights [4:1-10].

Some scholars question the next two verses. They may more properly belong after 2:3. Christians must not criticize each other. If a man criticizes or evaluates his fellow Christians, he is setting himself up as a judge and in doing so is evaluating God's law as well. A man who evaluates the law is not one who obeys it. God is the only law giver and he alone can condemn or acquit. By what authority do Christians place themselves in judgment over each other [4:11-12]?

How can any man be sure of his destiny? Some may say

that they will move to a city of their choice and spend a year there and make money in trade, but they don't even know what the next day will bring. Man's life is, after all, like a puff of steam that is only momentarily visible. Man should preface all his action on God's will. Instead man prides himself on his independence and evil attitude. If a man knows what is right and fails to do it, he is guilty of sin [4:13-17].

Rich people should weep and cry out in light of the miseries coming to them. Their riches have become rotten and their clothes moth-eaten. Their silver and gold have become tarnished, and the stain is evidence against them which will sear their flesh. They have accumulated wealth in the days close to judgment by withholding wages fraudulently. The very act cries out an accusation. God hears the cries of the swindled. The rich have lived well on earth and have enjoyed themselves and catered to their own selfish desires in times of judgment. They have even put to death innocent men who could not defend themselves [5:1-6].

Christians must be patient while they wait for Christ to come in judgment. As a farmer waits patiently from the beginning to the end of the season for the earth to produce crops, so must the Christian wait with patience because the time when Christ will come is very near. Christians must not complain lest they themselves be found guilty. The judge is about to enter the court. Christians must follow the example of the prophets who spoke in God's name. Men who have endured hardship for their faith are known as blessed people. That Job's patience was rewarded proved God's compassion and mercy [5:7-11].

Christians are not to take oaths under any circumstances. A man's simple word of honor should be good without need for further guarantees of veracity. He must be truthful or he will fall under judgment [5:12].

If a man is in trouble, he should pray for help. If all goes well, he should praise God. If a man is sick, he should ask the elders in the Christian community to pray for him in God's name and to anoint him with oil in which case God will heal him and forgive his sins.[7] Christians should, therefore, confess their sins to each other and pray for each other in order to be healed. A righteous man's supplications are powerful. Elijah was a devout man, and his prayer prevented rain for three and a half years; and when he prayed for rain, the rains came and the earth was fruitful again [5:13-18].

A man who succeeds in converting a sinner has saved a soul from death, and this action can save him from the consequences of a great deal of his own sins [5:19-20].

OUTLINE OF THE EPISTLE OF JAMES

I. Salutation and address, 1:1
Ch. 1

II. Temptation and reward, 1:2-18
- *a*) Temptation resisted produces Christian stamina, 1:2-4
- *b*) Christian wisdom obtained through prayer, 1:5-8
- *c*) Joy through God's service comes to both rich and poor, 1:9-12
- *d*) Temptation does not come from God, 1:13-18

III. The ospel to be heard and acted upon, 1:19-27
- *a*) The gospel to be heard, 1:19-21
- *b*) Faith implies action, 1:22-24
- *c*) Vain speech valueless, 1:25-26
- *d*) True religion is revealed in Christian activity, 1:27

IV. Warning against being unduly impressed by status and acting in contempt for God's law, 2:1-13
Ch. 2
- *a*) Distinctions must not be made between rich and poor, 2:1-4
- *b*) God chose the poor to receive his inheritance, 2:5-7
- *c*) Lawbreakers categorized and the fruits of mercy, 2:8-13

---

[7] Anointing with oil, the traditional and ancient method of healing.

V. Faith without works is valueless, 2:14-26

    a) True faith will motivate good actions, 2:14-20
    b) Abraham and Rahab examples of faith put into action, 2:21-26

VI. General warning against unchristian living, 3:1-4:10

Ch. 3   *a*) Teaching a grave responsibility, 3:1
        b) The dangers of an ignorant and unbridled tongue, 3:2-12
        c) Party strife is worldly and evil, true religious wisdom comes from above, 3:13-18
Ch. 4   *d*) Dissension, the result of man's base nature overcome by humility and God's grace, 4:1-10

VII. Forbearance recommended and the rich condemned, 4:11-5:6

    a) Judgment not man's province, 4:11-12
    b) God controls man's destiny, 4.13-17
Ch. 5   *c*) The rich castigated, 5:1-6

VIII. Exhortation to patience, 5:7-11

IX. Against perjury and an exhortation to prayer, 5:12-18

    a) Against perjury, 5:12
    b) Exhortation to prayer, 5:13-18

X. Fruitful ministry rewarded, 5:19-20

THE EPISTLE OF JUDE

Background

The purpose of the Epistle of Jude (Judas) is clear, but its author and destination, like those of the other Catholic Epistles, are obscure. The writing is also clearly a tract rather than a letter. It is addressed to a general Christian readership in those communities where Gnostic practices were corrupting the faith. Probably the practices of the Docetae are the main target. The writing begins and ends with a warning against the licentious behavior of theological errorists and bitterly denounces their activities.

The author was evidently a man so much a part of orthodoxy that he doesn't bother to refute heresy by argument. Rather, he contents himself with vehement castigation of unorthodox behavior. He unequivocally condemns those who do not accept Scriptural teaching and the authority of the apostolic college.

Evidence in the Epistle places it well outside the early apostolic age. Gnosticism was not an issue until the second century. Furthermore, the author admits that the first Christian era is past: (V.17) "But ye, beloved, remember the words which have been spoken before the apostles of our Lord, Jesus Christ." Both Verses 3 and 4 substantiate a late date. The faith had already been delivered to the first Christians (V.3), and V.4 refers to Christianity of ages past. Thus the writing could not have come from the pen of Jude, the brother of Jesus [Mk. 6:3, Mt. 13:55] as the salutation claims. It must have been written some time after 100 A.D. It is mentioned in the Muratorian Canon and by Tertullian, Clement of Alexandria and Origen, evidence that it was known in the middle of the second century. A guess within these limits might place the writing around 125-30 A.D. Although Rome may have been the place of origin, any prominent center of Christian activity fits its requirements as well. Some feel that its incorporation in II Peter, which is thought to be of Roman origin, makes Rome the most likely. Date and place substantiate pseudonymous authorship.

Structure

The Epistle, although very short, has four identifiable sections: salutation [1:1-2], denunciation of errorists [1:3-16], warning to be faithful to apostolic teaching [1:17-23], benediction and doxology [1:24-25].

Content

The salutation is brief. The author claims brotherhood to James in order to establish authority and terms himself a servant of Christ or Christian teacher. The writing is then addressed to the general readership of all Christians.

The next section constitutes the main body of the tract. The author asserts that he was about to write on the subject of salvation as a common Christian heritage, but changed his theme to a more pressing topic, an exhortation to preserve the purity of Christian faith, as it was understood by the apostles, against the erroneous influences of ungodly people who have for a long time been in line for condemnation. These people have perverted the gospel by lascivious activities and deny orthodox Christology [1:3-4].

Christians should remember some well-known past history. God saved the Israelites from Pharaoh's hand, but later those who did not believe in him were destroyed [Num. 14:24, 27; 26:64]. Even the angels who revolted against God did not escape divine wrath [Enoch Chs. 5-16, 21 ff, 54, 64, 67 ff]. The people of Sodom and Gomorrah who were given to gross sexual perversions were destroyed [Gen. 13:10ff, 19:24, Deut. 29:23]. Similarly men of the present time who have abandoned themselves to gross sexual immorality and perversion, show contempt for authority and laugh at godliness. Even the archangel Michael did not pronounce judgment on Satan with mockery, but left the matter to God.[8] The errorists, on the other hand, speak against authority which they do not understand without reason and as a result they will be destroyed. Woe will come to them for they have followed Cain's path [Gen. 4], have made Balaam's error [Num. 22-24], and, like Korah, have rebelled against God [Num. 16 ff]. Like hidden rocks to a ship, such people are a menace to Christian feasts. They feed themselves rather than those who are in need. They

[8] The line refers to an intertestamental writing, *The Assumption of Moses* in which the archangel Michael disputes with Satan for Moses' body.

are like rainless clouds, fruitless trees. They are completely dead because they don't have roots. They are like rushing seas producing only foam from their shameful character. They are like shooting stars that fall into eternal darkness. The Book of Enoch [Enoch 1:9, 27:2] foretold that it would be necessary for God to execute judgment on such people. They are chronic complainers who are motivated by their lusts and who speak boastfully, but who will pretend to be respectful if it seems to be to their advantage [1:12-16].

The next section reminds Christians that the apostles predicted that this sort of activity would occur in the days before judgment. These people break up communities, guided by fleshly appetites rather than spiritual motivation. Christians must build character through holy faith and by prayer under the aegis of the Holy Spirit. They must live in a relationship of love to God, expecting his mercy through Christ.

Christian activity with the errorists must be restrained, and mercy should be shown to those who are in doubt and are not yet completely committed to evil. Others can be saved only by snatching them away from sin while the completely depraved must be approached with pity as well as fear and hatred even for their contaminated clothes [1:17-23].

The tract closes with a comparatively long benediction and doxology [1:24-25].

OUTLINE OF THE EPISTLE OF JUDE

I. Salutation, 1:1-2

Ch. 1

II. Denunciation of errorists, 1:3-16

    a) Reason for writing, 1:3-4
    b) Warning against the consequences of evil activities, 1:5-11
    c) Evil character described, 1:12-16

III. Warning to be faithful to apostolic teaching, 1:17-23

IV. Benediction and doxology, 1:24-25

THE SECOND EPISTLE OF PETER

Background

Only one point is certain concerning the Second Epistle of Peter. The consensus considers it spurious. Certainly the author is neither Peter, the apostle, nor Peter the author of the first Epistle which bears his name. The style, slant, and posture are all totally different from First Peter. One large section of the Epistle is clearly a copy of Jude [2:10-22, Jude 9 ff]. An effort to appear prophetic by speaking from Peter's age concerning the subject matter of Jude is accomplished by substituting the future for the present tense in that section. That the "Assumption of Moses" is not, however, mentioned [Jude 9] confuses the passage as it appears in Second Peter

In spite of its fourfold claim, the Epistle can hardly have been written by the apostle: the salutation claims apostleship [1:1]; later the author identifies himself with Peter's predicted martyrdom by Jesus [1:14]; he claims to have been present at Jesus' transfiguration [1:17,18], and he claims to have written First Peter [3:1]. It has already been demonstrated [9] that First Peter was not written by the apostle Peter. Secondly, the writing clearly places itself outside the early apostolic age. Its use of Jude removes it at once from that period. Further the author admittedly knew the early fathers only by tradition [3:2-4], and lastly, the Pauline portfolio is known and accepted [3:16].

Like Jude the writing can best be described as a tract of the times apparently directed toward the general reader. Barnett describes it well as a manifesto of orthodoxy.[10] Although Chapter 2 is an attack on false teachers, Chapters 1 and 3 seem to be chiefly concerned with the need to reestablish faith in Christ's second coming and to denounce the lowered moral

[9] p. 316 this work on First Peter.
[10] The Second Epistle of Peter, Albert Barnett, *The New Testament, Its Making and Meaning*.

standards of the time [3:4]. As in Jude, the method for correction is castigation rather than argument.

The use of Jude, the fact that the first generation of Christians has passed, the reference to Paul, and the existence of doubt concerning the imminence of judgment not only preclude Petrine authorship, but place the letter well outside the time of Christ and well into the second century. The writing was known to Origen and Eusebius. Sometime between 125-175 A.D. which fits most of the specifications is a reasonable limit within which to place the writing. Rome, the center of orthodoxy, might be an educated guess for its place of origin. Lastly, the use of the pseudonym may be accepted as a means of establishing authority common in the period.

Structure

The book contains three main sections which follow roughly the chapter divisions: the first introduced by a short salutation [1:1-2] is concerned with the nature of Christianity in reference to man, morality and authority [1:3-19], the second taken largely from Jude tells of the judgment which will come to those who teach false doctrine [1:20-2:22], the third assures Christ's return and judgment and exhorts the reader to righteousness. It concludes with a doxology [3:1-18].

Content

In the salutation the author claims to be the apostle Peter. He emphasizes his claim by using the original Jewish name Simon. He tries to substantiate his assertion by reference to servant or teacher [1:1-2].

By God's divine commission Christians have been given all things necessary in order to live a godly life through an understanding of Christ's example. God fulfilled his promise by making it possible for Christians to acquire a divine nature and, in so doing, to escape from the worldly corruption of the flesh [1:3-4].

As a result Christians, for their part, must endeavor to cultivate their faith by living virtuously; their virtuous living must cultivate Christian understanding; their Christian understanding must cultivate self-control; self-control patience; patience godliness; godliness brotherly kindness; and brotherly kindness must cultivate love. If these things abound in a man, they indicate that Christian understanding is bearing fruit, not idleness. A person who lacks these characteristics is shortsighted and has forgotten the conversion experience which cleansed him from sin. Christians must, therefore, confirm their conversion and election by God. If they follow these virtuous actions, they won't fall into the way of sin, but will be granted entrance into the eternal kingdom of their Lord and Saviour Jesus Christ [1:5-11].

The author will always be ready to remind Christians of the facts surrounding their faith, even though these things are already familiar to them and are well established in their lives. He feels that it is his duty as long as he lives in this world to keep them active in the faith by reminding them of these things, for he knows that he won't live long because his demise was predicted by Christ.[11] In the meantime the author will work hard to make certain these things will be remembered after his death. The apostles did not make use of clever and spurious stories when they made Christ's second coming known. They witnessed his majesty personally. Christ received his commission from God himself for at the time of his birth God's voice said, "This is my well-beloved Son in whom I am well pleased." The apostles actually heard his voice when they were with Christ on the holy mountain. The Old Testament prophecies were fulfilled when they were heard. Christians should pay attention to these prophecies which shine like a lamp in darkness, giving illumination until dawn comes and light, like the morning star, enters their hearts [1:12-19].

Christians should know that no true scriptural prophecy is a matter of private interpretation. True prophecy doesn't

[11] The author's device for establishing himself as Peter, whose martyrdom was predicted by Christ, John 21:18-19.

come from man's spirit, but is the result of God's speaking through man by the Holy Spirit. False prophets lived in ancient days, like false teachers of present times who create destructive heresies that deny Christ, who saved them. These heretics will bring destruction upon themselves. Many people will be led astray by their wanton behavior thereby discrediting the truth. False teachers trade on Christian gullibility. With evil desires they convert the weak by false arguments, but they have been in a state of judgment for some time and their destruction is coming soon. If God didn't spare the angels when they sinned, but cast them into hell to wait in darkness until judgment day; and if he did not spare the ancient world, but drowned the ungodly in a flood and saved only Noah, a preacher of righteousness, with seven others; if he destroyed the cities of Sodom and Gomorrah by burning them to ashes as an example to those who lived an ungodly life, saving only the righteous Lot, who was desperately upset by the wanton life around him; if God acts in this manner, Christians may be certain that he can rescue the righteous and condemn the unrighteous until the punishment of judgment [1:20-2:9].

The next section of the writing is taken directly from Jude. God's condemnation will fall particularly upon those whose lives are motivated by fleshly appetites and who are contemptuous of authority. These daring and egotistical men are not afraid to hold divine authority in contempt. Even angels who are far more powerful and mighty respect divine authority. But these men, like unintelligent animals which are captured and killed, speak against things that they do not comprehend and, as a result of their destructiveness, will themselves be destroyed. They will receive God's punishment, the wages of their evil deeds.

These men find pleasure in open evil activity. They are filthy people who revel in deceiving Christians even while they feast with them. They always have an eye for adultery and they cannot cease from sin. They tempt the weak because they are experienced in the techniques of fulfilling their lusts. They are fathered by a curse. Like Balaam in the past, they forsake the way of righteousness. Balaam, son of Beor, was led into evil action for payment, but he was rebuked for his misconduct by a dumb animal that spoke with a man's voice and stayed his insane actions. These men are like dry springs. They are like clouds driven by a storm. They will end in utter darkness. By using ostentatious language, they appeal to fleshly appetites and corrupt people who are on the verge of breaking away from evil living. They promise liberty while they themselves are the slaves of corruption for men are slaves to that which controls them. A man who has been saved from worldly corruption through understanding and accepting Christ as Lord and Saviour and who lapses is in a far more terrible position than one who has never been converted. It is better never to have known righteous behavior than to have known it and then turned from God's way. Old proverbs speak to such people. The dog returns to his vomit and the sow to her wallow [2:10-22].

In the next section the Epistle leaves Jude and returns to the theme of Chapter 1. As Christ had not returned as quickly as expected, fear of impending judgment was lost as a deterrent to pagan immorality. The author now reiterates the belief that Christ will return and that judgment will come to those who deny the faith. In the first verse of Chapter 3 he claims to have written First Peter. Christians are to remember both the words of ancient prophecy and the teachings of Christ brought by the apostles. In the days immediately before judgment some people will ridicule the faith while living by standards created by fleshly appetites. They will ask, "What happened to the promise that Christ would come again?" Since the early days of the Christian movement after the first converts died, life has gone on exactly as before. In saying this they are deliberately forgetting that God created the world by separating heaven and earth and that the earth was surrounded by water. Furthermore, the ancient world was, on God's command, destroyed by water, but the present world and heaven are maintained by the same order until the day of judgment when ungodly men will be destroyed again.

One thing must not be forgotten. God is not bound by

time. God is not loose in his promises, as some may think, but is very patient; not wanting anyone to be lost. He gives all men an opportunity to repent. The judgment day will, however, certainly come unexpectedly. The heaven will disintegrate with a tremendous blast, the elements will be dissolved in searing heat, and the world with everything that it contains will be consumed. In light of the fact that everything will be annihilated, what sort of people should Christians be? Men who live a holy and godly life, searching for and wanting the day of judgment when annihilation of the present order will take place for according to God's promise Christians look forward to a new world and a new heaven ruled by righteousness [3:1-13].

As a result of these facts Christians should make a point of living so that they will be found flawless on judgment day. Christians should bear in mind that God's patience makes salvation possible, as Paul, with God-given wisdom, pointed out when he wrote them, even as he spoke of these things in all his letters, some of which are hard to understand. Ignorant and unstable people distort the material in the same way that they distort the scripture to their own destruction. Being aware of these things, Christians must be very careful not to be led into the evil ways of wicked men and fall from their solid faith before judgment [3:14-17].

Christians must grow in the grace and understanding of their Lord Jesus Christ to whom be glory now and forever. Amen [3:18].

OUTLINE OF THE SECOND EPISTLE OF PETER

Salutation, 1:1-2

Ch. 1

I. Concerning the nature of Christianity in reference to man, morality, and authority, 1:3-19

   a) The Christian heritage, 1:3-4
   b) Christians must behave accordingly, 1:5-11
   c) Christian faith of divine origin, 1:12-19

II. Judgment will come to those who teach false doctrine, 1:20-2:22

> a) Judgment awaits false teachers, 1:20-2:9
> Ch. 2 b) Evil character described, 2:10-22

III. Christ's return, judgment and an exhortation to righteousness, 3:1-17

> Ch. 3 a) Christ's second coming, 3:1-13
> b) Exhortation to righteousness, 3:14-17

Doxology, 3:18

THE EPISTLES OF JOHN

General Background

Although the Epistles of John are, as to authorship, date and direction, no less controversial than the other Catholic writings, and whereas other writers used pseudonyms, John may have penned at least two of the Epistles which bear his name. The question of which John, the Elder or the Son of Zebedee, remains. The first Epistle gives no direct clue. The salutations of the second and third identify the author with the Elder. Many scholars assume that John the Elder is the same John who wrote the fourth Gospel. Similarity of style and vocabulary indicate the possibility that the three letters share common authorship and may have originally been part of a single corpus.

The author was undoubtedly a man whose authority was known and accepted. This fact and the many similarities of style and thought to the fourth Gospel are sometimes accepted as sufficient evidence that John wrote both books. On the other hand, many dissimilarities can be found, and the issues which the Epistle considers clearly belong to a later period. Enslin suggests that the first and second Epistles may be the work of the fourth Evangelist's pen, directed against false teachers who in a later period misused his Gospel.[12]

The letters simply mention "The Elder," however, and no certain reason exists for identifying the author with "John, the Elder". The acceptance of John, the Elder, as the author of the fourth Gospel is also questionable. Further difficulty in determining authorship arises from the fact that the second and third letters do not treat the subject matter in the same way. Second John clearly opposes the Christian practice of welcoming itinerant preachers into established Christian communities, whereas third John urges their cordial reception. The last letter may be a skillful copy of the second, using the same style and format to neutralize the effect of its predecessor, in which case it may be considered spurious.

Although the place of composition is not mentioned in the Epistles, tradition has long associated them with Ephesus. They may well have been directed from there to general readers in Asia Minor. The reference to heretical ideas and the fact that the writings were known to Irenaeus and Polycarp and were used by Papias indicate a date within the first decade of the second century.

The purpose of the various writings is clear. The first was written against the particular form of Gnosticism which denied the complete humanity of Christ. The Docetists taught that Christ did not really exist in the flesh, but was a spirit that only appeared to suffer on the cross. The doctrine was incompatible with the Christian understanding of the atonement. The first Epistle is chiefly concerned with clarifying the nature of Christ as both the son of God and Jesus the man in conjunction with the new relationship he created between God and man by his sacrifice on the cross. Secondly, "John" seeks to establish an understanding of the love ethic in its application to life. Brotherly love is the second main theme of the first writing. "Believe in the name of his Son Jesus Christ, and love one another" [3:23].

The second and third Epistles are concerned with itinerant

[12] p. 349, Morton Scott Enslin, *Christian Beginnings*.

preachers who might possibly teach false doctrine or try to defraud the people. Overtones of church politics are also present. Men of recognized authority in their own locality probably resented new teachings from outsiders as well as the popularity of some of the itinerants.

THE FIRST EPISTLE OF JOHN

Structure

The Epistles are not true letters in spite of the format. Not only does the author use the phrase "we write" or "I write" [I John 1:4, 2:1, 12; 5:13], but he also seeks to indicate the existence of a close pastoral relationship. The phrase "my little children" appears repeatedly [2:1, 12, 18, 28; 3:7, 18; 4:4; 5:21]. In spite of its letter-like form, the writing is clearly a short tract-like document directed against Antinomianism, Docetism, and the teachings of Cerinthus[13] [2:22, 27]. It was no doubt directed to general readers in any locality where the Gnostic heresies flourished. The writing has been variously divided for the sake of study. The lack of clear-cut delineations and continuity makes several possible divisions acceptable. Six main sections, taken from the main themes of Christology and love, can be seen without difficulty. The first dealing with eternal life gained through fellowship with Christ [1:1-4] is followed by a long section on fellowship, sin, and the love ethic [1:5-2:11]; the theme is then broken by a short, direct appeal to the reader, emphasizing the love of God [2:12-17]; the next part dealing with the subject of antichrist [2:18-3:24] is followed by a short digression on the subject of true and false prophets [4:1-6]; the last section summarizes the author's position on love and exposes Gnostic fallacies [4:7-5:21].

[13] Cerinthus taught that divinity settled on Christ at baptism and withdrew again into heaven before the crucifixion. The teaching was popular in Ephesus in the last decade of the first century.

Content

The Epistle plunges at once into the main theme stressing Christ's tangible reality. Those who were first hand witnesses and ministers of Christ's word write about that which has always existed, that which they had seen and heard personally and which they had actually touched, that which was part of the eternal word of God and which was manifested to them, that which they had seen, they now declare to others that they too may become part of the fellowship of Christians on earth as well as with God and his Son Jesus Christ [1:1-4].

The message which Christ's ministers bring directly from him proclaims that God is righteous and that there is no righteousness in him. People who claim fellowship with God and live unrighteously lie and their life is a lie, but if they live righteously, because God is righteous, they share fellowship with each other and are cleansed from sin by the blood which Christ shed for mankind. People who claim to be sinless deceive themselves and are dishonest. If they confess their sins, God is righteous and true to his promises to cleanse them from sinfulness. People who claim to be sinless make God, who calls them sinful, a liar and are not part of his divine truth [1:5-10].

In the beginning of Chapter 2 "John" reiterates the material in 1:5-10 in language clearly directed at Gnosticism. He says he writes these things to indicate how sin can be avoided. If, however, a man sins, he has an advocate before God in the person of Jesus Christ, who atoned not only for the sins of Christians, but also for the whole world. Only by keeping God's commandments can a person be certain that he knows God. A man who claims to know God, but doesn't keep his commandments is a liar and deludes himself, but those who follow the teachings of Christ indicate that God's love has come to maturity within them. In this fashion a person knows he has become part of a godly life through Christ. A man who claims to be part of Christ must live in such a manner as to be an example of Christ's life [2:1-6].

The author writes nothing new, but reiterates an old commandment which was known to Christian communities from the first. This is the original word which continues to be true. The darkness of evil and untruth is passing away and the light of truth and righteousness already shines. A person who claims to be part of light and righteousness, but who hates his brother remains in the darkness of evil. A person who loves his brother lives in the light of righteousness; such a man won't fall, but a person who hates his brother lives in the darkness of evil and doesn't know where he will end, because evil has blinded him [2:7-11].

The letter is written to all Christ's children because their sins have been forgiven through Christ. The author writes to elders in the church, because they have known him who existed from the beginning of time; he writes to young men because they have been strong enough to vanquish the devil. Indeed he writes to all Christ's children because they know God, to the elders because they have known him who existed from the beginning, to the strong and devout young men who because of their strength have overcome the devil. Christians must not love worldly things. A materialist doesn't love God. Worldly things, fleshly appetites, things which appear glamorous, the vanities of the world, these things are not Godly, but originate in the world. Although the world and its desires are temporary and will some day be no more, a person who lives in accordance with God's will becomes part of things which are of eternal value and such a person will accordingly live forever [2:12-17].

In the section which follows, "John" writes from the belief that the judgment day is close at hand. The idea that the world's end would be heralded by a general out-break of evil activity is reminiscent of Paul [II Thess. 2:3-12]. The author warns that the last period before judgment is at hand, and even as Christians knew the prediction that the antichrist would come, so many antichrists have, in fact, appeared. Their appearance is clear indication that judgment is close. Although these evil men left the Christian community, they were never really a part of it. Had they been, they would never have left, but they did leave and in so doing indicate that not all who claim to be Christians are at heart part of the fellowship [2:18,19].

But Christians have been given insight into divine truth through Christ. The author doesn't write because they are ignorant of the truth, but indeed because they know it and can recognize truth from falsehood. The liar denies the reality of Christ's manhood. Anyone who denies the Father and the Son is antichrist. Anyone who does not recognize the Son cannot know the Father and anyone who knows the Son knows the Father well. Christians must adhere to the truth which they were originally taught. If they follow that teaching, they will live in fellowship with both the Son and the Father and partake in that which Christ promised, eternal life [2:20-25].

"John" now reiterates his statement concerning Christian insight and the need to remain steadfast in the faith. What has been written concerns those who would lead Christians into the acceptance of false teachings. Because those who remain steadfast possess an insight into divine truth through Christ, they do not need to be taught by anyone. Because this insight gives knowledge of all truth, because it is true not false, and because it teaches that man must live in Christ, Christians must live according to it. They must live in such a way that were Christ to come in judgment they would have no reason for fear or shame. If Christians recognize the fact that Christ is righteous, they must also know that everyone who lives righteously is part of his righteousness [2:26-29].

In Chapter 3 the Epistle turns to various ramifications of the love ethic and Christian salvation. Christians should see and understand the full implications of the love which God has bestowed upon them in calling them his children, for truly that is what they are. The world cannot recognize this fact, because it cannot recognize Christ. Christians are already God's children, although their future is not yet revealed. They know, however, that if Christ were to reveal himself, they would be like him, for when that time comes they will see him as he is. Anyone with the anticipation of such a future should keep himself as near Christ-like purity as possible. Anyone that sins breaks God's law. God's law specifies what sin is. Christ is sinless and was revealed to men to atone for their sins. A man who lives "in Christ" doesn't sin. A man who sins hasn't seen or understood Christ. Christians must not be led into sinful ways of life. A man who lives a righteous life is good even as Christ is good. A man who commits sin is devilish because the devil produced sin from the beginning of the world.[14] God's truth was revealed to the world through Christ in order to destroy the devil's works. A person who is one of God's sons is sinless because he inherits God's nature and so, coming from God, he cannot sin. Through these facts it is possible to differentiate between those who are God's children and those who belong to the devil. Anyone who doesn't live righteously is not one of God's children, nor is a man who doesn't love his brother one of God's children. From the very beginning the command has been to love one another. Christians must not be like Cain who killed his brother. Why did he kill him? Simply because his activities had been evil and his brother's were good. Christians should not be surprised then if the world hates them because of their goodness [3:1-13].

Christians know that they live in a new and eternal world, because of the relationship of love which exists between them. A man who doesn't love his brother lives in a world that ends. Anyone who hates his brother is capable of murder, and murderers do not inherit eternal life. Christians know about the love ethic and are part of it because of Christ's atoning action on the cross. As a result they should in turn be willing to give their lives for their brothers. How can God's love be in a rich man who sees his brother in need and closes his eyes to the situation. Christian love is not manifest simply in words or talk, but must be manifest in action and sincerity. By revealing Christian love in action, Christians can know for a certainty

[14] John understands Christ as the power of goodness and the devil as the leader of revolt against God and the source of evil in the world. To be righteous one is automatically part of Christ, Whereas to be sinful of necessity involves association with the devil.

that they are part of God's eternal truth, and their hearts can be confident in this knowledge. If Christians are condemned by their own conscience, they may find assurance in the fact that God is more charitable than they, although he knows everything. If Christians are not condemned by their own conscience, they may have complete confidence that they enjoy a good relationship with God. Whatsoever Christians pray for they will receive, because they keep God's commandments and do what he desires. God commanded men to believe in Christ and love each other. A man who obeys God's commandments lives in God's eternal world and God lives in him. Christians know that God lives in them because of the Holy Spirit which he gave them [3:14-24].

The next six verses are a digression concerning the familiar problem of true and false prophecy. Christians must not believe indiscriminately those who utter prophecy, but should put them to the test to find out if they speak truth, because the world is full of false prophets. The true spirit of God can be identified by the message (the author is now speaking directly against Docetism). Prophecy which proclaims that Christ came to earth in the flesh comes from God. Prophecy which denies this fact is not from God. Such prophecy comes from the antichrist that was predicted and is now here. Christians who belong to God have overcome the spirits of antichrist because God is stronger than evil. The spirits of antichrist are of this world and, therefore, speaking worldly language, can be heard and understood by worldly people. Those who know God understand Christians. Those who do not know God cannot understand them. It is, therefore, possible to differentiate between the true and the false [4:1-6].

In the next section the "John" returns to the main theme of love. Christians must love each other because the idea that God is love is the very essence of their faith. A man that really loves his fellows has been inspired by God and knows God. A man who doesn't know Christian love doesn't know God, because God is love. God's love was demonstrated in his sending his Son into the world that man might find eternal life through him. Real love is not revealed in man's love of God, but in God's love of man which was manifest when he sent his Son to atone for man's sins. If God loved man that much, surely men should love each other. No one has ever actually seen God, but if Christians live in a relationship of love with each other, God lives in them, and his love grows in them. Christians know that they live in God and God lives in them because he gave them the Holy Spirit. Christians give first-hand evidence to the fact that God sent his Son to be the Saviour of the world. Anyone who admits that Jesus is the Son of God has God living within him and he lives in God. Indeed God is love, and a man that lives in a relationship of love lives in God and God lives in him. Love grows in Christians so they may be confident on the day of judgment, because they are already living in God's world. Love is incompatible with fear. Perfect love destroys fear. Fear is a form of punishment coming from guilt. A man who fears is not completely ruled by love. Christians love God as a result of God's love for them. If a man claims to love God, but hates his fellow man, he lies because a man who hates his fellow man whom he has seen cannot love God whom he has not seen. Furthermore, Christians live under the command which implies that to love God one must also love his fellow man [4: 7-21].

The next section begins with a summary of John's theme and then turns again to the problem of Docetism in Christology. Anyone who believes in Christ is part of God's economy and anyone who loves God the Father of Christ must of necessity also love Christ. By loving God and following his commandments, Christians know they will also love all those who are God's economy. To love God means also to keep his commandments, and his commandments are not particularly trying, because anyone living within God's economy overcomes worldly desires. Christian faith is victorious for it can overcome the world. Who are the people that overcome the world? Those that believe Jesus is the Son of God. Jesus came to mankind by holy baptism and atoning sacrifice, not simply by one channel of grace, but by two. The activity of the Holy Spirit within man is a proof that this is true, and could not be otherwise, because the Spirit by its nature must be part of divine truth. (V.8 has been changed in some late MSS into a trinitarian formula.) Thus a triple testimony exists, the Holy Spirit in man, the baptism of water and the sacrifice on the cross, and all three testify to the idea that Christ is the Son of God. If Christian communities accept human testimony, so much the more should they accept divine testimony. God testifies to Christ's sonship. A man who believes Christ to be the Son of God accepts God's testimony in his heart, but a man who doesn't believe God's testimony makes God a liar by not accepting what God has said about his Son. This is the testimony. God has given man eternal life through his Son. A man who knows Christ and believes in him inherits thereby eternal life, and a man who does not accept Christ does not inherit eternal life [5:1-13].

These things have been written to assure Christians even though they already believe that they will inherit eternal life. Christians may be quite sure that their prayers will be answered when they follow God's will. Knowing this they know their petitions will be heard. If a man sees his brother commit a sin for which he will repent, he must pray that God will forgive him, because God will forgive those who can still repent. Sin can be committed, however, that goes beyond repentance. The letter is not written to request prayer for that type of situation. All unrighteousness is sinful, but some sin is not final [3:14-17].

Christians know that anyone who is part of God's economy does not sin, but such a man is under Christ's protection and the devil cannot reach him. Christians know that they partake of godliness, while the world around them is ruled by the devil. Further, they know that the Son of God came to this world and has given them an understanding of God's truth and that they partake of truth through his Son, Jesus Christ. This is the only true God and eternal life is real. The letter concludes with the command not to worship false gods [3:18-21].

OUTLINE OF THE FIRST EPISTLE OF JOHN

I. Fellowship with Christ, who was a tangible reality, 1:1-4

Ch. 1

II. Fellowship, sin and the five ethics, 1:5-2:11

    a) Sin destroys fellowship with God, 1:5-10
Ch. 2   *b*) Sin alienates man from God, 2:1-6
    c) The love ethic, 2:7-11

III. A direct appeal, 2:12-17

IV. The Subject of antichrist and the need for Christians to be strong in the faith, 2:18-3:24

    a) The activity of antichrist at hand, 2:18, 19
    b) Christians must seek the truth, 2:20-29
Ch. 3   *c*) The implications of salvation through Christ, 3:1-13
    d) The power of Christian love, 3:14-24

V. A digression dealing with true and false prophets, 4:1-6

Ch. 4

VI. Love summarized and Gnostic fallacies exposed, 4:7-5:21

    a) Love supreme, 4:7-21
Ch. 5   *b*) Love the basis of Christian understanding and Christology, 5:1-13
    c) Prayer, repentance and forgiveness, 5:14-17
    d) God assures Christians the final victory over evil, 5:18-21

THE SECOND EPISTLE OF JOHN

Background

The lady to whom the letter is addressed represents in all probability a church, and her children are the members of the congregation. If the little tract is for general readership, the lady no doubt represents the Church in Asia Minor and her children the Christians of the area.

Content

In the salutation John describes himself as the elder writing to one who has been chosen by God and to her children whom he truly loves and who are loved by all who know the truth of the Christian message. He writes for the sake of this truth which lives in Christians and which will live in them forever. He prays that God's grace, mercy, and peace may be bestowed on all Christians including himself [1:1-3].

The main body of the tract is a condensation of the material in its longer predecessor, First John, followed by a warning against the acceptance of false teachers who may come to Christian communities without proper authority.

He rejoices that he has met members of Christian communities who live according to the teaching of Christian truth as they were commanded to by God. He beseeches the members of the church to live in a relationship of love. This is no new commandment, but one familiar to Christians from the very beginning. Christian love is manifested by the fact that God's commands are obeyed. It has been known from the beginning that Christians must live in a relationship of love. But many impostors travel about who deny Christ's complete humanity. Such people destroy the truth and are antichrist. Christian communities must be careful not to lose all that has been given them by hard missionary work, but must continue strong in the faith until God finally rewards them [1:4-8].

Anyone who searches for knowledge and doesn't live according to Christ's teaching has lost God. A man who lives according to Christ's teaching knows both Father and Son as God. Anyone who comes to a Christian community and doesn't teach these things should not be received and really shouldn't be accepted at all, because to accept such a person is to become part of his evil activity [1:9-11].

John has much to say, but pen and ink are inadequate for the task. His coming to the community to speak in person will be a happy occasion. The community from which he writes sends greetings [1:12-13].

OUTLINE OF THE SECOND EPISTLE OF JOHN

I. Salutation, 1:1-3

Ch. 1

II. Christian love, antichrist and warning against errorists, 1:4-11

> *a*) Christian love and activities of antichrist, 1:5-8
> *b*) Criteria for Christian teaching and warning against errorists, 1:9-11

III. A visit planned and parting salutation, 1:12-13

THE THIRD EPISTLE OF JOHN

Background

The third letter of John is not so much concerned with doctrinal errors as with ecclesiastical organization and authority within the church. Contrary to the Second Epistle, this writing urges the acceptance of itinerant preachers. (The writing assumes them to be orthodox.) Apparently one, Diotrephes, has set himself up as sole authority in a community and does not welcome outside preachers of the word. On the other hand, Gaius, to whom the letter is addressed, seems to be a well-known and beloved preacher with a more liberal point of view. "John" praises Gaius and castigates Diotrephes.

Content

The writing opens with an extremely short salutation to Gaius [1:1]. "John" prays that the letter may find Gaius as prosperous and healthy in body as he apparently is in soul. John was very happy when Christians brought news that Gaius was a truly consecrated man and was living a Christian life. Nothing makes John happier than to know that his converts are living by the faith [1:2-4].

He commends Gaius for doing faithful work in his reception of strangers who are Christians. These men have told everyone in the church about Gaius' kindness. He has done well to help them in their journey because they travel in Christ's name and accept no assistance from non-Christians. Christians should welcome such people in order to be part of the fellowship [1:5-9].

John has written to the church in the past, but Diotrephes, who likes to be head man, doesn't recognize outside Christians. If John comes to the community, he will not, therefore, forget the things Diotrephes has done, his libelous statements, his discontent, his unwillingness to welcome outside Christians and his excommunication of those who do. Christians must not imitate evil, but must pattern their lives on godliness. A man that does good things is godly. A man who commits evil doesn't know God. Everyone speaks well of Demetrius. He is a truthful man. John's community testifies to his goodness and its testimony is known to be sound [1:10-12].

The last two verses [1:13-14] are nearly identical to those which conclude the second letter.

OUTLINE OF THE THIRD EPISTLE OF JOHN

I. Salutation, 1:1

Ch. 1

II. Prayer and news of Gaius, 1:2-4

III. Strangers to be received, 1:5-9
IV. Diotrephes castigated for not receiving itinerant Christians, 1:10-12
V. Conclusion and blessing, 1:13-14

XXII

The Revelation of John

Apocalyptic Literature

The word *apocalypse* means an uncovering, a bringing into view that which was previously unseen and thus a revelation. An apocalyptic writing is, therefore, primarily one which is revelatory. According to orthodox Jewry, the law was established and complete by the 3rd century B.C.; this meant that any writing after that period which purported to be prophetic and to represent divine revelation had to be pseudonymous, taking the name of some previously well-recognized and accepted authority. Furthermore, it had to use the recognized and accepted format of ancient prophecy. Prophetic utterances were usually spoken from ecstatic trances, induced either by whirling, inhaling noxious gas,or drunkenness, or from hypnotic or hysterical semi-consciousness induced by drum beats or strongly rhythmical music. The dreams thus experienced were thought to be revelatory. It was assumed that, for the purpose of revealing his will, God's spirit took possession of the prophet's body during the period of the trance. General characteristics of apocalyptic writing are, therefore, poetry, highly imaginative symbolism, rhythm, repetition, distortion,and poor continuity.

In the intertestamental period the motivation for apocalyptic writing came from a frustrated nationalism in conjunction with a desire to revive prophecy. First the forces of Greece and, after the fall of the Hasmoneans, Rome made it clear that victory and justice for Israel could only come as a result of divine interference in the world's political and military affairs. Accordingly a second general characteristic of Jewish apocalyptism was an attitude which despaired for the present, but which looked to an immediate future when a Messiah would come in judgment on the world and vindicate Israel's faith. Unlike the early prophets whose message was doom for a nation that had strayed from God's way, apocalyptic writers gave encouragement to a people who worshipped the one true God against the forces of evil. Written in what was clearly felt to be the end of an age, they foretold immediate judgment.

Background

The Book of Revelation is a Christian apocalypse. Although the writings whose form it copies were of necessity anonymous, the book establishes both the name and place of authorship. A second difference comes from the fact that it does not predict a new Messiah, but foretells the return of one already known. Otherwise it displays the general characteristics of its Old Testament and intertestamental predecessors. Like them it cries for undiscouraged and steadfast faith in the face of religious persecution and injustice.

At the turn of the first century prosperity and the Pax Romana had brought lush living to Asia Minor. Pagan religious rites were dominantly sexual in character, and the era pulsed with general immorality. At the same time emperor worship was enforced under Domitian's rule. Christian worship became, therefore, a crime against the state punishable by death. Nicolatism and persecution are the principal concerns of Revelation. The book is directed at strengthening Christians in the face of the double peril to their faith. Scholars generally concede that the book was, like the Epistles of John, written by one John, but they do not agree as to which John wrote it. Traditionally it is assumed that the book was composed on the Isle of Patmos where a large penal colony became the home of many Christians. John apparently knew Asia Minor well, as is evidenced by his knowledge of the churches there. His Greek is not, however, what might be expected from a man whose lifetime had been spent in a Greek colony such as Ephesus. He writes with Hebrew constructions that typify a Palestinian Jew. Because John, the son of Zebedee, is thought to have spent his late years in Ephesus, some scholars assume that he is the author of Revelation, as well as the fourth Gospel.

Objections must at once be raised to this assumption. In the first place it is highly unlikely that John, the son of Zebedee, was author of the fourth Gospel.[1] Secondly, the John of Revelation never refers to himself as an apostle, but rather assumes the position of prophet. Perhaps even more conclusive is the fact that the Gospel and the book do not share similarity of style, tone, or theology. The book cannot, therefore, be accepted as the work of John, the son of Zebedee, nor as the work of John the Elder if it is assumed that John the Elder wrote the fourth Gospel. The question of authorship remains unanswered. That John was a Palestinian Jew familiar with Asia Minor, who wrote from exile on the Isle of Patmos seems clear, but beyond this all is nebulous. Although some scholars date the writing as early as 64 A.D., assuming it to be the result of Neronic persecution, because the temple was no longer standing at the time of Revelation, a date prior to the fall of Jerusalem in 70 A.D. is not plausible. Although Vespasian passed an edict that all who did not partake in emperor worship were to be killed, Domitian's rule seems to fit more of the apparent circumstances of the writing than that of any other emperor. Sometime in the last decade of the first century is an acceptable date for the writing.

Throughout the ages the book has been variously interpreted. The early church fathers accepted a mystical and allegorical interpretation of the writing which ultimately leaves

[1] See p. 122.

its understanding to the imagination of each reader. The more popular historical approach is not, however, above criticism. The *futurists* think the book refers to the end of the world and to an age not yet begun. Others see it as representing a partially fulfilled plan of history. The apocalyptic style has led some to see in the book a description of the final battle between good and evil, and each successive age has interpreted its particular trial with "the beast." Mohammed, Luther, Napoleon, the Kaiser, Hitler, and even the Pope have been suggested as equivalents for "the beast." Contemporary scholarship is inclined to disagree with all of these positions. The book was written in and for the historical present of John's time with the expectation that God's judgment was imminent. Christians would be vindicated against the pagan power of Rome and those who were not among the righteous of God would be destroyed by his judgment.

Structure

The nature of the writing makes an outline and analysis difficult. Much of the interpretation will be forever obscure. In fact some question exists as to the legitimacy of any twentieth-century analysis and outline. Dreams and visions do not follow orderly sequences, nor can a work, if legitimate, which follows their pattern be expected to do so. The book does, however, have certain clear-cut divisions. It opens with statement of authorship, source, and significance followed by a salutation [1:1-8]; section two is a prologue describing John's vision [1:9-20]; section three consists of letters to seven churches in Asia Minor [2:1-3:22]; the fourth section describes John's vision of heaven [4:1-5:14]; the fifth, sixth, seventh and eighth sections consist of four series of visions and judgments broken at the end of each series by a vision of reward and reassurance for the righteous [6:1-20:15]; the last series concludes with visions of final judgment, the kingdom of God, a picture of the new Jerusalem, testimonials, and a benediction [21:1-22:21].

Content

God revealed himself to Jesus Christ, who in turn sent an angel to his teacher, John, who now testifies to all that he heard and saw. The end of the age has come. Those who read the word, those who hear the prophecies and those who adhere to the teachings thus set forth are blessed [1:1-3]. The salutation and designation of readers follows. John writes to the seven churches in Asia Minor. Although the use of the number seven probably comes from the tradition that seven was holy, the churches mentioned also represent the major centers of communication for the area. Grace and peace come from the Holy Spirit and from Christ who has created a community of followers, and who will come again from heaven to be seen by all. God is the beginning, the sustaining cause, and the end of all things [1:4-8].

There follows a description of John's vision, which evidently took place on Sunday (the first day of the week) on the Isle of Patmos. John, who is a persecuted Christian, fell into a trance and heard a great voice which commanded him to write to the seven churches in Ephesus, Smyrna, Pergamos, Thyatira, Sardis, Philadelphia,and Laodicea. John sees the Messiah standing a sovereign over all the churches. In the Lord's hand is a two-edged sword, symbolic of judgment. John is so shaken by this vision that he falls fainting, but is reassured by the Lord and commissioned to write concerning the things he sees [1:9-20].

The long section which follows contains the letters to the seven churches in Asia Minor, the first of which is Ephesus. The city was the chief outpost of the Christian movement in Asia, but it was also a hotbed of pagan superstition and vice. The Lord knows the stellar record of the Ephesian community for good work, patience, and abhorrence of evil-livers. The church is praised for its careful screening of true and false apostles. But the church has, in spite of this, apparently strayed from the original teachings of its founder (perhaps Paul). The vision urges that it return to the fold lest it fall into a state of judgment. One thing, however, is clear. It has resisted Nicola-itan practices. Christians who successfully resist persecution to the end (martyrdom) will inherit eternal life [2:1-7].

Smyrna was second only to Ephesus as a center of pagan culture. Apparently Christians were violently persecuted there and persecution from the Jews was particularly intense. The Lord is aware of this and urges Christians to remain steadfast unto death. If they remain faithful, neither death before nor after judgment can harm them. They will be given eternal life as a reward [2:8-11].

Although Pergamos was not as important a commercial center as either Ephesus or Smyrna, it outshone both in the number of pagan cults and temples. Not only did it boast temples to Zeus, Soter, Athena, Dionysus, and Aesculapius, but also a temple dedicated to emperor worship. The Lord knows the church has done well, existing in the very heart of evil, but still the Lord judges it for certain serious deficiencies. Some of its members eat idol meat and lead grossly immoral lives. These people must mend their ways quickly or they will be judged accordingly. Those who refuse to compromise with paganism at the risk of martyrdom will be given spiritual nourishment and the password to heaven [2:12-17].

Thyatira was a secondary city in the province. The church there was not troubled by direct religious influences, but by the presence of strong trade unions. Christians who might quite properly and naturally belong to such organizations took part in their feasts which were steeped in paganism. John writes that the Lord knows the steadfastness and fortitude of the Thyatirian church. It has grown steadily stronger, but it has one severe deficiency. Christians in the community have fallen under the influence of a modern Jezebel, who, claiming to be a prophetess, has lured them into immoral practices and persuaded them to eat idol meat. When she was given an opportunity to repent, she did not change her ways. As a result, she and all those who follow her example will be killed by plague so that she will be an example of God's wrath for all to see. The churches will then know that the Lord is one who knows all men's consciences and each will be judged accordingly. Those who have not followed false teaching, but who have remained steadfast to the end will stand with the Messiah at the time of judgment and inherit eternal life [2:18-29].

Sardis was an unimportant city in Lydia typical of the pagan moral decadence which the age produced. John says that the Lord knows that the church in Sardis was once active, but that it is now in moral decline. He wants them to be aware of their deficiencies. They have not fulfilled their Christian mission. They are warned to repent. If they do not, judgment will come quickly and unexpectedly. A few Christians have not, however, profaned their faith. Those who remain steadfast against temptation will be rewarded by eternal life [3:1-6].

Philadelphia was neither a large commercial center nor one of major religious significance. Its principal pagan cult was Dionysian. Apparently the Christian community there was strong and well-integrated. John writes that the Lord sees the community to be steadfast and strong. The Jews who claim to be in the tradition of their faith, but who are really following the devil in their persecution of Christians will someday be brought to hell. They will be converted to the faith and acknowledge the favored position of Christians before God. Because Christians in Philadelphia have kept God's commands they will be spared in the hour of trial which will come to the entire world. Judgment is imminent. Christians must be strong lest they lose out at the last minute. Those who endure to the end will inherit eternal life in God's kingdom [3:7-13].

Laodicea and her sister cities, Hierapolis and Colossae lie within a twenty-five mile circle in the Lycus valley. Already familiar to the readers of the captivity Epistles, the Phrygian city was best known as a wealthy manufacturing town and trade center. The indifference of the Laodicean Christians is castigated. They are neither hot nor cold. Because of their lukewarm attitude they will be rejected. The complacency of great wealth has blinded them to their spiritual poverty. The church is urged to become spiritually rich. Those whom God loves he chastises in order to correct their deficiencies. Christians must be jealous in their faith and show signs of repentance. The Lord is ready to enter any man's heart who is willing to hear his voice. Those who remain steadfast to the end will inherit eternal life [3:14-22].

The locale of John's vision now changes abruptly from earth to heaven. John continues to describe his vision. John sees a door opened and a loud voice commands him to come up and see the things which will occur in the future. He sees the Lord sitting on a throne and around the throne are twenty-four elders. Lightning and thunder come from the throne (similar to the theophany of Moses, Ex. 19:16). In front of the throne are seven lamps and a sea of glass and around the throne he sees four living, winged creatures embodying the characteristics of a lion, a calf, a man, and an eagle. These vigilant creatures and the twenty-four elders praise God without ceasing [4:1-11].

The description of the vision continues in Chapter 5. John sees a great book full of writing sealed with seven seals in the hand of him who sits on the throne. An angel asks who can break the seals on the book, but no one in either heaven or earth can do so. John weeps because the book cannot be opened. He is reassured by one of the elders who says that one in David's line from the tribe of Judah can open the book. He sees a sacrificial lamb standing in the midst of the heavenly host, and the lamb takes the book while all in heaven give praise saying that the lamb has been given in sacrifice to God for all mankind. John hears the heavenly host acclaim the lamb worthy to receive all power, riches, wisdom, might, honour, glory, and blessing. The section closes with a great doxology [5:1-14].

The next section describes the judgments revealed as Christ breaks the seals in the great book. After John sees the lamb open the first seal, a mounted archer comes forth in the act of conquest [6:1-2]. The breaking of the second seal reveals a red horse which will bring war and strife [6:3-4]. The third seal is loosed to reveal a black horse whose rider, probably representing famine, holds a balance to measure the produce of the land, [6:5-7]. When the lamb opens the fourth seal, death is revealed riding a pale white horse [6:8-9]. The fifth seal is broken to reveal the souls of the martyrs represented as sacrificial blood under the great altar. Persecution is thereby signified. In answer to the cry, "how long?" the saints are told they must wait until the number of martyrs is complete. The sixth seal is broken to reveal divine judgment on all the earth. Christ sits in glory to judge all mankind—princes, kings, military leaders, rich, poor, slave and free alike [6:12-17].

Chapter 7 is the first of three parenthetical interludes which assures salvation for the righteous. John sees four angels standing at the four corners of the earth withholding the winds so that none can blow on land, sea, or tree. Apparently they are making ready for the earth's final destruction, but they are stayed by an angel carrying God's commission who orders them to wait until the righteous have been sealed and so set aside from the destruction to come. The seal is a sign that they belong to God. John hears that 144 thousand from the tribes of Israel are to be saved. An inventory of the tribes follows. After this he sees those who have been saved standing in heaven glorifying God [7:1-17].

In Chapter 8 the seventh seal is broken and a new series of judgments begins, after silence has reigned in heaven for half an hour. The silence is explained as a period during which the prayers of the saints are heard. Seven angels then sound trumpets and judgment begins [8:1-6].

After the first trumpet sounds, one third of the earth is destroyed by hail and fire [8:7]. After the second trumpet sounds, one third of the sea, the ships on it and the fish in it are destroyed by a great burning mountain [8:8-9]. After the third trumpet sounds, one third of the springs and rivers of the earth are poisoned [8:10-11]. After the fourth trumpet sounds, one third of the heavens are destroyed. Woe is cried for the three judgments yet to come [8:12-13]. When the fifth trumpet sounds, an angel descends to the earth like a fallen star to release demonic forces of evil from within; in the form of locusts, evil tortures the unjust, but is not allowed to molest the righteous [9:1-12]. When the sixth trumpet sounds, a voice commands four angels of destruction to lead countless hordes of demon soldiers in the destruction of one third of all mankind [9:13-21].

The series of judgments is interrupted by a second parenthesis which tells that the final hour is at hand. This section consists of a book within the body of the writing dealing with the temple. John sees an angel from heaven with a little book who stands in judgment over all the earth and who speaks with a mighty voice. John is commanded not to write what he hears. The angel announces the judgment will be delayed no longer. The time has come. John is given the book to eat; after he eats it, he is commanded to prophesy to all the nations of the world [10:1-11].

John is told to measure the temple, but not to include the outer courtyard and the surrounding city, both of which will be trod under foot for three and a half years [11:1-2]. While this judgment is carried out two of the Lord's agents will prophesy against the enemies of righteousness. They will be protected until they have finished their task; then a beast will come from the depth of the earth and kill them. Their bodies will lie in the streets of the city for three and a half days during which time those who remain on earth will rejoice over their death, but after that time God will revive them, to the consternation of those who rejoiced. The two prophets ascend to heaven and in that instant the earth is stricken by an earthquake and one tenth of the city falls down and seven thousand people are killed; those who remain glorify God in fear [11: 3-14]. The seventh triumph of God's kingdom is heralded by praise from the elders in heaven. The last verse in the section pictures the Ark of the Covenant in its rightful heavenly situation [11:15-19].

The writing now begins the description of a second series of miracles. In Chapter 12 John sees a woman gorgeously arrayed with the sun and a crown of twelve stars with the moon under her feet. The woman is in labor. A terrible dragon which casts one third of the stars in heaven to the ground waits to devour the woman's child. The woman is delivered of her baby which is taken to God's throne, while its mother flees to the wilderness where she is protected for 1260 days [12:1-6]. The vision follows ancient pagan mythology, but may represent the author's adaptation of the story to the Israelite nation from which the Messiah was to come. The allegory goes on to show that the forces of evil are unable to destroy the child. The passage which follows might better have been placed before the vision of the baby, because it explains the cosmology and precedes it chronologically. Michael, captain of the heavenly host, is at war with the dragon (Satan) who leads the demonic forces of the universe. Satan loses the battle and is cast out of heaven. The time of the last battle which will end in victory for righteousness is at hand [12:7-13].

In the last part of Chapter 12 the vision returns to the myth of the woman and the dragon. The dragon, cast down to earth, persecutes the woman who gave birth to the child. The woman is given wings with which to escape to the wilderness where she remains for two and a half years. The dragon's attempt to destroy her by water is foiled by the earth. The enraged dragon leaves the woman and makes war on the righteous who follow God's commands and believe in Jesus [12:14-17].

Chapter 13 contains the vision of two beasts which symbolize the antichrist. The first beast probably represents the Roman empire and the second Satan, although it is possible that Nero or a contemporary Roman authority may have been in the author's mind. John sees a beast emerge from the sea and the dragon gives power to the beast. One of the heads of the beast is severed, but is healed. The people of the earth worship the dragon and the beast, because no one can fight successfully against such power. The reign of evil continues for three and a half years. Everyone on earth worships the beast except those righteous whose names are written in the Lamb's book, but even they must endure martyrdom [13:1-10].

John sees coming up from the depths of the earth a second beast which speaks like a dragon and which has authority over the first. It makes men worship the first beast and works great wonders by which it deceives mankind. All men who worship the beast are branded; these number 666. The number is thought by some authorities to indicate the followers of Nero [13:11-18].

Chapter 14 which begins the third parenthesis in the series of visions and judgments describes the rewards of faith. John sees the Lamb standing on Mt. Zion surrounded by 144 thousand people who are branded in his name. The people sing an anthem of praise to the Lamb quite the opposite of that sung by those who praise the beast. The righteous are pure and follow the Lamb in heavenly bliss [14:1-5]. John sees an angel flying in heaven who proclaims imminent judgment and asks all to worship God, who rules the universe, and who is the opposite of the dragon [14:6-7].

A second angel follows the first, proclaiming the fall of those who are against the righteous. Babylon probably represents Rome. A third angel follows pronouncing judgment and doom for all those who worship the beast and promising blessedness for all those who have endured suffering for their faith [14:8-13]. After John sees the Messiah sitting on a white cloud, an angel appears proclaiming the time of judgment to be at hand. The harvest is to be reaped and the grapes brought to press [14:14-20].

In the next section John describes a third series of visions and judgments. He sees another sign in heaven, seven angels in charge of seven plagues [15:1]. An interlude describes the redeemed who were successful in resisting the beast and were not numbered among its followers. These people sing praises to God in eternal bliss [15:2-4]. John now returns to the seven angels carrying seven plagues in their hands and representing the wrath of God. The temple in which God sits is filled with his mighty power, and none can enter therein until the plagues have been spent [15:5-8].

John hears a voice commanding the angels to pour the

seven plagues on the earth. The description of the plagues is reminiscent of the plagues sent against Pharaoh when Moses sought to liberate his people from Egyptian bondage [Ex. 7-11]. The first plague is boils [16:1,2]. The second poisons the sea killing all animal life [16:3]. The third plague poisons the rivers of the earth turning them to blood [16:4-7]. The fourth plague is searing heat, but the people of the earth do not repent [16:8-9]. The fifth is directed particularly to those who follow the beast; they are enveloped in darkness and pain [16:10-11]. The sixth plague dries up the Euphrates River, thereby removing the natural barrier between Rome and the East which made conquest by the Parthians a possibility [16:12]. The dragon rallies the forces of evil. Then a final battle is pictured as taking place on the ancient field of Megiddo [16:13-16]. The seventh plague is an earthquake which destroys all the cities of the world and Rome in particular [16:17-21].

In Chapter 17 the judgment to come upon Rome is made clear. The great harlot is Rome. The imagery is not without historical background. The ancient city was a place of utter moral debasement. One of the seven angels takes John to see the judgment which will befall the harlot who fornicates with the world's kings, and he sees her sitting on a scarlet beast which is full of the names of blasphemy. The reference here may be to the deification of the emperors. By Roman custom, harlots wore their names on their brows; so also does the woman in the vision. She is clearly identified with Rome by the word Babylon used as her name [17:1-6].

In the second part of the chapter the angel explains the meaning of what John has seen. The beast which he saw is a thing of the past, without any future, headed for perdition. Those whose names are not in the book of life will not understand what is happening. The city of Rome and her emperors will go to perdition. Furthermore, the world's rulers who take their authority from evil and war (against Rome as well) will all, in due time, be destroyed by the Lord and his heavenly hosts [17:7-18].

John then hears another voice from heaven calling the faithful to leave the city in order to escape the destruction to come [18:1-3]. The city's sin has been seen in heaven; she will receive double for all she has done, even though in her complacency she considers herself a queen above sorrow. In an instant the plagues will come with death, sorrow, famine and utter destruction, for God is mighty in judgment. The rulers of the world who associated with her will withdraw from her and cry in fear; all the merchants of the world who bought and sold all things, including slaves and the souls of men, will stand apart from her for fear of similar torture. They will cry and lament, and all who sail in ships will see the smoke of the burning city and will weep and lament, but the righteous in heaven will rejoice over God's judgment [18:4-20].

Finally, a strong angel picks up a huge millstone and throws it into the sea saying that thus, with a mighty crash, will Rome be cast down and cease to exist. All signs of life will vanish [18:21-24].

After Rome's doom is complete John hears the heavenly host of the righteous glorifying God with great hymns of praise. The Lord reigns victorious over both Satan and Rome. The marriage of the Lamb, probably signifying the union of Christ with the community of the righteous, is announced [19:1-10].

John sees a heavenly warrior mounted on a white horse leading the armies of heaven, clad in white garments and mounted on white horses, against the sinful nations of the world. An angel summons all the buzzards that fly in the air to come and feast on the flesh of the vanquished. The beast and the false prophet that misled him and those who received the mark of the beast are cast into a lake of fire and brimstone. All that remain are put to the sword and the buzzards eat their flesh [19:11-21].

The last three chapters of the book present chronological problems. Judgment continues, although in Chapter 19 the day of judgment is complete. Furthermore, within the chapters themselves, chronological continuity is confused: 20:4–21:8

describes events which follow the confinement of evil while the saints rule in the new order, but 21:9–22:2 which follows describes the new Jerusalem with pagan forces still in existence around it. In 20:11–15 the unredeemed have been destroyed, but 22:15 describes evil outside the city. Various explanations such as the use of different sources, a later addition to the book, the inconsistency of dreams, have been offered to reconcile the contradictions. Such solutions can be little more than speculative.

Chapter 20 begins the last series of visions and judgments. John sees an angel come down from heaven with a key to the depths of the earth and a great chain in his hand. Satan is bound and cast into the abyss for a thousand years after which he is to be set free for a short time [20:1-3]. John sees the righteous, who gave their lives for the faith and were not numbered among those who worshipped the beast, reign with Christ for a thousand years. Only those who have been martyred receive this reward. The second death has no power over these people [20:4-6].[2]

At the end of a thousand years Satan comes out of his prison and leads all the faithless people who are left on the earth in revolt against the heavenly city. Fire comes down from heaven and destroys them all. The devil is cast into the lake of fire and brimstone into which the beast and the false prophet have already been cast, where they will receive eternal punishment [20:7-10].

John sees the great white throne of judgment, the book of life is opened, and the dead from all places are judged according to what is written therein. Death and Hades are cast into the lake of fire with all those whose names do not appear in the book of life [20:11-15].

In Chapter 21 John describes the last vision. He sees a new heaven and earth in which there is no sea and he sees the

---

[2] Prof. Clogg understands the second death as signifying the death at the end of the Messianic Kingdom rather than physical death which is the lot of all men. F. Bertram Clogg, *Revelation*. Abingdon Bible Com., Abingdon Press.

holy city, the new Jerusalem, come down from heaven. God is united with his people. Sorrow, pain, death, and mourning are banished. Everything is made new. God is the beginning and end of all things. Those in need are cared for and those who suffered martyrdom inherit eternal life in the new universe, but those who do not believe are cast into the lake of fire and brimstone which is the second and final death [21:1-8].

One of the angels who held the seven plagues speaks to John and shows him the heavenly Jerusalem. A long and minute description of the city follows [21:9-27]. No unclean person can enter the city. Only those whose names are in the book of life can enter. In the middle of the city is a river reminiscent of the river that watered the garden of Eden, and on each side are trees of life. Those who live within the city live by God's great light in a state of heavenly bliss [22:1-5].

The concluding section begins with a testimonial to the validity of all that has been foretold and with the prediction that Christ will soon come to judge the world [22:6-7]. John himself gives testimony to the fact that he heard and saw all the things previously described in his vision. He says that he attempted to worship the angel who showed him the vision, but was forbidden to do so. This is apparently an injunction against angel worship [22:8-9]. John is then told not to seal up the book because the day of judgment is actually at hand. The inference from the lines is clear: it is too late for anyone to change his status. The unrighteous will continue so until the end. The same holds true for the righteous. Judgment is coming quickly. The blessed are in; the evil are out [22:10-15]. Christ's Messianic claim is made clear [22:16]. The righteous are invited to partake of eternal life. Those who have accepted the message are those who thirsted after truth and life; their thirst can be slaked by the eternal word of God alone [22:17]. John asserts that his testimony is not to be changed in any way [22:18-19]. The book closes with a prayer that Christ may come quickly followed by a benediction [22:20-21].

OUTLINE OF THE REVELATION OF JOHN

I. Authorship and salutation, 1:1-8

Ch. 1   *a*) Authorship and authority, 1:1-3
          b) Salutation and direction, 1:4-8

II. John's first vision, 1:9-20

III. The letters to the seven churches, 2:1-3:22

Ch. 2   *a*) The letter to the church in Ephesus, 2:1-7
          b) The letter to the church in Smyrna, 2:8-11
          c) The letter to the church in Pergamum, 2:12-17
          d) The letter to the church in Thyatira, 2:18-29
Ch. 3   *e*) The letter to the church in Sardis, 3:1-6
          f) The letter to the church in Philadelphia, 3:7-13
          g) The letter to the church in Laodicea, 3:14-22

IV. John's vision of heaven, 4:1-5:14
Chs. 4-5

V. A series of judgments, 6:1-11:19

Ch. 6 A. *Christ opens the seals, 6:1-17*
          a) Conquest revealed, 6:1-2
          b) War and strife revealed, 6:3-4
          c) Famine revealed, 6:5-7
          d) Death revealed, 6:8-9
          e) Persecution revealed, 6:10-11
          f) Final judgment revealed, 6:12-17

Ch. 7 B. *The righteous saved from worldly disasters, 7:1-17*
       c. *The seventh seal and judgments, 8:1-9:21*
Ch. 8   *a*) Silence in heaven while prayers of the faithful are heard, 8:1-6
          b) The first judgment, hail and fire, 8:7
          c) The second judgment, the sea destroyed, 8:8-9
          d) The third judgment, the waters of the earth are poisoned, 8:10-11
          e) The fourth judgment, the heavens destroyed, 8:12-13
          f) The fifth judgment, the forces of evil unloosed on the unrighteous, 9:1-12

Ch. 9   *g*) The sixth judgment, demon armies to destroy the unrighteous, 9:13-21

    D. *The time of final judgment and a secondary apocalypse,*
    10:1-11:19

Ch. 10   *a*) Final judgment announced, 10:1-11
Ch. 11   *b*) The temple to be measured, 11:1-2
      c) An interim before judgment, 11:3-14
      d) The seventh trumpet announces the establishment of
      God's kingdom, 11:15-19

VI. A second series of visions and judgments, 12:1-14:20

Ch. 12 A. *The vision of the woman and the dragon, 12:1-17*

    a) The woman in travail, 12:1-6
    b) The angel Michael at war with Satan, 12:7-13
    c) The woman and the dragon continued, 12:14-17

Ch. 13 B. *The vision of the two beasts, 13:1-18*

    a) The first beast, 13:1-10
    b) The second beast, 13:11-18

Ch. 14 C. *Four visions of reward, 14:1-20*

    a) The vision of the Lamb,14:1-5
    b) The vision of the angel who proclaims God's sovereignty, 14:6-7
    c) The vision of the angels who proclaim Rome's doom, 14:8-13
    d) The vision of judgment, 14:14-20

VII. A third series of visions and judgments, 15:1-19:21

Ch. 15 A. *Seven angels holding seven plagues, 15:1-16:21*

    a) Seven plagues, 15:1
    b) The vision of redemption, 15:2-4
    c) The vision of seven angels, 15:5-8
Ch. 16   *d*) The seven plagues, 16:1-21

Ch. 17 B. *The harlot and the beast, 17:1-18*

    a) The harlot, 17:1-6
    b) The vision explained in terms of the beast, 17:7-18

Ch. 18 C. *The vision of Rome's doom, 18:1-24*

    a) Rome's fall announced, 18:1-3

  b) Rome's doom in process, 18:4-20
  c) Rome's doom complete, 18:21-24

Ch. 19 D. *The vision of heaven in victory, 19:1-21*
  a) Exaltation in heaven over Rome's doom, 19:1-10
  b) The heavenly warrior, 19:11-21

VIII. A fourth series of visions and judgments, 20:1-22:21

Ch. 20 A. *The kingdom of God, 20:1-15*
  a) Satan bound for a thousand years, 20:1-3
  b) The righteous reign with Christ for a thousand years, 20:4-6
  c) The end of the kingdom, 20:7-10
  d) Final judgment, 20:11-15

  B. *The new Jerusalem, 21:1-22:5*
Ch. 21 *a*) The new universe, 21:1-8
  b) The holy city, 21:9-22:5

Ch. 22 C. *Testimonies and benediction, 22:6-21*
  a) Christ's testimony and imminent judgment, 22:6-7
  b) John's testimony, 22:8-9
  c) Final warning, 22:10-15
  d) Christ's Messianic claim, 22:16
  e) An invitation and promise for righteousness, 22:17
  f) A dire warning against changing the books' testimony, 22:18-19
  g) Prayer and benediction, 22:20-21

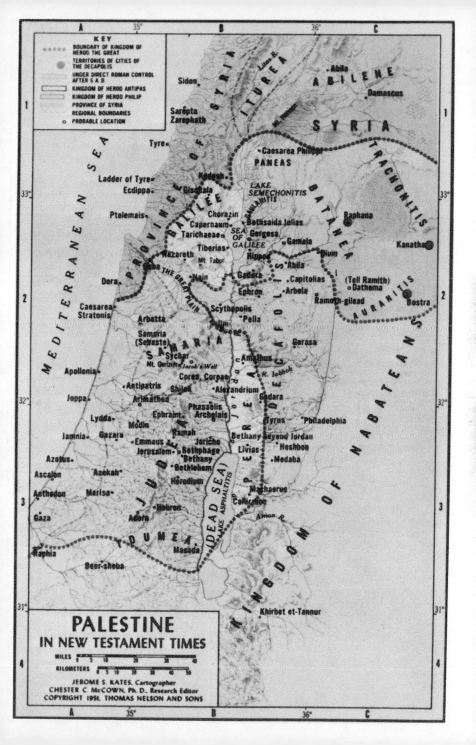

PALESTINE
IN NEW TESTAMENT TIMES

JEROME S. KATES, Cartographer
CHESTER C. McCOWN, Ph. D. Research Editor
COPYRIGHT 1951, THOMAS NELSON AND SONS

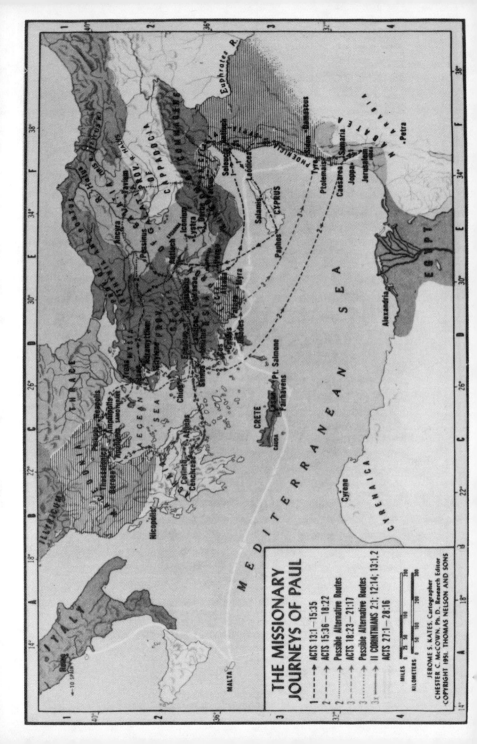

**THE MISSIONARY
JOURNEYS OF PAUL**

1 – – – – → ACTS 13:1—15:35
2 – – – → ACTS 15:36—18:22
2 ··········· Possible Alternative Routes
3 –·–·–·–→ ACTS 18:23—21:17
3 ············ Possible Alternative Routes
3x ─────── II CORINTHIANS 2:1; 12:14; 13:1,2
─────── ACTS 27:1—28:16

MILES 0 25 50   100   200   300

KILOMETERS 0 50 100   200   300

JEROME S. KATES, Cartographer
CHESTER C. McCOWN, Ph. D. Research Editor
COPYRIGHT 1951. THOMAS NELSON AND SONS

BIBLIOGRAPHY

Abingdon Bible Commentary.

Albert E. Bailey and Charles F. Kent, *A History of the Hebrew Commonwealth.* Charles Scribner's Sons, 1945.

Albert E. Barnett, *The New Testament: Its Making and Meaning.* Abington-Cokesbury Press, New York, Nashville, 1946.

Herbert Newell Bate, *A Guide to the Epistles of St. Paul.* Longman's Green and Co., London, New York, Toronto, 1953.

Dwight Marion Beck, *Through the Gospels to Jesus.* Harper & Bros., New York, 1954.

Gunther Bornkamm, *Jesus of Nazareth.* Hodder & Straughton, London, 1960.

Crane Brinton, Christopher, and others, *A History of Civilization.* Prentice Hall, Inc., n.d.

Frederick R. Crownfield, *A Historical Approach to the New Testament.* Harper & Bros., New York, 1960.

Martin Dibelius, *Paul.* Longman's Green & Co., London, New York, Toronto, 1953.

C. H. Dodd, *The Interpretation of the Fourth Gospel.* Cambridge University Press, 1958.

Will Durant, *The Story of Civilization,* Simon & Schuster, 1935-61.

Will Durant, *The Life of Greece.* Simon & Schuster, 1939.

Burton Scott Easton, *Early Christianity: The Purpose of Acts and Other Papers.*

Walther Eichrodt, *Man in the Old Testament.* SCM Press Ltd., London, 1951.

Morton Scott Enslin, *Christian Beginnings.* Harper and Brothers, New York, London, 1938.

Louis Finkelstein, *The Jews: Their History, Culture, and Religion.* Harper & Brothers Publishers, New York, 1949.

Henry Thatcher Fowler, *The Origin and Growth of the Hebrew Religion.* The University of Chicago Press, Chicago, Ill., 1943.

James George Frazer, *The Golden Bough* (Abridged). MacMillan, 1951

Reginald H. Fuller, *The New Testament in Current Study.* Charles Scribner's Sons, 1962.

379

Dr. P. Gardiner-Smith, *Saint John and the Synoptics*, 1938.

Maurice Goguel, *The Life of Jesus*. The Macmillan Co., New York, 1933.

Edgar J. Goodspeed, *How Came the Bible*. Abingdon-Cokesbury Press, 1940.

Norman K. Gottwald, *A Light to the Nations*. Harper & Bros. 1959.

Fred. C. Grant, Editor, *Early Christianity: The Purpose of Acts, and Other Papers*. Seabury, Greenwich, Conn. 1954.

Frederick C. Grant, *The Gospels: Their Origin and Their Growth*. Harper and Brothers, 1957.

Edmond Jacob, *The Theology of the Old Testament*. Harper Bros. Publishers, New York, 1958.

Ludwig H. Koehler, *Old Testament Theology*. Lutterworth Press, London, 1957.

George M. Lamsa, *The Modern New Testament from Aramaic*. Holman.

William L. Langer, *An Encyclopedia of World History*. Houghton Mifflin Co., 1952.

R. H. Lightfoot, *St. John's Gospel: A Commentary*. Oxford at the Clarendon Press, 1956.

James Moffatt, *Introduction to the Literature of the New Testament*. Charles Scribner's, 1925.

George Foot Moore, *Judaism in the First Centuries of the Christian Era—The Age of Tannaim*. Harvard University Press, 1927-30.

J. B. Phillips, *Letters to Young Churches*. The MacMillan Co., 1950.

James L. Price, *Interpreting the New Testament*. Holt, Rinehart Winston, 1961.

Charles A. Robinson, Jr., *Ancient History*. MacMillan, 1951.

J. H. Ropes, *The Synoptic Gospels*. Harvard, 1961.

M. I. Rostovtzeff, *A History of the Ancient World*. Oxford, Clarendon, 1926-8.

H. H. Rowley, *The Faith of Israel*. SCM Press, Ltd., 56 Bloomsburg St., London, 1956.

Charles A. Anderson Scott, *Christianity According to St. Paul*. Cambridge University Press, 1928.

Charles Edward Smith, Paul Grady Moorehead, *A Short History of the Ancient World*. D. Appleton-Century Co., 1939.

B. T. D. Smith, *The Parables of the Synoptic Gospels*, Cambridge University Press, 1937.

Henry Preserved Smith, *The Religion of Israel*. Charles Scribner's, 1914.

J. Paterson Smyth, *How We Got Our Bible*. James Pott & Co., New York, 1899.

Burnett Hillman Streeter, *The Four Gospels: A Study of Origins*. Macmillan & Co. Limited, St. Martins St., Lonon, 1936.

Frank Thilly, Ledger Wood, *A History of Philosophy*. Henry Holt & Co., 1959.

Williston Walker, *A History of the Christian Church*. Charles Scribner's Sons, 1959.

W. L. Wardle, *History and Religion of Israel*. Oxford, Clarendon Press, 1936.

Max Weber, *Ancient Judaism*. The Free Press, 1952.

C. S. C. Williams, *A Commentary on the Acts of the Apostles*. A & C. Black, London, 1957.

Herman Wouk, *This Is My God*. Doubleday, 1959.

INDEX

Acts of the Apostles: authorship, 145; miracles in, 150f.; outline, 151ff.; picture of Paul, 147; purpose, 146f.; structure, 148f.; "we-sections," 151
Ahriman, 13
Ahura Mazda, 13
Alexander the Great, 4f., 17
Alexandria, 299
Allegory, 58ff.
Ananias, 32, 167
Angels, 18
Anointed priest, 17
Anthropomorphism, 18, 20f.
Antigonus, 5
Antinomianism, 345
Antioch, 174, 236
Antiochus I & III, 5
Antiochus Epiphanes, 5
Aphrodite, 200
Apocalyptic literature, 358
Apocrypha, 104n.
Archelaus, 8
Aretas, 157f.
Aristobulus I & II, 7
Aristotle, 125
Ark, 19
Arnon River, 2
Artemis, 178
Asia Minor, 174f.
Assumption of Moses, 335n.
Astarte, 200
Astralism, 12
Athanasius of Alexandria, 34
Attis, 12
Augustine, 23, 246

Barabbas, 77
Barnabas, 161, 163
Bathsheba, 25
Beatitudes, 63, 87f.
Bithynia, 174
Blessedness, 22, 24

Bornkamm, Günther, 82, 87
Brutus, 7, 255

Caedman, 36
Caesar Augustus, 5, 7, 47, 255
Caiaphas, 49
Calendar, Jewish, 49
Calendar, Roman, 46f.
Calvin, John, 23
Canon, 315f., 435
Cassius, 7, 255
Castration, 12, 106
Catholic Epistles, 315f. (See also *James, I, II Peter, I, II, III John, Jude*)
Cerinthus, 345
Chalcedon, Council of, 83
Christology, 11
Circumcision, 187, 189
Claudius, 157, 164
Clement of Alexandria, 47, 334
Clement of Rome, 256, 296, 299n., 326
Codices, 42f.
Colossae, 264
Colossians, Letter to the: authorship, 264, 266f.; background, 264ff.; outline, 274; structure and content, 270ff. (See also *Ephesians* and *Philemon*)
Constantine, 46
Corinth, 174, 178, 200ff., 202, 236
Corinthian correspondence, analysis of, 203f.
I & II Corinthians: background, 200, 223f.; dating and origin, 201; outlines, 221ff., 234f.; structure, 202ff., 224ff.
Covenant, 14ff.
Coverdale, Myles, 38
Crispus, 164
Criticism, form, 41f.
Criticism, textual, 91

383